EL CUERPO
DE CRISTO

EL CUERPO
DE CRISTO

The Hispanic Presence in the U.S. Catholic Church

Edited by

Peter Casarella and Raúl Gómez, S.D.S.

A Crossroad Herder Book
The Crossroad Publishing Company
New York

The Crossroad Publishing Company
370 Lexington Avenue, New York, NY 10017

Printed in the United States of America

ISBN: 0-8245-1741-5

Library of Congress Catalog Card Number: 98-071206

1 2 3 4 5 6 7 8 9 10 02 01 00 99 98

Contents

The Extended Body: Faith Generates a Culture

Acknowledgments

Without the support and collaboration of various people and organizations it would have been impossible to offer this volume. Therefore, we are grateful to the following for their help in preparation for and during the 1997 conference on The Hispanic Presence in the U.S. Catholic Church sponsored by The Catholic University of America and the Instituto de Liturgia Hispana. We wish to express our deep gratitude to the members of the planning committee including Drs. Thomas M. Cohen, Catherine Dooley, O.P., Robin Darling Young, John Ford, C.S.C., Mario Rojas, and Sr. Doris Turek, S.S.N.D., J.C.D. Sr. Doris also deserves thanks for her role as on-site coordinator of the conference. We also wish to express our special thanks to Dr. Raymond Collins, Dean of the School of Religious Studies, for his encouragement, support, and enthusiasm. Furthermore, the conference was made possible through generous grants from the Louisville Institute and the Magi Foundation. Dr. James Lewis of the Louisville Institute has been particularly gracious in his support of the project. Without the tremendous speakers, moderators, respondents, and of course the participants drawn from all over the United States, there would have been no material from which to draw the contents of this volume. The following persons kindly offered their services in the form of moderating the workshops in which the papers were originally delivered or offering a final synthesis at the conference's end: Dr. Kevin Irwin, Dr. Charles Gravenstine, Dr. William Dinges, Dr. Mary Collins, Dr. David Power, Dr. Joseph Fitzmyer, S.J., Mr. Ron Cruz, Dean Elaine Walter, Rev. James Moroney, Dr. Patrick Granfield, Ms. María Angela Leal, Dr. James Provost, Ms. Elisa Montalvo, Rev. Agustín Escalante, and Rev. John Brogan. The respondents to the papers deserve mention because their contribution was so fundamental to the dialogical process of the conference. These included Mr. Abel López, Dr. Dean Hoge, Rev. Domingo Rodríguez, S.T., Dr. Brid Long, Dr. Frank Matera, the Most Rev. Alvaro Corrada, S.J., Rev. Rudy Vela, S.M., Dr. Margaret Mary Kelleher, Dr. Samuel Soliván, Dr. William Cenkner, Dr. Ovidio Pecharromán, and Dr. Mark Wedig, O.P.: *Que Dios haga redundarles su generosidad.*

We are grateful to the administrators of The Catholic University of America, particularly Br. Patrick Ellis, F.S.C., President, Sr. Rosemary Donelly, S.C., Executive Vice-President, Msgr. John Wippel, Provost, Dr. John Lynch, Vice Provost for Graduate Studies, Dr. Stephen Happel, Chair—Religion and Religious Education Department, Dr. James Wiseman, O.S.B., Chair—Theology Department, and Dr. Timothy Meagher, University Archivist. In addition, our special gratitude is extended to the Instituto de Liturgia Hispana and the past Executive Board, including Rev. Heliodoro Lucatero, current President, Ms. Sylvia Sánchez, Vice-President, Mrs. María Pérez-Rudisill, Dr. Lorenzo Florián, Rev. Rudolph T. Juárez, Mr. Raúl Mendoza Díaz, Ms. Margarita Roque, Mrs. Alejandrina Vera, and Mr. Rogelio Zelada. We say thank you to the Hispanic Pastoral Affairs Office of the Archdiocese of Washington; to the CUA Graduate Student Association, the Theological Students' Association, and the Religion Students' Association; to Ms. Virginia Sloyan of The Liturgical Conference; and to the Very Rev. James Brackin, S.C.J., President Rector of Sacred Heart School of Theology. Many thanks are also due to Rev. Msgr. Michael Bransfield, Revs. Daniel Maher and Walter Rossi, and Dr. Leo C. Nestor of the Basilica of the National Shrine of the Immaculate Conception. There were several volunteers who helped during the Conference; without their help it would have gone less smoothly. Our thanks goes to Robert Brancatelli, Mary Ann Buddenberg, Josefina Bush, Sara Casarella, Mario Casarella, Mary Dancy, Brian Doyle, Denise Eggers, Jack Figel, Barbara Galloway, Isabel García-Spiegel, Susan Grunder, Sr. Paulina Hurtado, O.P., Donald Kaufhold, Laurie Latuda, Maureen Macaleer, Richard McCarron, Sr. Eileen McGowan, S.S.J., Ann Riggs, Andrea Sargent, Bonnie Shrack, and Cindy Sobiesiak. The liturgies were enhanced by the Most Rev. Sean O'Malley, O.F.M. Cap, Mr. Richard Miller, and the Saint Camillus Spanish Choir as well as by Sr. Marilú Covani, C.P., Ms. Esmeralda Huízar Mendoza, Ms. Clare Mendoza, Mary Frances Reza, Deacon Noel Vivaldi, and Sr. Joan Williams, O.P. To all of you: *Que Dios los colme de mucha dicha.*

In terms of the production of this volume, we wish to express our special gratitude above all to the speakers who gave us permission to publish their talks. We only wish that there were more space to include all the discussions that took place, both formal and informal. We also wish to thank Dr. James Le Grys, Academic Editor at Crossroad Publishing for his encouragement and patience. We thank Mr. Philip A. Perry for his work in proofreading the final manuscript. Finally we owe a very special word of thanks to the tireless efforts of our two editorial assistants, Susan and David Dawson Vásquez. Their service in the editing and formatting of this volume was quite simply invaluable: *Que Dios se lo pague.*

PC & RG

Foreword

VIRGILIO ELIZONDO

I cannot begin to express the great joy and excitement that I felt as we started the symposium at the Catholic University of America on the Hispanic Presence in the U.S. Catholic Church. Just to see so many close friends and colleagues from the academic world gathered together to explore the meaning and challenge of the growing Hispanic presence in the Church and in society is itself life-giving and exciting. It is even with a greater joy and sense of profound satisfaction that I now have the privilege of introducing the proceedings of this ground-breaking conference to you, our readers.

The accomplishments of the last twenty-five years have been miraculous, the problems facing us today are scary, and the challenges and opportunities are the greatest ever! But like the Israelites of old, we can remember what the Lord has done for us in the past, and dare to dream and envision fascinating new times that are yet to come, in fact we go even further in daring to proclaim a new humanity in the new heaven and earth of the Americas that is already beginning.

There is no doubt that the more we recall our history in this country, the more we discover the oppression and the suffering that our people have endured. The Church was not always present when we needed it the most, and often we felt like abandoned and orphaned children, like unwelcome stepchildren in a family that not only did not care for us but was even ashamed of us for being who we were, and sometimes like a young daughter being raped while the parents shut their ears so as to ignore the cries for help.

It has been a painful past, but not a sad one, for our faith enabled us to contend with the harsh realities of daily life, rise above them and celebrate life as it is as a gift of God. Our dance, our music, and our art together with our home altars, rituals, and devotions have been our connection with the God of life who is always there to hear our cries and come to our rescue. Through them, God has been very much present in our daily lives and struggles. They have transmitted the faith of our

9

ancestors from one generation to the next and have been the power that
sustained us. In the past, our life of faith was lived more apart from the
Church than within the Church. More often than not, the institutional
Church was more an obstacle than a source of faith.

Even though the Church was not always present when we needed
it and even kept our people out of the structures of clerical, academic,
and religious life, if anyone was around to walk with us in our struggles,
encourage us, and to be an occasional voice in our defense, it was usually the Church. All of us remember heroic priests, religious, and teachers who went out of their way to encourage us, help us, and invite us
into full participation in the Church. Many religious communities dedicated themselves to working among our people, but they were so few
in relation to the growing numbers of our people.

I will never forget the pioneering and prophetic efforts of Archbishop Robert E. Lucey of San Antonio in awakening the U.S. Catholic
Church to the needs and the plight of the Latinos/as of our country. He
often incurred the ridicule of his fellow bishops for being concerned
about "all those Mexicans." Some forty years ago he dared to start serious efforts to get the entire U.S. Catholic Church involved with the Latino
population of this country. In the beginning, as the Archbishop used to
tell me, the efforts seemed hopeless.

MIRACLES OF THE PAST TWENTY-FIVE YEARS

There is no other way to describe the accomplishments of the last
twenty-five years than as truly miraculous! In prayer the Spirit has truly
worked wonders. It is as if we are living today the dynamism found in
the Acts of the Apostles.

Building upon the early efforts of the 1940s, today it is fascinating
to see the increasing involvement of Hispanic laypeople as well as increasing numbers of Hispanic religious, priests, bishops, and deacons.
Following upon the early efforts of that marvelous Puerto Rican lady
from New York, Dr. Encarnacion Armas, the Secretariat for Hispanic
Affairs under the visionary and tireless leadership of Pablo Sedillo became one of the most dynamic departments of the National Conference
of Catholic Bishops. They encouraged and helped local efforts, promoted
comunidades eclesiales de base (ecclesial base communities) and even organized national meetings of Hispanic Catholics to design a National
Pastoral Plan. Today, Ron Cruz, head of the U.S. bishops' Secretariat for
Hispanic Affairs, is not only continuing the work but moving it to new
levels of involvement in the entire work of the Church.

Our Hispanic liturgists have multiplied. Organizing the Instituto de Liturgia Hispana, they have not only promoted music, dance, Church decoration, popular rituals, and liturgical forms that truly rise out of the faith tradition of our people, but organized workshops and conferences to bring anyone who is interested into the excitement of Hispanic liturgy. Our U.S.-produced Hispanic music can now be heard worldwide. I have personally heard the "Padre Nuestro" of Carlos Rosas sung in many parts around the world. Our common soul is expressed through our music and our composers are providing for the expression of this soul.

Many more parishes are having liturgies in Spanish, and the popular rituals of our people are being more and more accepted by the Church in general. We are truly enriching the liturgical life of the Church through our popular and family rituals.

Hispanic catechists have also organized and are providing leadership and understanding in relation to the various catechetical needs of our people. A few years ago, we had not a single Hispanic theologian in this country. Today we not only have many, but we even have a serious academic association—ACHTUS (Academy of Catholic Hispanic Theologians of the United States)—with annual meetings to further our theological research. We publish a journal, mentor new students, teach in various universities, and participate actively in various professional organizations—national and international. Our Hispanic Catholic social scientists have organized the Program for Analysis of Religion Among Latinos (PARAL), which investigates the origins, meaning, and function of our beloved popular religious practices.

Ecumenically, we are preparing for a yet uncharted future as our seminarians and religious study theology together with future ministers of other ecclesial communities, become friends, and learn to work together across denominational lines.

In the field of communications, I dare to say that from being totally absent, today we are way ahead of the rest of the Church in the United States. The weekly nationally televised Mass from San Fernando Cathedral is unique and reaches millions every Sunday. The efforts of the Hispanic Television Network (HTN) in producing Hispanic programs that reach throughout the United States and abroad are beyond comparison. Other productions such as the educational videos of South East Pastoral Institute (SEPI), the Mexican-American Cultural Center (MACC), and Father Nuñez in New Orleans are serving many people throughout the country. The new programming of CTSA-22 (Catholic Television of San Antonio) is offering many new possibilities.

We have also pioneered, through community organizing projects, the most effective means today for neighborhoods to work together for the common good. Our National Hispanic Catholic Leaders are gathering together to form a common agenda and work together in more effective ways. More and more Hispanics (usually from Latin America) are found in our seminaries and houses of formation.

The "Hope Center" in the Bronx has prepared hundreds of poor, working Hispanics not only to learn English but to prepare for citizenship in the country. Centers like this should exist in every Hispanic parish in the country.

And finally, our pride and joy, we have two struggling but thriving institutions that we can truly call "mi casa"—MACC and SEPI. These are the two institutes that own their own property, have their own facility, and can truly invite others with the traditional "Mi casa es su casa, bienvenidos." These two institutes, along with other programs of formation around the country, are transforming the life of the U.S. Church by giving a new vision of pastoral life, evangelization, and mission to the many people who come to participate in the programs of formation. Out of the suffering of the past, we are offering a new vision for the future.

I have named but a few of the many efforts that are multiplying around the country for the sake of our Hispanic Catholics. But unfortunately, it is not all good news.

PROBLEMATIC: AN APOCALYPTIC END? THE REALITY OF SUFFERING

As much as we have accomplished, we still have a lot to do. A quick look at our contemporary situation is both scary and alarming. Abandoned, undernourished, and homeless children are found everywhere around our country. Teenage drugs, violence, sex, and early pregnancies are extremely high among our people. Our Hispanic school dropout rate is at an all-time high at all levels of the educational spectrum. So few of our people reach the college level, much less the Ph.D. Jails, prisons, detention centers, and the cells along death row are packed with our people. Medical care for our elderly, abandoned children, children of recently arrived immigrants, and even our ordinary Hispanic is becoming more and more impossible. Many of our people are "underemployed," working only occasionally with no benefits whatsoever.

What has been most sacred for us in the past is quickly disappearing with the breakdown of family. There are multiple "couples" wherein each child has a different last name, no extended family, and the worst: no grandparents present around the family. I personally contend that the absence of grandparents is one of the greatest roots of violence in this country. The elderly have a special way of transmitting love and affection that even the best parents cannot give.

Our seasonal (migratory) workers have it worse than ever. Often they are paid the same wages (with no benefits) that they were paid twenty years ago but have to do four times as much work. More people are around looking for the same jobs, and old jobs are disappearing. Migratory workers are still the least protected and the most ignored workers in this country—very large percentages of them are Hispanic.

Benefits are being taken away from our senior citizens. Since many of the elderly came to this country a very long time ago and worked seven days a week for twelve to fourteen hours a day, they never had time to become legalized. Those who worked the hardest for the welfare of this country and for the enrichment of many are today being denied their just retirement rewards. This crime cries to God for justice! Families are being broken up by the deportation of some of their members. The undocumented migrants are being hunted down worse than ever, and the new wall between the United States and Latin America is the most effective wall that has ever been built to keep "unwanted people" out. It is a very friendly-looking wall but much more powerful in intent than the Berlin Wall ever was. The prophets of old would not have hesitated to raise their voices in sharp criticism of this injustice— but where are the voices of our bishops, our priests and religious, our theologians, academicians, and liturgists?

Many of our Hispanics are recently-arrived immigrants who are suffering because of the immigrant bashing that is increasing throughout the country. We, the citizens of this country, often forget that we were once aliens ourselves. The scripture tells us never to forget our former status as aliens, but we quickly seem to forget this in this country, so as to keep others from what we ourselves or our ancestors enjoyed before.

For many reasons, including the fact that often our Church ridicules and gets rid of what it does not understand, there is a breakdown of our religious heritage and traditions. The many devotions and rituals that initiated us into the faith and transmitted the faith from one generation to the next are disappearing. Add to this the rise of fundamentalist Christianity and liberal Catholicism that discredit all these living treasures as ignorance and superstition, coupled with the elimination of elders from the family unit, and we end up with a religious vacuum that leads to many disastrous consequences.

Whereas great strides have been made by the Catholic Church in the United States to include Hispanics fully in every aspect of Church life, we still have a long way to go in really being welcomed. As I travel around the country, I still hear horror stories of Hispanics being denied the most basic services of the Church, being ridiculed and even insulted for our tradition of Christian faith, even being told: "This is not your Church—the Mexican church is over there." Often our people go to the Methodist, Presbyterian, or Episcopal Church for *Quinceañeras,* weddings, and funerals. Once they go and are warmly accepted, they just keep on going. Thanks be to God there is an ecclesial community to welcome them when we ourselves drive them away.

I often have the feeling that the U.S. Catholic Church wants us, but not as Hispanics with our tradition of faith, our language, our customs, music, sense of beauty, and our festivals. The Church still wants to re-make us not into Christians but into Nordic European Americans. Our God-designed culture with its rich religious expression is still looked upon as backward and alien to Church life by many in the Church. The Church still continues to insult us and tell us we are not wanted when it denies us the feast of Our Lady of Guadalupe because December 12 happens to fall within Advent. A humanly designated liturgical season (which is more important to the clergy than to the people) is given more importance than God's own precious gift of a Mother for all the people of America. How can anyone dare to keep us from celebrating our Mother's birthday?

We have come a long way and we still have a long way to go. But we are determined, and through prayer and the power of the spirit, we will usher in a new humanity of the Americas—that is our task and our mission. In and through us "every other" will become one flesh and soul, the one body and blood of the American people from the tip of North America to the tip of South America and everything in-between.

Challenge and Opportunities: The Greatest Ever!

Out of the sufferings of the past, a new beginning is in the making. We cannot just wait around for it to happen, and neither can we wait for others to do things for us. This new beginning must begin with us and within the deepest depths of our personal and cultural being!

Conversion of Our Own!

If Jesus triumphed through the scandal of his birth, Galilean identity, and the suffering of the cross, then through the very scandal of our birth, identity, and suffering we too can become victorious over the forces that have oppressed us. Our spirit of endurance—*aguante*—which enabled us to withstand the harsh insults, oppression, and sufferings of the past for the sake of the survival and betterment of our families, can today become the divine energy that will triumph over the chaos and create a new Church and a new humanity.

In the beginning of the Hispanic movement, it was necessary to bring out the many ways in which our people had been victimized by others and even by our very own. Unfortunately, many of these practices still continue. Today, we are moving from seeing ourselves as victims to recognizing that we are not only the survivors who need to celebrate our presence, but equally the ones who are charged with the responsibility of creating something truly new. Even though unjust practices against our people continue, it is time to stop blaming others—for there will always be others to blame—and assume responsibility for our lives and those of our people. With or without others, we will create a new humanity. As we grow in numbers, so grows our responsibility to take charge of our lives and our destiny.

We can no longer believe what those who disseminate the negative stereotypes say about us! We are human beings and we must believe in ourselves. Conversion begins when we stop believing negative and ugly things others say about us and begin to believe in ourselves, our self-worth, our abilities, and our people. Enslaving and destructive feelings of inferiority have often paralyzed our ability to think, speak, and act. The belief in ourselves and our self-worth is the *first* step towards the new life of responsible freedom.

Jesus calls us to recognize, celebrate, and actualize the good in us that has remained hidden and inactive for too long. We must convert from the sin of not believing in ourselves, from the sin of believing that we are inferior or not as valuable as others, from the sin of being ashamed of our customs and traditions. Jesus calls us to recognize the good, the true, and the beautiful that is within every one of us. That is why conversion is good news and a cause of rejoicing.

To believe in Jesus is to believe in ourselves, for he certainly believes in us. To be followers of Jesus is to come out of the tombs of victimhood unto the life of the children of God; to believe in the Spirit given to us by Jesus is to believe that nothing is impossible to accomplish and no tragedy too massive to overcome. But freedom implies responsibility.

The more we experience our innermost freedom, the more we have to accept responsibility for our lives and that of our Church and society. We should no longer waste time and energy blaming others for our situation. Hence we must begin with a reclaiming of our basic Creed, the commandments, sacraments, and prayer. The basics of our faith have been a deep source of strength in the past, and they will be the foundation of the new future that we hope to construct. Our unquestioned belief in the goodness of our God is the strength that will carry us through any and every tribulation of this world. The internalization of the ten commandments will give us the basic interior freedom to be the masters of our bodies and not the other way around. Through the sacraments and other religious expressions of our people, we will consciously feel the touch of God in our lives, and prayer will allow us to converse with God and enter into the divine friendship.

One of the greatest sins of modern Western culture is the attempt always to shift the guilt for our mistakes onto someone else. Christians do not have to blame anyone, for we can recognize our guilt, receive God's healing forgiveness, and begin anew. We, like many others in our contemporary culture, are falling victim to this irresponsible behavior that is destroying our country—rather than admitting responsibility, we seek others to blame for whatever is going wrong in our lives.

Today, we have an urgent need within our Hispanic communities to call each and every person to personal responsibility. Husbands and wives need to eliminate the "D" word from their consciousness and work at becoming better and more loving husbands and wives, fathers and mothers, and responsible parents. Grandparents need to be welcomed into the homes, for they can give a love that is beyond what the parents can provide. Children need to obey, respect, and love not only their parents, but all those who assist the parents in the socialization process: *padrinos y madrinas*, teachers, coaches, catechists. I am convinced that one of the greatest roots of the escalating violence in this country is the breakdown of family life and the absence of grandparents and relatives from the normal growing-up process of children.

This sense of personal responsibility must carry over into the ordinary life of our Church. Through baptism we all participate in the priesthood of Jesus Christ, which means that we are all responsible for the life and ministry of the Church. We need to get rid of the old attitude of waiting for the *padrecito* or *la monjita* or the bishop to do things for us. We need to invite everyone to develop into dynamic leaders within the Church.

We need to convert from the old attitude of just attending church and leaving the work of the Church to the bishop, priests, and religious. We are all responsible in the Church. Remember that most of the creative breakthroughs in the life of the Church have come from the creativity of the grassroots. The hierarchy safeguards and manages while the faithful at large create and innovate new movements. We must convert from the passive attitude of waiting for others to start things and become self-starters. This is happening in many ways, but it has to happen even more.

ARTISANS OF A NEW HUMANITY

As we Hispanics become a greater percentage of U.S. Catholics, our responsibility for leadership within the Church becomes all the greater. The time for demanding of others is over but the challenge is now to ourselves. We need to be creative and bold in developing ministries within the Church. As Archbishop Patrick Flores has often told us "No tengan miedo ser atrevidos" (Don't be afraid to assert yourself). And as the folk wisdom of our ancestors tells us: "Mejor pedir perdon que permiso" (Better to ask for forgiveness than permission). We need to develop a healthy aggressiveness, boldness, and creativity.

In the new Church that we will all build together, there will be no foreigners because everyone will belong fully and will experience acceptance, belonging, and respect! Out of the painful memory of having been rejected and marginalized by others, treated as aliens and foreigners in our own home, we must work so that others today will not have to suffer what we were forced to endure in days gone by.

The first priority of the Church must always be the needs of the poor, the immigrant, the abandoned, the unwanted, and those in special need. There is no question about this. This is the priority of the gospel and it must be our own today. It must be the ever-present priority in all our deliberations and pastoral planning. We must not only minister to the poor but recognize how the poor minister to the rest of the Church.

The Church is with the poor not so that they may remain poor and marginalized but to help them in the struggles for new life. Hence the Church also has to accompany those who are succeeding in breaking forth from the enslavement of poverty and misery. The leaders of our Church have an obligation to those who are in the process of success—university students, professionals, executives, business leaders, artists, and sports figures. The Church must accompany them on their road to success so that by advancing in society—and we hope more and more of our people will—they will not destroy themselves in the process.

In building the new Church and society of the Americas, those who have succeeded in various ways have a special obligation to help those who are still outside the structures of opportunity in this country. The Christian challenge to reach out to the other in need as the true measure of our human success must be an essential ingredient in the spirituality of Christian success, which we must develop and promote among our successful Hispanics. Unfortunately, this has not happened in Latin American Christianity; in fact, it is totally missing. The Latin American rich are arrogant and feel that they have a divine right to exploit the poor, treat them as trash, and ignore their misery. We must challenge and condemn this attitude both in the United States and in Latin America. The Church should not be afraid to assist and challenge our Hispanic rich and wealthy to Christian justice, generosity, and commitment. The more one succeeds in this world, the greater the obligation one has to be of service to others.

The Church needs to have an active and dynamic presence in the Catholic and secular university campuses. It is not sufficient simply to accompany students. The Church must also walk and converse with the faculty as they struggle to create and develop a new "mestizo" knowledge. This knowledge (philosophical, historical, scientific, technological, theological, and literary), which truly emerges out of our *mestizo* worldview, can make its legitimate contribution to the various fields of knowledge of the university and world community. We do not want to be a ghetto people, but we do want to take our legitimate place in the global community.

The Church must also be involved in conversations with artists, musicians, playwrights, poets, and the like, for artists have a great role in the shaping of a civilization. We have sinned in being very absent from the world of our Latino/a artists in the United States. We should not dictate to them, but we certainly should be partners with them so that through their artistic expression, the wonders of God might be known and appreciated.

The Church will best accomplish this not through new dogmas or episcopal pronouncements but by becoming a prophetic/festive Church that dares to celebrate in a truly festive way the unquestioned fact that life is not only possible but worth celebrating. Yet in the midst of these celebrations we dare to proclaim the truth about the human situation, about the daily injustices people suffer. Archbishop Oscar Romero certainly did this, Bishop Samuel Ruíz is doing this today, as Archbishop Flores has always done through his cathedral in San Antonio: they speak the truth while always offering hope and joy to our people and to the world.

BUILDUP OF GOD'S REIGN: SPIRITUALITY OF OTHERNESS

Today's rapidly expanding multicultural and multiracial society cannot survive and live in peace and harmony without a radically new paradigm of society. The segregation and ethnically "superior and normative" models of Church and society that we have had until the present moment are not adequate and can only lead to ongoing divisions and destruction. A mere respectful coexistence is no solution and will only create new problems.

It is precisely at this level that our *mestizo* reality has the most to offer. Whereas in the beginning of America our *mestizaje* was not a product of love but of conquest, bringing with it the profound curse of being ashamed of our bodies, our mothers, and our mother cultures, today we are happily recognizing it as our greatest blessing and potential: the synthesis in our body and spirit of two and even three great racial and cultural traditions: Native American, African, and Iberian-European.

In our *mestizo* identity we have lived every moment of our lives within the world of the other, for we were never considered fully one or the other of our ancestral roots while actually being both at the same time. Because we were never *just* Indian or *just* European, or *just* African, our very being was "being in the other and for the other." Groups that feared and even despised one another become one flesh and spirit in our *mestizo* body and blood. In this new body the deepest blood barriers of separation are dissolved, and in our very selves the distant and feared "other" is now included.

We are what the rest of society is just beginning to recognize itself becoming and needing to become for the survival of humanity! Separation and segregation are simply not possible in today's shrinking world. The mixture of peoples is a growing fact of life. We *mestizos* can help to make it something good and beautiful. The future has already begun in us, thus we can offer others valuable insights into the process that the rest of society is just beginning to experience.

Today, *mestizaje* is the way of the future, but hopefully no longer through conquest and rape, but through love. It is the natural result of truly living out the new commandment of Jesus that we should love one another. No human taboo of segregation and separation should ever be so absolute or sacred that it cannot be transgressed for the sake of love. Love is that divine energy that seeks to unite without destroying. It is the very energy of the Christian movement and the very characteristic by which the movement is recognized. Our Christian community will be prophetic and visionary insofar as it is a community of true love and fellowship that dares to transgress even the deepest and most sacred taboos in favor of the other as other, so that all may truly become one!

In the past we had been ashamed of our *mestizaje* because of the deep and soul-penetrating scars of the conquest, but today we are rejoicing with pride and gratitude for all the ancestral traits that flow through our veins and animate our spirit. We are assuming our past and transforming it into the new personality of the future. We know that this is the ultimate way of ushering in the family of Jesus that goes beyond all human families and unites us in that one thing that can destroy all human barriers of separation: God's will, that is love without limit or condition.

Christ broke his own body and spilled his own blood that we might all share in the one body and blood, that we might all truly be one. Each time I celebrate the Eucharist with the multiple *mestizajes* that surround the altar, I realize more and more the full implications of Christ's body and blood: that each one of us might break with our body and blood barriers of separation so that we might become united in love to produce a new humanity. This is truly the celebration of our redemption that is working its way through our *mestizaje*. As the scandal of the cross was transformed by the glory of the resurrection, so too is the scandal of our original *mestizaje* being transformed today as we go from shame to pride, from denial to acceptance, from anger to gratitude, from sadness to joy, from inferiority to self-affirmation.

Our historical journey, as painful as it has been, was as necessary as the way of the cross for the emergence of a truly new humanity. We want to forgive the abuses of the past but never forget the wounds as we rejoice in what has come, through what is just the beginning of a new future. With the help of God, we will construct it not just for ourselves but for the sake of a new peace and harmony in the human family. This new family will regard and love every human being and cultural tradition as a beautiful expression of the greatness and glory of God.

We do not have a plan of action to propose, but we do know that if we can develop a true spirituality of the sacredness of others, we will find a way of creating a truly sacred human family wherein no one will be rejected; no one will be forced to live as an unwelcome alien; no one will be ashamed of the color of their skin, the shape of their eyes, or the size of their bodies; no one will be denied the basic opportunities of life; and people, institutions, and governments will truly care for the welfare of every single person. Thus will society become the temple of the Living God.

This symposium and the articles that follow are a clear proof of the new boldness, creativity, and seriousness that our Hispanic scholars are developing and offering to our own people and equally to Church and society at large. It is just beginning, but it is great! Much more is yet to come. As Archbishop Flores has always said: "Just give us a chance, that is all we ask for. You will be surprised in what we have to offer." ¡*VÁMONOS!*

Introduction

PETER CASARELLA AND RAÚL GÓMEZ, S.D.S.

On the afternoon of October 26, 1997 precisely at the intersection of California and Connecticut Avenues in Washington, D.C., at least two worlds met. Coming from the east on California Avenue was a procession of several hundred people buoying a twenty-five foot tall *paso*, a type of float, on which is depicted the Peruvian icon of Christ crucified, the Lord of the Miracles. Modestly cold rain fell upon them in a steady drizzle. The slow, funereal rhythm and loud trombone blasts of the drum and bugle corps contrasted with the monotonous whir of traffic speeding down Connecticut Avenue. The passengers heading south on this main artery might have been traveling to the Washington Monument or even the White House. Yuppies gawked in amazement from the upper story balconies of their high-rise apartment complexes. One such onlooker, eager to preserve the image of an intruding, fraternal mass of purple-caped pilgrims, snapped a picture with a telephoto lens. Just off Connecticut Avenue lay the swooping, high modern entrance to the Washington Hilton Hotel, the site of the 30 March 1981 attempt on the life of President Ronald Reagan by the would-be assassin, John Hinckley, Jr. Towering above the cars, pedestrians, and float was an equestrian memorial dedicated to General George McClellan of the Union Army. Just before the procession reached the intersection, two police cars marked with emblems representing the District of Columbia stopped the stream of automobiles and taxis on Connecticut Avenue to allow the drenched pilgrims to pass.

From their conversations one knew that the participants in the procession felt in their hearts they were really walking through the streets of Lima. By accompanying the Lord of the Miracles, they adopted a gait that conforms ineluctably to a strategy of resistance to the culture and ethos of their immediate surroundings. They intend no irreverence to the venerable memorials of History in their midst, for they do not see themselves as acting in a manner the least bit counter-cultural. They are so absorbed in the rhythms and movements enlivened by the One who has been raised up in their procession that the markers of the passing of the *saeculum* fail to divert their gaze.

The procession took the participants out of History and inserted them into a new dimension of liturgical time. The celebration of the Lord of the Miracles by itself is a unique synthesis of time and eternity. The feast predates the U.S. Civil War by over two hundred years and is over a century older than the institution of the U.S. Presidency. The crucified Christ depicted on the *paso* is a replica of an icon painted by a liberated Angolan slave on the walls of an adobe chapel in the Peruvian village of Pachacamilla.[1] First in 1655 and then again in 1687 and 1746, violent natural disasters struck this locale. On each occasion the wall with the sacred image was the sole part of the chapel to survive.

The groups represented in the procession in Washington, D.C. were laypeople hailing from parts of the U.S. eastern seaboard ranging from New Jersey to Puerto Rico. They arranged themselves in accordance with the tightly organized structures of the *cofradías* or lay confraternities that date back to the origins of the devotion in the seventeenth century. The flyer announcing the event spoke of "Festividades en Honor a Nuestro Cristo Morado" (a celebration in honor of the 'purple' Christ), and the capes that the leaders wore reflected the same hue as that found in the habits of the Nazarene nuns who guard the sanctuary of the icon in Pachacamilla even today.

The procession is essentially liturgical even if some would prefer to label it with a name like "popular religion" or "popular Catholicism." The event is genuinely *popular* in the sense that the march of the *pueblo* (people) transpires on the streets outside the ecclesiastical edifice, beyond the temporal boundaries of the official Mass, and devoid of priests or any other ordained officials of the Catholic Church. It is nonetheless rooted in the liturgy because it follows directly upon a lengthy Eucharistic service in the nearby Latino parish and never leaves behind the central theme of the bishop's homily that Christ's sacrifice on the cross is wholly transformative for those who incorporate it into each individual step of their daily lives.

The Lord of the Miracles' procession contrasts with other marches with which the inhabitants of downtown D.C. are quite familiar. Their presence is not a gathering of outright social protest nor is it just a nationalistic assertion of Latin American pride. The carrying of both Peruvian and U.S. flags testifies to what has been identified as the bicul-

---

1. See, inter alia, Rubén Vargas Ugarte, *Historia del Santo Cristo de los Milagros*, 4th ed. (Lima, 1984) and Vicente Santilli, *El Señor de los Milagros*, 2nd ed. (Lima, 1980).

tural, "hyphenated" existence of the participants.[2] Without sacrificing what sets them apart from the hegemonic culture of North America, the Hispanic American pilgrims nonetheless deserve to be considered of this very place. Their overtly eschatological march is at the same time the planting of a seed of hope. Far from either protest or even its polar opposite, the romanticization of a bygone era and a distant place, the pilgrims reflect with pride what Virgilio Elizondo has referred to as a new way of being American.[3] As living icons of a very visible God, the joint religious *and* cultural identity (How can these two be separated?) of the (post)modern confraternities resists the centripetal pull of the more than proverbial melting pot and asserts itself as a new presence on the urban topography of America.

The unexpected, expanding, and ever changing newness of Hispanic/Latino Catholicism in the United States is the subject of this volume. All the essays originated in a conference that took place 29–31 May 1997 also in Washington, D.C. under the joint sponsorship of The Catholic University of America and the national Instituto de Liturgia Hispana. Presentations from that conference, by itself an important collaborative venture on the part of the two sponsoring institutions as well as the participants who came from all over the United States, were rewritten, edited, and brought together in this volume so that others might be able to benefit from them.

At the same time, this volume represents more than just the published proceedings of an academic conference. Reflecting not only on the written texts but also on the experience of the conference, the editors feel that the essays in this volume all center around the reality of

2. This term originates with Fernando F. Segovia and reflects Segovia's long-standing concern to defend the nonassimilation of the U.S. Hispanic American into the hegemonic "melting pot." Segovia notes that non-Hispanic U.S. citizens commonly use the word "America" synecdochically, i.e., a word that signifies the whole continent is used to refer to just one part (the United States). When a U.S. Hispanic American uses the same word, Segovia argues, it is precisely the synecdoche that collapses. See Fernando F. Segovia, "Aliens in the Promised Land: The Manifest Destiny of U.S. Hispanic American Theology," in *Hispanic/Latino Theology: Challenge and Promise*, ed. Ada María Isasi-Díaz and Fernando F. Segovia (Minneapolis: Augsburg/Fortress, 1996), 15–42, here at 35. See also the contribution by Jean-Pierre Ruiz below.

3. Virgil Elizondo, *The Future is Mestizo: Life Where Cultures Meet* (Bloomington: Ind.: Meyer-Stone, 1988), 110–1: "The old Nordic cultures of Europe, which formed the cultural/religious base of the U.S.A., are meeting and merging with the Latin mestizo cultures of the old Iberian world, which mesticized with the native nations of the Americas. . . . Differences are not being destroyed, but they are being transcended and celebrated as together we usher in the beginning of the new race of humanity."

the transfigured but still scarred body of Christ.[4] The title *El Cuerpo de Cristo* was chosen to highlight that the Hispanic presence can no longer be viewed as just a marginal or additive presence in the U.S. Catholic Church. Several of the essays document sociologically and empirically how the Hispanic presence is growing at a far more rapid pace than many people realize. But an even greater concern was to demonstrate that this unmistakable trend has repercussions not just for the sociologists of contemporary Church life but for all who care about the spiritual *and* cultural vitality of U.S. Catholicism.

The pregnant phrase *Cuerpo de Cristo* could be understood in the sense of what the theologian Henri de Lubac, S.J. called "the heart of the Church."[5] For de Lubac the original, Pauline conception of the Church as a body of Christ allows for no sharp separation of a natural, physical body from a "mystical" or spiritual body.[6] The heart, the point from which and around which love and life circulate outwards, is also the point of contact between the increasingly *mestizo* constituency in Church and society and the non-utopian eternal kingdom in which the communion of all races, nations, and ethnicities with one another and the triune God will be fully achieved. The spiritual dimensions of the Church emerge from the very flesh and blood of the Latino corporate body working six days a week at two jobs to support extended family in both North and South America and taking a much deserved respite on the Sabbath to offer praise to the Lord. The Church and the world intersect precisely at the point at which the Hispanic presence brings about a surprisingly new marriage of faith and culture. The Hispanic presence embodies the heart of the Church because it contributes a liv-

---

4. Fittingly, the conference concluded with a procession from the university to the nearby Basilica of the National Shrine of the Immaculate Conception. Once in the Shrine the conference participants celebrated the Solemnity of the Body and Blood of Christ at a liturgy presided over by the Most. Rev. Sean O'Malley, O.F.M. Cap., bishop of Fall River, Mass. Bishop O'Malley was instrumental in the founding of the *Capilla Latina* in the Archdiocese of Washington, the Church from which the liturgical procession described at the outset of the introduction originated.

5. Henri de Lubac, *The Splendor of the Church* (San Francisco: Ignatius Press, 1986), 127–61.

6. De Lubac shows that the phrase "mystical" (as opposed to natural) body first came into usage in the second half of the twelfth century as a quality used to describe the Church. Prior to this point the distinction was employed only in the discussion of the Eucharist. This way of describing the Church persists up to the important encyclical of Pius XII, *Mystici corporis*, in which it is asserted that the difference [between a mystical and moral body] "is by no means slight but, on the contrary, of the very highest importance." H. de Lubac, *The Splendor of the Church*, 127–9.

ing Catholic tradition, one deeply rooted in American soil, to the complex and unique intermingling of Church and world in the United States today. By publishing these essays, we wish to make the religious and cultural dimensions of the Hispanic presence better understood. We thereby hope to show that realities as seemingly disparate as liturgical processions, educational advancement, the overcoming of economic oppression and gender discrimination, Church architecture, prison theater, and the pivotal role of grandmothers in child-raising all contribute corporately to the building up of the Latino community of faith and thereby to the common good of Church and society.

The essays can accordingly be divided up into three categories: (1) *The Wounded Body*, which addresses questions relating to theology, biblical interpretation, liturgy, metaphysics, and spirituality; (2) *The Latino Body*, which considers the interrelated themes of Church, family, and ecumenism; and (3) *The Extended Body*, in which the contributors demonstrate how Hispanic/Latino Catholicism generates its own multifaceted cultural reality. By way of introduction, let us briefly survey some of the riches we have assembled.

I. *COMO DEGOLLADO*: THE WOUNDED, TRANSFIGURED BODY OF THEOLOGY, LITURGY, AND SPIRITUALITY

The cross is not the only place to turn to view the woundedness of Christ. Revelation 5:6, for example, states: "Then I saw standing in the midst of the throne and the four living creatures and the elders, a Lamb that seemed to have been slain" (NAB). The image could not be more graphic, for it depicts a Lamb whose throat appeared to be slit, in Spanish, *como degollado*. This eschatological image is a fitting starting point for theological reflection on Hispanic life, liturgy, and spirituality. The passage makes the startling claim that in the kingdom of God, the body of Christ will not have its scars surgically removed. Like the blood that pours from the Paschal Lamb of old, the promise for the future is that the wounds will ascend unto a throne in order to be glorified and praised. By taking such a deliberately spiritual stance towards the present travails of the community, both separatist self-aggrandizing and an irresponsible sense of victimization are excluded. Theological reflection that proceeds from the reality of an eternally wounded human nature of Christ must return to the real sacrifices of the every day. Like the pilgrims engaged in an eschatological march through the streets of Washington, D.C., a spirituality centered on the eternally wounded side of Christ still requires a daily commitment to family, Church, and society. The theology of the wounded body reassures the Hispanic community in realistic terms that the one who struggles daily is *already* a participant in the march to the kingdom. This is not utopian wishfulness. It is an essential part of the very fabric of a community's faith.

In his essay "'Why Are You Frightened?': U.S. Hispanic Theology and Late Modernity," Roberto Goizueta reflects on the role of U.S. Hispanic/Latino Theology in the light of Christ's wounded body. He takes note of the increasing awareness of the inherently ambiguous character of human history in these last years of the twentieth century. He cites Walter Benjamin's admonition that "every great work of civilization is at the same time a work of barbarism." This final decade of the present century, a period that has been called both "postmodernity" and "late modernity," challenges us to confront the truth of Benjamin's dictum, according to Goizueta. Although modernity has stressed progress, the central task before us as we come to the threshold of the third millennium is to forge our future alongside the bodies scarred by modern progress. Christians who have persisted in regularly recounting the stories of suffering and crucifixion, like Paul who preached Christ crucified, have been reviled. The first gnostics wanted to deny the suffering and cross of Christ and to celebrate instead the victory over suffering and death in the glorified Christ. In Goizueta's judgment, this is also the case with modern "gnostics" who continue to deny the still-bleeding wounds on the Body of Christ and who want us to look beyond them to a pure, unscarred future.

However, the Hispanic/Latino community will not surrender to the illusory belief in a resurrection without the cross. Thus the task of Hispanic/Latino theology in the United States is to challenge the attempts by modern gnostics to interpret Jesus' crucifixion and resurrection through the lenses of an ideology of progress. For Christ's suffering on the cross is not forgotten after the resurrection; it is taken up into the glorified life of Christ and is thereby transfigured, not eliminated. Modernity has preached a Jesus whose resurrection erases all memories of his violent death. Hispanic/Latino theology in the U.S. witnesses to Jesus' resurrection without pretending that the resurrection somehow justifies and erases the past. Goizueta notes that, grounded in the Crucified Jesus of popular religion, Hispanic/Latino theologians are retrieving the intimate connection between the Crucified Christ and the glorified Christ. Hispanic/Latina theologians in particular are in the forefront of current attempts to uncover the wounds that are obscured by modernity's attempt to make the home all-but-invisible, and thereby recover the experiences of women, children, and the elderly as sources of theological insight and wisdom. They stress the significance of *lo cotidiano* ("the everyday") as a key *locus theologicus* since it is the very heart of human history. He stresses that it is in *lo cotidiano* where Christ has been born and where he continues to accompany us. The task of the theologian is to reflect on this and thus also to broaden our very conception of history itself to include not only the life of the public square but also the life of the family. From Goizueta's perspective, the modern worldview maintains that only what is purely rational and abstract counts as the really real. This does not allow for ambiguity or contradiction. Such a polarized worldview cannot encompass the *mestizo* experience of a God who is known not through rational concepts alone, but through the embodied relationships lived out in symbols, narratives, and rituals of popular religion. For Goizueta we find in and through these relationships a God who pleads with us: "Why are you frightened? *Touch* me." This is what modern Western theologies have been afraid of doing; this is what Hispanic/Latino theology in the United States invites us all to do.

In his contribution, "Hispanic Liturgy and Popular Religiosity: A Reflection," Juan Sosa observes that those who are to minister among Hispanics/Latinos must understand how this people moves and is moved at worship. It is important to attend to myth and ritual since they arise to shape the heritage of a community of faith that seeks to transmit its powerful message of hope. Hispanic/Latinos, Sosa asserts, have a dual experience of worship: Hispanic/Latino liturgy and popular religion. These phenomena of public worship provide a sense of pageantry that can draw the curious. Nonetheless, they are also two ingredients in today's pastoral life that are far from defined, accepted or understood by all. Thus they form a dual, ambiguous reality in the United States. Sosa believes that liturgy and popular religion in the hands of pastoral agents are not only tools for evangelization now, but sources of deep spiritual nourishment that place us all in touch with the core of human experience, the religious self. As for the roots of popular religion among Hispanics/Latinos, he posits that possibly the centralization of Church life by the hierarchy and monks at the time of the Gregorian reform in the eleventh century, particularly in the celebration of the liturgy and spirituality, gave birth to parallel forms of culturally mediated expressions of faith. Sosa observes that converts to Catholicism in Latin America, after the incorporation of the Tridentine liturgy into the official worship of the Church, continued to express their newfound faith in Jesus and his Mother with symbols that emerged from their own cultural-religious experience. Thus Hispanic/Latino liturgy and popular religion embody a language of worship that is unique and enriching; it is open-ended and, therefore, accessible to growth. Liturgy and popular religion represent "siblings" that are only in competition with one another when pastoral leaders choose to neglect one or the other. Sosa notes that popular religion and liturgy have become for Hispanic/Latino Catholics the language of faith and prayer in the Church. For Sosa, they are the avenue through which pastoral agents can reinterpret the stories and symbols that shape the Hispanic/Latino worldview. Furthermore, they constitute the avenue to a healthy inculturation of the Gospel and the path to the new evangelization needed today.

In light of Sosa's contribution, it is important to reiterate that liturgy and popular religion in the Hispanic/Latino context of the United States have a symbiotic relationship. That is, popular religion among Hispanics/Latinos gets many of its themes, symbols, and practices from the liturgy, and the celebration of the liturgy among Hispanics/Latinos reflects many of the attitudes, values, and symbols that emerge from popular religion.[7] One cannot hope to understand Hispanic/Latino popular religion without reference to the liturgy. Moreover, one cannot hope to understand Hispanic/Latino liturgical celebrations without reference to popular religion.

The next essay concerns "A Reading of the Apocalypse: Biblical Interpretations from a U.S. Hispanic American Perspective." In it Jean-Pierre Ruiz lays out an insightful biblical hermeneutic of the book of Revelation and its relation to the devotion to Our Lady of Guadalupe. He notes that the affirmation of the importance of ethnicity and gender for biblical interpretation by various scripture scholars has provided the opportunity for new voices to make themselves heard within and beyond the circles of academy and Church. Thus in this article he begins to sketch a "U.S. Hispanic American reading" of the book of Revelation. Ruiz observes that many Hispanic/Latino authors have devoted much attention to a broad range of biblical texts, but Revelation has received little notice in print. On the other hand, it plays a prominent role in the liberationist hermeneutics of many Latin American authors with whose work Hispanic/Latino theologians in the United States claim affinity. Furthermore, Ruiz notes the frequent citations of Revelation 12 in connection with Our Lady of Guadalupe and is surprised by the relatively little deliberate reflection on the hermeneutical implications of the "readings" of the Tepeyac Mariophany as conscious rereadings of Revelation 12.

In analyzing the connection between the book of Revelation, the experience of diaspora by Hispanics/Latinos in the United States, and

7. See for example Raúl Gómez, "The Day of the Dead: Celebrating the Continuity of Life and Death," *Liturgy: There is a Balm . . . , Journal of the Liturgical Conference* 14, no. 1 (1997): 28–35.

the prominence of devotion to Our Lady of Guadalupe, Ruiz highlights two characteristics of the Apocalypse: its urban setting and its overtly liturgical character. This is particularly significant since the great majority of Hispanics/Latinos live in urban areas, and the liturgy for them is the primary experience of Church life. They will resonate with the Apocalypse since it is written to seven urban Churches in Asia Minor that are experiencing the difficulties associated with being a minority within a larger society marked by the pervasive influence of the imperial cult. The contemporary urban experience of violence, unemployment, and substance abuse helps Hispanic/Latinos in the United States to "foreground" the undeniably urban character of the book. Moreover, the hymnic quality of key passages suggests a liturgical setting for the book in which the legitimate object of praise and reverence is God and the Lamb, not the powers of this world. Ruiz notes that the image of Guadalupe itself is a type of "text" that is meant to be "read" as it is was originally done by the *tlamatinimes*, the wise men and women trained to "sing" in a liturgical manner the painted codices of the Nahuatls. The image and words of the Guadalupan event lead the people to turn to the true God-by-whom-one-lives. This disposes latter-day U.S. *tlamatinimes* and their audiences to recognize the liturgical quality of the Apocalypse so that the activity of worship is recognized in every activity that expresses uncompromising commitment to God and to the Lamb. Thus, reading the urban and liturgical qualities of the Apocalypse with the reading of Guadalupe extends the maxim that *lex orandi* (rule of prayer) constitutes *lex credendi* (rule of belief) to include *lex agendi* (rule of action). In other words, worship involves prayer, and such prayer manifests a commitment of faith by which believers can engage in action that establishes the reign of divine justice within the context of U.S. Hispanic American life.

In its scope, Alejandro García-Rivera's essay on "Wisdom, Beauty, and the Cosmos in Hispanic Spirituality and Theology" is clearly the broadest of any in the volume. It sets a wholly new standard for what is normally understood by Hispanic "spirituality." He argues that a renewed understanding of the spiritual must take place, whose focus is neither "worldly" nor "other-worldly." García-Rivera proposes the retrieval of a theological aesthetics that would provide no less than a new foundation for a reconceived metaphysics. He employs semiotic analysis as a primary tool in this retrieval and examines elements of the iconography used by Hispanics/Latinos. In the latter he finds important clues for understanding the mediation of reality itself. This is significant in that postmodernism has provided the insight that all knowledge, indeed all reality, is mediated by an indeterminate variety of forms of expression that include the poetic and symbolic.

García-Rivera finds in the image of Our Lady of Mercy of El Cobre, in particular, a "new world theodicy" that combines Iberian and indigenous elements of creation and redemption. The image of Our Lady of El Cobre lifts up sign/symbol as the reigning paradigm for a specifically Hispanic/Latino theological aesthetics. The image of Our Lady of El Cobre is expressive at the encounter of creation and redemption, for she represents the cosmological middle, which García-Rivera identifies as the spiritual realm in which cosmic order and suffering are found. From this particular Cuban devotion one can show how the Christian experience of prayer can be redirected to a spirituality that speaks to the whole of reality and away from a spirituality that is confined within one's own private experience. In this way, prayer brings to (rather than finds in) experience comfort and thus also the sense that there is a possibility of transcending human experience.

García-Rivera observes that a proper theology of the spiritual must draw its inspiration from a theology of creation. Key to this is the assumption that aesthetic value is an intrinsic reality of the cosmic order. The recognition of aesthetic value in the contingent world of creation makes spiritual discernment possible: ". . . the spiritual within the graded aesthetics of a created cosmos can act as a compass of ultimacy." Rather than theorizing about different views of God, this way of life actually leads to God. García-Rivera redefines the ancient practice of ἀναγωγή (anagoge or contemplative ascent) in terms of the capacity of the human imagination to harmonize the affective, volitional, and cognitive aspects of human life. Playing off of David Tracy's much discussed "analogical imagination," García-Rivera posits an "anagogical imagination." By means of the anagogical imagination, a life of discernment emerges that continually transforms the human creature toward the divine glory.

This form of spiritual exercises reflects the spirituality of Hispanics/Latinos as they gather insights from Amerindian, African, and Roman theology into an authentic inculturation of the Christian faith. Hispanic/Latino expressions of faith therefore ought to be studied not only because they represent a deeply felt and profoundly understood expression of the Christian message. Contemporary theology needs to take the role of cosmology in Hispanic/Latino spirituality seriously, for Hispanic/Latino spirituality proclaims with power and vigor that the universe is a cosmos full of intrinsic value and beauty. By developing a theological aesthetic from the Hispanic/Latino perspective, García-Rivera concludes, one can lend tangible support to a community of discernment that in the midst of turmoil sees the vision of a wonderful world yet to come.

Ana María Pineda's contribution, "The Place of Hispanic Theology in a Theological Curriculum: Systematic and Pastoral Implications," sets out the curricular implications of the various developments with which all the authors of essays in this volume are concerned. Pineda provides illustrative examples of some of the significant steps taken over the last twenty-five years toward the assessment and creation of appropriate forms of theological education for Hispanics/Latinos in the United States. She notes that the three national *encuentros* (encounters) (1972, 1977, and 1985) were formative experiences that provided the participants in these events with a context in which to learn theology as a community. Subsequent efforts have been undertaken by various organizations, institutions, and individuals, which have resulted in the identification of major issues and implications for the theological enterprise in the United States. Entities such as the Fund for Theological Education, the Catholic Theological Union, and the Hispanic Theological Initiative have identified a number of present needs. These include: (1) augmenting the pool of Hispanic/Latino professors (both male and female), (2) providing financial support for Hispanics/Latinos as they pursue theological education, (3) fostering forms of theological reflection that reflect the diversity and complexity of the Hispanic/Latino reality in the United States, (4) broadening the knowledge and pedagogical skills of non-Hispanic/Latino faculty members to reflect the Hispanic/Latino presence in the United States, and (5) mentoring Hispanic/Latino scholars as they pursue theological education.

Pineda observes that publishing houses and funding agencies have begun to acknowledge the growing importance of the developing Hispanic/Latino theological enterprise. This has been aided by the establishment of professional organizations such as the Academy of Catholic Hispanic Theologians of the United States (ACHTUS) and La Comunidad. Significant contributors to this development have been the Lilly Endowment and the Pew Charitable Trust.

Unresolved issues still remain. For example, she wonders why a community blessed with so much charismatic leadership is not adequately represented in the established leadership. The efforts hailed by Pineda indicate that the answer to this question is being pursued by Hispanics/Latinos, both Catholic and Protestant, as well as by non-Hispanics. She affirms that "if the Church is to be true to its mission, the respectful inclusion of these new voices is not only important but necessary."

II. *EN MARCHA*: CHURCH, FAMILY, AND ECUMENISM
WITHIN THE LATINO BODY

A word like "assimilation" creates the impression that Latino membership in either ecclesial or civic bodies is only possible if the individuals
involved sacrifice their unique cultural and religious heritage for the
sake of participating in a Church or society already dominated by the
mainstream, non-Hispanic culture. Assimilation cannot accord respect
even if it is a constant temptation to those who would be otherwise
marginalized. Yet not all forms of adaptation need to be shunned. U.S.
Hispanics do in fact choose to adapt themselves to their new home in
ways that inevitably involve some distancing of their lives from the
religious and cultural traditions of Latin America and the Caribbean.
The real problem is with the all too prevalent idea of a "melting pot."
The pressure to assimilate into a homogenous social entity whose precise contours, values, styles of social interaction, and spiritual orientation is not made explicit until after one has already been accepted as a
member demands careful and critical attention. Assimilation is particularly questionable inasmuch as the lure of social advancement distances
Hispanics from their own communities in the United States and creates
undue fragmentation within these communities. The process of critical
evaluation must therefore remain fundamentally open to a re-assertion,
now on the level of conscious awareness and transformative self-knowledge by both the individual and the community, of distinctively Latino
perspectives on faith and culture.

In the essays that follow there are noteworthy differences of opinion on the issues of assimilation and resistance to assimilation. The editors nonetheless felt that all of them focus on the Latino body of Christ
because of the specific issues that are addressed: the Hispanic vision of
Church and society and the need for Hispanic models of leadership
within both, the fragile reality of (and urgent need for) ecumenism in
the U.S. Hispanic community, and the place of the family and familial
models of interaction as a *locus theologicus* and pastoral task. Although
divergent opinions are presented and in some cases the same reality is
viewed from different angles, in each case what is at stake is how the
Latino body as an ecclesial and social reality needs to be taken seriously on its own terms.

In her essay on "The Hispanic Challenge to U.S. Catholicism, Colonialism, Migration, and Religious Adaptations," Ana María Díaz-Stevens
demonstrates with compelling detail just how Latinos and Latinas will
allow the U.S. Catholic Church in the next generation to grow in new
and unexpected ways. Three major factors that mark these challenges

are the youthfulness of the Hispanic population, its widespread poverty, and its low educational attainment. She also shows that 70 percent of those identified as Hispanics are native-born U.S. citizens and that future growth in the Latino population will come more from natural demographic increase than from immigration.

There have been definite improvements in all areas, and Hispanics have begun to acquire political clout within both Church and state. She acknowledges that Hispanics are increasing so rapidly that they can outpace the resources of the total Church. However, Latinos and Latinas have already experienced not only the shortage of priests but often institutional neglect. Díaz-Stevens observes that Hispanics often respond to this situation by maintaining their faith through lay-led organizations and community leaders, both male and female, but especially the latter. Despite the increasing numbers of Latinos/Latinas joining non-Catholic Churches, the great majority continue to identify themselves as Catholic and seek to continue contributing to the life of the Church through a *pastoral de conjunto*, a holistic approach to ministry that integrates liturgy, catechesis, and social justice. Latinos/Latinas contribute as well through lay participation in Cursillos, *comunidades eclesiales de base*, and other more traditional organizations.

This presents a challenge to the non-Hispanic Church in that it needs to be willing to learn from the Hispanic success as well as learn how to integrate lay men and women into the life of the Church. Nonetheless, Hispanics also have the challenge of establishing a "national identity" forged from their experience of working together for the common good. As Latino peoples descendent from the various Spanish-speaking nations come together to negotiate their differences and similarities, an authentic multi-Hispanic reality comes onto the scene. The liturgy has played a significant role in developing a new Hispanic consciousness as it brings together the various groups to worship together while balancing local traditions and general respect for the common doctrine that unites them. The liturgy among Hispanics has been able to do this while emphasizing the Spanish language and those parts of history and culture that are most common to peoples of the Southwest, Latin America, and the Caribbean. According to Díaz-Stevens, there has been a greater desire on the part of Latinos and Latinas to participate in active ministry, but many such women and men have sought their education in other Christian seminaries due to the inaccessibility of adequate training within the institutional programs of the Catholic Church. She expresses a concern that a "brain drain" among Hispanic Catholics may result as these students convert to other Churches where their ministry is often officially recognized through ordination. The largest challenge to the U.S. Hispanic/Latino Catholic Church comes from the migration to other denominations and the downsizing of the Catholic clergy, which will push the Church once again toward "innovative" approaches. She predicts that these approaches will incorporate what Hispanics/Latinos in their lands of origin have found effective for hundreds of years: an increase in the importance of the role of lay persons, especially women, in the ministry of the Catholic Church.

Having written about the emergent role of Latinos in the Churches and society for many years, Allan Figueroa Deck, S.J., applies this sagacity to "Latino Leaders for Church and Society: Critical Issues." He describes an initiative for Hispanic leadership development recently undertaken by the National Catholic Council for Hispanic Ministry (NCCHM) and contextualizes that initiative within the contemporary Latino Catholic presence. Recognizing that the ultimate target of Hispanic ministry are the children of immigrants, including the many youth who are either bilingual or English speakers only, Deck stresses the need to form the future members of a Latino professional class so they still maintain their distinctive religious and cultural identity without having to sacrifice the legitimate opportunities for personal advancement made available to them in modern U.S. society. "By no means is the vibrant heritage of the past erased," he states. "Rather it takes on new life and forms in the more complex cultural matrix of today's United States."

Deck wants to form Latino models of leadership that take into account the cultural values that the Hispanic community has to contribute, values that contrast with the stance of individualistic self-assertion that is often used to characterize the North American ethos. He critically evaluates virtues prevalent among Latinos such as proportion, realism, and respect for others. His goal is not to postulate that Hispanic culture is the sole bearer of virtue. Rather he claims that the Hispanic experience of deferring towards others may complement the prevailing North American ethos of being direct, pragmatic, and self-reliant. The process of evaluating differing and new models of leadership, Deck avers, is essential for the Church as it contemplates the awesome task of evangelization that will confront it in the next millennium.

Drawing upon his wide-ranging expertise as an ecumenist and theologian, Jeffrey Gros addresses the delicate subject of "Ecumenism in the U.S. Hispanic/Latino Community: Challenge and Promise." He faces the difficulties of ecumenical dialogue squarely. For example, he admits that the ecumenical agreement over the last thirty years, as well as Vatican II's call for efforts toward dialogue with other Christian denominations, have met with spotty success in the Hispanic/Latino community, both here and abroad. Gros indicates that part of the reason for this is that Hispanic/Latino theologians are not well represented in the "classical ecumenical literature." This is partially due to the fact that much of Hispanic/Latino theology does not take into account the results of the ecumenical dialogue. Thus he seeks to encourage these theologians to take their rightful place in the ecumenical research. On the other hand, he acknowledges the work of theologians such as Virgilio Elizondo and Justo González as well as the work of Bishops Plácido Rodríguez, C.M.F. and Ricardo Ramírez, C.S.B. The latter have been particularly assertive in calling Hispanic/Latino pastoral agents and ecumenical leaders to engage in dialogue. Nonetheless, Gros recognizes that at the grassroots level, where the majority of Hispanics/Latinos interrelate with other Churches, difficulties arise with those denominations that are less ecumenical or positive about Catholicism. In addition, many immigrants arrive unprepared for pluralism and for a free interchange of ideas. Gros has come to understand that, as with liturgy and spirituality, ecumenism must be inculturated in order to be successful. One way this can take place is by identifying the specific ecumenical programs and priorities of the various Hispanic/Latino communities in the United States. For, according to Gros, the most significant pastoral impetus will come from those committed and converted Hispanic/Latino leaders who equip themselves to provide "leadership in knowing how to be attentive to the needs, theological issues, and institutional forms that will best serve the ecumenical dimension of Church ministry for the future."

José Antonio Rubio discusses "Bearing False Witness" in the Latino Christian body. He takes his cue from the stories of Susanna (Daniel 13) and Anna (Tobit 2–3), biblical narratives that offer ample evidence of mistrust, false accusations, and unjust recriminations. He then complements Gros's survey of the academic literature by identifying in the popular literature available in most religious bookstores the perceptions that Catholics and Protestants harbor toward one another.

The first part examines Pentecostal misinformation and misconceptions. It is not unusual in their popular literature, Rubio argues, for Pentecostals to distort Catholic attitudes toward the Bible, the extent of the Church's persecution of heretics, and Catholic mariology. The second part looks at the way in which Catholics bear false witness toward their Protestant brethren. This is evidenced when Catholics proliferate the essentially pejorative term *sectas* (sects), when they refuse to distinguish properly between true Pentecostal movements and "holiness" movements that have disavowed speaking in tongues, and when they fail to define their terms in impugning "proselytism" by non-Catholics.

Rubio's essay also contains practical guidelines for eliminating the false witness in both Catholic and Protestant quarters that wounds the Latino body. The fostering of scholarly exchange and joint participation in research projects is a necessary but not sufficient condition for eliminating the level of mistrust that perdures. Beyond intellectual collaboration he enjoins genuine face-to-face interaction at all levels of Church life. Sometimes the old Hispanic wisdom of inviting one another to coffee is exactly what is needed. No one is being asked to give up his or her identity; Rubio states: "I do not want Pentecostals to light candles before a statue of the Virgin Mary. On the other hand, I do not want them to say I am not a Christian because I do." Mutual respect will ensue only if there is a real context in which conversations can take place. Interfaith services, joint participation at funeral rites of families that are split between Catholicism and Protestantism, mutual support in local and national civic organizations—all of these initiatives contribute at the level of the grass roots to the common unity of the Church for which all Christians are called to hope. Finally, more attention needs to be paid in the popular literature not to disseminate the misconceptions that in the past have borne false witness and bred deep mistrust.

David Traverzo Galarza contributes an essay on the "Historical Roots of the Contemporary U.S. Latino Presence: A Latino Protestant Evangelical Contribution." As editors of a volume on the Hispanic presence in the U.S. Catholic Church, we feel honored to have a contribution from a Protestant Evangelical. We recognize that the Latino body of Christ may extend beyond the visible limits of the Catholic Church and hope that this fine presentation will encourage the type of ecumenical discussions that took place in Washington in 1997.

Traverzo begins by noting that while the larger society identifies the U.S. Hispanic/Latino population as a distinct community, there is still great diversity within the particular Hispanic/Latino groups. According to Traverzo, the sum of common experiences and understandings outweighs the differences among U.S. Latinos/Hispanics. It is this common heritage that makes it possible to speak of a U.S. Hispanic/ Latino presence. One of the overarching factors that binds U.S. Hispanics/Latinos together in his opinion is that it is a history of Spanish-European and then Anglo-American invasion, conquest, colonization, and Christianization. Examining the contemporary plight of U.S. Hispanics/Latinos and the roots of this plight, it is possible to see a history of disfranchisement and disempowerment. He avers that the Hispanic/Latino presence in the United States had its birth in two major historical periods: the Spanish colonial era and the U.S. neocolonial phase. Therefore, he posits that the roots of U.S. Hispanic/Latino Christianity is found in these two eras as well, first Roman Catholic and then Protestant. Under both, the process of Christianization was marked by conquest and the use of religion as an instrument of societal control.

Despite this there are today indications of a vibrant and vital U.S. Hispanic/Latino Christianity. Traverzo argues that the role of U.S. Hispanic/Latino Christianity has had a positive and liberating character to it, both in its Roman Catholic and Protestant expressions. Many hopeful signs and new directions have emerged. There are a growing number of ecumenical training centers or programs to train clergy and laity from a Hispanic/Latino perspective. As a result, after five hundred years of struggle, U.S. Hispanic/Latino religion is developing a sense that new paradigms are required for a new day. In the forms of Roman Catholicism, mainline Protestantism, and Pentecostalism, U.S. Hispanic/Latino Christianity is united in its effort to foster a spirit of cooperation, common ground, and authentic community according to Traverzo. As we move toward the millennium and as the U.S. Hispanic/Latino community continues to grow, it is plausible that the role of U.S. Hispanic/Latino Christianity in both the religious and sociopolitical realms will increase. In the meantime, he is confident that the seeds of a Hispanic American social ethic can already be discerned.

The essay by Vicente López, O. Carm., "Cuando Lleguemos a Casa: The Journey to be Church," is an impressive example of the many lively conversations that took place during the weekend of the Washington conference on the topic of pastoral theology. By means of anecdotes, López reflects on his pastoral experience and raises the question of where to begin to prepare ministers to accompany people of faith, the *pueblo en marcha* (the people on the way). As one intimately involved in the various programs and movements that have given life to ministry among Hispanics/Latinos in the United States, he notes that stress has been placed on the "how to" rather than on the "what for" of ministerial preparation. López laments that for too long the issues of *el pueblo* have been a "bothersome novelty, a distraction from the main course of business" so that, although there have been all sorts of creative responses in the more popular, informal, and ad hoc programs, Hispanics/Latinos are not a part of the mainstream commitment of the Church. In particular he observes the lack of "a serious, generous, or creative response to [Hispanic/Latino] needs in the formal, more academic institutions under Church auspices." As a result, Hispanics/Latinos are waiting to be welcomed by the Church where they can recognize that *ésta es su casa* (this is your home). This requires that preparation for ministry among Hispanics/Latinos not just focus on pragmatic needs but also try to identify the grace and favor that the Hispanic presence adds to an evolving U.S. Catholic Church. López sees the *National Pastoral Plan for His-panic Ministry*[8] as a key element in this effort. He points to the necessary tension Hispanics/Latinos live in as they bridge two models of Church and ministry, namely "the authoritarian, hierarchical remains of a cleri-cal culture . . . stretched and challenged by the communal, shared, and consensual struggle of the *pueblo en marcha.*" This *encrucijada* (crossing) is a painful existence that tries to bridge the two seemingly contradic-tory means to the realization of the kingdom. However, existence at the *encrucijada* also gives birth to new life. Thus he maintains that the model of Church that Hispanics/Latinos declare for themselves will provide in the future the vision from which processes of formation will develop.

Another important contribution to the pastoral field is made by Gelasia Márquez Marinas in her essay "Hispanic Ministerial Prepara-tion: Pastoral Care and Hispanics." Márquez offers specific strategies for pastoral care primarily addressed to Hispanic/Latino immigrant families. She notes that in the parish setting it is particularly necessary to affirm, support, and welcome these families to the Church and to U.S. society. Immigrant families are especially vulnerable and in need of tools to negotiate the transition from one cultural context to another. These families are immersed in a threefold process of cultural transi-tion that includes psychosocial development, adaptation and adjust-ment by means of acculturation, and changes to the family structure. She acknowledges the dearth of theoretical and conceptual frameworks that might guide the pastoral care of newcomers and immigrants. How-ever, she names two interventions that offer the most promise, namely education and counseling directed toward the family. The family in par-ticular is the person's most important, reliable, and external resource for psychosocial development as well as the key social group that me-diates the larger world to the individual family member. The family has to be *the* matrix for healing according to Márquez since its stability contributes to the minority group's adaptation to the larger society. Thus Family Ministry needs to be directed to Hispanic/Latino families as they struggle to contribute to Church and society in the United States. Furthermore, this ministry should encourage families in their efforts to maintain their Christian and cultural sense of self, meaning, and worth as they learn to cope with a new and radically different environment. Education, as a strategy for pastoral care, is an important element in regaining a sense of belonging while counseling, especially if concrete, directive, and immediate, can help the family cope constructively with

8. The National Conference of Catholic Bishops, *National Pastoral Plan for Hispanic Ministry* (Washington, D.C.: United States Catholic Conference Office of Publishing and Promotion Services, 1987).

the stress produced by the new environment. Márquez notes that mediating structures, such as bilingual/bicultural liturgies and similar activities, are especially effective in the pastoral care of immigrant families, but these programs are still in need of a great deal of additional assistance. Moreover, the Church will be better able to carry out its mission only if we seek to learn more about the effects of immigration on Hispanic/Latino families and develop programs that support Family Life Ministry for these groups.

III. *LA FE ES GENERADORA DE CULTURA*: THE EXTENDED BODY OF U.S. LATINO CATHOLICISM

The faith of Hispanics never existed in a vacuum or in the purely interior realm of an individual's private religious experience. Without sacrificing the truly transcendent dimensions of the gift of faith, U.S. Hispanic Catholicism bears a cultural tradition with roots in the Iberian peninsula, colonial Latin America, diverse Amerindian and African traditions, present day Latin American and Caribbean countries, and the varied and changing Latino landscape of many different regions of the United States. Too often the cultural heritage of Hispanic Catholicism has been relegated to the realm of folklore, sentimentality, and vestiges of a past that is better left dead and buried. Latino theology today is not just unearthing cultural treasures in order to put them on display behind glass cases. Perhaps it is because faith and culture in the Hispanic tradition have always been inextricably intertwined that present day Latino theologians in the United States have taken a strong interest in the aesthetic character of human action.[9] Latino theologians today are saying that the always plural cultural tradition of Hispanic Catholicism is expressing itself in new ways even as it continues to testify to the same beauty of an incarnate Savior that itself transcends each and every particular cultural expression.

In the keynote address at a 1995 convention celebrating fifty years of Hispanic ministry in the United States, the speaker noted the ten-

---

9. Cf. Roberto S. Goizueta, *Caminemos con Jesús: Toward a Hispanic/Latino Theology of Accompaniment* (Maryknoll, N.Y.: Orbis Books, 1995), especially chapter 5, "Beauty and Justice: Popular Catholicism as Human Action"; Ana María Díaz-Stevens, "In the Image and Likeness of God: Literature as Theological Reflection," in *Hispanic/Latino Theology: Challenge and Promise*, ed. Ada María Isasi-Díaz and Fernando F. Segovia (Minneapolis: Augsburg/Fortress, 1996), 86–103; and Alejandro García-Rivera, *The Community of the Beautiful: A Theological Aesthetics* (Collegeville, Minn.: The Liturgical Press, forthcoming).

dency in U.S. Protestantism to separate faith from culture.[10] With its strong and noble tradition of defending the juridical right to religious liberty, the speaker argued, Anglo-American Protestantism as a cultural tradition can also err on the side of an absolutized private choice. Latino Catholicism need not "solve" the problem of free choice any more than it can ignore the modern Catholic defense of religious liberty. Instead Hispanic Catholics need to begin by understanding why their Catholic faith is generative of culture and why that same faith allows itself to be transformed into a culture that evangelizes.[11] In the words of the National Conference of Catholic Bishops of the United States:

> Although addressed to each person, the invitation to follow Jesus Christ has a necessary cultural dimension. Without it the Gospel becomes an abstract system of ideas and values that can be manipulated to excuse individual sin and social sin . . . [A] faith that does not generate culture is a sterile faith.[12]

Culture is accordingly a plural reality that has as its aim the cultivation of souls through process of personal, moral, intellectual, spiritual, aesthetic, and emotional maturation.[13]

Out of the cultural heritage born from faith emerges not only fervent religiosity but forms of social solidarity that witness a preferential option for the poor, the marginalized, and otherwise outcast. The essays that follow testify to the unique way in which the Hispanic body of Christ extends itself into the realm of culture and society and thereby can serve as a source of religious and social renewal in the United States.

10. Msgr. Lorenzo Albacete, "La Presencia Hispana y la Nueva Evangelización en los Estados Unidos," reprinted in ¡En Marcha! ed. the Secretariat for Hispanic Affairs, the United States Catholic Conference (Washington, D.C.: United States Catholic Conference Office of Publishing and Promotion Services, 1995), 10.

11. Ibid., "Para aprovechar bien esta oportunidad, es necesario comprender, comenzando por nosotros hispanos, el por qué nuestra fe católica es generadora de cultura, el por qué la fe se convierte en una 'cultura de evangelización.'"

12. National Conference of Catholic Bishops, The Hispanic Presence in the New Evangelization in the United States (Washington, D.C.: United States Catholic Conference Office of Publishing and Promotion Services, 1996), 17–9.

13. Ibid., 17: "The word culture comes form the Latin verb colere, which means to cultivate the ground. Eventually, the expression cultura animi, the culture of souls, came to designate the personal formative process of the individual. When the process of personal formation is understood in intellectual terms, a "cultured person" is someone who knows a lot ("una 'persona culta' es aquella que simplemente tiene muchos conocimientos"). However, personal formation is a process with intellectual, affective, ethical, and practical components. It touches on everything that is characteristically human."

In "The Sacramented Sun: Solar Eucharistic Worship in Colonial Latin America," Jaime Lara deftly unfolds a heretofore unexamined aspect of the dynamics of liturgical inculturation that took place in colonial Mexico and Peru. The term "sacramented sun" refers to the substitution of solar cults among the Amerindians with the Eucharist by means of conscious, selective, and deliberate inculturation on the part of the first Spanish evangelizers of the Americas. For example, Lara reveals that the Eucharistic monstrance in the form of a solar disk has its origins in the Americas: the evangelizers took the symbol of the sun worshiped by the Incas as a god in itself and converted it into a symbol of Christ by building on the solar imagery already present in Christian iconography and theology.

He argues that these efforts contributed to the unique heritage that the Hispanic/Latino presence in the United States brings with it. This heritage is one which *Sacrosanctum Concilium*, the *Constitution on the Sacred Liturgy* of the Second Vatican Council, affirms when it declares respect for the genius and talents of people in an attempt to incorporate their faith into the Church's life, including its liturgy.[14] Lara refrains from indicating what specific relevance his historical exposition has for Hispanics/Latinos in the United States in this era; however, he presents two tools that can help them inculturate faith in this context: (1) dynamic equivalence, i.e., taking existing symbols and reinterpreting them in light of Christianity, and (2) ritual substitution, i.e., the replacement of a non-Christian religious ritual with a Christian ritual, such as the Eucharist. Utilizing these strategies, the evangelizers of the Americas were able to change the root metaphors already operative in the belief systems of the Amerindian civilizations and incorporate them into the life of the Church.

Lara's article raises several questions for contemporary Hispanics/Latinos of the United States. For instance, what are the root metaphors that will need to be changed so that the presence of Hispanics/Latinos in the Church will be more readily recognized as a leavening source of change and renewal? How will the faith of Hispanics/Latinos be inculturated in the U.S. context? Hispanics/Latinos are likely to take the root metaphors of U.S. culture and adapt them to their own understanding of the activity of the triune God in the Church and in secular history. At the same time, those whose ministry involves work with Latinos must learn to understand and even participate emotionally, intellectually, and spiritually in the realities signified by the metaphors

14. *Sancrosanctum Concilium*, n. 37, in *Documents on the Liturgy 1963–1979: Conciliar, Papal, and Curial Texts* (DOL), comp. the International Commission on English in the Liturgy (Collegeville, Minn.: The Liturgical Press, 1982), 1.37.

and symbols that are incarnated in Hispanic/Latino cultures. Otherwise, they will not be able to appreciate the genius and talents in the Hispanic Catholic traditions or the genuine contribution of U.S. Latinos to the life of the Church in the United States.

Mario T. García examines "Catholic Social Doctrine and Mexican American Political Thought." His essay counters the trend that he notes in Chicano Studies to downplay the role of religion in Chicano life and in the early development of the field. His interest in the topic remains nonetheless that of a historian, viz., to highlight the way in which religion operates as a central cultural variable in the political identity of Chicanos and other Latino groups.

Drawing upon his extensive research into the generational history of Mexican communities in the United States, García looks at the influence of Catholic social teachings on the Mexican American generation, namely, that generation of Chicanos who were mainly of immigrant parents and who came of political age prior to and during the Great Depression and World War II. Their struggle with ethnic and political identity was made all the more difficult by the fact that most Mexican Americans in the Southwest were viewed primarily as a cheap pool of labor and suffered harsh forms of racial discrimination and segregation.

He documents the tangible influence of Catholic social teachings on two key political figures whose views helped to shape Mexican American political thought: Alonso Perales of San Antonio and Cleofas Calleros of El Paso. Two social encyclicals in particular were formative in the thought and lives of these two men: *Rerum Novarum* (1891) and *Quadragesimo Anno* (1931). In Calleros's case a long-term association with the National Catholic Welfare Conference (a predecessor of the current U.S. Catholic Conference) solidified his immersion in Catholic social thought, especially after he began to serve as the head of its Immigration Bureau in 1926. Perales came from a middle-class Mexican family in Texas, was educated in Washington, D.C., and returned to Texas to serve as cofounder of the League of United Latin American Citizens (LULAC), the predominant civil rights group for Mexican Americans in Texas. Both figures drew upon Catholic social teachings to argue for just wages and against illegal deportation, segregated schools, and the false stereotyping of Mexican workers as lazy and unproductive. They supported New Deal labor legislation and rebutted the widely prevalent charge that the recent influx of immigrant labor was somehow a cause of the Depression.

To the balanced thought on class conflict embodied in the social encyclicals, Calleros and Perales added their own hard-won wisdom regarding race. Even though many Mexican Americans served as loyal soldiers in World War II, there was little prospect that these same citizens would be treated upon their return to the States with equal dignity and with the same opportunities as their Anglo counterparts. As Perales admonished: "'Equal in the trenches, but also equal in the factories, in the stores, in the schools, in the Churches, in the restaurants, in the barbershops, in the theaters, and everywhere else.'" In sum, the rhetoric of social justice among the advocates of Mexican American rights in this period was certainly not antithetical to the American constitutional tradition of advocating the equal rights of all citizens, but it had an even firmer and perhaps even more effective foundation in the specifically Catholic articulation of the priority of labor over capital and the equal dignity of all creatures before their Creator. Much like John Courtney Murray, S.J., the famed North American Catholic theologian who several decades later defended religious liberty at the Second Vatican Council, neither Calleros nor Perales were afraid to assert that there was no outright inconsistency between holding strong Catholic views and being American. Operating with more boldness than even Courtney Murray, these men articulated a Catholic view of the human person at a time when the language of equal dignity for immigrants and other Hispanics was hardly commonplace. They thereby demonstrated in both word and deed the prophetic nature of a Catholic view of the human person.

Marcos Martínez addresses the relationship of "Community and the Sacred in Chicano Theater." His essay both develops a theoretical approach to the religious dimension of Chicano theater and cites numerous concrete examples of religious themes treated in recent Chicano productions. Martínez begins with the presupposition that contemporary Chicano theater is both similar to and different from earlier religious drama in the Hispanic tradition such as the didactic religious plays or *autos sacramentales* of the sixteenth-century colonizers of the Americas. The positive aspect of the analogy is visible on the levels of both the sacred and the profane. In both instances the dramatic instrument serves to represent the communal relationship of a people to God. While the colonizers drew upon an explicitly liturgical tradition, contemporary drama theorists note a para-liturgical "sacrifice" in the modern actor's sense of giving himself or herself over to an audience. The vacuum created by the absence in modern secular life of an explicitly dramatic relationship to the divine is in a sense filled by modern drama's tendency to exalt its own function in quasi-theological terms.

Martínez examines both anti-ecclesiastical and pro-Church attitudes in recent Chicano drama in order to identify what distinguishes the

new expression of community and the sacred from its colonial forebears. In the 1970s, for example, it was quite typical for theater troupes
to depict the Church as a retrograde, neocolonial institution whose clergy
were capable only of operating in collusion with the status quo. In these
plays the missionary impulse is redirected completely to the
antihegemonic purpose of building up audiences for Chicano theater.

More recently, new initiatives such as La Compañia de Teatro de
Alburquerque have taken a new tack. La Compañia sees itself as a ve-
hicle for Christian ethics in action. The actors prepare for their productions by defining their goals and offering a small prayer. Their selection
of material follows a model of community development. Themes are
chosen that fuse classical Spanish religious drama with modern issues
of social justice. Most remarkable was the production of a nonconfron-
tational drama about three undocumented Mexicans who end up in an
American jail. One prisoner in the New Mexico State Penitentiary was
so moved by the production of *La Pasión of Jesus Chavez* that he tattooed
the playbill's image of a suffering Christ onto his back! Clearly, the new
relationship between the community and the sacred opens up a realm
in which a highly compelling call for social justice is articulated by means
of an explicitly religious endeavor and by drawing upon explicitly Christian themes and devotional traditions. Authentic Chicano theater,
Martínez argues, must still ward off the Church's tendency to censure
material; nonetheless, a collaborative paradigm has been struck for renewing drama following the Church's historical interest in sustaining a
culture of life based upon a model of "sacred love."

Because of its brevity, one might be tempted to view the last essay
in the volume as a mere coda. In fact, it addresses provocatively and
incisively issues that Hispanic/Latino theologians in the United States
have sometimes shirked. In "Spain in Latino Religiosity," William A.
Christian, Jr. offers a brief but intriguing critique of several presupposi-
tions underlying much discourse on Hispanic/Latino religion. Specifically, he questions the notion that much of Hispanic/Latino religion
has its roots solely in Spanish pre-Tridentine spirituality. He suggests
instead that the spirituality of the Iberian peninsula has continued to
influence Hispanic/Latino religion to this day. An example of this is the
Cursillo de Cristiandad which made its way into the United States by
means of Spanish lay persons in the 1950s. Moreover, Christian observes
a mutual influence between Latin America and Spain in terms of religious practices. Some scholars have claimed that the Hispanic/Latino
stress on Mary and on Jesus as a child or as the suffering Christ is
pre-Tridentine. Christian argues on the basis of extended research into
the religious practices in Spain that the stress on Mary and Jesus actu-

ally reflects a long-term effect of the Council of Trent on Spanish and Latin American spirituality. In Spain, this meant the substitution of devotion to local saints by devotion to local images of Jesus and Mary. Instead of differentiating between pre- and post-Tridentine religiosity in order to distinguish Hispanic/Latino from Euro-American religion, Christian attributes the differences to different kinds of European Catholicism. Furthermore, Christian questions the use of the term "popular" to qualify Hispanic/Latino religion. He points to the fact that many clergy and religious share aspects of "popular religion" with lay persons and suggests that careful ethnographic study is required to discover the degree to which Hispanic/Latino religion is influenced by Amerindian and African religion. As more ethnographic study takes place, various practices thought to be Amerindian in origin have been found to be rooted in the ritual practices of rural Spain. In addition, he advocates the examination of the elements of Hispanic/Latino religiosity to see which can "travel" into the realm of a dominant religion and survive in a plural society in which Hispanics/Latinos form a minority.

IV. CONCLUSION

El Cuerpo de Cristo: The Hispanic Presence in the U.S. Catholic Church should be read as part of a larger conversation. The conference sponsored by The Catholic University of America and the Instituto de Liturgia Hispana was somewhat unique in that it brought together the resources of a research university and a national organization dedicated to the study of Hispanic liturgy with a wide array of pastoral agents whose expertise— as much *conocimientos* or personal knowledge as factual information— was an even more valuable contribution and stimulant to further thought and action. Academics who had had no previous acquaintance with the leadership of U.S. Hispanic ministry came away impressed. Pastoral agents noted with satisfaction that a conference in English on a wide variety of themes enabled them to learn and participate in a new and enriching manner. We are obviously not able to reproduce in this volume these conversations in the precise manner in which they played themselves out over the course of those three days.[15] Instead we have compiled a book that we think will help others to imitate the level of reflection and the type of collaboration that emerged in our own *encuentro*.

We hope that this volume signals a new level of participation of both the U.S. Catholic Church and the correlative academic and pastoral institutions. We were not able to include essays on every possible topic. Some topics that needed more attention, for example, the expanding diversity of Latina voices in Church and academy or the theology of the immigrant, were not covered as adequately as we would have liked. The essays nonetheless reflect a level of self-awareness, intellectual vitality, and spiritual renewal that is genuinely new in the context of the larger U.S. society. We are not making a plea that the Hispanic presence be assimilated into the mainstream of cultural life nor are we enjoining in any way the maintenance of a *barrio* Catholicism. The central leitmotif of the book, *el Cuerpo de Cristo,* calls us to seek the greatest possible unity without having to be at all ashamed of skin color, ethnic and social background, cultural heritage, devotional life, or familial and other personal commitments.

During the conference we felt that a distinctive enthusiasm emerged from the joint collaboration of academy, Instituto, and Church. The experience of the conference made us realize that the Hispanic presence in the U.S. Catholic Church can be a force mediating the polarities that split us up. In our view, the Hispanic presence forces us to rethink the dichotomies that make people feel that they must choose to be *either* liturgical purists *or* defenders of popular piety, *either* research scholars *or* pastoral agents, *either* defenders of the clergy *or* advocates for the laity, *either* religious traditionalists *or* social progressives, *either* ecumenists *or* evangelizers, *either* U.S. Hispanics *or* Latin Americans. On the basis of this experience we feel with great conviction that Hispanic ministry, Latino theology, and the diverse cultural traditions of Hispanic Catholicism can no longer be pushed to the margins as the province of a small group of scholars and professional activists. These concerns need to be viewed as central, we feel, because they issue simultaneously from the heart of the Church *and* the very fabric of life today in the United States. We offer this volume knowing that each of these essays displays the renewed seriousness with which Hispanics/Latinos are now taking themselves and deserve to be taken by the wider community in the ecclesial body of Christ and the world.

15. In particular, constraints of space and other limitations prevented us from including the excellent presentations of the following individuals: Rev. Joseph Augustine DiNoia, O.P., Dr. Eduardo Fernández, S.J., Dr. Lorenzo Florián, Dr. Mark Francis, C.S.V., Ms. María Luisa Gastón, Dr. Marina Herrera, the Most Rev. Sean O'Malley, O.F.M. Cap., Mr. Mario Paredes, Ms. Mary Frances Reza, Rev. Arturo Pérez Rodríguez, the Most Rev. Agustín A. Román, and Dr. Samuel Solivan.

The Wounded Body

Theology, Liturgy, and Spirituality

1

"Why Are You Frightened?"

U.S. Hispanic Theology and Late Modernity

Roberto S. Goizueta

These days we are repeatedly reminded that, during this last decade of the twentieth century, we stand on the threshold of Christianity's third millennium. Interestingly, the last decade of each century thus far has often been a time of great turmoil and change. Recall just a few of the history-altering events that took place during these crucial decades: the sacking of Byzantium in 196; the First Crusade in 1096; the so-called "discovery of the New World," the expulsion of the Jews from Spain, and the Catholic Monarchs' "reconquest" of Spain from the Moors—all in 1492; the issuance of the Edict of Nantes in 1598, ending the French wars of religion; the invention of the steam engine in 1698 and the cotton gin in 1792; the French Revolution and its aftermath in the last decade of the eighteenth century; the ratification of the U.S. Bill of Rights in 1791; the fall of the Berlin Wall in 1990, and the aftermath of that momentous event, in which we are still living.

In retrospect, we know that, while all of these events have left their enduring mark on history, the precise features of that mark have often been ambiguous and complex. Who can think of the great motto of the French Revolution, "liberté, egalité, fraternité," without also conjuring up images of priests and nuns being led to the guillotine? Who can read about the first steam engine, or the cotton gin, and the magnificent economic and industrial development that they precipitated without, at the same time, recalling images of polluted streams and razed rain forests? Who can extol the great courage and commitment of the Christian missionaries during the conquest and evangelization of the Americas without, at the same time, mourning the human toll exacted by that "evangelization," whose victims numbered in the millions? Who can celebrate the destruction of the Iron Curtain without weeping with the many victims of the ongoing conflicts in Eastern Europe?

History is fraught with such ambiguities. Perhaps the most significant trait of these last years of the twentieth century, a period that we have come to call postmodernity, or late modernity, has been humanity's increasing consciousness of the inherently ambiguous character of human history. Our consciousness has been raised—not by political leaders or intellectuals, not by popes or theologians—but by the many victims of that history, whose barely-muffled cries can no longer be silenced, the victims whose scars and bleeding wounds can no longer be ignored. In a century that has witnessed more human victims of violence than all other centuries combined, the modern ideology of progress, the belief that human history is a process of uninterrupted improvement, is under attack like never before. Yes, there has been progress, but too often at the point of a gun, either literally or figuratively. To be living in the late modern period is to have discovered that, in the words of the German Jewish philosopher Walter Benjamin, "every great work of civilization is at the same time a work of barbarism."[1]

The challenge that this last decade of the twentieth century presents to us is that of honestly confronting the truth of Benjamin's dictum, the truth written on the scarred bodies of the victims of progress, and entering the next millennium with the humbling conviction that those scars will and must forever remain the privileged criterion of what we are wont to call "human progress." In the presence of those scars, and the many wounds still being inflicted today, any talk of human progress, development, or freedom is obscene. Any talk of economic growth, bridges to the twenty-first century, technological revolutions, the victory of capitalism, or the end of history is obscene. Yet, as we stand on the brink of a new millennium, the modern ideology of progress has not loosed its hold on our society. Though the cries of the poor have begun to break through, these continue to be muffled by other cries, coming from Wall Street, Madison Avenue, and Silicon Valley, cries proclaiming a future of limitless, universal economic growth and consumption, a world where technology will humanize everything and everyone it touches.

Nevertheless, however strong our nostalgic desire to relive some supposedly idyllic time when the victims' voices were still being successfully silenced, we cannot turn back the clock. Our future surely will and must be forged alongside the scarred bodies, the victims of modern progress. *That* is the situation of late modernity and the central task before us as we come to the threshold of the third millennium.

---

1. Walter Benjamin, quoted in David Tracy, *Plurality and Ambiguity: Hermeneutics, Religion, Hope* (San Francisco: Harper and Row, 1987), 69.

What has been, is, and will be the role of U.S. Hispanics in this late modern context? More specifically, what might be the role of U.S. Latino theology in this historical context? It is my conviction that perhaps the primary role of Latinos and Latinas is, in the words of Justo González, to "bring our fellow citizens to an acknowledgment that the present order is the result not merely of hard labor, daring enterprise, and rugged individualism but also of theft."[2] In performing this role, Latinos and Latinas will be reviled and calumnied; we will be accused of ingratitude and disloyalty, of reopening old wounds and ignoring the great progress that has already been made.

From the time of St. Paul, who always insisted that what he preached was Christ Crucified, those Christians who have persisted in regularly recounting stories of suffering and crucifixion have been reviled. From the early gnostics on, others have found the story of Jesus Christ's own passion and crucifixion at best uncivil and at worst unbelievable, preferring to worship a heavenly Christ, a Christ without wounds, a civilization without barbarism. Surely Christ's victory over death through his resurrection has healed those wounds—if they were ever really there in the first place! Let us celebrate that victory! Let us forget those old wounds and move on! Get over it! Stop wallowing in suffering! Those were the cries of the first gnostics, and they are the cries of contemporary gnostics who, in the face of the still-bleeding wounds on the Body of Christ, would have us look beyond them to a pure, unscarred future.

To these modern gnostics who will not surrender their illusory belief in a resurrection without the cross, a progress without cost, the Latino community today cries out "put your fingers here, and see our hands; and put out your hands and place them in our side" (John 20:27). To them, we, like St. Paul before us, "preach Christ crucified" (1 Cor. 1:23). And, like St. Paul, we do so not to condemn but to make a genuine reconciliation possible.

The apostles themselves had abandoned Jesus during his own passion and crucifixion. After proving themselves untrustworthy friends who fled from Jesus' side when the going got rough, the apostles surely needed to be reconciled with him. And the resurrected Jesus sought such a reconciliation when he approached them in his glorified body. But the Jesus who sought reconciliation with his friends who had abandoned him was a Jesus who still bore the physical wounds of that abandonment and its violent consequences. His resurrection had not erased the wounds; instead, the wounds themselves became the instruments

---

2. Justo González, *Mañana: Christian Theology from a Hispanic Perspective* (Nashville: Abingdon Press, 1990), 40.

of Jesus' reconciliation with his friends. "See my hands and my feet" (Luke 24:39). "Put your finger here, and see my hands; and put out your hand, and place it in my side" (John 20:27).

Whenever we read the accounts of Jesus' post-resurrection appearances, especially his appearance to Thomas in John's Gospel, our tendency is to assume that the wounds on his glorified body made possible the apostles' reconciliation with Jesus because those wounds were the visible proof that Jesus had indeed risen, that their faith had not been in vain. Yet, as surely the apostles themselves knew, their faith had long ago vanished when they abandoned Jesus to his persecutors. And surely they knew that they themselves had helped inflict the wounds on Jesus' hands, feet, and side. Surely, upon seeing the wounds, the sound of the cock crowing must have echoed in Peter's ears. Is it possible that, when Jesus invited them to see and touch his wounds, he was inviting them not only to believe in the truth of the resurrection but also, concomitantly, to acknowledge, confess, and repent of their own complicity in his crucifixion? Is it possible that the visible wounds engendered belief not only because they allowed the apostles to see the truth about the resurrected Jesus Christ but because, at the same time, the wounds allowed the apostles to see the truth about themselves? Could it be that it was this *twofold* revelation that ultimately effected their reconciliation and conversion? Could it be that the wounds on Jesus' glorified body were the mirrors not only of God's glory but also of the apostles' own humanity, of their own souls?

Maybe that is why, upon seeing the wounds, the apostles did not immediately rejoice. At first, they were startled and terrified, they were frightened (Luke 24:36–37). "Why are you frightened?" Jesus asks them (Luke 24:38). Were they frightened simply because they did not recognize this strange apparition? Or, perhaps also, because they recognized it only too well?

And yet, through the recognition of their own complicity in Jesus' crucifixion, the apostles became reconciled to Jesus and came to know the truth of the resurrection, the victory of love over death, the victory of reconciliation over division. The sign of the reconciliation between the apostles and Jesus is that, having showed the apostles his wounds, the resurrected Jesus immediately invites the apostles to break bread with him, thereby renewing his table fellowship with them and foreshadowing that ultimate symbol of reconciliation, the eucharistic meal: "Have you anything here to eat? They gave him a piece of cooked fish which he took and ate in their presence" (Luke 24:41–43).

In contemporary U.S. society, a fundamental role of Latinos and Latinas is that of bearing witness to the wounds, remembering and recounting the passion, giving voice to the memories of suffering, thereby reminding contemporary men and women that "every great work of civilization is at the same time a work of barbarism," that the resurrected Body of Christ will always—must always—remain marked by the violence out of which new life was born. (Aren't we all Doubting Thomases? Don't we all need to see the wounds?) To pretend otherwise would be to crucify the victims once again, to murder them a second time, this time by *forgetting* their passion, their crucifixion, their wounds, the price of the resurrection. The entire U.S. Hispanic experience—from the *mestizo* heritage and the experience of exile to the popular religion of our Latino communities—makes manifest those wounds and, in so doing, reveals the very ambiguities that the victors, those who prefer a resurrected body without wounds, dare not confront.

The memories of crucifixion are what the German theologian Johann Baptist Metz has called "dangerous memories, memories which make demands on us."[3] Within the modern ideology of progress, all such memories are extinguished; what remains is mere nostalgia, the memory of the "good old days," where the atrocities of war and conquest are transformed into tales of adventure, genocide is romanticized at the Alamo, and the period of slavery is wistfully recalled in the idyllic images of "Gone With the Wind."[4] "It is not by chance," continues Metz, "that the destruction of memory is a typical measure of totalitarian rule. The enslavement of men [*sic*] begins when their memories of the past are taken away. All forms of colonialization are based on this principle. Every rebellion against suffering is fed by the subversive power of remembered suffering. The memory of suffering continues to resist the cynics of modern political power."[5] No amount of progress, success, or liberation ever extinguishes those memories anymore than Jesus' resurrection extinguished his wounds:

> The history of freedom remains much more and always a history of suffering. Pain, sorrow, and melancholy remain. Above all, the silent suffering of the inconsolable pain of the past, the suffering of the dead continues, for the greater freedom of future generations does not justify past sufferings nor does it render them free. No improvement of the condition of freedom in the world is able to do justice to the dead or effect a transformation of the injustice and the non-sense of past suffering. Any emancipative history of freedom in which this whole history of suffering is suppressed or supposedly superseded is a trun-

---

3. Johann Baptist Metz, *Faith in History and Society: Toward a Practical Fundamental Theology* (New York: Seabury Press, 1980), 109.
  4. Ibid.
  5. Ibid., 110.

cated and abstract history of freedom whose progress is really a march into inhumanity.[6]

In other words, however much we may want to "put the past behind us," to do so would be to put behind us our own fathers and mothers, our grandfathers and grandmothers, those who came before us and whose struggles gave us birth as a people. Modern ideologues of progress would have us believe that the present is unconnected to the past, which has forever been erased by the historical achievements of modern men and women. We, however, know that the past will always remain a part of who we are, and who our children are. Acknowledging that fact is a precondition for true human progress, true liberation.

The unhappy and, indeed, dangerous task of serving as a mirror to U.S. society is not one which, as many pundits argue, exacerbates divisions; on the contrary, it is a necessary precondition for unity, reconciliation, and authentic human progress. A reconciliation between those social and ecclesial groups that today remain polarized will be authentic and long-lasting only insofar as it is grounded in the *truth*, or what Jon Sobrino has called an "honesty about the real":

> The poor show the reality of this world for what it is: sin. Sin is not the only reality in this world. But whatever else the reality of this world may be, unless we see flagrant sin, we shall miss the mark—if we really want to discover the truth of that reality. . . . Human beings act first and foremost in terms of precisely how they see reality. . . . Precisely as sin, this reality tends to conceal itself, to be relativized, to pass itself off as something secondary and provisional in the larger picture of human achievements. It is a reality that calls on men and women not only to recognize and acknowledge it, but to take a primary, basic position regarding it. Outwardly, this reality demands that it be stated for what it is and renounced. This is the stage of prophetic denunciation. But inwardly, this same reality is a question for human beings as themselves participants in the sin of humankind. It is the call for their first great conversion.[7]

In the case of Latinos and Latinas in the United States, such "honesty about the real" implies an honesty, not only about the unprecedented opportunities that we have enjoyed in this country, not only about the resurrection that many of our people have experienced here, but also an honesty about the very real wounds that still mark our community, wounds that cannot be simply wished away without thereby wishing away the blood, sweat, and tears shed by so many of our forebears. If we are indeed a people who value community and family above all,

---

6. Ibid., 128–9.
7. Jon Sobrino, *Spirituality of Liberation: Toward Political Holiness* (Maryknoll, N.Y.: Orbis Books, 1988), 30–1.

then we are a people who will not easily surrender our memories, for these are our link to past generations, whose toil, suffering, and unquenchable hope in the ultimate victory of life over death made possible whatever resurrection we may experience today and in the future.

The historical experience of *mestizaje* that unites U.S. Hispanics subverts the modern ideology of progress, the belief that civilization precludes barbarism, or that the resurrection precludes the crucifixion. The *mestizo/a* knows otherwise, for he or she is a child of both "civilization" and "barbarism." What is more, when we review our history, we have a difficult time distinguishing civilization from barbarism. It is astonishing what atrocities have been committed and justified by the very peoples considered to be the guardians of civilization and the torchbearers of human progress. Conversely, how courageous, generous, civilized, and, indeed, Christ-like has so often been the behavior of those peoples dismissed as "barbarians."[8] The memory of *mestizaje* forces the United States, as a nation, to be honest about the real by reminding us that "we are all *ladrones* [thieves]."[9] Such a mutual acknowledgment is the first step toward reconciliation.

This, it seems to me, will be the central task of the next century: we must move toward a reconciliation that takes as its starting point the scarred bodies of the many victims of modern progress, a reconciliation that proclaims the resurrection without pretending that the crucifixion never took place or that its scars can ever be completely erased. That task, furthermore, is at the very heart of U.S. Latino theology, which challenges modern gnostic attempts to interpret Jesus' crucifixion and resurrection through the lenses of an ideology of progress.

U.S. Latino theology takes as its starting point the preferential option for the poor; it calls us to read the Christian faith, the Christian Scriptures, and the Christian tradition through the eyes of the poor—and the poor have a *history* that is not identical with the history of progress. The preferential option for the poor in no way promotes conflict or division; on the contrary, the option for the poor reflects a profound commitment to human unity, human reconciliation.

Any reconciliation based upon a dishonesty about historical reality denies the human dignity of the victims, the victims' right to their *own* history, their *own* memories; such a supposed reconciliation can only be

8. One of the most profound analyses of the barbarism of the "civilized" and the civilized behavior of the "barbarians" was that articulated by the great Spanish missionary and theologian Bartolomé de Las Casas; see Gustavo Gutiérrez, *Las Casas: In Search of the Poor of Jesus Christ* (Maryknoll, N.Y.: Orbis Books, 1993).
9. González, *Mañana*, 40.

fraudulent and illusory. The command, "if you want peace, work for justice," has important implications not only for the present and future, but also for the past. As we proclaim at every eucharistic liturgy, the past, present, and future are intrinsically related: "Christ has died, Christ is risen, Christ will come again." Christ's resurrection and Second Coming themselves have a history, a history of suffering. Christ's suffering on the cross is not forgotten after the resurrection; it is taken up into the glorified life of Christ and is thereby transformed—not eliminated.

To make a preferential option for the poor, then, is to claim that any authentic reconciliation must take as its starting point the ongoing crucifixion of the marginalized members of our society; it is to claim that the starting point for any appropriate Christian understanding of the resurrection is the cross; it is to claim that the starting point for any appropriate Christian understanding of the glorified body of Jesus Christ are the wounds on his hands, feet, and side; it is to claim that the starting point of any appropriate Christian understanding of history is the history of the victims. The apostles saw the wounds on Jesus' body and believed—they believed in the truth of the resurrection as the victory of God's gratuitous love over their own sinfulness. The wounds revealed to the apostles that, even though they had abandoned Jesus, Jesus would not abandon them.

The task of U.S. Hispanic theologians is to articulate the theological significance of this resurrected, though still-scarred body of Jesus as he is today present in the Hispanic community. It is this Jesus who is revealed, above all, in the Latino experience of *mestizaje* and in our popular Catholicism. If, in its blind subservience to the gods of historical progress, modernity has preached a Jesus whose resurrection erases all memories of his violent death, U.S. Hispanic theology witnesses to Jesus' resurrection without pretending that *that* resurrection somehow justifies and erases the past. In the remainder of this paper, I would like to briefly single out just four of the important ways (there are many more) in which U.S. Hispanic theology is today helping Christianity proclaim such a resurrection, by retrieving: (1) the nature of religious faith as necessarily and inescapably "cultured"; (2) the lived faith of the people as the fundamental *locus theologicus;* (3) the centrality of "lo cotidiano" to that lived faith; and (4) the importance of the body as mediating the human encounter with God.

The modern ideology of progress cannot abide the existence of particular cultures for, insofar as these may not share in that ideology, they will be perceived as obstacles to progress. Native American culture was and is such an obstacle, so today we have the reservations. Mexican culture was such an obstacle so, in the last century, we had the Treaty of

Guadalupe Hidalgo and, today, Proposition 187. Ideologues of progress will use whatever instruments are at their disposal. In the five centuries since 1492, the primary instruments have been military and political. In the United States, the most effective and most subtle of these instruments has been the ideology of the "Melting Pot"; for a people to participate in and benefit from historical progress, they would have to leave behind their pre-modern, backward, inferior cultures, languages, and religious practices.

During the last half of this century the preferred instruments of progress have been economic. The unprecedented advances we are witnessing today in the areas of technology and communications media are providing uniquely powerful instruments for assimilating other cultures into this seemingly autonomous and inexorable march of history to an ever greater, ever more digitized future. Technology, we are assured, equals freedom. The modern ideology of progress has rejected the Natural Law theory of Thomas Aquinas only to replace it with the Natural Law theory of Bill Gates: the inexorable direction of history is inscribed—or, rather, encrypted—in the computer chip, and we have no choice but to acquiesce in this predestined natural order. What U.S. Hispanics must challenge here is not the unquestionable potential of technological and economic progress but the illusion that such progress can come, and has come without tremendous human cost.

In the Americas, in 1492, Christianity itself was born from this illusion. With the conquest, the centuries-old gnostic temptation to deny the wounds on Christ's glorified body resurfaced in the guise of the missionary blind to the wounds on the body of the converted, Christianized Amerindian, or the Christianized African slave. The soul having been saved, those wounds could and should be forgotten, for they had served their purpose. Crucifixion was merely a stepping stone on the way to resurrection. And to preserve that illusion, the sacredness of *all* particular cultures as mediations of the divine, as revelations of God, had to be denied—except, of course, Western culture.

From the outset, and at its very foundations, U.S. Hispanic theology has rejected such an understanding of the Christian faith. By grounding our reflections in the U.S. Hispanic history of *mestizaje*, U.S. Hispanic theologians are retrieving the central role of culture as mediator of the Christian faith and, in so doing, are making visible to the entire Church the resurrected, though still scarred body of Jesus Christ. To insist that *all* faith is culturally mediated and incarnated is to unmask the totalitarian pretensions of modernity, which views particular cultures (except, of course, Western culture) merely as "objects" of modernization, and the pretensions of modern Christianity, which views particular cultures (except, of course, Western culture) merely as "objects" of evangelization. U.S. Hispanic theology understands culture not merely as a sinful human reality in need of evangelization, but *also* as a place of grace, a mediator of divine revelation, an encounter between a people and their God.[10] The physical scars on the body of Christ are precisely what reveal it and make it recognizable as the *resurrected* body of Christ. A Christian faith without culture is no more visible or real than a resurrected Jesus without the wounds—and no more recognizable. However sinful and in need of transformation, human culture is also the place where we encounter the resurrected Christ.

Virgilio Elizondo, especially, has articulated the profound theological implications of U.S. Hispanic culture as, above all, a *mestizo* culture. In its most profound sense, the historical experience of *mestizaje* is, as Elizondo has demonstrated, an experience of the ultimate inseparability of crucifixion and resurrection. The birth of the *mestizo* people from the violence of the conquest—in both its Spanish and Anglo-American versions—makes manifest the power of the resurrection in history; out of the ashes of conquest, a new people are born, new life emerges, the Latin American peoples.[11]

Yet, even today, that new life bears the visible marks of its violent birth. Our countenances, our music, our language, and, especially, our popular religion all testify to the failure of modern Western progress to eradicate the lingering vestiges of pre-modern cultures. Just as the resurrected Jesus would not hide his wounds from his friends, neither will the Latina hide her dark skin, or the African rhythm of her music, or her halting accent, or her devotion to Our Lady of Guadalupe or to the Crucified Jesus, or the stories her grandmother has passed down to her. Like Jesus' scars, these are the living memories of a still-wounded resurrection. In the midst of our daily struggles as a people, the crucifixion is being transformed into new life; every day we see new signs of hope. Yet, whether we like it or not, this hope, this new life, cannot be one which transcends the painful past, one that transcends the struggles of those who came before us. For the *mestizo*, the memories of suffering and crucifixion will forever be borne into the present and the future.

If the *mestizo* history of U.S. Hispanics serves as an enduring reminder that civilization and barbarism always accompany each other,

10. On the necessary connection between revelation and culture, see, for example, Orlando Espín, *The Faith of the People: Theological Reflections on Popular Catholicism* (Maryknoll, N.Y.: Orbis Books, 1997), 93–9.

11. See especially Virgilio Elizondo, *The Future is Mestizo: Life Where Cultures Meet* (Bloomington, Ind.: Meyer-Stone, 1988), and *Galilean Journey: The Mexican American Promise* (Maryknoll, N.Y.: Orbis Books, 1983).

and that the wounds of barbarism cannot be erased even from the resurrected body of a new civilization, then the single place where that *mestizo* history is most powerfully manifested is in the popular religion of the Latino people, in our lived faith. In the symbols, narratives, and ritual practices of Latino popular religion, hope and liberation are born in the very midst of our memories of suffering. Here, especially, the future is never simply an overcoming of the past, or the resurrection an overcoming of the crucifixion.[12]

The hope-against-hope symbolized by Our Lady of Guadalupe is not one which demands that we forget the pain of the past or the struggles of our ancestors. The new life she symbolizes is not one unmarked by the scars of violence. By virtue of her *mestizo* countenance, her many indigenous attributes, and, above all, her identification with the indigenous man Juan Diego, *la Morenita* stands before us like the resurrected Jesus before the apostles, witnessing to the power of a divine love that, while redeeming and liberating us from our own inhumanity, will never allow us to forget that inhumanity. For the racial, cultural and religious *mestizaje* of the Guadalupan symbol serves as a mirror of modernity's soul as much as the scars on the resurrected Jesus' body served as a mirror of the apostles' souls. And that is why, as Elizondo has demonstrated, modern Western society rejects the *mestizo/a,* and why modern Christianity rejects Guadalupe and, indeed, Latino popular religion as a whole. And, like Jesus, *la Morenita* continues to ask us today: "Why be frightened?"

If modern Christianity cannot understand Guadalupe, even less can it understand that other great symbol of Latino popular religion, the Crucified Christ. More specifically, what modern Christianity cannot understand are, once again, the wounds. Seen through the lenses of the modern ideology of progress, the wounds vanish with the resurrection, the resurrection obviates the crucifixion, and we all live happily ever after. What most effectively unmasks the gnostic undercurrents of modern Christianity is its fear of the wounds.

For all of modern culture's obsession with the body, the body is still treated as little more than a machine to be oiled and fitted properly or a mannequin to be sculpted and made up properly. What ultimately makes the body a *human* body is the unique history inscribed in its wrinkled and drooping skin, its graying hair, and, yes, its "unsightly" scars—but these, we are told, must be eliminated. The beautiful body, the resurrected body, must have no unsightly scars. These must be covered up.

---

12. On the way in which suffering and hope are mediated through Latino popular religion, see especially Espín, *The Faith of the People,* 156–79.

So too, then, must the scars on the body of Western civilization be covered up.

As Gustavo Gutiérrez avers, however, the true criterion of our respect for the beauty of the human body is not whether we treat our own body well, but whether we treat the body of *the poor person* (i.e., the wounded person) well; before asking the question "Is my body beautiful?" I must answer the question "Is the poor person's body beautiful?" and must do so not simply in rhetoric but in action.[13] In that light, the modern glorification of the body is unmasked as, once again, simply another gnostic repudiation of human physicality. And, whether by simply eliminating the corpus from the cross altogether, or whether by presenting the wounds as a timid afterthought, modern Christologies reveal this same gnostic heritage.

The Christologies being articulated by U.S. Hispanic theologians, however, reflect and present a very different Jesus Christ. Grounded in the Jesus of Latino popular religion, the Crucified Jesus, U.S. Hispanic theologians are retrieving the intimate connection between the Crucified Christ and the glorified Christ. That connection is never completely severed, not even after the resurrection; the scars and the memories remain, even in the midst of the Easter celebration. Indeed, it is precisely by touching the wounds on the body of Christ and the neighbor that we acknowledge and make real that love that conquers death. The victory of life over death is made manifest when, standing at the foot of the cross, Mary accompanies Jesus even to the bitter end; it is made manifest when the Roman Centurion, looking with compunction at the wounds, proclaims "Truly, this was God's Son"; the victory of life over death is made manifest when the Apostles dare to touch the wounds on the glorified body of Jesus, or whenever each of us dares to see and touch the wounds of our neighbor and invites the neighbor to touch our own wounds. "Why are you frightened?"[14]

And the wounds that modernity has been most terrified of touching—indeed, the wounds most invisible to modernity—are those on the bodies of women and children. Historical "progress" takes place in history, that is, in public, in government offices, in the streets, in corporate boardrooms, in the offices of the Vatican, in palaces, in the marketplace. That is where history is "made," where human progress and achievement are measured. History is not "made" in a child's bedroom, or on a living room sofa, or in a kitchen, or on the patio, or the front steps.

13. Gustavo Gutiérrez, *We Drink From Our Own Wells: The Spiritual Journey of a People* (Maryknoll, N.Y.: Orbis Books, 1984), 102–3.
14. See Roberto S. Goizueta, *Caminemos Con Jesús: Toward a Hispanic/Latino Theology of Accompaniment* (Maryknoll, N.Y.: Orbis Books, 1995).

Human progress is not measured by the time spent listening to your spouse's fears about losing his or her job, or the time spent preparing meals, or playing ball with the children, or struggling to survive as a family in a crime-ridden environment, or tending to the needs of an aging parent, or praying at the foot of the *altarcito*. Thus, it is precisely here, in the home, that one is likely to find the deepest of the wounds inflicted by the ideology of progress—simply because, in modernity, the home has become all-but-invisible. Like nature itself, the home is, at best, a repository of resources to be used for promoting economic growth and productivity (e.g., by raising children to become good productive workers, or by providing a "good wife" who will tirelessly patch up the wounds inflicted on her husband by a dehumanizing work environment). And, like nature itself, the life of the home is, at worst, nothing but an obstacle to human progress and achievement; the incessant demands of spouses, children, and family stand in the way of human progress, whose arena is not the home but the public square, the marketplace.[15]

What are the "wounds," the "acts of barbarism" that are obscured when the home becomes invisible? Who bears these? The persons who bear the brunt of modernity's costs are, of course, those persons who have historically been relegated to the home, outside the scope of history: the women, the children, and the elderly. It is no coincidence that a greatly disproportionate number of the poor in our nation are precisely women, children, and elderly. If the gnostic illusion of modernity—that human progress can come without cost, or the resurrection without visible scars—is to remain inviolable, the wounds of the women, children, and elderly must remain hidden, indeed invisible.

Latina theologians are in the forefront of current attempts to uncover these wounds and recover the experience of women, children, and the elderly as sources of theological insight and wisdom. In their insistence on the significance of "lo cotidiano" as a key *locus theologicus*, *Latinas* are insisting that the daily struggle of Latinas, the everyday struggle to survive with dignity in a hostile environment, is at the very heart of human history. *Lo cotidiano* is at the very heart of that history into which Christ has been born, in which he continues to accompany us, and upon which it is the task of the theologian to reflect. Consequently, Latina theologians argue that the proper response to sexism in modern society is not simply to make the public square, the professional world, and the institutional Church—those places where history is made—more accessible to women, but also to transform our very

15. See ibid., 111–9.

conception of history itself to include not only the life of the public square but the life of the family as well. If the achievements of women do not appear in our history books, it is not only because the contributions of women to human history have been ignored but, even more so, because our very conception of what counts for human history is itself skewed, or distorted. Conversely, if more men participated in the everyday life of the home, and if this were our primary context for theological reflection, our conceptions of what counts for historical experience and human progress would almost certainly change.[16]

The expulsion of the home from the realm of human history and progress also has important implications for the Church's appreciation of popular religion. To identify human progress or, in theological language, salvation history only with those human activities undertaken in the public square is, in the case of U.S. Hispanics, to devalue our popular religious practices, for these are based primarily in the home and neighborhood rather than in the public square or, its ecclesial analogue, the parish. And the devaluation of popular religion, in turn, contributes further to the exclusion of women and the laity from participation in the public life of the Church and society since popular religious practices are not usually led by male clergy but by women and laypersons.

Insofar as it participates in the modern identification of human progress with the public square and its criteria of truth, then, the Church will continue to dismiss popular religious practices as "backward," infantile vestiges of a pre-modern era. Once the Church locates itself at the center of the modern public arena, it becomes beholden to the rational, economic, technological criteria of that arena. Consequently, popular religious practices like "El Día de los Muertos" (The Day of the Dead) or symbols like the "Divino Rostro" (Divine Countenance) are likely to be perceived as reflecting an irrational, even morbid preoccupation with death. Popular religion is depreciated not only because it is primarily practiced outside the boundaries of the public square, but because, in so doing, it does not participate in the "rationality" of public life.[17]

Logical reason is neat and tidy; it resolves contradictions and ambiguities. In modernity, truth becomes identified with that which can be demonstrated logically, and human existence becomes identified with our capacity for such logical, rational thinking (viz., Descartes' famous

16. See especially María Pilar Aquino, *Our Cry for Life: Feminist Theology from Latin America* (Maryknoll, N.Y.: Orbis Books, 1993), 38–9 and Ada María Isasi-Díaz, *Mujerista Theology: A Theology for the Twenty-First Century* (Maryknoll, N.Y.: Orbis Books, 1996), 66–73, 128–47.

17. Goizueta, *Caminemos Con Jesús*, 111–9.

axiom "I think, therefore I am"). Reality can ultimately be understood through the use of logical reason; as Galileo explicitly argued, the entire universe is ultimately reducible to and knowable through mathematics. The abstract concept—the most abstract of which is the number—becomes the measure of all things. Truth is whatever a computer decides is true; anything else is mere subjective opinion. Rationalism is the language of industry, government, the academy, and, too often, the Church itself.[18]

The modern ideology of progress is essentially an abstract, conceptual construction of historical reality. Abstract concepts do not allow for ambiguity or contradiction: two plus two must always equal four, not five; black cannot also be white; truth cannot also be falsehood; civilization cannot also be barbarism; intellect cannot also be emotional. Therefore, Benjamin's assertion that every act of civilization is at the same time an act of barbarism literally makes no sense within the modern worldview; neither does the notion of a resurrected body that still bears its wounds, a Jesus Christ who, even after the resurrection, will always remain *both* crucified *and* risen; or the notion of a Virgin who is both Mary and Tonantzín; or the notion of an everyday struggle that is both painful and liberating; or a history that is both public and private. Such an "either/or" worldview cannot encompass the Latino experience of *mestizaje* or our experience of a God who is known primarily not through rational concepts alone but through the embodied relationships lived out in the symbols, narratives, and rituals of our popular religion, a God who pleads with us: "Why are you frightened? *Touch* me." To know the truth about reality, the truth about God, the truth about ourselves is to *touch* the wounds. And this is precisely what modern Western theologies have been afraid of doing; this is what U.S. Hispanic theology invites us all to do.

Jesus, however, does not ask us to touch his wounds either out of self-pity or out of a desire to condemn us for what we have done to him. He invites us to do so in order that we may experience the resurrection. When we touch the wounds of our neighbors, we will see ourselves—our own souls—reflected in those wounds. We will come to know the truth of our *common* humanity, that our lives are intimately bound together, that the wounds inflicted on one ultimately affect us all. Yes, we will initially be terrified and frightened. But then we will hear a voice call out, "Why are you frightened?" And we will no longer remain blind or passive in the presence of our wounded neighbors; instead, like the Apostles, we will commit ourselves to destroying the violent barriers that inflict the wounds, we will invite our neighbors to break bread

18. Ibid., 132–72.

with us: "Have you anything here to eat?" And then—only then—will
we know the truth of the resurrection.

As surely as the memories of his own crucifixion were inscribed on
Jesus' hands, feet, and side, these memories are inscribed in U.S. Hispanics' culture, our language, our faces, and our popular religion. Ours
are the memories of Juan Diego, repeatedly humiliated, ignored, silenced, and rejected by the Spanish bishop; the memories of the
Villaseñor family who, fleeing poverty and war in their native Mexico
for the promise of "El Norte," were forced to beg and scavenge through
manure piles for undigested grains of corn to feed their children.[19] They
are the memories of Osvaldo Martínez, a young middle-class Puerto
Rican forced to hear cries of "hey spic, go back where you came from"
when walking through his own neighborhood in New England; memories of Virgilio Elizondo, ridiculed by his seminary professors and fellow students for the "stupid practices of Mexican Catholics";[20] memories of the young Latina college student I knew who wanted to be a
doctor but who, though valedictorian of her high school class, had been
advised by her college counselor to "study something you can handle";
memories of thousands of men and, especially, women struggling to
keep their families together while holding down two, three, and even
four jobs merely to make ends meet; memories of a family who will
never again be together, never again celebrate or mourn together, forever separated by that cruel fate that Cubans have learned to call "el
exilio."

Yet this is by no means the whole story; there is another side. With
the help of *La Morenita*, Juan Diego eventually converts the Spanish
bishop. The Villaseñores thrive today in Southern California. Osvaldo
Martínez is a successful labor attorney. Virgilio Elizondo is today . . .
well . . . *Virgilio Elizondo*. That young Latina undergraduate is currently
a student at Loyola University Medical School in Chicago. And the
Latino community has established itself at the very heart of U.S. society. All of these memories are also part of our collective memory. We are
indeed a resurrected people, but a people who—out of love and respect
for those who went before us—cannot forget that we remain a wounded,
scarred people: "Put your finger here, and see our hands; and put out
your hand, and place it in our sides" (John 20:27). With those words,
the resurrected victims of modern progress, whose voices can no longer
be silenced, proclaim the possibility of human reconciliation. If we heed
them, those words may yet become the seedbed of reconciliation:

19. Victor Villaseñor, *Rain of Gold* (New York: Dell, 1991).
20. Elizondo, *The Future is Mestizo*, 24.

The truth of the matter is . . . that we do not destroy the reality of the past. The unremembered past endures. This is that part of the truth that each section of society is required to face. It can do so thoughtfully and carefully or risk the possibility that it will erupt in an uncontrollable manner. Suppressed and forgotten truth is part of the inclusive truth that must be uncovered if a polarized society is to be united in the healing process. More realistically, it is only as we pursue the *possibility* of uncovering the full truth that the *possibility* of healing is there.[21]

Why are you frightened?

21. Charles Villa-Vicencio, "Telling One Another Stories: Toward a Theology of Reconciliation," in *The Reconciliation of Peoples: Challenge to the Churches,* ed. Gregory Baum and Harold Wells (Maryknoll, N.Y.: Orbis Books, 1997), 36.

2

Hispanic Liturgy and Popular Religiosity

A Reflection[1]

JUAN J. SOSA

Imagine that you are standing before the magnificent Cathedral of the small town of Orvieto, not far from Rome, on the solemnity of Corpus Christi, with thousands of people, some of whom are dressed in Medieval costumes representing the various "offices and functions" of the township, preparing to embark on their annual procession through the streets.

"The ones who are dressed up," someone says, "are all descendants of the original families of Orvieto." "The Cardinal will go up to that balcony after Mass," another spectator claims. Indeed, the loudspeakers are blurting brief announcements to guide inhabitants and visitors alike in some form of an orderly fashion—as orderly as you can expect anywhere in Italy.

"What about Mass, the Eucharistic Liturgy? It must be concluding; look, there must be some First Communions too." The bronze gates to the beautiful Cathedral open and behind the elaborate canopy that highlights and protects the presider, who is carrying a sumptuous golden monstrance, follow the few thousand worshipers who attended the sa-

1. The following sources were useful in preparing this article: José Manuel Bernal, *Iniciación al Año Litúrgico* (Madrid: Ediciones Cristiandad, 1984); J. Castellano, "Religiosidad Popular y Liturgia," *Diccionario de Liturgia: Documentos completos del Vaticano II* (Bilbao: Ediciones Mensajero, 1980); Richard P. McBrien, *Catholicism*, rev. ed. (New York: HarperCollins, 1994); A. G. Martimort, *The Church at Prayer*, one-volume ed., ed. A. G. Martimort (Collegeville, Minn.: The Liturgical Press, 1992); Juan J. Sosa, "Liturgia Hispana en Estados Unidos," *Notitiae: Sacra Congregatio Pro Culto Divino* 20 (1984): 688–96; Juan J. Sosa, "Renewal and Inculturation," in *Liturgy: A Journal of the Liturgical Conference* 9, no. 2 (1990): 17–23; P. Manuel Traval y Roset, *Milagros Eucarísticos* (Quito, Ecuador: Librería Espiritual, 1989).

cred liturgy inside the Cathedral. Such numbers, however, can never supersede the many thousands of pilgrims who are about to enjoy the 'other' sacred liturgy, the liturgy that takes place every 'Corpus Christi Day' outside of the Cathedral doors, the very reason—many claim—why people continue to visit Orvieto every year on this solemnity.

Behold, the canopy passes by us. We can see the Blessed Sacrament on top of the monstrance, in the customary *lunetta*. Yet, we notice that the monstrance itself is not round, in the shape of the sun, as the monstrances that Latin American communities developed during the centuries of evangelization,[2] but rather square, a square and large frame encased in glass. Inside the glass, as if enshrined for all eternity, one can see a piece of cloth covered with stain. It is a relic, indeed, the subject of a mythical story that still awes the listener and inspires the believer.

Most people, we notice, have come to see the relic. Do they forget that the Blessed Sacrament stands above it? Not so, but the relic seems to evoke feelings and reactions of tremendous significance for them at a point in this 'public' liturgy in which bodily movement, music, colorful banners, prayer, and tradition blend in space and time in a unique fashion. The Eucharist itself helps them remember the reason for the relic, and the relic, I hope, brings them to a better awareness of the Eucharist.[3]

It was the year A.D. 1263, during the Pontificate of Urban IV, who found himself in Orvieto together with his attendants. A German priest had embarked on a pilgrimage to Rome to recharge his spiritual batteries, for indeed many doubts pursued him. As he stopped in Bolsena to celebrate the Eucharist at St. Christina's Church, he noticed that at the elevation, the host turned to flesh, and blood began to drip consistently from the sacred host on the corporal set on the altar. At the urging of the Pope, the sacred relic of the stained corporal was brought to Orvieto's Cathedral where it has remained over the centuries. Under the impact of these events, Pope Urban IV himself established the feast of Corpus Christi for the universal Church one year later. Some even claim that the phenomenon of Bolsena, now in Orvieto, inspired a young theologian named Thomas Aquinas to write one of his most famous poems, *Pange Lingua Gloriosi*.

2. See Jaime Lara, "The Sacramented Sun: Solar Eucharistic Worship in Colonial Latin America," elsewhere in this volume.

3. For the relationship of popular devotions to the liturgy see *Sacrosanctum Concilium* (SC), in *Documents on the Liturgy 1963–1979: Conciliar, Papal, and Curial Texts* (DOL), comp. the International Commission on English in the Liturgy (Collegeville, Minn.: The Liturgical Press, 1982), 1.13.

The story, the celebration, the liturgy—official and nonofficial—all blend together to form a mosaic of faith, unique yet popular, local yet universal in its intent, festive and yet reflective. Myth and ritual imbue themselves in the collective unconscious of a people in touch with the fibers of their human experience and motivating them to search for the Sacred at its best.[4] Myth and ritual work together to suspend space and time, allowing the divine to appear before the human at its most vulnerable moment of existence, a moment of crisis for the Pope, who was besieged by persecutors, and for the priest who was besieged by unbelief, a moment of crisis, perhaps, for a people in search of the divine at a time of misery and oppression. Myth and ritual arise in human tradition to shape the heritage of a community of faith that seeks to transmit its powerful message of hope, as conceived by the repetitive character of its annual celebration.[5]

All of this, and even more, constitute the dynamic interplay of ingredients involved in the dual treatment of our topic. For the Eucharistic phenomenon of Orvieto and its impact on human culture and Church life has been paralleled by the multiple, festive, Church-rooted celebrations that encompass—at least for Hispanics in Latin America and in the United States—a dual experience of worship: *Hispanic liturgy and popular religiosity.*

While these phenomena of public worship, held outside or inside a Church building and alongside so-called official liturgies, provide a sense of pageantry that may satisfy the curious mind, the reality of these two ingredients in today's pastoral life is far from defined, accepted, or understood by all. To say the least, Hispanic liturgy and popular religiosity appear before our bishops, pastors, theologians, catechists, liturgists, and musicians in many parts of the world, and of course, here in the United States, as an *ambiguous reality.*[6] I would like to examine such ambiguity in three sections: (1) The ambiguous nature of this combina-

4. See Theodor H. Gaster, *Thespis: Ritual, Myth and Drama in the Ancient Near East,* rev. ed. (New York: Harper & Row, 1961); Ronald L. Grimes, *Beginnings in Ritual Studies,* rev. ed. (Columbia, S.C.: The University of South Carolina Press, 1995).

5. See Victor W. Turner, *The Ritual Process: Structure and Anti-Structure* (Chicago: Aldine, 1969).

6. The fourth instruction on the implementation of *Sacrosanctum Concilium* (SC), *Instruction: Inculturation and the Roman Liturgy* (Washington, D.C.: United States Catholic Conference Office of Publishing and Promotion Services, 1994), §45, appears to modify SC 13 in its approbation of popular devotions that accord with the liturgy. Though neither SC 13 nor the fourth instruction prohibit the practice of employing popular devotions as a source of inculturation of the liturgy, they certainly add to the ambiguity. *Eds.*

tion of liturgy and popular religiosity (What is it?); (2) The ambiguous reasoning behind its appearance in the Church and its persistence in the Hispanic heart (Why is it what it is? Why has it persisted over time and continued to rise above the reforms of the Church?); and (3) the ambiguous search for a means to approach this phenomenon today (How do we handle it?; How do we deal with it now and tomorrow?). Finally, I will offer some conclusions that hope to summarize my key points in this reflection.

TENSION 1: THE AMBIGUOUS NATURE OF HISPANIC LITURGY AND POPULAR RELIGIOSITY

The tension about the nature of these two ingredients for worship, some claim, stems out of the growth of the Church itself, particularly after the Edict of Constantine in A.D. 313, when, despite much documentation about the catechumenate, the *mystagogia* for neophytes in certain areas where the Church grew rapidly was not deep enough or substantial enough for their understanding. Some writers claim this lack of catechetical depth actually led some of the neophytes to maintain a series of non-Christian practices to which they had grown accustomed before their initiation.[7]

Others claim that the liturgical families of the East and the West during subsequent centuries did not distinguish between what was "official or magisterial" and what was "popular," for there was a continuous and healthy interplay between the two.[8] At any rate, this pre-medieval period witnessed both the ever-present tension and ultimate rift between the East and the West, manifested at the Council of Chalcedon in 451 by theological discussions and reaching a definite peak in the eighth century when the Eastern emperor attempted to impose a policy of iconoclasm (the abolition of all religious images). Not only did the Church resist such an attempt, but it opted for an elaborate iconography that would be both aesthetic to the eyes and didactic—those who

7. See especially Josef A. Jungmann, *The Early Liturgy: To the Time of Gregory the Great*, trans. Francis A. Brunner (Notre Dame: The University of Notre Dame Press, 1959).

8. See for example Adolf Adam, *Foundations of Liturgy: An Introduction to Its History and Practice*, trans. Matthew J. O'Connell (Collegeville, Minn.: The Liturgical Press, 1992); Anscar Chupungco, *Worship: Progress and Tradition* (Washington, D.C.: The Pastoral Press, 1995); and Herman A. J. Wegman, *Christian Worship in East and West: A Study Guide to Liturgical History*, trans. Gordon W. Lathrop (Collegeville, Minn.: The Liturgical Press, 1990).

could not read or write would learn about the mystery of God's revelation and love through mosaics and paintings.

We need not turn so far back in time to remember witnessing this particular tension particularly after Vatican II, when, in the iconoclastic vein of those early centuries or in this century's attempt at simplification, many pastors interpreted the liturgical reform brought about by *Sacrosanctum Concilium* as a justification to get rid of statues, images, novenas, and other devotions, ignoring the call of paragraph 13 of the document to update and reform, not eliminate, the *pia exercitia*.[9] At the same time, we need not forget that still today we witness in many sanctuaries such an overabundance of cluttered symbols. This points not only to a misconceived iconography, but to what most would simply consider "poor taste," communicating more a sense of the "mediocre" than a sense of the sacred.

The medieval reform of Leo IX and, later on, Gregory VII in the early part of the eleventh century provided the Church with both a sense of freedom from the influence of emperors, princes, and political figures and an autonomy that established it as a spiritual society organized with its own legal, juridical, and governing rights. Many claim this centralization of Church life, expressed in institutional centralization and the concomitant development of the liturgy and the spirituality of Christians by the hierarchy and the monks, gave birth to parallel forms of faith-expressions mediated by the cultures of the people: *popular religiosity*.[10] As a progressive devotion to the humanity of Christ evolved during this medieval period—a result in part of many apocryphal stories about the birth of Jesus and his passion—a greater sensibility toward sentiments and feelings in public expressions of popular worship also evolved, while the official liturgy of the Church, a patrimony of monks, hierarchy, and the clergy which was celebrated in Latin and transformed by the beauty of Gregorian Chant, rooted itself in a reality apart from the feelings of the people.

What did the evangelizers bring to the Americas after 1492? A sense of the sacred permeating the need to convert all native peoples to the one, true faith, probably motivated by the need to face the upcoming end of a century and the apocalyptic spirituality of the era, but also by a sense of freedom—at least before the Council of Trent in 1547—to

9. DOL 1.13.

10. See for example Anscar J. Chupungco, *Liturgical Inculturation: Sacramentals, Religiosity, and Catechesis* (Collegeville, Minn.: The Liturgical Press, 1992); A. G. Martimort, "Definitions and Method," in *The Church at Prayer*; and Orlando O. Espín, *The Faith of the People: Theological Reflections on Popular Catholicism* (Maryknoll, N.Y.: Orbis Books, 1997).

adapt the rites and symbols of the Church to the needs of her new members in the New World.[11] As the the Risen Christ and his pure, Immaculate Mother were substituted for the Sun and the Moon, and the temples of ancient divinities gave way to the building of Churches and Basilicas, the testimony of many local American saints began to embody the gospel for the people in unique ways. And even though the official demands of the Tridentine liturgy eventually reached the shores of the new Catholic communities, the people continued to express their new-found faith in Jesus and His Mother with symbols that emerged out of their own cultural-religious experience: *la Cruz de Mayo, los aguinaldos y pastorelas, las novenas y procesiones, el culto a los santos y a sus reliquias, las imágenes y las velas.*[12] They still do this today.

Liturgy and popular religiosity may be perceived from this brief historical perspective as distant as vinegar and oil, or as near as two sides of the same coin. In the hands of pastoral agents, they are not only tools for evangelization now, as they have always been in the past, but sources of deep spiritual nourishment that place us all in touch with the core of human experience, our religious self. Particularly among Hispanic Catholics, liturgy and popular religiosity are and should be viewed as complementary and not exclusive of one another.

In describing our first tension, and in attempting to answer the question, "What is it?" we can say that among Hispanics, liturgy and popular religiosity embody a language of worship that is unique and enriching, open-ended and thus accessible to growth, a marriage and not a divorce—as in early medieval times—sisters that, though siblings, are not in competition with one another, unless our pastoral leaders make them compete by ignoring and neglecting them.

In the last few decades, these two components have become the source of theological interest as a result of the reflection of Latin American Church leaders and as a reaction to secularism at all levels of life.[13] However, one must admit that the connection is mentioned only lightly in the Medellín documents of 1968, officially targeted by the magisterium for the first time by Pope Paul VI in 1974 both in *Marialis Cultus* and in *Evangelii Nuntiandi,* explored more fully by the gathering of bishops at Puebla in 1979, most recently assumed under the heading of in-

11. See Jaime Lara, "Precious Green Jade Water: A Sixteenth-Century Adult Catechumenate in the New World, *Worship* 71 (1997), 415–28.

12. . . . . the May Cross, the gifts and mystery plays, novenas and processions, the cult of the saints and their relics, images and candles. *Eds.*

13. For an overview of the importance of popular religion to Hispanic/Latino theological reflection see Arturo J. Bañuelas, "U.S. Hispanic Theology: An Initial Assessment," in *Mestizo Christianity: Theology from the Latino Perspective,* ed. Arturo J. Bañuelas (Maryknoll, N.Y.: Orbis Books, 1995), 53–82.

culturation by John Paul II, and constantly referred to by liturgists, pastors, and some theologians in their writings.[14] Nonetheless the interplay between liturgy and popular religiosity continues to be ignored by most Church leaders and pastoral agents today even though it continues to be extremely important for many people. Even for the sects and other syncretistic groups, it has become an avenue of recruitment and integration into a new identity.

TENSION II: THE AMBIGUOUS REASONING BEHIND ITS APPEARANCE IN THE CHURCH AND ITS PERSISTENCE OVER THE CENTURIES
(THE WHY OF THE WHAT)

Certain sciences such as anthropology, sociology, and psychology, among others, can definitely assist theology in its quest to reinterpret the interaction between liturgy and popular religiosity.

Three reasons, among many, seem to prevail as ways of answering the question that permeates our focus now: Why? The heart of the answer lies in understanding the *religious person (homo religiosus)*[15] in all of his or her complexity as the religious person faces him/herself and others under these global realities.

THE NEED FOR SALVATION

More than ever today one feels the hunger for spirituality and meaning in people. More than ever Hispanic Catholics find themselves at the crossroads of life when, after leaving their culture of origin, they tend to neglect and abandon the foundations of their "meaning" level—the religiosity that fosters and sustains their identity. They proceed to substitute their religious heart for economic improvements at the risk of losing the best of their heritage and tradition. Some in the past had been forced to abandon externally the expression of that religious heritage under the assimilating pressures of a society foreign to them and hostile to their development. In the present, many Hispanics themselves seem to buy into our consumer-oriented society as the answer to all problems. More evident in the urban centers of our country toward which

14. For a summary and interpretation of these see Michael S. Driscoll, "Liturgy and Devotions: Back to the Future?" in *The Renewal that Awaits Us,* ed. Eleanor Bernstein and Martin F. Connell (Chicago: Liturgy Training Publications, 1997), 68–90.

15. This term was coined by Mercea Eliade; for an interpretation of Eliade's concept see David Cave, *Mircea Eliade's Vision for a New Humanism* (New York: Oxford University Press, 1993).

Hispanics move in ever greater numbers, the result of this process is dismal: the disintegration of their personal and family life, which, in turn, echoes in them the need to find wholeness and harmony by rediscovering their myths and rituals in a new way and under new circumstances. Who can help? If we, the Church, are not present to them, someone else will be.

INCLINATION TOWARD THE SACRED

The sacred is not institutional nor can it be institutionalized. People have their own inspiration and treasure of faith-expressions. In the sacred the religious person experiences a proximity to nature, lost in most of our industrial society at large. Before the sacred, the religious person becomes a protagonist at worship, not a spectator. The religious person, especially, though not exclusively, under a crisis, seeks to receive the unveiling of the mystery as the healer of all crises. In the sacred, those categories of social life by which we distinguish one another, such as race, denomination, social and economic status, disappear, for all religious persons experience the oneness of God. As tribal members set aside time and space to experience "liminal" moments by which they could be in touch with the power of their roots, transmitted by their elders,[16] Hispanic Catholics today seek to withdraw from the deafening noises of human life to experience the "rumor of angels," the whisper of God and the affirmation of their present reality. They recognize in the sacred that ultimate reality without which they could not live and toward which they journey. In the sacred, they begin to find themselves, if their 'elders' are willing to lead them to the sacred.

WORSHIP/RITUAL AS LIBERATION AND TRANSFORMATION

As rational, logical, disciplined, and orderly existence becomes unbearable, the source of constant strain and continuous pain for Hispanic Catholics at the non-rational level (i.e., sentiments, feelings, passions), the search for liberation and peace from this personal and family crisis begins. When confronted with the difficulty of human existence and without much solution, Hispanic Catholics find in religious rituals both the gift of God as presence and the space and time to play in the midst

16. Liminality as a ritual concept was introduced by Arnold Van Gennep and further developed by Victor Turner and Ronald L. Grimes. See Arnold Van Gennep, *The Rites of Passage,* trans. Monika B. Vizedom and Gabrielle L. Caffee (Chicago: The University of Chicago Press, 1960); Victor Turner, *The Forest of Symbols: Aspects of Ndembu Ritual* (Ithaca, N.Y.: Cornell University Press, 1967); Ronald L. Grimes, *Beginnings in Ritual Studies.*

of strains and tensions. Religious rituals liberate them and allow them to mediate through their own culture their perception of God and humanity. Religious rituals allow them to speak a language distinct from that of society, not the language of economics or technology but a language of faith, which remains understood only by those who share the same faith. It also allows them to mediate, through their own culture, those symbols that emerge out of their own collective memory and identify them as one.

In answer to our second question, the 'why' of the 'what,' we must turn not only to history but rather to the signs of the times. In times of crisis, our people seek more than an answer, a way toward liberation. They bring to our table their own dialogue with human existence and religious symbols. Are we prepared to dialogue with them?

The U.S. Church, through our Hispanic Catholics, is witnessing an ongoing tension that requires attention and focus. In the dialogue between liturgy and popular religiosity, we need to perceive other ongoing dialogues that should become part of the pastoral life of the Church in a more serious way. We need to address the broader dialogue between faith and culture that calls for a reinterpretation of our pastoral life in light of the needs of the people and not of our needs, as structured by previous experiences not present today. Secondly, we also need to enter into the dialogue between our Catholic culture and non-Christian cultures still prevalent in the religious symbolism of our Hispanic Catholics, who, in turn, come from areas of Latin America in which several cultures and non-Christian religious practices prevail, some of native American ancestry, others, of African roots.

I propose that we are still in diapers about this last dialogue, and the previous one has merely begun to catch our attention. I would furthermore like to propose that popular religiosity and liturgy—rather than remaining opposed and distant elements of our pastoral life—can become for us the avenue through which we can reinterpret those stories and symbols that shape the Hispanic worldview. I venture to propose that, for Hispanic Catholics, this constitutes the avenue to a healthy inculturation of the Gospel and the path to the new evangelization so badly needed in our culture of death.

TENSION III: THE AMBIGUOUS SEARCH FOR A MEANS TO APPROACH HISPANIC LITURGY AND POPULAR RELIGIOSITY TODAY
(HOW THE WHY OF THE WHAT CAN MAKE SENSE)

The essence of this third section lies in a tension that we have discussed before at previous meetings of the Instituto de Liturgia Hispana, first in

Alburquerque, New Mexico in 1984[17] and, later, in Phoenix, Arizona in 1992[18]: the balance between *tradition* and *creativity*.

Tradition does not mean "archaic," old-fashioned, or obsolete. Tradition is dynamic and, by its very nature, encompasses the core heritage of a people's belief system.[19] Popular religiosity, more than liturgy, has embodied the best of the Hispanic traditions particularly during the last five hundred years. The various groups of Hispanics all feel at home at one another's popular celebrations of faith. Tradition may have its limitations: it may not lend itself to innovations, but—properly guided by authentic elements of faith and the patience of pastoral agents—it may become open-ended to accept new forms of expression.

Creativity, on the other side, does not mean "anarchy," relativism, or individualism. Creativity is based on a healthy appreciation of diversity as a criterion channeled both by anthropology and theology. Through creative endeavors that respect the best of the tradition and use the core of symbolic expression, Hispanic Catholics can rediscover themselves on a journey of spiritual enrichment.

Consider a concrete example. When a Good Friday procession begins at the conclusion of the English Good Friday service and one allows the English-speaking participants to carry the statue of Christ out of the church into the street while the image of Mary, already outside of the church and surrounded mostly by the Hispanic members of the community, awaits and St. John the Evangelist is carried by the youth of the parish, who long to be near to the Lord and not give up on life despite family and social difficulties and misunderstandings, we Hispanics are trying to be creative within a traditional framework of liturgy and popular religiosity. Such is a service that, at the conclusion of this triple-imaged procession, allows the English-speaking participants to go home, the Hispanics to enter the Church for their liturgical service, and the youth to reflect at prayer and fasting in a different setting. But, for once, they have found unity and support around the imagery of their cultural and Catholic tradition.

Tradition and creativity must remain in constant dialogue with each other. We, the Church's pastoral agents, must make it happen; this is a dialogue of deep respect for the many prayerful forms that the people display in their search for a new beginning and a better tomorrow.

17. This conference, entitled Somos Peregrinos: La Conferencia Nacional de Liturgia Hispana, took place from 27–30 September 1984.

18. This conference, entitled Quinta Conferencia Nacional: La Religiosidad Popular de los Hispanos: Mitos, Símbolos y Creatividad, took place from 25–28 October 1990.

19. See Chupungco, *Worship: Progress and Tradition,* as well as Espín, *The Faith of the People,* for particularly germane analyses of tradition and creativity.

The Paul VI Roman Missal provides us with avenues of adaptation for the interplay between liturgy and popular religiosity to "happen" at the level of both Cathedral and parish celebrations.[20] The openness in the monitions, the carefully crafted texts at certain celebrations in which the Introductory Rites involve the entire assembly in body and song, such as the Blessing of Palm Branches on Palm Sunday, the Blessing of Candles on the Feast of the Presentation of the Lord, the Blessing of the New Fire at the Easter Vigil, provide us with good models of interaction. The Book of Blessings and the subsequent revision of other rites, such as the Marriage Rite, will continue to provide us with good spaces in which the people can find their role as a ministerial assembly. But these texts are not enough; more work must continue in bringing the rites of our Church closer to the people for whom they are intended.

In essence, the efforts of the Instituto de Liturgia Hispana and collaborative academic bodies, such as The Catholic University of America, must continue to ensure that the "how" of the "what" may find expression once the "why' is more and more appreciated by our people. The efforts of all pastoral agents in their spiritual growth and the service of God's people must become apparent for many other organizations to focus on the promotion of this interplay between liturgy and popular religiosity as the treasure of an authentic spirituality among our Hispanic Catholics.

CONCLUSIONS

The challenge is ours to face and to confront. Before a culture of death, on the way to the third millennium and called to announce and recreate a civilization of love, are we willing to take Hispanic liturgy and popular religiosity seriously?

Hispanic liturgy and popular religiosity are not only here to stay, but to grow. Just as one cannot abandon liturgy to itself, for it might tend to lack its focus—the people for whom it is intended—one cannot abandon popular religiosity to itself, for it can be easily manipulated by other entities and for other ends that might deviate it from its liberating power.

The anthropological and theological analysis, already available from the Mexican-American perspective and the Caribbean worldview,[21]

20. Of particular interest is the *General Instruction of the Roman Missal*, ch. 2, DOL 208.7–57.
21. In addition to Espín, the work of Virgilio Elizondo, Arturo Pérez, and the Instituto de Liturgia Hispana can be useful for seminaries and universities addressing the question of the anthropological and theological aspects of His-

among others, must reach our seminaries and the curriculum of all universities and centers of learning. Our future priests must understand how our people move and are moved at worship. Our pastoral agents must also learn how not to rationalize liturgy and popular religiosity and, thus, not to relegate them to "Cinderella" roles, the "filler" courses and independent studies, thereby diminishing their importance in relation to other areas of theological research.

All of us must heed the voice of the liturgical reform uttered by *Sacrosanctum Concilium* and the subsequent documentation discerned and issued by the post-Conciliar group of *periti* known as the *Consilium*.[22] If the motivating force of the reform became grounded in the criteria of *participation, the rediscovery of the Scriptures, the use of the language of the people, the development of ministries,* and *the cultural adaption currently referred to as "inculturation,"* then we would already have with us an overwhelming treasure of spiritual wealth in the interaction between liturgy and popular religiosity.

Lastly, all of us must heed the voice of our people, whom we serve and for whom we exist. In their need, they cry for worship that can heal them and free them. In their joy, they long for worship that can help them share their humanity through its best possible cultural mediation— their symbols. And in their hope they look toward us with pride so that we can help them become pilgrims of love on this journey to the year 2000, not messengers of despair and death. Are we willing and ready to walk with them these extra miles by reaching out to them at the deepest core, their "circle of intangibles," and help them experience the liberating presence of the Spirit-at-work within and among them through the powerful interplay between (our/their) Hispanic liturgy and (our/their) popular religiosity?

---

panic devotional practices and liturgy.

22. *Consilium ad exsequendam Constitutionem de sacra Liturgia* (The Council for the Implementation of the Constitution on the Sacred Liturgy). See Annibale Bugnini, *The Reform of the Liturgy 1948–1975,* trans. Matthew J. O'Connell (Collegeville, Minn.: The Liturgical Press, 1990), 49–53.

3

Biblical Interpretation from a U.S. Hispanic American Perspective

A Reading of the Apocalypse

JEAN-PIERRE RUIZ

Juan vio el número de los redimidos
y todos alababan al Señor.
Unos oraban, otros cantaban
y todos alababan al Señor.[1]

INTRODUCTION

The first verse of the popular hymn, "Alabaré," widely known in Spanish-speaking and English-speaking congregations both Catholic and Protestant, provides what I hope will prove an appropriate overture for these reflections on biblical interpretation from a Hispanic/Latino perspective. After all, the importance of music as a medium for the transmission of key social and religious values resounds in texts as ancient as the psalter itself, and this hymn's reference to the Apocalypse's vision of the redeemed invites earthly choirs to participate in an interpretive move that responds in kind to the heavenly choruses of praise.[2] While congregations singing "Alabaré" might not explicitly identify that activity as a matter of biblical interpretation, our willingness to take it as such in the context

---

1. Manuel José Alonso and José Pagán, "Alabaré," in Oregon Catholic Press, *Flor y Canto* (Portland, Ore.: OCP Publications, 1989), 450.
2. See William L. Holladay, *The Psalms through Three Thousand Years: Prayerbook of a Cloud of Witnesses* (Minneapolis: Augsburg/Fortress Press, 1993); Carlos Rosas, "La música al servicio del Reino," in *Voces: Voices from the Hispanic Church*, ed. Justo L. González (Nashville: Abingdon Press, 1992), 153–8; Edwin David Aponte, "Coritos as Active Symbol in Latino Popular Religion," *Journal of Hispanic/Latino Theology* 2, no. 3 (1995): 57–66.

of this discussion of the Hispanic presence in the U.S. Catholic Church is a sign of the progress that biblical scholarship has made in its turn to the reader as a matter of recognizing the importance of the real concerns of real readers, beyond the interest of reader-response criticism in such constructs as the "implied reader."[3]

Two publications signify the entry of this sort of reader-oriented biblical interpretation into the ecclesiastical mainstream in a fashion somewhat analogous to the ways in which the promulgation of *Divino Afflante Spiritu* and *Dei Verbum* affirmed the value of the historical-critical approach for biblical interpretation by Roman Catholics. The first of these is the 1993 instruction of the Pontifical Biblical Commission, *The Interpretation of the Bible in the Church*, with its nuanced attention to contextual approaches, actualization, and inculturation. The Biblical Commission recognized that "the interpretation of a text is always dependent on the mindset and concerns of its readers. Readers give privileged attention to certain aspects and, without even being aware of it, neglect others."[4]

A second significant publication that marks the mainstreaming of this trend toward contextual interpretation is the appearance in 1994 of the first volume of the *New Interpreter's Bible*. Like its predecessor, the original *Interpreter's Bible*, which began to appear in 1951,[5] this twelve volume commentary aims "to bring the best in contemporary biblical scholarship into the service of the Church to enhance preaching, teaching and the study of the Scriptures."[6] Unlike its predecessor, though, the *New Interpreter's Bible* includes an article by James Earl Massey entitled, "Reading the Bible from Particular Social Locations: An Introduction,"[7] followed by Massey's treatment of "Reading the Bible as

3. On this deliberate, self-conscious, self-critical, self-implicating turn in academic biblical interpretation, see the essays in *Semeia* 72 (1995), an issue guest-edited by Janice Capel Anderson and Jeffrey L. Staley entitled, *Taking It Personally: Autobiographical Biblical Criticism*.

4. Pontifical Biblical Commission, *The Interpretation of the Bible in the Church* (Boston: Pauline Books and Media, 1993), 66. See Joseph A. Fitzmyer, *The Biblical Commission's Document "The Interpretation of the Bible in the Church": Text and Commentary* (Rome: Editrice Pontificio Istituto Biblico, 1995).

5. 12 vols., ed. George Arthur Buttrick (Nashville: Abingdon Press, 1951–57).

6. Leander E. Keck, et al., eds., *The New Interpreter's Bible*, vol. 1, *General Articles on the Bible, General Articles on the Old Testament, the Book of Genesis, the Book of Exodus, the Book of Leviticus* (Nashville: Abingdon Press, 1994), xvii. On the difference between the *Interpreter's Bible* and the *New Interpreter's Bible*, see Leander E. Keck, "Introduction to the New Interpreter's Bible," *The New Interpreter's Bible*, vol. 1, 1–6.

7. Keck, *The New Interpreter's Bible*, 1:150–3.

African Americans," then Chan-Hie Kim's "Reading the Bible as Asian Americans," Fernando F. Segovia's "Reading the Bible as Hispanic Americans," George E. Tinker's "Reading the Bible as Native Americans," and Carolyn Osiek's "Reading the Bible as Women."[8] These affirmations of the importance of ethnicity and gender for biblical interpretation are an encouraging sign that new voices have begun to make themselves heard within and beyond the circles of academy and Church in ways that challenge, stimulate, and enrich.

In this essay, I will begin to sketch a U.S. Hispanic American[9] reading of the book of Revelation. First, I will set the stage with a survey of recent U.S. Hispanic American biblical interpretation and of the initial assessments of this first generation of readings. I will move on to identify two currents in Latin American interpretation of the Apocalypse, first considering liberationist readings and then readings of Revelation 12 that identify the "woman clothed with the sun" with Our Lady of Guadalupe. In the light of that discussion, I will suggest that the U.S. Hispanic American experience provides yet another vantage point for the interpretation of the Apocalypse, and I will trace some features of one such reading from that context.

New Voices

It would not be inaccurate to speak of a "boom" of sorts during the past two decades in publications by Protestant and Catholic U.S. Hispanic American specialists in biblical studies and in other theological disciplines, offering readings of a variety of texts from the Hebrew Bible and from the New Testament.[10] Treatments of texts from the Hebrew Bible include Francisco O. García-Treto's "El Señor guarda a los emigrantes (Salmo 146:9)," and his treatment of Joshua 9 in "The Lesson of the Gibeonites: A Proposal for Dialogic Attention as a Strategy for Reading

8. Keck, *The New Interpreter's Bible,* vol. 1. Massey's essay can be found on pages 154–60, Kim's on 161–6, Segovia's on 167–73, Tinker's on 174–80, Osiek's on 181–7.

9. Because no single term in current use is entirely satisfactory, here I am using the terminology adopted by Fernando F. Segovia in "Aliens in the Promised Land: The Manifest Destiny of U.S. Hispanic American Theology," in *Hispanic/Latino Theology: Challenge and Promise,* ed. Ada María Isasi-Díaz and Fernando F. Segovia (Minneapolis: Augsburg/Fortress Press, 1996), 15–42.

10. On the broader "boom" in U.S. Hispanic American theology, see Allan Figueroa Deck, "Latino Theology: The Year of the Boom," *Journal of Hispanic/Latino Theology* 1, no. 2 (1994): 51–63; Jean-Pierre Ruiz, "U.S. Hispanic/Latino Theology: The 'Boom' and Beyond," *American Catholic Issues Online* (http://www.adelphi.edu/~catissue/RUIZ96.HTM).

the Bible;" the reading of Psalm 137 by Ada María Isasi-Díaz, "'By the Rivers of Babylon': Exile as a Way of Life;" as well as Robert D. Maldonado's "¿La Conquista? Latin American (*Mestizaje*) Reflections on the Biblical Conquest" and Maldonado's "Reading Malinche Reading Ruth: Toward a Hermeneutics of Betrayal." Readings of the prophets include C. Gilbert Romero's "Amos 5:21–24: Religion, Politics and the Latino Experience," Michael Candelaria's "Justice: Extrapolations from the Concept Mishpat in the Book of Micah," and my own modest "Exile, History and Hope: A Hispanic Reading of Ezekiel 20."[11]

Recent U.S. Hispanic American readings of New Testament texts include "Reading from My Bicultural Place: Acts 6:1–7" by Justo L. González, Efraín Agosto's "Paul, Leadership and the Hispanic Church," Fernando F. Segovia's treatment of the Fourth Gospel in "The Gospel at the Close of the Century: Engagement from the Diaspora," and my own "Four Faces of Theology: Four Johannine Conversations." Also worth mentioning among U.S. Hispanic American perspectives on biblical interpretation is the multivolume Comentario Bíblico Hispanoamericano series edited by Justo L. González, with its pastoral and homiletic orientation.[12]

11. Francisco O. García-Treto, "El Señor guarda a los emigrantes (Salmo 146:9)," in *Voces: Voices from the Hispanic Church,* ed. Justo L. González (Nashville: Abingdon Press, 1992), 35–9; Francisco O. García-Treto, "The Lesson of the Gibeonites: A Proposal for Dialogic Attention as a Strategy for Reading the Bible," in *Hispanic/Latino Theology: Challenge and Promise,* ed. Ada María Isasi-Díaz and Fernando F. Segovia (Minneapolis: Augsburg/Fortress Press, 1996), 73–85; Ada María Isasi-Díaz, "'By the Rivers of Babylon': Exile as a Way of Life," in *Reading from This Place,* vol. 1, *Social Location and Biblical Interpretation in the United States,* ed. Fernando F. Segovia and Mary Ann Tolbert (Minneapolis: Augsburg/Fortress Press, 1995), 149–64; Robert D. Maldonado, "¿La Conquista? Latin American (*Mestizaje*) Reflections on the Biblical Conquest," *Journal of Hispanic/Latino Theology* 2, no. 4 (1995): 5–25; Robert D. Maldonado, "Reading Malinche Reading Ruth: Toward a Hermeneutics of Betrayal," *Semeia* 72 (1995): 91–109; C. Gilbert Romero, "Amos 5:21–24: Religion, Politics and the Latino Experience," *Journal of Hispanic/Latino Theology* 4, no. 4 (1997): 21–41; Michael Candelaria, "Justice: Extrapolations from the Concept Mishpat in the Book of Micah," in *Voces: Voices from the Hispanic Church,* ed. Justo L. González (Nashville: Abingdon Press, 1992), 40–5; Jean-Pierre Ruiz, "Exile, History and Hope: A Hispanic Reading of Ezekiel 20," *The Bible Today* 35 (1997): 106–13.

12. Justo L. González, "Reading from My Bicultural Place: Acts 6:1–7," in *Reading from This Place,* vol. 1, *Social Location and Biblical Interpretation in the United States,* ed. Fernando F. Segovia and Mary Ann Tolbert (Minneapolis: Augsburg/Fortress Press, 1995), 139–48; Efraín Agosto, "Paul, Leadership and the Hispanic Church," in Eldin Villafañe, *Seek the Peace of the City: Reflections on Urban Ministry* (Grand Rapids, Mich.: Wm. B. Eerdmans Publishing Company, 1995), 103–22; Fernando F. Segovia, "The Gospel at the Close of the Cen-

Charting the Territory

The increasing proliferation of U.S. Hispanic American readings of biblical texts has not gone without its interpreting angels. These analysts, apologists, critics, and chroniclers have begun to engage in the interrelated processes of advocacy on behalf of such reading strategies within and beyond U.S. Hispanic American audiences, academic and ecclesiastical, of mapping the convergences and the differences among the readings set forth thus far, and of exploring the hermeneutical ground on which these readings stand.[13] Among them, two scholars have gained particular prominence both because of the U.S. Hispanic American hermeneutics they have articulated and because of their activity as *padrinos* of a sort in the work they have done to stimulate biblical interpretation by U.S. Hispanic Americans. These two Cuban-Americans are Justo L. González, a Methodist historical theologian, and Fernando F. Segovia, a Roman Catholic who is professor of New Testament and early Christian literature at Vanderbilt University Divinity School.[14]

---

tury: Engagement from the Diaspora," in *What is John? Readers and Readings of the Fourth Gospel*, ed. Fernando F. Segovia (Atlanta: Scholars Press, 1996), 211–6; Jean-Pierre Ruiz, "Four Faces of Theology: Four Johannine Conversations," in *Reading from this Place*, vol. 3, ed. Fernando F. Segovia and Mary Ann Tolbert (Minneapolis: Augsburg/Fortress Press, forthcoming). Volumes published in the Comentario Bíblico Hispanoamericano series thus far include Pablo Deiros, *Santiago y Judas* (Miami: Editorial Caribe, 1992); Justo L. González, *Hechos* (Miami: Editorial Caribe, 1992); Washington Padilla, *Amós—Abdías* (Miami: Editorial Caribe, 1993); and Marcos Antonio Ramos, *I Timoteo, II Timoteo y Tito* (Miami: Editorial Caribe, 1992). Also published in this series as a companion volume to the commentaries is Cecilio Arrastía, *Teoría, práctica de la predicación*, rev. ed. (Miami: Editorial Caribe, 1993).

13. Some of these are Ada María Isasi-Díaz, "The Bible and *Mujerista* Theology," in *Lift Every Voice: Constructing Christian Theologies from the Underside*, ed. Susan Brooks Thistlethwaite and Mary Brooks Engel (New York: HarperCollins, 1990), 261–69; Pablo A. Jiménez, "In Search of a Hispanic Model of Biblical Interpretation," *Journal of Hispanic/Latino Theology* 3, no. 2 (1995): 44–64; Jean-Pierre Ruiz, "Beginning to Read the Bible in Spanish: An Initial Assessment," *Journal of Hispanic/Latino Theology* 1, no. 2 (1994): 28–50.

14. González was the guiding spirit behind *Apuntes*, a journal of Hispanic theology published jointly since 1980 by the Mexican-American Program at Perkins School of Theology and the United Methodist Publishing House. In 1989 he established the Hispanic Summer Program, which provides Hispanic seminary students with an opportunity to study in a Hispanic setting, with Latino peers and professors. More recently, González was responsible for the development of the Hispanic Theological Initiative, a program funded by the Pew Charitable Trust with the goal of increasing the presence of Hispanic faculty in seminaries, schools of theology, and universities through scholarship awards for graduate study and through mentoring of scholarship recipients

In *Mañana: Christian Theology from a Hispanic Perspective,* González proposed "Reading the Bible in Spanish" as a metaphor for biblical interpretation "in the 'vernacular,' not only in the cultural, linguistic sense, but also in the sociopolitical sense," recognizing at the same time that "in the high Andes, the equivalent of our reading in Spanish would be a reading in Quechua, and from the perspective of the Quechua-speaking peoples oppressed by the Spanish-speaking."[15] The "grammar" González sets forth for this reading strategy involves four key principles. First is the awareness that the Bible is a political book, and this awareness that the Bible deals with issues of power and powerlessness means that reading the Bible in Spanish is to do so "as exiles, as members of a powerless group."[16] A second principle of this grammar calls for an awareness that "even when we read Scripture in private, God is addressing all of us as a community of faith."[17] The third core principle of González's grammar for reading the Bible in Spanish is the availability of Scripture to the *neipioi*. Drawing on Matthew 11:25, González suggests that "to read the Bible 'in Spanish' means to give attention to what the 'babes' find in it."[18] The fourth principle of González's grammar for reading the Bible in Spanish is the call to read the Bible "in the voca-

---

by Latino faculty. Segovia, who served as president of the Academy of Catholic Hispanic Theologians of the United States (ACHTUS) in 1994–95, also served as a member of the Society of Biblical Literature's Committee on Underrepresented Racial and Ethnic Minority Persons in the Profession. See Segovia's ACHTUS presidential address, "Theological Education and Scholarship as a Struggle: The Life of Racial and Ethnic Minorities in the Profession," *Journal of Hispanic/Latino Theology* 2, no. 2 (1994): 5–25. With Mary Ann Tolbert, Segovia was responsible for organizing the 1993 conference at Vanderbilt University that resulted in the publication of the first two volumes of *Reading from This Place*: volume 1, *Social Location and Biblical Interpretation in the United States,* ed. Fernando F. Segovia and Mary Ann Tolbert (Minneapolis: Augsburg/Fortress Press, 1995); volume 2, *Social Location and Biblical Interpretation in Global Perspective,* ed. Fernando F. Segovia and Mary Ann Tolbert (Minneapolis: Augusburg/Fortress Press, 1995). Together with Ada María Isasi-Díaz, Segovia was responsible for organizing a 1994 conference at Drew University entitled, "Aliens in Jerusalem: The Emerging Theological Voice of Hispanic Americans," which resulted in the publication of *Hispanic/Latino Theology: Challenge and Promise,* ed. Ada María Isasi-Díaz and Fernando F. Segovia (Minneapolis: Augusburg/Fortress Press, 1996).

15. (Nashville: Abingdon Press, 1990), 84. On readings of the Bible by indigenous peoples of the Americas, see Elsa Tamez, "Quetzalcóatl Challenges the Christian Bible," *Journal of Hispanic/Latino Theology* 4, no. 4 (1997): 5–20.

16. González, *Mañana,* 85.

17. Ibid.

18. Ibid., 86.

tive," because "the purpose of our common study of Scripture is not so much to interpret it as to allow it to interpret us and our situation."[19]

In *Santa Biblia: The Bible Through Hispanic Eyes,* González explains that reading with "Hispanic eyes" is to read from the perspective "of those who claim their Hispanic identity as part of their hermeneutical baggage, and who also read Scripture within the context of a commitment to the Latino struggle to become all that God wants us and all the world to be—in other words, the struggle for salvation/liberation."[20] González offers five paradigms that inform Hispanic biblical interpretation either explicitly or implicitly: (1) marginality, (2) poverty, (3) *mestizaje* and *mulatez,* (4) exile and alienness, (5) solidarity.

While devoting considerable attention to the Fourth Gospel, Fernando F. Segovia has also invested substantial effort in charting the direction of U.S. Hispanic biblical hermeneutics and in developing what he has called a hermeneutics of the diaspora that grounds the practice of intercultural criticism.[21] According to Segovia,

> intercultural criticism entails an analysis of texts, of "texts" or readings of texts, and of "selves" or readers of texts. As such, it is a reading strategy that calls upon its practitioner to deal with issues of interpretation, hermeneutics, and culture/ideology. . . . It is also a reading strategy that sees itself not as *the* one, sole, and definitive reading strategy but as a reading strategy among many, grounded in and addressing the reality of the diaspora, my diaspora, and committed to the values of otherness and engagement.[22]

19. Ibid.

20. (Nashville: Abingdon Press, 1996), 28–9.

21. Fernando F. Segovia, "Hispanic American Theology and the Bible: Effective Weapon and Faithful Ally," in *We Are a People! Initiatives in Hispanic American Theology,* ed. Roberto S. Goizueta (Minneapolis: Augsburg/Fortress Press, 1992), 21–49; Segovia, "In the World but Not of It: Exile as Locus for a Theology of the Diaspora," in *Hispanic/Latino Theology: Challenge and Promise,* ed. Ada María Isasi-Díaz and Fernando F. Segovia (Minneapolis: Augsburg/ Fortress Press, 1996), 195–217; Segovia, "Reading the Bible as Hispanic-Americans," in *The New Interpreter's Bible,* vol. 1, ed. Leander Keck, et al. (Nashville: Abingdon Press, 1994), 167–73; Segovia, "The Text as Other: Towards a Hispanic American Hermeneutic," in *Text and Experience: Towards a Cultural Exegesis of the Bible,* ed. Daniel Smith-Christopher (Sheffield: Sheffield Academic Press, 1995), 276–98; Segovia, "Towards a Hermeneutics of the Diaspora: A Hermeneutics of Otherness and Engagement," in *Reading from This Place,* vol. 1, *Social Location and Biblical Interpretation in the United States,* ed. Fernando F. Segovia and Mary Ann Tolbert (Minneapolis: Augsburg/Fortress Press, 1995), 57–73; and Segovia, "Towards Intercultural Criticism: A Reading Strategy from the Diaspora," in *Reading from this Place,* vol. 2, *Social Location and Biblical Interpretation in Global Perspective,* ed. Fernando F. Segovia and Mary Ann Tolbert (Minneapolis: Augsburg/Fortress Press, 1995), 303–30.

22. Segovia, "Towards Intercultural Criticism," 330.

The diaspora of which Segovia speaks and in which he situates himself identifies "that large and growing segment of people from the Third World who are forced to live—for whatever reason, though usually involving a combination of sociopolitical and socioeconomic factors—in the First World, whether in Europe, Japan, or the United States."[23] This condition, Segovia holds, gives those who belong to the Hispanic American diaspora two places and no place on which to stand, a bicultural identity, a hyphenated existence with the accent sometimes falling before the hyphen, sometimes after it, and sometimes squarely on the hyphen itself.[24]

As for otherness and engagement, the two complementary concepts we find at the core of the intercultural critical strategy that Segovia proposes, otherness

> is grounded in and reflects the reality and experience of otherness on the part of individuals from non-Western civilizations who reside on a permanent basis in the West, the children of the colonized who live among the children of the colonizers. . . . Such "otherness" implies a biculturalism with no home, no voice, and no face: as the ones who left, we are no longer accepted where we came from, and, as the ones who do not fit, we are not accepted in our present home.[25]

As for its impact on biblical interpretation, Segovia suggests that the experience of otherness disposes diaspora readers to deal with biblical texts as *others,* that is, "as realities to be acknowledged, respected and engaged in their very otherness rather than overwhelmed and overrriden."[26]

Segovia characterizes engagement as the positive side of otherness:

> Such otherness embraces biculturalism as its very home, voice, and face: instead of no home, no voice, no face, it argues for two homes, two voices, and two faces. Such otherness also holds that all reality— all homes, all voices, and all faces—is construction and, as such, has both contextuality and perspective. . . . From this point of view, we find ourselves, following the dynamics of decolonization and liberation, in a position of critical engagement in the world, both with regard to ourselves and others: as self-affirming and self-defining others . . . also engaged in critical dialogue with all other voices and faces.[27]

23. Segovia, "Toward a Hermeneutics of the Diaspora," 60.
24. Also see Fernando F. Segovia, "Two Places and No Place on Which to Stand: Mixture and Otherness in Hispanic American Theology," *Listening* 27 (1992): 26–40. For an example of how such biculturalism affects biblical interpretation, see Justo González, "Reading from My Bicultural Place," 139–48.
25. Segovia, "Toward Intercultural Criticism," 322.
26. Ibid., 323.
27. Ibid., 322. Segovia's debt to the insights of postmodernism is clear here. Also see his "Cultural Studies and Contemporary Biblical Criticism," in

Following Segovia's intercultural critical hermeneutics of the diaspora, the texts of early Christianity and ancient Judaism are among the other voices engaged within this positive reading of otherness. Here, he writes, "the operative attitude is not one of ancestral obeisance or search-and-destroy demolition but rather one of critical dialogue and struggle in the light of one's reality and experience."[28]

READING THE BOOK OF REVELATION IN THE AMERICAS

Given the broad range of biblical texts to which U.S. Hispanic American authors have devoted attention, it is remarkable that the book of Revelation has received relatively little notice in print. This omission is especially striking in view of the prominence of the Apocalypse of John among Latin American authors with whose liberationist hermeneutics many U.S. Hispanic American theologians claim some affinity.[29]

In that vein, the testimony of Brazilian biblical scholar Gilberto da Silva Gorgulho about the importance of the Apocalypse among basic Christian communities in Latin America is worth quoting at some length:

> The Book of Revelation is the favorite book of our popular communi-
> ties. Here they find the encouragement they need in their struggle
> and a criterion for the interpretation of official persecution in our so-
> ciety. The communities plumb the depths of the book that is revela-
> tion, witness and prophecy (Rev. 1:1–6), a book whose purpose is to
> encourage and maintain the prophetical praxis of the new people—
> this priestly, royal and prophetic people. The meaning of the life of
> the Church in the persecuting Empire proceeds from the need to
> "prophesy again" (Rev. 10:11). It is in prophetical witness that this
> people finds its living liberty.
>   The meaning of the Church in history is rooted in the witness of
> the gospel before the state imperialism that destroys the people's life,

---

Reading from this Place, vol. 2, *Social Location and Biblical Interpretation in Global Perspective,* ed. Fernando F. Segovia and Mary Ann Tolbert (Minneapolis: Augusburg/Fortress Press, 1995), 1–17. On the complexities of this discussion, see Justo L. González, "Metamodern Aliens in Postmodern Jerusalem," in *Hispanic/Latino Theology: Challenge and Promise,* ed. Ada María Isasi-Díaz and Fernando F. Segovia (Minneapolis: Augusburg/Fortress Press, 1996), 340–50; and Roberto S. Goizueta's "Rationality and Irrationality? Modernity, Postmodernity and the U.S. Hispanic Theologian," in his *Caminemos con Jesús: Toward a Hispanic/Latino Theology of Accompaniment* (Maryknoll, N.Y.: Orbis Books, 1995), 132–72.

28. Segovia, "Toward Intercultural Criticism," 326. Segovia's essay, "The Gospel at the Close of the Century," provides an example of intercultural criticism at work.

29. See Elisabeth Schüssler Fiorenza, *Revelation: Vision of a Just World* (Minneapolis: Augusburg/Fortress Press, 1991), 10–2.

looming as an idol and caricature of the holy Trinity. Testimony against the state and imperial idolatry has but one weapon: the force of the gospel. A discerning judgment strips away the mask, the radical lie of the society that oppresses, to reveal its antithesis, the monarchy of Christ. Witness enters into the process of liberation—liberation from domination, and liberation to life in the heavenly Jerusalem in the communion of the Lamb who was slain.[30]

Further evidence of the impact of the Apocalypse among Latin American theologians is provided in Enrique Dussel's liberationist treatment of social ethics. Citing Revelation 17:4–7, Dussel asserts that

> the mystery revealed in the Book of Revelation is actually more current today than ever, and merits our close attention. The Dragon, the Beast, the kings and authorities at their disposal, their envoys or angels, their servants, their customs, laws, and powers, all constitute a full-fledged order, that of *this world*—as category—and its prevailing morality.[31]

Dussel goes on to formulate the "Babylon principle": "for 'Babylon' signifies the order of oppression, that of the Devil. 'All, great and small, rich and poor, slave and free, he made that they mark them on the right hand or the forehead' (Rev. 13:16)."[32] Dussel also formulates a contrasting "Jerusalem principle":

> Confronted with the persecution and murder of Christians in the first century of our era, which took place at the hands of the imperialism of that age ("suffered under Pontius Pilate"), today other Christian-murdering empires carry on the Roman empire's tradition of sin. The author of the Book of Revelation has formulated an explicit political theology. Christians are murdered because they are "witnesses" ("martyrs") of the "heavenly Jerusalem," the *"new* Jerusalem"—called "new" lest it be confused with the "old" Jerusalem, the empirical one, the one that killed Jesus and was destroyed for its infidelity. The *new* City of God—and future Christendoms will be the "earthly city" of Cain, still claiming to be the City of God—is utopian. It comes from the future, and is built of the blood of the heroes, the saints, and the martyrs.

Thus Dussel suggests that

30. Gilberto da Silva Gorgulho, "Biblical Hermeneutics," in *Mysterium Liberationis: Fundamental Concepts of Liberation Theology,* ed. Ignacio Ellacuría and Jon Sobrino (Maryknoll, N.Y.: Orbis Books, 1993), 146. Together with Ana F. Anderson, Gorguhlo himself wrote *No Tengan Miedo: Apocalipsis y comunidades cristianas* (Buenos Aires: Ediciones Paulinas, 1978).

31. *Ethics and Community,* trans. Robert R. Barr (Maryknoll, N.Y.: Orbis Books, 1988), 28.

32. Ibid., 31.

the hope of the new Jerusalem is the "Jerusalem principle." It is a utopian Christianity that believes in the reign of God, hates the Prince of "this world" and his reign, and inaugurates a praxis of liberation where all will receive "on the basis of each one's need." But in order for Jerusalem to exist, obviously Babylon must be destroyed, and the poor, the heroes, the saints, and the martyrs rejoice at its fall: "Alleluia! Triumph, glory, and power to God! . . . He has condemned the great prostitute . . . and has lost count of the blood of her slaves" (Rev. 19:1–2).[33]

LATIN AMERICAN LIBERATIONIST READINGS OF THE APOCALYPSE

Readings of the Apocalypse from within the Latin American context abound, and many of them can be grouped under one of two headings, headings that reflect two key concerns of liberationist biblical interpretation. First, we find popular introductions and commentaries on the Apocalypse that reflect the emphasis of liberationist hermeneutics on grassroots biblical interpretation, especially as practiced in basic Christian communities.[34] One example of such a commentary now available in English translation is Pablo Richard's *Apocalypse: A People's Commentary on the Book of Revelation.*[35] The author, a Chilean working in Costa Rica, lists the following as the first of the principles that guided his reading of the Apocalypse:

33. Ibid., 52.
34. See Carlos Mesters, "The Use of the Bible in Christian Communities of the Common People," in *The Bible and Liberation: Political and Social Hermeneutics,* ed. Norman K. Gottwald (Maryknoll, N.Y.: Orbis Books, 1983), 119–33; reprinted from *The Challenge of Basic Christian Communities: Papers from the International Ecumenical Congress of Theology, 20 February–2 March 1980, São Paulo, Brazil,* ed. Sergio Torres and John Eagleson (Maryknoll, N.Y.: Orbis Books, 1981), 197–210. Also see Paulo Fernando Carneiro de Andrade, "Reading the Bible in the Ecclesial Base Communities of Latin America: The Meaning of Social Context," in *Reading from this Place,* vol. 2, *Social Location and Biblical Interpretation in Global Perspective,* ed. Fernando F. Segovia and Mary Ann Tolbert (Minneapolis: Augusburg/Fortress Press, 1995), 237–49.
35. (Maryknoll, N.Y.: Orbis Books, 1995). Originally published in Spanish under the title *Apocalipsis: Reconstrucción de la esperanza* (San José, Costa Rica: Editorial DEI, 1994). Other popular commentaries and introductions to the Apocalypse in this vein include Ricardo Foulkes, *El Apocalipsis de San Juan: Una lectura desde América Latina* (Buenos Aires: Nueva Creación; Grand Rapids, Mich.: Wm. B. Eerdmans Publishing Company, 1989); F. S. Gorgulho and Ana F. Anderson, *No tengan miedo: Apocalipsis y comunidades cristianas* (Buenos Aires: Ediciones Paulinas, 1980); Carlos Mesters, *El Apocalipsis: La esperanza de un pueblo que lucha. Una clave de lectura* (Santiago de Chile: Ediciones Rehue, 1986); Juan Snoek and Rommie Nauta, *Daniel y el Apocalipsis: Una lectura introductoria* (San José, Costa Rica: Editorial DEI, 1993).

Revelation arises in a time of persecution—and particularly amid situations of chaos, exclusion and ongoing oppression. In such situations, Revelation enables the Christian community to rebuild its hope and its awareness. Revelation transmits a spirituality of resistance and offers guidance for organizing an alternative world. Revelation is a liberating book, one full of hope; its utopia is political and unfolds in history.[36]

The liberation hermeneutical emphasis on the socioeconomic and sociopolitical realities of power and powerlessness (both local and global) provides a second heading under which a number of recent Latin American contextual readings of the Apocalypse can be grouped. "Apocalyptic and the Economy: A Reading of Revelation 18 from the Experience of Economic Exclusion," by Néstor Míguez, is an example of this body of literature, written mainly with academic audiences in mind.[37]

Making explicit reference to Dussel's "Babylon Principle," Míguez asserts that

behind the mask of luxury and progress lies the true visage of human destruction. The repulsive spirits of violence, racial hatred, mutilation, and exploitation roam the streets of our Babylons in Latin America (and the globe); their presence is clear once one looks be-

36. Richard, *Apocalypse: A People's Commentary*, 3.
37. In *Reading from this Place*, vol. 2, *Social Location and Biblical Interpretation in Global Perspective*, ed. Fernando F. Segovia and Mary Ann Tolbert (Minneapolis: Augsburg/Fortress Press, 1995), 250–62. Other examples of this current in Latin American interpretation of the book of Revelation (and other apocalyptic literature) are Xavier Alegre, "El Apocalipsis, memoria subversiva y fuente de esperanza para los pueblos crucificados," *Revista Latinoamericana de Teología* 26 (1992): 201–29, 293–323; J. Severino Croatto, "Apocalíptica y esperanza de los oprimidos (contexto socio-político y cultural del género apocalíptico)," *Revista de Interpretación Bíblica Latinoamericana* 10 (1990): 9–24; J. Severino Croatto, "Desmesura y fin del opresor en la perspectiva apocalíptica: Estudio de Daniel 7–12," *Revista Bíblica (Argentina)* 39 (1990): 129–44; J. Severino Croatto, "El discurso de los tiranos en textos proféticos y apocalípticos," *Revista de Interpretación Bíblica Latinoamericana* 8 (1991): 39–53; Néstor Míguez, "Las víctimas en el Apocalipsis: Estudio de Apocalipsis 5 tras 500 años de incorporación de América al dominio occidental," *Revista de Interpretación Bíblica Latinoamericana* 12 (1992): 167–85; D. Ramírez Fernández, "El juicio de Dios a las transnacionales: Apocalipsis 18," *Revista de Interpretación Bíblica Latinoamericana* 5 (1990): 55–74; D. Ramírez Fernández, "La idolatria del poder. La Iglesia confesante en la situación de Apocalípsis 13," *Revista de Interpretación Bíblica Latinoamericana* 5 (1989): 109–28; Pablo Richard, "El Pueblo de Dios contra el Imperio: Daniel 7 en su contexto literario e histórico," *Revista de Interpretación Bíblica Latinoamericana* 7 (1991): 25–46; J. Stam, "El Apocalipsis y el imperialismo," in *Capitalismo: Violencia y antivida. La opresión de las mayorías y la domesticación de los dioses* (San José, Costa Rica: Editorial DEI, 1978), 359–94.

yond the glimmering lights of the neon signs. It is the accumulation
of goods as such that gives birth to these spirits. The vision of John is
thus "revelation" in this sense as well.[38]

Thus Míguez reads Revelation 18 "from the perspective of the victims of the neoliberal capitalist marketplace and its imposed instrumental logic,"[39] suggesting in the end that "for those of us who nourish an
apocalyptic faith (a faith that trusts in the power of revelation to unmask and the power of the God of justice), the earth is more than Babylon
. . . the power of Babylon is finite, temporal. The hope in the justice of
God is infinite, eternal."[40] Another reading of Revelation 18 from the
Latin American context is offered by Dagoberto Ramírez Fernandez,
who moves from exegetical analysis of Revelation 18 to an actualization of this text as an expression of divine judgment against multina-
tional corporations.[41] The same author approaches Revelation 13 seeking to understand how the Church can confront the powers of this world,
suggesting significant similarities between the situation of Christians
living under Roman rule during the first century and twentieth-century
Latin American Christians.[42]

The publication of Apartheid-era and post-Apartheid South African contextual readings of the Apocalypse indicate that Latin America
is not the only geographical and sociopolitical context within which
such liberationist readings of the Apocalypse have emerged.[43]

A WOMAN CLOTHED WITH THE SUN
OUR LADY OF GUADALUPE AND REVELATION 12

In 1648, more than one hundred years after the apparitions of the Virgin Mary to Juan Diego at Tepeyac in 1531, the first published account
of the apparitions appeared, written by the Mexican-born Oratorian
priest Miguel Sánchez and entitled, *Imagen de la Virgen María Madre de
Dios de Guadalupe milagrosamente aparecida en México. Celebrada en su
historia, con la profecía del capitulo doce del Apocalipsis.*[44] When Sánchez

38. Míguez, "Apocalyptic and the Economy," 260.
39. Ibid.
40. Ibid.
41. D. Ramírez Fernández, "El juicio de Dios a las transnacionales."
42. D. Ramírez Fernández, "La idolatria del poder," 109.
43. For example, Allan Boesak, *Comfort and Protest: The Apocalypse from a
South African Perspective* (Philadelphia: Westminster/John Knox Press, 1987);
Tim Long, "A Real Reader Reading Revelation," *Semeia* 73 (1996): 79–107.
44. (Mexico City: Imprenta de la Viuda de Bernardo Calderón, 1648). Reprinted in *Testimonios históricos guadalupanos,* ed. Ernesto de la Torre Villar and
Ramiro Navarro de Anda (Mexico City: Fondo de Cultúra Económica, 1982),
153–267.

died in 1674, his obituary testified to the impact of this volume: "He wrote a learned book about her apparition, which has seemingly been the means by which devotion to this holy image has spread throughout all Christendom."[45] Jacques Lafaye speaks of the "invention" of the Guadalupe apparition by Sánchez, by which he means that no one prior to Sánchez "had explicitly referred to an 'apparition' of the image of Tepeyac."[46] As for the contents of Sánchez's book, Stafford Poole reports that it contains "a brief exegesis of the principal verses of Revelation 12, then a second exegesis applying these verses to the Virgin Mary, and then a narration of the apparitions. After this account there is a third exegesis of Revelation 12, a word-by-word application to the Virgin of Guadalupe."[47] The first chapter, "Prophetic Original of the Holy Image Piously Foreseen by the Evangelist Saint John, in Chapter 12 of Revelation," sets forth Sánchez's view that the woman clothed with the sun of Revelation 12 corresponds to the image of Tepeyac.[48] Poole characterizes *Imagen de la Virgen* as baroque in character, its style ornate and repetitious."[49] As for its aims, Poole observes that Sánchez

> had a messianic view of Mexico City, which he sought to put on a par with the great religious centers of the Catholic world. He compared

45. Antonio Robles, *Diario de sucesos notables (1665–1703)* (Mexico City: Ediciones Porrua, 1964), 1:145, as cited in Stafford Poole, *Our Lady of Guadalupe: The Origins and Sources of a Mexican National Symbol, 1531–1797* (Tucson: University of Arizona Press, 1995), 108. On the other hand, Poole suggests that "Although Sánchez's work was influential in encouraging the Guadalupan devotion, its overall impact seems to have been blunted by the small number of volumes printed and his ornate, gongoristic style" (Poole, *Our Lady of Guadalupe*, 109). The anonymous publication in 1660 of an abridged version of Sánchez's book in 1660 (by the Jesuit Mateo de la Cruz), entitled *Relación de la milagrosa aparición de la Santa Virgen de Guadalupe de México, sacada de la historia que compuso el Br. Miguel Sánchez* (Puebla de los Angeles: Viuda de Borja, 1660) had a significant impact on the diffusion of Sánchez's account. The abridgement excised much of Sánchez's exegesis. On Mateo de la Cruz, see Poole, *Our Lady of Guadalupe*, 109–10. It is important to note that Poole's revisionist history, useful for its extensive documentation of the written sources, has provoked much controversy. See the review of Poole's *Our Lady of Guadalupe* by Allan Figueroa Deck in *Journal of Hispanic/Latino Theology* 3, no. 3 (1996): 62–5. Also see the discussion of Poole's book in Orlando O. Espín, *The Faith of the People: Theological Reflections on Popular Catholicism* (Maryknoll, N.Y.: Orbis Books, 1997), 7–10.
46. Jacques Lafaye, *Quetzalcóatl and Guadalupe: The Formation of Mexican National Consciousness 1531–1813*, trans. Benjamin Keen (Chicago: University of Chicago Press, 1976), 243.
47. Ibid., 101.
48. Ibid., 249.
49. Ibid., 106.

Zumárraga [Juan de Zumárraga, the first bishop of Mexico, to whom
Juan Diego reported the apparitions at Tepeyac] to Saint John the Evangelist and Mexico to Patmos . . . and he interpreted Revelation 12 in
terms of Mexico and the Spanish empire. The woman clothed with
the sun was the city of Mexico. Mary, he asserted, had aided the Spanish conquest, she was the "assistant conquistador." New Spain was
her homeland. His emphasis, which took up most of the first part of
the work, was that Revelation 12 prefigured Mexico, Guadalupe, and
the destiny of the sons of the land.[50]

Historians of this period in Mexican history recognize that *criollismo*
was the agenda that Sánchez sought to advance, and his book's interpretation of Revelation 12 was directed towards that goal. Sánchez took
up the traditional account of Guadalupe, a story directed towards the
indigenous Nahuatl-speaking people of Mexico, and recast it on behalf
of the criollos, the Mexican-born descendants of the Spanish *conquistadores*, according to the conventional European apparition genre. Emphasizing the very limited freedom enjoyed by painters of religious
subjects in Spain and in New Spain during the Counter-Reformation,
Patricia Harrington notes that Spanish artist Francisco Pacheco, who
was an inspector of painting for the Inquisition at Seville, published a
book in 1649, entitled *El arte de la pintura*. In this work Pacheco directed
that painters were to use Revelation 12 as a guide to their representation of the Immaculate Conception.[51] Whether or not Sánchez had access to a work like Pacheco's, it seems likely that his interpretation of
Guadalupe in the light of Revelation 12 was influenced by the prevailing spirit of Iberian Counter-Reformation aesthetic orthodoxy.

As for the fanciful allegorical application of Revelation 12, Sánchez
offered in his own Mexican context; the following serves as an illustra-
tion. Noting that the woman of Revelation 12 is clothed with the sun
(Rev. 12:1), Sánchez suggests that it was Mary's special intervention
that rendered the climate of New Spain hospitable for European settlement:

We have learned, as something evident, that by nature this land and
new world were a torrid zone and a region burned by the sun and
presumed to be uninhabitable. Most holy Mary took control of the
sun, moderated its rigors, reduced its heat, calmed its fire, tempered
its rays, served as a cloud.[52]

50. Ibid., 106–7.
51. Patricia Harrington, "Mother of Death, Mother of Rebirth: The Mexican Virgin of Guadalupe," *Journal of the American Academy of Religion* 56 (1988):
35–7. Harrington cites Jonathan Brown, *Images and Ideas in Seventeenth Century
Spanish Painting* (Princeton: Princeton University Press, 1978).
52. *Imágen de la Virgen María*, folio 57 verso; *Testimónios históricos
guadalupanos*, 219; as cited in Poole, *Our Lady of Guadalupe*, 107.

Sánchez's *Imágen de la Virgen* was eclipsed by the appearance some six months after its publication of Luis Laso de la Vega's Nahuatl account of the apparitions at Tepeyac, the *Huey tlamahuiçoltica* ("by a great miracle"), a work which includes the *Nican mopohua* ("here is recounted"), which has become the standard account of the Tepayac Mariophany.[53] Yet, whatever else might be said of Sánchez's book and its aims, its interpretation of Our Lady of Guadalupe in the light of Revelation 12 had a powerful and lasting impact.

That impact is evident, for example, in the one sonnet that Sor Juana Inés de la Cruz (1648–1695) specifically devoted to Our Lady of Guadalupe:

> This Marvel, composed of flowers,
> Divine American protectress
> who from a rose of Castile,
> is transformed into a Mexican rose;
> She whose proud foot made the dragon
> humbly bend his neck at Patmos. . . .[54]

In print, in poetry, and in preaching, the allegorical reading of Revelation 12 in connection with Our Lady of Guadalupe took broad and effective hold. In the preface to a published sermon preached On 12 December 1748 by the Jesuit Francisco Javier Carranza, for example, we find the following: "In Chapter 12 of Revelation, which so truthfully describes the miraculous apparition of our Lady of Guadalupe, following the evangelist's ecstatic vision of this prodigy, the celestial woman . . ."[55]

Thus, reflecting on the trajectory set in motion in 1648 by Sánchez, Lafaye concludes,

53. Luis Laso de la Vega, *Huey tlamahuiçoltica omonexiti in ilhuicac tlatocacihualpilli Santa Maria totlaçonantzin Guadalupe in nican huey altepenahuac Mexico itocayocan Tepeyacac* (Mexico City: Imprenta de Iuan Ruiz, 1649). A Spanish translation of this work is available in *Testimonios Históricos Guadalupanos*, 284–308. See the translation into English of the *Nican mopohua* in Virgil Elizondo, *Guadalupe: Mother of the New Creation* (Maryknoll, N.Y.: Orbis Books, 1997), 5–22. English, French, and Spanish translations of the *Nican mopohua* are also available online at the Our Lady of Guadalupe website (http://ng.netgate.net/~norberto/materdei.html).

54. Sor Juana Inés de la Cruz, *Obras completas*, ed. Mendez Plancarte (Mexico City: Fondo de Cultura Económica, 1951–57), 3:107; as cited in Jacques Lafaye *Quetzalcóatl and Guadalupe*, 74.

55. *La transmigración de la iglesia a Guadalupe. Sermon, que el 12 de Diciembre de 1748 años Predicò, en el templo de N. S. de Guadalupe de la Ciudad de Santiago de Queretaro, el P. Prefecto Francisco Xavier Carranza, Professo de quarto voto de la Sagrada Compañia de Jesús* (Mexico City: En el Colegio Real, y Mas Antiguo de S. Ildefonso de Mexico, 1749); as cited in Lafaye, *Quetzalcóatl and Guadalupe*, 245–6.

what was the contribution of Miguel Sánchez to the oral tradition? ... Most important of all, he gave it prophetic roots whose eschatological significance would fully emerge a century later, when the millenarian fever was reborn. Over the bridge thus thrown between Tepeyac and the Revelation of John, the eighteenth-century preachers, followed by the nineteenth-century revolutionaries would boldly advance.[56]

Sánchez's contribution fueled a Mexican millenarianism that found symbolic expression in the Virgin of Guadalupe as identified with the Apocalypse's woman clothed with the sun.[57]

What makes our attention to the interpretation of Revelation 12 in Sánchez's *Imagen de la Virgen* more than merely an exercise in the history of biblical interpretation in the Americas, and far more than a study in the ideological history of the colonial Mexico, is the abiding power of Our Lady of Guadalupe for Mexicans and, more broadly, even for U.S. Hispanic Americans who are not of Mexican descent.[58] U.S. Hispanic American scholars have justly devoted substantial energy and attention to understanding the place of Our Lady of Guadalupe in the religious experience of Latinas and Latinos.[59] Only rarely, however, have

56. *Quetzalcóatl and Guadalupe*, 248–9.

57. On Mexican millenarianism during the colonial period, see Lafaye, *Quetzalcóatl and Guadalupe*, 32–6. "In 1810, Miguel Hidalgo y Costilla, parish priest of Dolores, rallied the people in revolutionary ardor under the banner of Our Lady of Guadalupe, an event about which an 1883 public school textbook instructed Mexican schoolchildren in question-and-answer format: What was the flag of that army? When he passed through Atotoniclo, the parish priest Hidalgo took from the church a standard with the effigy of the Virgin of Guadalupe. He hung the cloth, cherished and revered by all Mexicans, on the staff of a lance and made it the flag of that strange and improvised army. What was the war cry of that army? 'Long live religion! Long live our very holy Mother of Guadalupe! Long live America and down with the rotten government!'" Manuel Payno, *Compendio de la historia de Méjico para el uso de los establecimientos de Instrucción pública de la República Mexicana*, 8th ed. (Mexico City: NP, 1883) 120–1; as cited in Lafaye, *Quetzacóatl and Guadalupe*, 112.

58. See Espín, *The Faith of the People*, 73–7. Virgilio Elizondo contends that "If our Lady of Guadalupe had not appeared, the collective struggles of the Mexican people to find meaning in their chaotic existence would have created her. The cultural clash of sixteenth-century Spain and Mexico was reconciled in the brown Lady of Tepeyac in a way no other symbol can rival," "Our Lady of Guadalupe as a Cultural Symbol: 'The Power of the Powerless,'" in *Liturgy and Cultural Religious Traditions*, ed. Herman Schmidt and David N. Power, Concilium 102 (Maryknoll, N.Y.: Orbis Books, 1977), 25.

59. See, for example, Jeanette Rodríguez, *Our Lady of Guadalupe: Faith and Empowerment among Mexican-American Women* (Austin: University of Texas Press, 1994); Roberto S. Goizueta, *Caminemos con Jesús*, 37–46. On Guadalupan devotions, see Timothy M. Matovina, "Our Lady of Guadalupe Celebrations in San Antonio, Texas, 1840–41," *Journal of Hispanic/Latino Theology* 1, no. 1

U.S. Hispanic American theologians attended to the connection between Our Lady of Guadalupe and Revelation 12, the "reading" of the Mariophany at Tepeyac as a rereading of Revelation 12. Virgil Elizondo's *Guadalupe: Mother of the New Creation* is a noteworthy exception, with its use of Rev. 12:1–2 as an epigraph.[60] This citation notwithstanding, Elizondo emphasizes the Nahuatl symbolism of the Mariophany at Tepeyac:

> The story of Our Lady of Guadalupe is the indigenous account of the real new beginnings of the Americas. The story of her appearances and compassion is sacred narrative as remembered by the victim-survivors of the conquest who were equally the first-born of the new creation. The entire Guadalupe event as recorded in the *Nican Mopohua* is a Nahuatl communication par excellence. . . . Each detail had special significance for the Nahuatl peoples. The story came from their world, and if we are to discover its regenerative signification, we must seek to understand it through their cosmovision.[61]

For Elizondo, as for other U.S. Hispanic American theologians, it is the *Nican mopohua* and not Miguel Sánchez's *Imagen de la Virgen Maria* that furnishes the narrative background for reflection on the significance of Our Lady of Guadalupe. The former, written in Nahuatl and intended to promote Guadalupe among Nahua audiences, appealed to its intended audience by drawing upon the canons of indigenous religious symbolism.[62] The latter, written in Spanish, sought to advance its author's *criollo* agenda by clothing the Mexican Virgin in the raiment of the New Testament canon, in keeping with prescribed conventions. Thus, despite the frequently recurrent citations of Revelation 12 since 1648 in

---

(1993): 77–96; Timothy M. Matovina, "Guadalupan Devotion in a Borderlands Community," *Journal of Hispanic/Latino Theology* 4, no. 1 (1996): 6–26.

60. Virgil Elizondo, *Guadalupe: Mother of the New Creation*, ix. Elizondo returns to this text at the very end of the book (134).

61. Ibid., xviii.

62. As Espín points out: "Among the important ancient deities there was one Tonantzin, 'our mother,' as she was called by the Nahuas. She was frequently said to be pregnant or to be carrying a small child on her back or arms. When depicted as pregnant the religious symbol representing the fundamental reconciliation of opposites was placed over her womb. Her sacred place had been precisely on the hill of Tepeyac. She dressed in a particular type of tunic, wore a mantle, and was connected in myth to the serpent high god. The woman that spoke with Juan Diego (in his native Nahuatl) did so on the hill of Tepeyac, wore that particular style of dress with a mantle, appeared to be pregnant, and had the symbol of the reconciliation of opposites over her womb" (*The Faith of the People*, 74). While Espín denies he is implying that Juan Diego saw Tonantzin, he insists that the similarities are too important to be dismissed, and that the differences between the Tonantzin and the Virgin of Guadalupe also warrant close attention. He notes that "Juan Diego's Mary assumes the

connection with the Virgin, there has been relatively little deliberate reflection on the hermeneutical implications of these "readings" of the Tepeyac Mariophany as conscious rereadings of Revelation 12.[63]

TOWARDS A U.S. HISPANIC AMERICAN READING OF THE APOCALYPSE

At this juncture, I would like to venture that the articulation of a U.S. Hispanic American reading of the book of Revelation is a project with some urgency. Despite the explicit acknowledgment by U.S. Hispanic American biblical scholars of their debt to the liberation hermeneutics developed in the Latin American context,[64] political readings of the Apocalypse have not yet appeared from the pens of U.S. Hispanic Americans.[65] At the same time, despite the burgeoning attention to popular religion among U.S. Hispanic American theologians and to the place of Our Lady of Guadalupe within that constellation, reflection on Revelation 12 as a lens through which the Mariophany at Tepeyac and the image of Our Lady of Guadalupe have been viewed has also been lacking. Curiously, then, neither of the two currents I have identified in Latin American interpretation of the Apocalypse—the one relatively recent and the other centuries-old—has generated much of a resonance in the Latin American "diaspora."[66]

The urgency of the call for such readings from a U.S. Hispanic American perspective stems in part from the disturbing prominence of the Apocalypse in contemporary U.S. public discourse. This was tragically manifested most recently in the mass suicides of members of Heaven's Gate, the two founders of which identified themselves as the

---

symbols that are useful for Christianity but rejects those that could identify her with the old religion or that appear to at least condone it" (75).

63. We might also venture to speculate that this omission reflects a certain distaste among twentieth century biblical scholars for what they would qualify as "premodern" or "popular" biblical interpretation.

64. See, for example, Segovia, "Toward Intercultural Criticism," 328–29; González, Santa Biblia, 26–7.

65. However, it may still be too soon to expect these relatively recent readings by Latin American scholars to influence their U.S. Hispanic American counterparts.

66. I find some encouragement toward the development of a U.S. Hispanic American reading of the Apocalypse in the work of Christopher Rowland and Mark Corner, "Exploring the Implications of a Liberation Exegesis in a First World Context 2: The Challenge of the Book of Revelation," in their Liberating Exegesis: The Challenge of Liberation Theology to Biblical Studies (Philadelphia: Westminster/John Knox Press, 1989), 131–55.

two lamp stands and two olive trees of Revelation 11:4,[67] in an episode that stirred the nation's not-yet-distant memory of the 1993 apocalypse at the Branch Davidian compound outside Waco, Texas.[68] While I would never imply that these incidents or the media coverage that surround them constitute what it means to "read the Apocalypse in English," in the late twentieth-century U.S. context, events like these arouse both sufficient curiosity and anxious concern to warrant close and careful consideration of Revelation from various contexts, including the U.S. Hispanic American context.[69]

I would like to identify two characteristics of the Apocalypse to which a reading from the U.S. Hispanic American context might draw particular attention: (1) the Apocalypse of John is an urban book; (2) the Apocalypse of John is a liturgical book. By doing so, I am also suggesting that a U.S. Hispanic American foregrounding of these two characteristics of the Apocalypse can facilitate a productive conversation with the two Latin American currents identified earlier.

While I do not believe that the U.S. Hispanic American context confers any hermeneutical privilege, I recognize that, in the words of the Pontifical Biblical Commission's 1993 instruction mentioned earlier, that "the interpretation of a text is always dependent on the mindset and concerns of its readers. Readers give privileged attention to certain aspects and, without even being aware of it, neglect others."[70] Though I would not dare to speak for all U.S. Hispanic Americans, or to paint in broad strokes that cut across the many differences that are gathered under that umbrella expression, I read the Apocalypse as a U.S. Hispanic American, the son of a Puerto Rican father and a Belgian mother, as a Roman Catholic priest of the Brooklyn diocese, as a professional interpreter of the Bible by training, employed in undergraduate and graduate teaching.

67. Barry Bearak, "Eyes on Glory: Pied Pipers of Heaven's Gate," *New York Times*, 28 April 1997.

68. See James D. Tabor, "Apocalypse at Waco," *Bible Review* 9 (October 1993): 24–33.

69. Another current, U.S. feminist interpretation of the Apocalypse, includes, for example, Tina Pippin, *Death and Desire: The Rhetoric of Gender in the Apocalypse of John* (Philadelphia: Westminster/John Knox Press, 1992); Tina Pippin, "The Revelation to John," in *Searching the Scriptures*, vol. 2, *A Feminist Commentary*, ed. Elisabeth Schüssler Fiorenza (New York: Crossroad, 1993), 109–30.

70. Pontifical Biblical Commission, *The Interpretation of the Bible in the Church*, 66.

THE APOCALYPSE IS AN URBAN BOOK

Although the island of Puerto Rico is far from the island of Patmos, and the seven cities of Asia are not New York, Washington, Miami, Chicago, El Paso, Denver and Los Angeles, the fact that, as of 1988, eighty-eight per cent of U.S. Hispanic Americans lived in urban areas has a significant bearing on their interpretation of the Apocalypse. In a book that draws its title from Jeremiah 29:7, *Seek the Peace of the City: Reflections on Urban Ministry,* Puerto Rican Pentecostal minister and social ethicist Eldin Villafañe offers pointed observations on the urban reality confronted by millions of U.S. Hispanic Americans. He recognizes that "our cities are not what they were fifty years ago, twenty-five years ago, or even ten years ago. Our cities are multiethnic, multicultural, and increasingly multilingual. They are increasingly divided between the 'haves' and the 'have nots' and between people of color and white."[71]

In the face of this increasingly complex and ambiguous social context, Villafañe admits, "I am concerned for the city—particularly that inner-city reality that is being shaken by the mindless violence of its youth and undermined by the cold indifference of institutional violence," and this concern is profound, for, "the prevalent . . . mentality of many urban youth, the unrestrained, rudderless, and destructive subculture so visible in our cities, is but a prophetic manifestation of a people perishing for lack of a *vision.*"[72]

Violence, unemployment, substance abuse, inadequate educational and health care services, the subtle and not-so-subtle racism of the rising anti-immigrant sentiment directed principally against immigrants from Latin America—all of these have their impact on U.S. Hispanic Americans with particular intensity in the cities of the United States. This experience, I would submit, disposes U.S. Hispanic American readers of the Apocalypse to foreground its undeniably urban character.

In an earlier study I pointed out that

> cities are violently ambiguous places in the Apocalypse of John. . . .
> In this book where rulers, merchants and seafarers lament the demise
> of Babylon, and where the advent of the eschatological Jerusalem is
> greeted with hopeful acclamation, first-century Christians in the cities of Asia Minor were invited to consider the ambiguities of their
> own urban existence, together with the uneasiness with which their
> own Christian convictions promised to infuse them.[73]

71. Eldin Villafañe, *Seek the Peace of the City,* 77.
72. Ibid., 1–2.
73. Jean-Pierre Ruiz, "No Temple in the City," in *Humanizing the City: Politics, Religion and the Arts in Critical Conversation,* ed. Patrick D. Primeaux

Recent studies have made considerable gains in advancing our knowledge of the cities of the Roman Province of Asia to which the Apocalypse of John was directed. For example, Steven Friesen's work on Ephesus amply documents the complexities of the sociopolitical situation, of the pervasive influence of the imperial cult within the province of Asia, and of the situation of the Asian Christians who were Revelation's original audience.[74] At the same time, attention to the Apocalypse from the standpoint of literary criticism has drawn attention to the vision that the book sought to communicate to its late first-century audience. Here Leonard Thompson suggests that "The seer is constructing an *encompassing* vision that includes everyday, social realities in Asia Minor.[75] Thus, as Friesen understands Thompson's argument, John's

> attempt to speak to the public order from the apocalyptic perspective required him to have an ambivalent relationship with the Roman world. He both rejected that order and attempted to absorb it into his vision. The result of an apocalyptic text that did not require its hearers to withdraw from the world into a sectarian social setting: they only needed to be willing to engage that world as an enemy from a particular Christian perspective.[76]

A thoroughly cosmopolitan document, the Apocalypse is

> grounded in first-century Asian life and necessarily entangles itself in all power structures in all dimensions of human society. But it entangles itself as opposition. It opposes the public order and enters the fray as other 'deviant' groups in the empire, not by joining rioters in the streets but by a literary vehicle, a written genre—in John's case, a genre offering revealed knowledge as an alternative to the knowledge derived from the public order.[77]

As for the appeal of the Apocalypse beyond first-century Asian audiences, Thompson cautions,

> to be sure, the book does communicate an alienation from the larger society that may be attractive to those who are persecuted and oppressed, but it may be just as attractive to those who are momentarily

(Bethesda, Md.: Catholic Scholars Press, forthcoming).

74. See Steven Friesen, "The Cult of the Roman Emperors in Ephesos: Temple Wardens, City Titles, and the Interpretation of the Revelation of John," in *Ephesos, Metropolis of Asia: An Interdisciplinary Approach to its Archaeology, Religion and Culture*, ed. Helmut Koester (Valley Forge, Pa.: Trinity Press International, 1995), 229–50; Helmut Koester, *Twice Neokoros: Ephesus, Asia and the Cult of the Flavian Imperial Family* (Leiden: E.J. Brill, 1993).

75. Leonard L. Thompson, *The Book of Revelation: Apocalypse and Empire* (New York: Oxford University Press, 1990), 74.

76. Friesen, "The Cult of the Roman Emperors," 248.

77. Thompson, *The Book of Revelation*, 196.

frustrated or dissatisfied with the public order or to those who are disengaged from some aspect of public knowledge.[78]

First of all, the Apocalypse of John is an urban book because it explicitly addresses the Churches of Ephesus, Smyrna, Pergamum, Thyatira, Sardis, Philadelphia, and Laodicea, directing a specific message from the risen Christ to each of the seven Churches (Rev. 2:1–3:22). These messages challenged the Churches to consider those features of their situations that are singled out for attention, with some singled out for encouragement and praise, and others diagnosed for the sake of reform. The Churches are praised for their fidelity and for their resistance to assimilation, and they are warned of the dangers of wavering in their commitment, and warned about internal and external enemies.

There is broad agreement that the seven messages never circulated independently apart from the rest of the Apocalypse, either as individual messages or as a group. As I noted in an earlier study, "the messages to the seven Churches are specific but not private: the message addressed to each Church is available to all of the others."[79] This availability promotes a sort of sanctioned eavesdropping, an authorized reading of other people's mail that established the sort of distance from each Church's particular situation that encouraged comparison. The repeated exhortation, "let the one who has ears listen to what the spirit is saying to the Churches" urges listeners to consider all seven messages, and that invitation "effectively extends to hearers beyond the circle of the seven Churches."[80] At a distance of many centuries and many thousands of miles, Xavier Alegre takes up this invitation in an appendix to his article, "El Apocalipsis, memoria subversiva y fuente de esperanza para los pueblos crucificados," adding messages to the Church in El Salvador and in Cuscatlán that are modeled after the messages of Rev. 2:1-3:22.[81]

78. Ibid.
79. Jean-Pierre Ruiz, "Betwixt and Between on the Lord's Day: Liturgy and the Apocalypse," *1992 Society of Biblical Literature Seminar Papers,* ed. Eugene H. Lovering, Jr. (Atlanta: Scholars Press, 1992), 669.
80. Ibid.
81. *Revista Latinoamericana de Teología* 26 (1992): 315–6. Here is Alegre's message to the Church in El Salvador: "Escribe el [sic] ángel de la Iglesia de San Salvador: Esto dice el que está de pie sobre el mundo, el que rige a las naciones, el Alfa y Omega, principio y fin de todo. Conozco tu conducta, tu caridad, tu fe, tu paciencia en el sufrimiento. He visto tu sufrimiento y tu lucha contra la Bestia. Pero tengo contra ti que estás perdiendo tu amor primero, que toleras a los emisarios de la bestia, estás cediendo al miedo y dejas que tus hijos sean devorados. He posado mi mirada sobre la tierra, he visto los cadáveres en el camino, ruido de la fiesta en los altozanos, el grito del hombre en el valle; salgo al campo y tus hijos mueren a espada, el crujir de la muerte en la

The urban quality of the Apocalypse of John is by no means restricted to the messages to the seven Churches. It extends to the elaborate contrasting metaphors of Babylon and Jerusalem, the former the dystopia par excellence and the latter the eschatological utopia, the former doomed by divine judgment and the latter the longed-for goal of believers' hopes, the former a place from which the faithful are urged to flee (Rev. 18:4), the latter a place the saints long to enter after sharing in the victory of Christ the Lamb. U.S. Hispanic American readers of the Apocalypse are poised between Babylon and Jerusalem, the ambiguity of their existence leading them to recognize both their entanglement in Babylon's unclean commerce and their hope for an end to the mourning and crying and pain (Rev. 21:4) in the new creation.

In the hearing of today's U.S. Hispanic American interpreters of the Apocalypse, the sevenfold admonition in the messages to the seven Churches, "Let anyone who has an ear listen to what the Spirit is saying to the Churches" (Rev. 2:7, 11, 17, 29; 3:6, 13, 22) is a call for discernment, a call for attention amid the ambiguities of life in the streets of their cities, a call to "keep the words of the prophecy of this book" (Rev. 22:7).

THE APOCALYPSE IS A LITURGICAL BOOK

Jeanette Rodríguez explains that "the Nahuatl believed that only the heart was capable of obtaining truth. Words were not enough: only through *flor y canto* (flower and song) can truth be obtained and communicated. The Nahuatl wise men and wise women did not believe that they could form rational images of what is beyond, but they were convinced that through metaphors, by means of poetry, truth was attainable.[82] The *tlamatinime*, the caretakers and interpreters of the painted Nahua codices, were responsible for breathing life into these documents that preserved the sacred traditions of the people. In one poetic description of the art of the *tlamatinime*, we read:

---

tierra y en el cielo. He visto cómo de entre los tuyos se postran ante los baales que ha colocado la bestia. Acuérdate, por tanto, de cómo recibiste y oíste mi palabra, no acalles la voz de mi profeta (Monseñor Romero), no adulteres la sangre de tus mártires, guárdala y arrepiéntete. No temes beber la copa, mira que está rebosando; no temas ir al Gólgota, mira que ahí te esperan tus hijos. Tienes, sin embargo, en San Salvador unos pocos que no han manchado sus vestidos con los ídolos de las bestias. Ellos andarán conmigo vestidos de blanco, porque lo merecen; a ellos les daré la palma del que ha vencido. El que tenga oídos que oiga lo que el Espíritu dice a las iglesias."

82. Jeanette Rodríguez, *Our Lady of Guadalupe*, 8.

I sing the pictures of the books,
and see them widely known,
I am a precious bird
for I make the books speak,
there in the house of the painted books.[83]

Ana María Pineda explains that "The *tlamatinimes* were given to
search deeply for the meaning contained in the painted codices. . . . Often their answers emerged in the composition of songs and poetry. . . . It
was their task to bring before the community the 'mirror' of tradition as
a way of making it prudent and cautious."[84] The Spanish conquest did
not put an end to this social function, or to the musical and poetic mode
of communication that characterized it. The following verses from a
sixteenth-century Nahuatl song in honor of the Virgin Mary, one of the
Cantares Mexicanos, offer an example of its transposition into a Christian key:

I took delight in all the many-colored flowers, so sweet-smelling,
that, startled and magnificent, were scattering,
with petals half-opened, in your presence, O Mother, Our Holy
    Mary.

By the water's edge (Mary) sang:
I am the precious plant of youthful buds;
I am a creation of the one perfect God, but I am the best of his
    creatures.

Your spirit, O Holy Mary, is alive in the picture. We men [*sic*]
    praised her,
taking after the Great Book [Bible], and danced the perfect dance,
and you, Bishop, our father, preached by the shore of the lake.

Artistically your spirit was imprinted.
Oh! In the worshipped canvas your spirit was hidden.
A perfect creation.
Oh! I would live securely here.[85]

The image of the Virgin Mary is "read" as though it were a text,
with the parallelism between the picture and the Great Book underlin-

83. *Cantares mexicanos,* folio 14 verso, as cited in English translation in
Miguel León-Portilla, *Fifteen Poets of the Aztec World* (Norman, Okla.: University of Oklahoma Press, 1992), 5.
84. Ana María Pineda, "The Oral Tradition of a People: *Forjadora de rostro
y corazón,*" in *Hispanic/Latino Theology: Challenge and Promise,* ed. Ada María
Isasi-Díaz and Fernando F. Segovia (Minneapolis: Augsburg/Fortress Press,
1996), 110.
85. As cited in Harrington, "Mother of Death, Mother of Rebirth," 34–5.
Various translations from the Nahuatl have been offered. See Poole, *Our Lady
of Guadalupe,* 44–7, who concludes that this song "says nothing about Guadalupe, either in terms of the apparitions or the devotion" (47).

ing the equal eloquence of image and document. The fact that the abiding power of story and song for the descendants and heirs of the *tlamatinime* and their audiences has not diminished over the centuries since the Spanish Conquest either in Latin America or in the United States disposes latter-day *tlamatinime* and their audiences to foreground the liturgical quality of the Apocalypse (together with an appreciation of the sorts of signification and symbolism that liturgy entails). The first verse of the hymn, "Alabaré," with which I introduced this presentation, substantiates that claim, and invites us to listen "in Spanish," as it were, to the hymns found within the Apocalypse itself.[86]

Taking note of the expressions of praise rendered by attendants at God's heavenly throne throughout the Apocalypse (e.g., Rev. 4:8–11; 5:9–14; 7:9–17; 11:15–19; 12:10–12; 15:2–4; 19:1–8), some have suggested that these hymns were drawn from the liturgy of the Churches to which the Apocalypse was first addressed. However, the majority of commentators suggest instead that these texts are *ad hoc* compositions that draw upon ritual imagery (biblical and imperial) in order to evoke the traditional language of praise. Sung by heavenly voices and not by worshippers on earth, they served to direct the attention of the Apocalypse's original audiences to the only legitimate object of their praise and reverence. As the angel instructs the seer in Rev. 19:10, "Worship God!" the Churches in the seven cities are challenged to do likewise.

By emphasizing the Apocalypse's liturgical quality, I am not advancing the claim that it provided a script for first-century Christian ritual, or that it reflects the liturgical practice of first-century Christians in western Anatolia. On the other hand, the blessing pronounced on the reader and on the listeners in Rev. 1:3, and the indication in 1:9-10 that the seer's inaugural vision took place on the Lord's day combine to indicate that the Apocalypse was destined for oral recitation within a ritual setting in the Churches of the Roman province of Asia.[87]

Accordingly, "hearing the Apocalypse within the ritual liminality of their assembly for worship afforded the book's earliest audiences among the seven Churches of Asia with the opportunity for critical reflection on their everyday experience."[88] This is because ritual makes it possible for participants "to objectify their action and experience in the context of the rite, and to stand back and distance themselves from their action within the rite so that they can reflect upon their own and others'

86. See Jean-Pierre Ruiz, "The Apocalypse of John and Contemporary Roman Catholic Liturgy," *Worship* 68 (1994): 482–504.

87. See David L. Barr, "The Apocalypse as Oral Enactment," *Interpretation* 40 (1986): 243–56; Ruiz, "Betwixt and Between on the Lord's Day," 663.

88. Jean-Pierre Ruiz, "The Politics of Praise: A Reading of Revelation 19:1–10," *1997 SBL Seminar Papers* (Atlanta: Scholars Press, forthcoming).

actions and understandings."[89] As for the liturgical character of the Apocalypse, I have argued elsewhere that the Apocalypse significantly

> redefines what worship involves. As the characteristic activity of the Churches, worship is not simply and exclusively a matter of prayer either public or private. Understood in this light as a stance rather than particular ritual activity circumscribed spatially and temporally, worship serves as a way of describing *every* activity, both cultic and otherwise, by which the ekklesia expresses its exclusive and uncompromising commitment to God and to the Lamb.[90]

In a similar vein, Elisabeth Schüssler Fiorenza has pointed out that "John's prophetic-apocalyptic rhetoric employs conventional cultic vocabulary . . . not for the sake of persuading his audience to participate in the daily or weekly liturgy. Rather, he uses such cultic language . . . for the sake of moving his audience to political resistance. He seeks to motivate them either to give obeisance to the power and empire of God and the Lamb or to the dominion of Babylon/Rome."[91]

Thus the foregrounding of the liturgical quality of the Apocalypse that can occur within a U.S. Hispanic American reading extends the maxim *lex orandi, lex credendi* to *lex agendi,* from prayer that manifests the commitment of faith to the sort of prayer that moves believers to engage in the sort of action that works to establish the sovereignty of divine justice.[92]

CONCLUSION

> The song was established
> the drums were set up.
> Thus, it is said
> were the cities born,
> when music came to be in them.

89. Bruce Kapferer, "The Ritual Process and the Problem of Reflexivity in Sinhalese Demon Exorcisms," in *Rite, Drama, Festival, Spectacle: Rehearsals Toward a Theory of Cultural Performance,* ed. John J. McAloon (Philadelphia: Institute for the Study of Human Issues, 1984), 180–1.
90. Ruiz, "No Temple in the City."
91. Elisabeth Schüssler Fiorenza, *Revelation: Vision of a Just World,* 103.
92. In an analogous manner, the research of Jeanette Rodríguez (*Our Lady of Guadalupe*) discloses that the prominence of Our Lady of Guadalupe among Mexican-American women is more than merely devotional. For the Mexican-American women Rodríguez interviewed, Our Lady of Guadalupe is a powerful source of resilient, resistant faith and of genuine empowerment.

Quoting these lyrics of an ancient indigenous song, Miguel León Portilla explains that it was music that brought the ancient cities of Mexico to life.[93] These verses offer a fitting way to bring these reflections to a close, with its interconnection of the two qualities—the urban and the liturgical/lyrical—which stand in the foreground of the U.S. Hispanic American interpretation of the Apocalypse that I have only begun to outline here. I have suggested that the foregrounding of these qualities of the Apocalypse makes it possible for U.S. Hispanic American readers of the Apocalypse to engage in productive conversation with two important currents in the Latin American interpretation of that book. This dialogue of engagement and otherness recognizes the distinctiveness of U.S. Hispanic Americans while recognizing their links across time and space with the peoples of their lands of origin.

As a dialogue of engagement, this effort has adopted what Segovia qualifies as an operative attitude that is "not one of ancestral obeisance or search-and-destroy demolition but rather one of critical dialogue and struggle in the light of one's reality and experience."[94] As a dialogue that respects both the otherness of the text and of differently situated contextual readings of the text, such a U.S. Hispanic interpretation of the Apocalypse acknowledges that reading the Apocalypse "in Spanish" in the United States is not quite the same as reading it "in Spanish" in Latin America, and that reading the Apocalypse at the end of the twentieth century is not quite the same as reading it in the seventeenth and eighteenth centuries.

By the same token, both Latin American and U.S. Hispanic American readings of the Apocalypse offer instances (interrelated instances at that) of the processes of inculturation and actualization that yield productive encounters with the biblical text. Such attention to "what the Spirit is saying to the Churches" through their experience, through their engagement with the sacred texts (both the printed texts and the signs and symbols that function with equal impact as "texts") holds great promise. These are conversations well worth pursuing.

93. Miguel León Portilla, *Los antiguos mexicanos a través de sus crónicas y cantares* (Mexico City: Fondo de Cultura Económica, 1961), 37. My translation.
94. Segovia, "Toward Intercultural Criticism," 326.

4

Wisdom, Beauty, and the Cosmos in Hispanic Spirituality and Theology

ALEJANDRO GARCÍA-RIVERA

INTRODUCTION

She stands on a down-turned sliver of moon, with menacing clouds and a terrible thunderbolt under her feet and a promising hopeful opening sky with the nascent sun behind her back. Surrounding her head are nine stars, and her baby holds the planet in his hands. Beneath her a rowboat rocks under threatening rolls of boiling, foaming sea and a black, a *mestizo,* and a white man cry for deliverance from this powerful storm.[1] She is La Virgen de la Caridad del Cobre, Cuba's Patroness and subject of Cuba's most significant spiritual devotion. A semiotic analysis provides some clues to the significance such a devotion holds not only for Cuban people in particular, but for Hispanic/Latino spirituality in general.[2] Perhaps the most striking element about La Caridad is cosmic. Stars, clouds, rain, lightning, sea, sun, and moon appear to be signs that say something significant about her. In this sense, the cosmic elements of La Caridad are not unique. They may be found in almost all Hispanic/Latino Marian devotions. Our Lady of Guadalupe, for ex-

1. The original story concerns two *mestizos* (half indian, half white), known as the two Juanes, and a mulatto (half black, half white). Recent depictions of La Caridad have shown either two whites and a mulatto, or a *mestizo,* mulatto, and a black. I have picked the latter depiction as being the most interesting.
2. Semiotics is the science and study of signs and symbols, pioneered by Augustine. I have used semiotics as a way to understand the theological significance of not only Hispanic/Latino spirituality but even French Cathedrals. See, e.g., Alejandro García-Rivera, St. Martin de Porres: The "Little Stories" and the Semiotics of Culture (Maryknoll, N.Y.: Orbis Books, 1995) and Alejandro García-Rivera, "A Tale of Two Altars: The Pilgrim Church of Vatican II," in Pilgrimages, ed. C. Duquoc and Virgil Elizondo, Concilium 1996/4 (Maryknoll, N.Y.: Orbis Books, 1996), 123–35.

ample, wraps herself in a mantle of stars, stands on the moon and is embraced by the sun. The cosmic symbolism surrounding the Marys of Hispanic/Latino spirituality ought to alert us that something profound is being said about the role creation plays behind these devotions. La Virgen de la Caridad del Cobre, in particular, provides an important clue. The popular contemporary image is evenly split between a world caught in a furious storm whose humanity is caught in desperate suffering and a world where storm clouds have begun to disappear, where sunlight filters through in peaceful promise focused by La Caridad's tender and loving gaze. In other words, the striking semiotics of this image of La Caridad suggest a theodicy.

A semiotic consideration of such theodicy raises the issue of the retrieval of a theological aesthetics that may provide a foundation for a reconceived metaphysics. The suggestion of the need for a reconceived metaphysics is the underlying suggestion of La Caridad that a profound unity exists between moral and natural evil at the level of the "middle." Such unity has traditionally been made through a metaphysics. It is a concern that combines indigenous and Iberian spirituality in the theodicy implicit in the image of La Caridad. A constructive project is then developed that attempts to fill in this suggestion of a New World theodicy. That project turns out to be a theological aesthetics that substitutes sign or symbol for form as reigning paradigm. The center of such a theological aesthetics, however, is the transformation of the universe into a *cosmos*, i.e., a created reality full of value that must be discerned by the human heart. The nature of such discernment is further explored through the notion of the anagogical imagination that transforms the human creature in its discernment. As such, wisdom, beauty, and the cosmos merge into a New World theodicy based on an anthropology of the anagogical imagination that creates communities of discernment and transformation.

La Caridad del Cobre

Nuestra Virgen de la Caridad del Cobre is Cuba's Guadalupe. It is not an exaggeration to say that Cuba and the Virgen de la Caridad are synonymous to Cuban hearts. Our Lady of Charity was declared the patroness of Cuba in 1916 by Benedict XV who fixed her feast date as 8 September. The Eucharistic Congress held in Santiago de Cuba in 1936 solemnly confirmed Benedict XV's declaration. Pope Paul VI raised her sanctuary to the category of Basilica in 1977.[3] Legend only remains, how-

3. This information can be gleaned off the Internet. See the University of

ever, concerning the origins of the devotion of La Caridad del Cobre. One legend has it that the first *conquistadores* to explore Cuba left an image of a Spanish Virgen de la Caridad as a gift to a Cuban Cacique. The Indians apparently became quite devoted to it. When the *conquistadores* returned, the Cacique and his community feared that they were coming to take her back and thus hid her in the mountains until she reappeared again in the more familiar story of the three Juanes.[4]

Under her feet, a violent sea churned revealing a desperate situation.[5] A small rowboat with three men, two Indians and an African slave, was about to be torn apart, her diverse human cargo to be offered to the inky violet of the deep. Such was my mother's gift to me when I moved to California, a tiled image of La Virgen de la Caridad del Cobre, Cuba's patroness and beloved virgin. The tile depicts in image a holy story that dates to the late seventeenth century. Around 1598, copper mines in the eastern mountains of Cuba, a region known as del Prado, began to be mined extensively. Near the mines a thriving cattle industry also began to feed the miners. The meat from this cattle was preserved with generous portions of salt creating what Cubans call *tasajo,* a tasty delicacy. The salt itself was gathered from a beautiful bay just north of the mountains called Nipe. It was the need for salt that brought two Indian brothers and a nine year old African slave *moreno* to the shores of Nipe. Upon their arrival, a great storm came in from the sea and kept them ashore for three days.

On the third day, however, they awoke to a beautiful Cuban morning and set out in a canoe seeking their precious salt. On the way there, one of the Indian brothers noticed what looked like a little girl floating on the sea. As they rowed closer, they saw that it was not a girl but a statue floating by itself on a wooden plank. As they approached the statue, they realized it was a statue of the Virgin Mary dressed in a dazzling white dress with the baby Jesus in one hand and a cross on the other. Even more amazing, the dress on the statue was thoroughly dry! As the men picked up the statue to put it in the canoe, they noticed something written on the plank: "I am the Virgen de La Caridad." They realized then that this statue was very special. So the brothers and the boy brought her to their small town near the bay where the community

---

Dayton's Web Page and their informative page on Latin American Marian devotion. The University of Dayton has, amazingly, the largest library and resources on the topic of Mary and Marian devotion. This is due to the unflagging efforts of the founding Marianist brothers.

4. This story comes from her most famous researcher.

5. See Alejandro García-Rivera, *Nuestra Parroquia,* Claretian Publications for what follows in this passage.

erected a small shelter for the statue. Then curious happenings began to take place. The statue disappeared at night only to return in the morning! This happened several times, and the folks realized that perhaps the Virgen wished to be somewhere else.

In order to discover the Lady's wishes, the statue was passed from town to town but the disappearances continued. Everyone was mystified. Then, up in the mountains of the Sierra Maestra, a young girl, Apolonia, began to chase butterflies. At one point, she looked up and saw la Caridad smiling down at her from a craggy outcropping of a copper mine. The mystery had been solved and Cuba's beloved Virgen de la Caridad del Cobre had herself pointed to the place she wanted to be placed.

La Virgen de la Caridad is now pictured in a storm clearing floating above a tempest-tossed boat carrying the three "Juanes" who, in our day, are pictured as either being two whites and one mulatto or one white, one *mestizo,* and one mulatto.

The enigmatic Caridad, I believe, can be analyzed by using a method I developed from a suggestion by Robert Schreiter, the semiotics of culture.[6] Semiotics *per se* studies signs and the relationships between signs.[7] The semiotics of culture attempts to study the signs and the relationship between signs in what might be called a cultural "text." Just as the grammar and words of a sentence can be analyzed, so can the signs and the relationship between signs in a particular cultural product be analyzed. The popular image of La Caridad del Cobre is just such a cultural "text." A full semiotic analysis is impossible in this brief paper, but some significant elements can be identified that point towards a profound theology of suffering. Notice, once again, the number of cosmic elements. Clouds, sea, lightning, the sun, moon, and the stars all surround La Caridad. True, all these elements have their counterpart in indigenous spirituality as gods or near-gods, but in this cultural text I believe they are more than syncretic additions or indigenous remnants. A brief consideration of the numerous other *virgenes* of Latin American and Hispanic/Latino devotion[8] reveals that such cosmic elements ac-

6. See García-Rivera, *St. Martin de Porres.*

7. St. Augustine pioneered semiotics in order to make sense of obscure passages in Scripture. Cf. Marcia L. Colish, *The Mirror of Language: A Study in the Medieval Theory of Knowledge,* rev. ed. (Lincoln, Nebr.: University of Nebraska Press, 1968).

8. For example, Argentina: Nuestra Señora de Luján; Bolivia: Nuestra Señora de Copacabana; Brazil: Nuestra Señora Aparecida; Chile: Nuestra Señora del Carmel del Maipú; Colombia: Nuestra Señora de Chiquinquirá; Costa Rica: Nuestra Señora de los Angeles; Dominican Republic: Nuestra Señora de la Altagracia; Ecuador: Nuestra Señora del Quinche; El Salvador: Nuestra Señora de la Paz; Guatemala: Nuestra Señora del Rosario; Honduras: Nuestra Señora

company most of these Marys. The Marys of the New World have something to say of cosmic significance. Surely this reflects an indigenous concern. The early ethnography of the first missionaries tell us the major religious category for Native religion was not human salvation but cosmic order.[9] Such a clue allows us to see a major constellation of sign relationships in the popular image of Nuestra Virgen de la Caridad.

Notice, for example, the humanity that is the three "Juanes" tossed about by an angry sea, illumined by startling lightning, and blown by a violent wind is counterbalanced by the gentle gaze of La Caridad serenely opening up a clearing in the storm clouds, the moon at her feet and the sun gently silhouetting her head, which, in turn, is crowned with nine stars. Here in this image, cosmic chaos is seen to be ultimately not chaos at all. Under the feet of our Lady, the cosmos is under control. What is more striking is the picture of cosmic order and human redemption mixing in semiotic relationship suggesting deeper waters of analysis. There even appears to be a semiotic "hot zone." La Caridad dominates the *middle*. Indeed, the three "Juanes" appear to be helplessly drawn up into it. A preliminary analysis suggests that something significant is being said about the relationship between creation and redemption and the role of a cosmological *middle* in such a relationship. This cosmological *middle* I will propose as the spiritual.[10] The significance of this image of La Caridad, I believe, is, above all, what is being said about spirituality in the midst of human suffering. As such, an understanding of spirituality (and human suffering) born out the tradition as well as the springs of New World piety may be retrieved.

Towards A New Theodicy

The suggestion of a theological statement being made that combines the concern for cosmic order and human suffering may surprise con-

de Suyapa; Mexico: Nuestra Señora de Guadalupe; Nicaragua: Nuestra Señora de la Inmaculada Concepción de El Viejo; Panama: La Inmaculada Concepción; Paraguay: Nuestra Señora de los Milagros de Caacupé; Peru: Nuestra Señora de la Merced; Puerto Rico: Nuestra Señora de la Divina Providencia; Uruguay: Nuestra Señora de Los Treinta y Tres; Venezuela: Nuestra Señora de Coromoto.

9. See especially Ricard's marvelous account of the difficulties of the Friars in explaining the concept of sin to the Mexicans in Robert Ricard, *The Spiritual Conquest of Mexico* (Berkeley and Los Angeles: University of California Press, 1966).

10. I have dealt with this issue in Alejandro García-Rivera, "Creator of the Visible and the Invisible: Liberation Theology, Postmodernism, and the Spiritual," *Journal of Hispanic/Latino Theology* 3, no. 4 (1996): 35–56. Although much of the material that follows can be found in this article, it is being given new connotations through its explicit connections to a theodicy.

temporary theologians. In our day, human suffering has been analyzed mainly in sociological and political terms. Cosmology has played little if any role in contemporary theology except in current dialogues with the natural sciences. Indeed it is our secular cosmology that would make this particular image, even all the popular images of Latin American and Hispanic/Latino Marian devotions, sentimental pious pap or misguided superstition. I would propose that it is the lack of an adequate contemporary Christian cosmology that prevents popular spirituality from being given serious attention by contemporary theologians.[11] Yet cosmology has played a central role in both Scriptures and theology. In the Scriptures, one finds cosmology an integral element of the Wisdom Literature. In theology, cosmological considerations became the battleground for the tradition's earliest theodicies as response to the twin challenges of Gnosticism and Manichaeism. It may be said that at the heart of those challenges was the nature of the relationship between creation and redemption. An understanding of such relationship depended, in turn, on a Christian understanding of evil and its experience, human suffering. What is striking about the tradition's reflections on evil and human suffering is its dependence on a theological aesthetics. Thus, if one is to understand the full implications suggested by the image of La Virgen de la Caridad, wisdom (cosmic order), beauty, and the cosmos must become the threads by which we weave the accounting of a New World spirituality and theodicy.

The term theodicy comes from the Greek, *theos* (God) and *dike* (justice). As John Hick so aptly put it: "The word is thus a kind of technical shorthand for: the defence of the justice and righteousness of God in face of the fact of evil."[12] Theodicy has become, in our day, an almost intractable dilemma. The reason for this, I believe, lies in the nature of the modern spirit and theodicy itself. Theodicy is an intellectual exploration of the nature of evil that emerges out of the concrete but agonizing reality of human suffering. Thus, theodicies speak of abstract evil to explain the concrete experience of suffering. If making abstract the concrete experience of evil is, for our day, injury to our sensibilities, then the use of abstract categories at all adds insult to that injury. Indeed,

11. By contemporary, I am speaking of the period after Vatican II—1965 and after. In contrast, theologians before Vatican II saw spirituality as a resource for their reflections. A brief examination of Rahner's *Theological Investigations*, e.g., would reveal numerous articles ranging from devotion to the Sacred Heart to the theology of the spiritual senses. Unfortunately, few theologians today would even consider such reflection.

12. John Hick, *Evil and the God of Love* (London: Macmillan, 1966), 6. Indeed, Hick's work provides a great summary of the nature and issues of theodicy.

our times tolerate little abstraction. There is good reason for this. Human suffering after Auschwitz, Hiroshima, and the ethnic cleansings of Cambodia and Bosnia leave little sympathy for traditional theodicy. The concrete experience of evil appears to explode any abstract category by which we attempt to measure the contemporary experience of human suffering. Moreover, recent postmodern thought admits of no abstractions. The ultimate reality is human experience. Yet images such as La Caridad continue to comfort the afflicted of our day. What is their power? What is the nature of their theodicy that may speak to our day?

The very image of La Caridad provides a clue. Traditional theodicy makes the distinction between *moral* evil, evil that originates in human actions, and *natural* evil, evil independent of human actions. Yet in La Caridad, natural evil appears to symbolize all human suffering. In the eyes of pious faith, the distinction between natural and moral evil is not overcome but permits a profound unity to be suggested. Such suggestion is not new to the theological tradition. It is a foundational element to an Augustinian theodicy.[13] Augustine traced the origins of natural and moral evil to what Leibniz called "metaphysical" evil, the finitude and limitation of the created universe. The very suggestion of a metaphysics, however, sends shudders down the spines of most contemporary theologians. The notion of both a "wholeness" to reality as well as an "in-between" reality, implicit components of a metaphysics, find little if any support among contemporary academic circles. Lest the reader come to the premature conclusion that I am suggesting the retrieval of a traditional metaphysics, let me be direct about my proposals.

Rather than suggesting the retrieval of a traditional metaphysics, I am articulating the spirituality of an "in-between" reality that founds a "whole" reality. In other words, I am speaking of the retrieval of a theological aesthetics (rather than a metaphysics) that may serve as a new approach to a *reconceived* metaphysics. Indeed, the traditional theological component in all theodicy is an aesthetics.[14] Though all theodicies relate the Christian doctrines of creation and redemption, the original contribution I see suggested in the semiotics of the image of *Nuestra Señora de la Caridad* is a closer relationship between creation and redemption than may be found in the two major theodicies of the theo-

13. Ibid., 13.
14. My proposal for such a reconceived metaphysics will be forthcoming in a chapter tentatively entitled "The Whole" in a book project on Latino Systematics to be published by Orbis Books in the not too distant (I hope) future. My proposal for a theological aesthetics will be forthcoming as *The Community of the Beautiful: A Theological Aesthetics* (Collegeville, Minn.: The Liturgical Press).

logical tradition.[15] As such, a New World theodicy may be discerned that combines the inherited Western theological tradition with the indigenous New World concern for cosmic order. But to make the claim, I must reflect on the first claim made in the first sentence of the first article of the Nicene Creed: *I believe in the Creator, Maker of Heaven and Earth, of all visible and invisible.*

CREATOR OF THE VISIBLE AND THE INVISIBLE

Why do Catholic Christians bother with prayer at all? Why do they even pray for one another? Why, indeed, do we even dare praying to La Caridad to intercede and pray for us? Why the insistence on *mediacy* rather than directness? Surely there are enough cultural anthropological, sociological, and ritual studies to give some measure of understanding. Yet these do not let the theologian off the hook. There is, in the tradition of the faith, a reality being addressed by our way of life. This reality reveals itself in the image of La Caridad as a *middle*. There is in the nature of things an *in-between*, a demand for mediation. Modernity has not been kind to the proposal of an in-between to reality. Direct access to an ultimate reality may be proposed as the reigning paradigm of Modernity. Whether in the natural or human sciences,[16] the in-between has been sloughed off in favor of an ultimate originating reality. Whether the spirit of the marketplace, the social contract, the inevitable laws of demographics, or the fixed, eternal laws of Nature, Modernity has tried to explain all reality in terms of the "really real," an originating principle or law, a "spirit," if you will, that undermines the *experience* of reality towards an abstract, original reality.[17] As such, Modernity has thrived on abstraction. Such abstraction, however, has been bought at a

15. I am referring, of course, to the theodicies associated with Augustine and Irenaeus. If Augustine exaggerated the distinction between the orders of Creation and Redemption in his theodicy, Irenaeus almost dismissed it. By downplaying the difference between Creation and Redemption, Irenaeus did not bring about a closer understanding of their relationship. The point being made is that the distinction must be appreciated before a claim for their interconnectedness can be made. Augustine's theodicy left little room to make such a claim. Irenaeus did not see the necessity to make it. Note the discussion in Hick, *Evil*, ch. 2.

16. What C. P. Snow called the "two cultures" of Modernity. Cf. C. P. Snow, *The Two Cultures* (Cambridge: Cambridge University Press, 1969).

17. On this matter, Funkenstein's discussion of the natural sciences' use of the counterfactual conditional is quite appropriate. Amos Funkenstein, *Theology and the Scientific Imagination: From the Middle Ages to the Seventeenth Century* (Princeton: Princeton University Press, 1986).

price. Modernity has brought the dissection of reality: Nature vs. Culture, Spirit vs. Matter, Male vs. Female, etc. The dichotomies of Modernity go on forever.[18] An emerging school of thought known as postmodernism has begun to contradict Modernity's assumptions. As will be explored in more detail later, postmodernism makes the *in-between* the actual criterion of reality. The proposal of an *in-between* reality has once again been made intellectually feasible through the powerful currents of postmodern thought. Nonetheless, the New World metaphysical aesthetics explored here is not meant to be another postmodern product. Postmodernism opens up the discussion for this new metaphysics, but, as will be seen, postmodernism itself will be challenged by the proposal.

Postmodernism is notoriously difficult to describe and has many "flavors" and approaches ranging from the psychological insights of Lacan to the archaeology of Foucault.[19] I am going to concentrate on the semiotic approach of Derrida for reasons that will become, I hope, quite clear (if such is possible with postmodern thought!).[20] Towards that goal, I find the approach of the semiotician John Deely particularly helpful.[21]

18. See, e.g., the illuminating discussion in Louis Dupré, *Passage to Modernity: An Essay in the Hermeneutics of Nature and Culture* (New Haven, Conn.: Yale University Press, 1993).

19. The literature on postmodernism is vast. Some basic works consulted for this paper include Jean-François Lyotard, *The Differend: Phrases in Dispute,* trans. Georges Van Den Abbeele (Minneapolis: University of Minnesota Press, 1988) and Jean-François Lyotard, *The Postmodern Condition: A Report on Knowledge,* trans. Geoff Bennington and Brian Massumi (Minneapolis: University of Minnesota Press, 1984); Jacques Derrida, *Of Grammatology,* trans. Gayatri Chakravorty Spivak (Baltimore: Johns Hopkins University Press, 1976); Jacques Derrida, *Writing and Difference,* trans. Alan Bass (Chicago: University of Chicago Press, 1978); Mark C. Taylor, *Erring: A Postmodern A/theology* (Chicago: University of Chicago Press, 1984); and John Deely, *New Beginnings: Early Modern Philosophy and Postmodern Thought* (Toronto: University of Toronto Press, 1995).

20. In the discussion that follows I will be using the term "postmodernism" in the Derridean sense with hopes that much of what is said also applies to other "flavors" of postmodern thought—being aware, however, that such an universal claim cannot be made. Nonetheless for clarity of narrative and adequacy of coverage, I believe it is not inappropriate.

21. John Deely's thesis ought to be of particular interest to Hispanic/Latino theologians. His claim is of a lost history of philosophy between Ockham and Descartes. Late Hispanic philosophy included the works of Soto (1495–1560), Araújo (1580–1664), Fonseca (1548–1599) and John Poinsot (1589–1644). This period between the end of Latin scholasticism and the beginning of the Modern Age sees Hispanic philosophy flowering into a new understanding of sign, which is at the same time postmodern yet goes beyond. Deely sees a parallel connection between the semiotics of the Hispanic philosopher of this period,

The Greeks and Latins took Being as "what had reality and existence independently of human thought and feeling." Being was immediate to human experience. For the Greeks, experience did not go much farther than acknowledging it as *empeiria*. The Latin's notion of experience, *experimentum*, consisted of "the action of the sensible thing making itself an object by its own action upon the organ of sense." As such, human experience was the mediation of Being. Modernity expanded the notion of experience by bringing into consideration the "activity of the mind itself." This had the effect of shifting talk away from *being* to *discourse*: "the rational activity of the human mind whereby it is able to know whatever it comes to know." The basic assumption was that the "mind knows only its own products." Thus, the issue of the "external" world was raised as it relates to experience. As such, human experience gets dissected by modernity. Human experience consists of rational elements provided by the mind and natural elements provided by the "world." The relationship between the natural and the rational elements of experience became the great projects of modernity. Thus, modernity led to the dissection of human experience into the subjective (Idealism) and the objective (Realism).[22]

Postmodernism, on the other hand, seeks to find room for all aspects of human experience: "the affective no less than the cognitive, the conative no less than the intellective, the cultural and artifactual no less than the natural." Indeed, postmodernism asserts that the realities of feeling, deception, and illusion are every bit as much a piece with our experience as are the "realities of rational communication and order and sensible intrusions from the environment upon our experience."[23] What Postmodernism has done is to take the *whole* of experience seriously. In doing so, postmodernism has placed all elements of human experience on an equal epistemological level. The natural carries as much weight as the mental. Indeed, such a difference cannot be made within the totality of human experience. Human experience is an unbroken fabric. Postmodernism arrives at this conclusion through its own analysis of the "middle."

Postmodernism sees experience as constructed of the *différance*, i.e., mediation of the "other."[24] The "other" as difference attacks modernity's notion of subjects or objects as "original" to experience. *Différance*

John Poinsot, and the semiotics of Charles Peirce. It is not, however, a straight parallel, and John Poinsot said a few things about sign that would improve upon Peirce's system. Deely, *New Beginnings*, 3–11.

22. Deely, *New Beginnings*, 16.

23. Ibid., 17.

24. Jacques Derrida, "Structure, Sign, and Play in the Discourse of the Human Sciences," in *Writing and Difference*.

amounts to nothing more than an attempt to understand experience in terms of a pure intersubjectivity. Postmodernism finds its model of intersubjectivity in language, or more specific, the linguistic semiotics of Ferdinand de Saussure. Saussure's semiotics are based on the sign as dyadic: the sign consists of a signifier and a signified. The dyadic sign distinguishes itself by exclusion of the referential object. It is absolutely arbitrary. Thus, language only brings meaning to human experience. Reference or the "objective" cannot exist in human experience.[25] As such, Saussure's dyadic sign presents language as a closed sign-system with unlimited semantic productivity and complete arbitrariness in the production of signs. Saussure's dyadic sign-system lays the foundation for postmodernism's attack on modernity's dissection of human experience.

Derrida, for example, begins his attack on modernity by assuming that it is absolutely impossible to achieve self-knowledge by intuitive self-reflection. This implies that thought must externalize itself into repeatable structures such as the signs that make up language. These signs mediate thought yet never complete a semantic circle. Their meaning is constantly pulled this way or that by their many semantic connections. Thus, the mediation of thought, the signs of language, postpone the end of their mediation and fail to complete the origin of their meaning through the inevitable play of chance or the aleatory on meaning. Indeed, postmodernism sees any hermeneutic circle (such as Hegel's) as philosophical *hubris*. Difference and alterity can not be mastered.[26]

25. This has severe consequences for the nature of language. The loss of reference means the loss of "meta-narrative." One cannot stand outside of language. All we can hope from language is "meaning." As such, this appears to aid a claim to the primacy of aesthetics as a theological approach. But such an aid is illusory. A totally "meaningful" world may find sympathy in what Balthasar calls an "aesthetic theology" but not in "theological aesthetics." A theological aesthetics has as its primary assumption that "human being lives to see God." This means an aesthetics not only capable of meaning but also of reference, albeit reference to an ultimate reality. Nonetheless, a theological aesthetics does not directly contradict postmodernism's claim that reference is illusion but mitigates it as the rest of this paper will show. On the normative character of semiotic aesthetics, see Vincent G. Potter, *Charles S. Peirce: On Norms & Ideals* (Worcester, Mass.: University of Massachusetts Press, 1967).

26. Leonard Lawlor, *Imagination and Chance: The Difference Between the Thought of Ricoeur and Derrida* (New York: State University of New York Press, 1992), 2. This is good news for Hispanic/Latino theology. Their claim that cultural and racial differences are fundamental is supported. This is bad news for any theology that has as its method an absolutely closed hermeneutic circle. As such, liberation theology's method escapes the fiery furnace of postmodernism. Critical reflection on praxis is more a spiral than a circle. Cf. Juan Luis Segundo, *Liberation of Theology* (Maryknoll, N.Y.: Orbis Books, 1979).

Postmodernism carries astounding implications. Mediation is prior to thought or perception. "Nonpresence, discontinuity, and difference . . . are prior to presence, continuity, and identity."[27] Thus, the "middle" of *différance* does not function traditionally as a "passage from thought back to thought, from the present back to the present" but rather is turned away from its destination by the "unforeseeable accident" of meaning rather than the "novel product" of a subject's imagination or the forcible intrusion of an object outside experience. *Différance* relies on the intrinsic nature of sign to stand for another, classically stated as *aliquid stat pro aliquo*. As such, the sign is an intrinsic *mis*-use of meaning. The sign takes us somewhere *else*. Unexpected meaning intrinsically accompanies the sign sending "us indefinitely back and forth to rethink the origin and transform the end." Mediation, as Derrida is fond of repeating, is a zigzag and not a dialectic. Without "origin" or "end," the experience woven by signs becomes an unbroken fabric in which a most curious situation exists. Human experience consists of a collage of arbitrary and repeatable encounters with difference that has no author to comment nor listener to address. As such, human experience is rather "seen" than "read." "Otherness," i.e., the difference of the sign, resists its reading. "Otherness," on the other hand, lends itself to "seeing." This is the insight of postmodernism. A "seeing" that has no subject to "see," nonetheless, is a curious matter. The astounding conclusion of postmodernism asserts that such is possible for what is "seen" is nothing more than the mirror reflection of the "other's" mirror. Thus, Andy Warhol could say, "When I look into a mirror, I see nothing. People call me a mirror, and if a mirror looks into a mirror what does it see?"[28] Surprisingly, the taking of human experience seriously appears to dissolve the author, the subject of experience, into the unchartable expanses of the intersubjectivity of experience.

Postmodernism (as understood here) has been most helpful in retrieving the taking seriously of human experience, and thus the experience of spirituality, yet it differs from the Christian experience of prayer, indeed, from the semiotic import of the mulatto "Juan" praying with hands folded to Mary. Prayer beckons *beyond* experience an "other." In doing so, prayer *brings to* (rather than *finds in*) experience comfort. Postmodernism, on the other hand, has little to say about comfort. There is little comfort to be found in the postmodern labyrinth of mirrors. Indeed, postmodernism knows of no project of human emancipation, little

27. Lawlor, *Imagination,* 3.
28. A. Warhol, *From A to B and Back Again* (London: Cassell, 1975), quoted in Richard Kearney, *The Wake of Imagination: Toward a Postmodern Culture* (Minneapolis: University of Minnesota Press, 1988), 5.

less of redemption. There exists in this image of *La Caridad* a spiritual intuition of ultimate reality, not the experience of a world ultimately unreal. Neither is such intuition of ultimacy due to a proleptic "future" emancipation but to emancipation in the "here and now," born of the immediacy of human suffering. Instead, a "middle," La Caridad, grounds this sense of ultimacy, an intercessor, another subject that stands on our behalf at that place where one can say: "the buck stops here." A "middle" makes possible our "Juanes's" prayer—a call for ultimate accounting based on confidence and comfort on the ultimately Accountable. Indeed, the sense of an ultimate reality came not from a subject's *immediacy* with ultimacy but an intersubjectivity, a *mediacy,* that brought ultimate reality to the subject. In other words, Christian spirituality speaks of the possibility of transcending human experience through the existence of the *middle* in reality. This type of metaphysics allows the possibility of abstraction not as a way to elude the concrete but by allowing the concrete "here and now" to emerge and interconnect. Such creaturely transcendence provides a clue to the nature of redemption.

Redemption lies at the feet of an ultimate reality if not entirely at the feet of the subject of salvation. Ultimate reality, however, addresses the subject of redemption somewhere in the "middle," i.e., the spiritual. Direct access to ultimate reality would conflate creation and redemption. The "middle" keeps both orders distinct but not mutually exclusive.[29] Such assertions, however, are difficult to make. The spiritual has fallen on hard times. Associated (wrongly) with an ascent to an "other-worldly" world, the spiritual has been criticized as leaving human experience behind for an experience-less, ultra-terrestrial world. This made the spiritual little less than a Platonic form. Nonetheless, a renewed understanding of the spiritual must take place. At faith's door lies the challenging conclusion of postmodernism—redemption is only a "meaning" *found in* the *immediacy* of human experience not also a reference to an ultimate reality *brought to,* i.e., mediated through human experience.[30]

This "bringing to" belongs to the theological tradition of the spiritual. A "bringing to" already says something about the spiritual. It is

29. In this respect, Lawrence Sullivan's account of the importance of a "middle" that keeps the Original myth of Creation from exploding the symbolic categories of present existence, i.e., of the function of a middle that allows making sense of the world is important. Lawrence E. Sullivan, *Icanchu's Drum: An Orientation to Meaning in South American Religions* (Chicago: University of Chicago Press, 1988).

30. I am referring, of course, to Frege's famous distinction between sense and reference.

not a Platonic form. The spiritual "brings to" human experience ultimate reality; it does not exist there. A proper theology of the spiritual, then, must draw its inspiration from a theology of creation. The spiritual exists on *this* side of ultimate reality. I am proposing that a recovery of the spiritual that goes beyond Platonism and postmodernism must ground itself in a theology of creation. A starting point for such a theology may be found in the familiar article of faith: "I believe in God, Maker of all things, visible and invisible." If God is the creator of the visible and the invisible, then matter and spirit may not be related as absolute formlessness and absolute form.[31] Matter and spirit must relate, rather, as creatures—the visible and invisible. But what does belief in the invisible mean for faith today? Creation, through the paradigm of the natural sciences, has come to consist simply of the visible, i.e., the empirical. The invisible, on the other hand, has become associated, through the paradigm of the human sciences, with the purely human invention of the imagination. As such, the spiritual fits within postmodernism's paradigm quite nicely. Postmodernism accommodates the imaginary by making human experience a meaningful irrationality rather than a referential reality. Thus, the reality of the spiritual becomes co-opted under postmodernism as a meaning within experience. As meaning rather than reality, the spiritual cannot be a compass of ultimacy.

The spiritual seen from a theology of creation, on the other hand, proposes something different. Belief in the creator of the visible and the invisible suggests that there exists in the *intellectus* of faith a distinction between the *created* invisible and the *uncreated* invisible.[32] As such, the created invisible stands in the "middle" between the uncreated invisible and the created visible. The created invisible mediates the uncreated invisible by affecting human being, the juncture of the visible and the invisible, towards the invisibility of the uncreated, i.e., the divine. This "turning towards ultimacy," in a sense, describes the traditional notion of repentance. Repentance, in turn, is the foundation for any theology of redemption. Thus, the connection between creation and redemption may be found in describing the nature of such turning towards ultimacy. In terms of the creator of the visible and the invisible, such turning to ultimacy becomes an act of making visible the invisible.

31. Ernst Cassirer, *The Individual and the Cosmos in Renaissance Philosophy* (New York: Barnes & Noble, 1963), 9.

32. This is, in fact, a Cappadocian insight used against the negative judgments of the creation by Christian Gnostics. Jaroslav Pelikan, "Creator of the Visible and the Invisible," in *Christianity and Classical Culture: The Metamorphosis of Natural Theology in the Christian Encounter with Hellenism* (New Haven, Conn.: Yale University Press, 1993).

As such, belief in the creator of the visible and the invisible suggests a theology of redemption based on a theological aesthetics that involves both the cosmos and the creature where the invisible becomes visible, the human.[33]

A theological aesthetics avoids many of the problems associated with systems that focus on a mediating principle for their dynamics. Theological aesthetics, for example, does not lose the subject of redemption in some mediating principle of ultimate reality like Hegel's dialectic of absolute Reason. Theological aesthetics does not reduce the irreducible alterity between creature and creator. Rather, it speaks of the mystery of human being, a mystery best encapsulated by Irenaeus: "The glory of the Lord is living human being and human being lives to see God."[34] Human being not only has the capacity to "see" God but also his and her very life depends on it. This is not a spirituality of Platonic forms. Human contingency (the "glory of the Lord") founds human transcendence ("lives to see God"), the "seeing" of the "invisible." A theological aesthetics, then, that flows from belief in the creator of the visible and the invisible sees in human being an intrinsic connection between creation and redemption, between creature and creator. The connection has qualities that have at the same time the nature of an aesthetics and the nature of a sign—making visible the invisible, i.e., a semiotic aesthetics. Indeed, the New World theological aesthetics would substitute the traditional notion of form for the notion of sign or symbol as the foundation for such an aesthetics.[35] As a semiotic aesthetics, the "middle" that is the created invisible safeguards the subject of redemption (which must still discern a reality beyond experience) as well as the nature of redemption (redemption is not identical with the subject).

33. Theological aesthetics, before Modernity, was the *conditio sine qua non* of theological approaches to the question of spirituality. Theological aesthetics, notwithstanding Hans Urs von Balthasar's majestic work *The Glory of the Lord: A Theological Aesthetics* (San Francisco: Ignatius Press, 1982–91), is rarely discussed today as a viable approach to theology. The reason for this lies, in my estimation, with the loss of confidence in the possibility of metaphysics or the notion of Being. While not convinced that metaphysics is to be assigned the status of a historical fact rather than a living tradition of study, my approach to aesthetics is based on the science of semiotics rather than a metaphysics of being. Indeed, my approach to the spiritual is a semiotic aesthetics. My proposal for such an aesthetics may be found in the forthcoming, "A Matter of Presence" in *Journal of Hispanic/Latino Theology*. An alternative but complementary proposal for a theological aesthetics may also be found in Roberto S. Goizueta, *Caminemos Con Jesús: Toward a Hispanic/Latino Theology of Accompaniment* (Maryknoll, N.Y.: Orbis Books, 1995).

34. Ireneaus, *Adversus Haereses*, Book 3.

35. This claim is developed more fully in García-Rivera, *The Community of the Beautiful*.

The encounter of the faith's tradition of the spiritual with postmodern thought has emphasized the importance of retrieving a sense of the *in-between* of reality. Proposed here is an aesthetic metaphysics that has not form but sign or symbol as its reigning paradigm. This semiotic aesthetics provides a way of speaking of the spiritual that acknowledges the insights of postmodern thought without succumbing to its fatal assumptions about the possibility of redemption. Such aesthetics, however, must also acknowledge the insights of modernity without also succumbing to its assumptions of a "middle-less" reality. Towards that end, the issue of a Christian cosmology is now addressed through an exploration of the theodicy inherent in the Wisdom tradition.

The Wisdom Tradition[36]

"Vanity of vanities. . . . I saw all the deeds that are done under the sun; and see, all is vanity and a chasing after wind" (Eccles. 1:2, 14 NRSV).[37] The Preacher's words to his (assumed) tutor could just as easily have been written by any postmodernist such as Derrida. Indeed, Qoheleth shares the postmodern conclusion that human achievements are neither novel nor significant. Such a conclusion, however, throws cold water on liberation theology's claim of a fundamental project of human emancipation. If human projects are a "chasing after wind," then can hope exist for the human condition? Yet one must not ally Ecclesiastes too readily with postmodernism. Ecclesiastes' vanity is more subtle than postmodernism's. Indeed, the reigning metaphor of Ecclesiastes is *hebel* whose semantic field includes "vanity," "absurdity" as the irrational, "absurdity" as the inconsistent, and "ephemeral."[38] The literal meaning of *hebel*, however, is "breath," and is closely associated with a similar term *ruah* (1:14; 2:11, 17, 26; 4:4, 16; 6:9) that means "spirit" or "wind." *Ruah* "is the vital power originating with God that activates and sustains both human life (Job 27:3; Isa. 42:5; Zech. 12:1) and creation (Ps. 104: 29–30). Their combination gives Ecclesiastes' tragic theme: the "ephemeral" nature of human existence together with the innate desire for the vital breath of life.[39] *Hebel* and *ruah*, breath and spirit, intertwine

---

36. Much of the treatment immediately before and after comes directly but in somewhat modified form from my previous article, "Creator of the Visible and the Invisible."

37. Unless noted, all biblical quotations derive from the New Revised Standard Version, or NRSV.

38. Leo G. Perdue, *Wisdom & Creation: The Theology of Wisdom Literature* (Nashville: Abindgon Press, 1994), 206.

39. Ibid.

in Ecclesiastes the cosmic and social dimensions of human life. Ecclesiastes' "vanity" is meant to hold these two dimensions in tension:

> There is a vanity that takes place on earth, that there are righteous people who are treated according to the conduct of the wicked, and there are wicked people who are treated according to the conduct of the righteous. I said that this also is vanity. (Eccles. 8:14)

The vanity of Ecclesiastes appears as an ancient *topos*: the *verkehrte Welt*, i.e., the cosmic order turned upside down and reflected in the social order.[40] There is great injustice in the human condition. The wicked prosper while the righteous suffer (Job 21:7). The vanity lies, however, in believing this injustice to be the "natural" way of things. Indeed, the "natural" way of things speaks of a different order:

> LORD, our Sovereign, how majestic is your name in all the earth! You have set your glory above the heavens. Out of the mouths of babes and infants you have founded a bulwark because of your foes, to silence the enemy and the avenger. When I look at your heavens, the work of your fingers, the moon and the stars that you have established; what are human beings that you are mindful of them, mortals that you care for them? Yet you have made them a little lower than God, and crowned them with glory and honor. (Psalm 8:1–5)

The vanity of Ecclesiastes bears little relationship to the glorious order mentioned above. Indeed, Ecclesiastes' vanity carries a profound tension: a cosmic order that is the "glory of the Lord" versus a social order that is the vanity of human work. Such tension speaks of a subtle but decisive distinction between Ecclesiastes' skepticism and postmodern nihilism. Ecclesiastes' skepticism revolves around the difficulty between distinguishing human "breath" and life-giving "spirit." Postmodern nihilism has no notion of distinguishing. All "spirits" are "welcomed" in the wistful, aleatory play of signs.

Ecclesiastes is part of the biblical corpus known as the Wisdom literature. The Wisdom literature includes several Psalms and the books of Proverbs, Job, Ecclesiastes, Sirach, and the Song of Songs. Ecclesiastes' skepticism must be considered in terms of the entire Wisdom corpus. As such, the Wisdom literature adds another dimension to Ecclesiastes' skepticism. It may be "measured" against a glorious order bounded at creation by its creator:

> Then the LORD answered Job out of the whirlwind: "Who is this that darkens counsel by words without knowledge? Gird up your loins like a man, I will question you, and you shall declare to me. "Where were you when I laid the foundation of the earth? Tell me, if you have

40. R. W. Scribner, *Popular Culture and Popular Movements in Reformation Germany* (London: Hambledon Press, 1987).

understanding. Who determined its measurements—surely you know! Or who stretched the line upon it? On what were its bases sunk, or who laid its cornerstone when the morning stars sang together and all the heavenly beings shouted for joy? Or who shut in the sea with doors when it burst out from the womb?—when I made the clouds its garment, and thick darkness its swaddling band, and prescribed bounds for it, and set bars and doors, and said, 'Thus far shall you come, and no farther, and here shall your proud waves be stopped'?" (Job 38:1–11)

The vanity of human works lies in their failing to "measure up" to the divine cosmic order. The author of the social order has an Author, the creator of the cosmic order. The works of the human author compared to the works of the cosmic Author always prove themselves to be contingent vanities. Thus, the contingency of human works provides a subtle but amazing corollary: the social order may be "measured" against the cosmic order! The great founder of liberation theology, Gustavo Gutiérrez, sees the same correlation in his own commentary on Job:

> The whole of this first speech (chaps. 38–39) expresses the delight that the created world gives God. . . . Utility is not the primary reason for God's action; the creative breath of God is inspired by beauty and joy. Job is invited to sing with Yahweh the wonders of creation. . . . The reasoning in God's discourse seems to be this: what holds for the world of nature, holds with all the greater reason for the world of history.[41]

But how can such a "measure" be taken? Are we talking of some sort of "natural law" by which to judge the human social order? Here lies the crux of Wisdom theology, a theology difficult to discern because the paradigms of modernity's natural sciences and postmodernism's analysis of human experience obscure its vision. The "measure" taken between the cosmic and social orders has as its basic unit of measurement neither the binary unit of logic, truth or falsehood, nor of ethics, good or bad, but the graduated and relative unit of Wisdom's cosmic aesthetics—spirit.

A Cosmic Aesthetics

This still begs the question. How can such a "measure" of spirit be taken, i.e., what sort of aesthetics is being proposed? Wisdom gives few clues to a detailed answer but one may discern a basic assumption: *aesthetic value is an intrinsic reality of the cosmic order.* In other words, the contin-

41. Gutiérrez, *Job*, 75.

gency of creation introduces value into the cosmos. This insight of Wisdom follows from the nature of the contingency between creator and creature: "And God saw it was good." Contingency in the context of an ultimate reality amounts to a cosmic aesthetics, a cosmos of values. One speaks of values instead of value because as contingent realities all creatures are accountable to the creator. As such, not all creatures carry the same value. The most capable of responding to the creator's love are also the most contingent, i.e., dependent on that ultimate love and thus bearing the most value. The aesthetic values of the cosmos are relative, not absolute. As such, a cosmic aesthetics based on the contingency of its creatures carries the possibility of discernment. Such discernment is made even more possible with the created invisible. In-between the created visible and the uncreated invisible, spiritual realities carry relatively higher aesthetic values. In other words, the spiritual within the graded aesthetics of a created cosmos can act as a compass of ultimacy.[42]

This does not mean that the aesthetic *value* of the cosmos resides with the spiritual. Such would be a misunderstanding of Wisdom's creation theology. Wisdom's creation theology has as intrinsic and inseparable complement an aesthetic anthropology. Such an anthropology can be discerned in the distinction Wisdom makes between the cosmic and social order. As such, it suggests a further distinction: the intrinsic realities of the spiritual carrying aesthetic values and their conscious adoption as ideals within the social order. Human "measure" of the cosmic order, then, involves the conscious adoption of such intrinsic values as ideals to be pursued.[43] Such "measurement" is not the determination of ultimate reality. It is not simply a type of "natural" law nor purely an act of ethical discernment. Rather it is a discerning towards a deliberate and willing shaping of one's life to ultimacy, i.e., an anthropological aesthetics. It is not so much adopting a *view* of God as it is adopting a *way of life* that leads to God. It is not "thought" about God but an aesthetic response to the creator through the aesthetic realities present in creation.

Such an aesthetics, however, does not yet make clear the role of redemption. Is such an aesthetic response merely a fulfillment of an intrinsic anthropology? Such a conclusion leaves unsatisfied the tragic experience of human suffering. The aesthetic realities of Christian cosmology ought not to serve to harmonize away suffering but to trans-

42. I am indebted here to the thought of one of my students, Robert Marsh, S.J., who worked out some of the implications of the Cappadocian distinction between the created and uncreated invisible for his project on Ignatian discernment.
43. The following develops the reasoning in Potter, *Norms & Ideals*, 48–51.

form our humanity so that God's Glory ultimately be seen. Thus, we come to the crux of our reflection begun through the image of our Lady of Caridad. Not all aesthetic values lead to God. A theological aesthetics must give principles by which one may judge the aesthetic cultural values that lead a particular religious cultural tradition to God. A theological aesthetics is by its very nature a normative science. Indeed, the adoption of a false norm, a false aesthetic principle, can lead far away from the presence of God.

Roberto Goizueta, for example, warns of the dangers of an "insufficient Cultural-Racial aesthetics," an aesthetic epistemology that can lead to "idealist abstractions."

> [Idealist aesthetics] overlook the concrete sociohistorical and, hence, ethical-political character . . . beauty. That is, they overlook the fact that, like reason, beauty . . . is always mediated by social, cultural, political, and economic practices, structures, and institutions—in short, by the very ethical-political praxis that Vasconcelos, the Mexican Aesthetician, had hoped to transcend through aesthetics. Without attention to that mediation, an aesthetic philosophy remains hopelessly abstract and, yes, disembodied: social structures and institutions are an important form of historical embodiment.[44]

Furthermore, if aesthetics is to be truly redemptive,

> aesthetic unity must be grounded in the experience of unjust sociohistorical disunity. If its to be genuinely liberative, aesthetics must be mediated by the preferential option for the poor.[45]

Goizueta's warning, in my opinion, is well taken and must be heeded by a practicioner of Hispanic/Latino theological aesthetics. Indeed, Goizueta seems to be suggesting an aesthetic principle: "a preferential option for the poor." Although my sentiments lie with such a rallying cry, I believe the phrase as formulated is inadequate for a theological aesthetics. I intend, however, to take Goizueta's insight to heart in an approach to a proper aesthetic principle.

A NORTH AMERICAN APPROACH TO AESTHETIC VALUE

Western ideas of art and beauty continue to be profoundly influenced by Hellenic aesthetics, the idea that "the world of beauty was rather that of imitative representation than of interpretive origination."[46] In

44. Roberto Goizueta, "La Raza Cósmica: The Vision of José Vasconcelos," *Journal of Hispanic/Latino Theology* 1, no. 2 (1994): 23.
45. Ibid.
46. Bernard Bosanquet, *History of Aesthetic* (Cleveland, Ohio: World Publishing, 1957), 12.

other words, Hellenic aesthetics are governed by a principle of representation rather than presentation.[47] Bosanquet, in fact, feels he has discovered a tension inherent in aesthetic theories of representation or
imitation:

> Even the idea of imitation, indeed, contains the germ of a fuller aes-
> thetic truth than was ever attained by Hellenic thought; for the trans-
> lation of an object into a plastic medium involves a double and not
> merely a single element,—not merely a consideration of the object to
> be represented, but a consideration of the act of imaginative produc-
> tion by which it is born again under the new conditions imposed by
> another medium.[48]

Bosanquet points to an inherent tension in all aesthetics. Beauty is
as much a "making" as a "beholding." As John Dewey puts it:

> The process of art in production is related to the esthetic in percep-
> tion organically—as the Lord God in creation surveyed his work and
> found it good. Until the artist is satisfied in perception with what he
> is doing, he continues shaping and reshaping. The making comes to
> an end when its result is experienced as good—and that experience
> comes not by mere intellectual and outside judgment but in direct
> perception. . . . As we manipulate, we touch and feel; as we look, we
> see; as we listen, we hear. The hand moves with etching needle or
> with brush. The eye attends and reports the consequence of what is
> done. Because of this intimate connection, subsequent doing is cu-
> mulative and not a matter of caprice nor yet of routine. In an em-
> phatic artistic-esthetic experience, the relation is so close that it con-
> trols simultaneously both the doing and the perception.[49]

True beauty, then, lies as much in the art as in the aesthetics of the
beautiful. Implicit in John Dewey's suggestion above, a theology of aesthetic imagination that takes into account both the artistic and aesthetic
elements may be found in the biblical doctrine of creation. When God
"formed" the world, it was good. The beauty of God's creation is found
not only in its beholding but in the very act of its forming. Thus, I believe, a proper theological aesthetics must take into account these twin
acts of beauty—"making" and "beholding." Such an account begins with
the biblical notion of creation as "forming," an act that, biblically, has
the dimension of the imagination.[50]

47. At least, this is how I interpret Bosanquet's sense of "interpretive origination."
48. Bosanquet, *Aesthetic,* 12.
49. John Dewey, *Art As Experience* (New York: Perigee, 1980), 50.
50. The pursuit of such an enterprise is, necessarily, an interdisciplinary
venture with perils for all those trained in one discipline but not the other.
Nonetheless, it is an enterprise that must be undertaken. The peril, however,
is not letting a philosophical framework guide a biblical interpretation. True,

The Hebraic Imagination

A place to start for a biblical aesthetics given the previous analysis may be the biblical word for the imagination. In the Hebrew scriptures, the closest equivalent is the word *yetsêr*. The basic meaning of the semitic root, יצר, i.e., *yetsêr*, is "shape, form." Other meanings include "potter," "form," "purpose," "sketch," "plan," and "determine." Forms derived from this root occur some seventy times in the Old Testament. The word *yetsêr*, in the main, denotes forms of craftsmanship such as pottery. Those passages, however, rarely describe the potter in an everyday context but theologically. The potter may refer to the creator or pottery to the act of creation. Such uses of the word refer to the notion found in both Israelite and non-Israelite religions that God formed the human race from clay *like* a potter. Thus yetsêr, itself, can refer to the creation of the human race. Yetsêr, however, also refers to the creation of Israel such as in Deutero-Isaiah (Isa. 43:1, e.g.) where Yahweh is referred to as the "former" or *yotsar* of Israel. Moreover, *yetsêr* is also used to describe God's shaping of history such as in Jer. 18 where Yahweh through the image of the potter shapes the destiny of the people of Judah. Such meaning has surprisingly modern connotations when referred to the modern notion of culture. Yahweh, e.g., may be seen as the "former" or *yotsar* of the culture that is Israel. Other occurrences of *yetsêr* also connote the sense of framing a plan. Such occurrences frequently occur in conjunction with לב (leb) or "heart," which is the Hebraic locus for the seat of thought. As such, *yetsêr* takes on the meaning of "imagination of the heart," the heart's thoughts and purpose (Gen. 8:21). Thus, when *yetsêr* stands alone, it must be translated as something like "purpose," or following the Rabbinic commentators of the Talmud and Mishnah, the "imagination."[51]

Indeed, at the "heart" of the Hebrew Scriptures stands the great exhortation of Deut. 6:5, "you shall love the Lord your God with all your heart and with all your soul and with all your might." This exhortation is part of what is known as the *Shema* and constitutes the religious ideal of Israel.[52] Thus, the imagination as "shaper, former" plays a significant role of Israel's self-understanding as a cultural being as

the biblical material has an integrity all its own. Nonetheless, such material must be interpreted, and in its interpretation a theologian may, indeed must, bring some sort of framework to guide him or her.

51. G. Johannes Botterweck and Helmer Ringgren, eds., *Theological Dictionary of the Old Testament*, trans. David Green (Grand Rapids, Mich.: Wm. B. Eerdmans Publishing Company, 1974–) s.v. לב.

52. Michael Fishbane, *The Kiss of God: Spiritual and Mystical Death in Judaism* (Seattle: University of Washington Press, 1994) 3.

well as the source of its spirituality. The earliest Rabbinic interpretation of Deut. 6:5, e.g., is found in the Mishnah, *Berakhot* IX. 5. In reference to the phrase *"with all your heart,"* the comment reads: "with your two inclinations, with the good inclination (*yetzêr*) and with the evil inclination (*yetzêr*)." The comment puzzles until one realizes that ancient Judaic psychology saw the human heart as having two distinct inclinations: one towards evil (the *yetsêr hara*) and one towards good (the *yetsêr hatov*).[53] These two inclinations form the core of an Old Testament doctrine of sin. The Talmud, for example, contains several passages that see the imagination as the most "primordial drive" of the human being, the gift of God to his most excellent creation, the power to "form" or "shape" as the creator. This primordial drive, however, can either lead to idolatry or can

> if sublimated and oriented towards the divine way (Talmud), can serve as an indispensable power for attaining the goal of creation: the universal embodiment of God's plan in the Messianic Kingdom of justice and peace. . . . In short if the evil imagination epitomizes the error of history as a monologue of man with himself, the good imagination (*yetsêr hatov*) opens up history to an I-Thou dialogue between man and his Creator.[54]

Thus the Talmud says: "God created man with two *yetsêr*s, the good and the evil" (*Berach,* 61a). Martin Buber's commentary on the Deuteronomic passage is illuminating:

> Evil is lack of direction and that which is done in it and out of it as the grasping, seizing, exploiting, humiliating, torturing, and destroying of what offers itself. Good is direction and what is done in it . . . with the whole soul, so that in fact all the vigour with which evil might have been done is included in it.[55]

Thus, one possible interpretation of the Old Testament understanding of "forming" may be the imagination of the heart, which directs human creativity and activity. This human creativity has moral dimensions. Not all uses of the creative imagination lead to divine presence. At the same time, the imagination of the heart is God's gift to the human creature. Through the imagination, we become, in Philip Hefner's words *created co-creators,*[56] able to participate in divine presence. The

53. G. Cohen Stuart, *The Struggle in Man Between Good and Evil: An Inquiry into the Origin of the Rabbinic Concept of Yetser Hara* (Kampen: Kok Publishing House, 1984).

54. Richard Kearney, *The Wake of Imagination* (Minneapolis: The University of Minnesota Press, 1988), 46.

55. Martin Buber, *Good and Evil* (New York: Scribner's, 1952), 130–1.

56. Hefner, Philip, *The Human Factor: Culture, Evolution, and Religion* (Minneapolis: Augsburg/Fortress Press, 1993), 32.

human imagination, then, "forms" or "shapes" the conditions by which divine presence, the self-communication of God, can be perceived.

A New Testament Understanding of the Imagination

Tracing the literal Hellenic equivalent of *yetsêr* into the New Testament is disappointing. A more productive approach concentrates on the role the "heart" plays in the New Testament corpus. Such an approach reveals a certain continuity with the previous discussion of the role of the *yetsêr* in the Old Testament. The New Testament appears to continue the Hebraic theme of "forming" but adds the nuance of "beholding." Some have suggested that this takes place through a Hellenic shift of the understanding of the heart, καρδία (*kardia*) from a center of moral deliberation to a center of metaphysical deliberation,[57] i.e., νοέω (*noeo*). Indeed, in the Septuagint, the heart is the organ or seat of *noeo*, which means "to direct one's mind to."[58] In Gen. 8:21, e.g., the Hebrew term *yetsêr leb*, is translated in the Septuagint as *dianoia tou anthropou. Dianoia* is a derivative of *noeo. Noeo* is an important New Testament verb occurring (along with its derivatives) very frequently. *Noeo* also has a rich history of connotations in Greek philosophical thought especially as it applies to metaphysics. It would be a mistake, however, to conclude that the New Testament sense of *noeo* follows slavishly the Hellenic metaphysical sense. The New Testament appears to have in its use of *noeo* less a metaphysics than an anthropology. It appropriates the Hebraic *yetsêr* towards articulation of a new human reality. This appropriation may be seen in the analysis of three important derivates of νοέω: νοῦς (*nous*), μετάνοια (*metanoia*), and διάνοια (*dianoia*).

Nous, e.g., originally meant an "inner sense directed on an object." As such, it is a special type of seeing or beholding. *Nous* beholds "mental formations," i.e., *noemata*, objects "invisible" to the eye but visible to the *nous*. Thus, the sense of "forming" and the sense of "making" join together in the New Testament use of *nous*. The objects of *nous* are, at the same time, "formed" by the *nous* as well as "beheld" by it.[59] This double sense of "making" and "beholding" is clear in the other derivative term of *noeo*—*metanoia. Metanoia* is a very common term in the New Testament, especially in the Synoptics and Acts. As such, *metanoia* calls for a fundamental change in a human reality through a holistic "change

57. Kearney, *Wake of Imagination*, 79.
58. Gerhard Kittel and Gerhard Friedrich, eds., *Theological Dictionary of the New Testament*, trans. Geoffrey W. Bromiley (Grand Rapids, Mich.: Wm. B. Eerdmans Publishing Company, 1964–1976) s.v. "νοέω."
59. Ibid., s.v. "νοῦς."

of mind." Indeed, *metanoia* calls for a reshaping or re-"forming" of mental structures (the imagination), which is at the same time a new "form" or "shape" of a human life.[60]

Another New Testament word relevant to the Old Testament notion of *yetsêr* is *dianoia*. This common word for "thought" has the nuances of resolve or intention. Thus, *dianoia* appears to contain the sense of the evil or good imagination found in the Hebraic notion of *yetsêr*. Matt. 22:37, in fact, uses *dianoia* in a direct reference to Deut. 6:5. Furthermore, Col. 1:21 uses *dianoia* to refer to the impulses of the will. More interestingly, Ephesians calls *dianoia*, the "eyes of the heart" (Eph. 1:18), a visual metaphor, which may be "enlightened" or "darkened" depending on the "hardness of the heart" (*porosis kardia*, Eph. 4:18), a metaphor of "form." Indeed, Heb. 8:10 refers back to Deuteronomy in which God intends to "put my laws in their minds (*dianoia*), and write them on their hearts (*kardia*), and I will be their God, and they shall be my people." Thus, God intends to "form" or "shape" the laws of the imagination of our hearts so that our imaginative activity will lead us to God. As such, *dianoia* also has the sense of "forming" a people such as the *yetsêr*'s sense of the "forming" of Israel.[61]

All these senses, I believe, come together in what I consider the most significant occurrence of the word, the passage in Luke known as the *Magnificat*: Luke 1:51

> He has shown strength with his arm; he has scattered the proud in the thoughts (*dianoia*) of their hearts. He has brought down the powerful (*katheile dunastes*) from their thrones, and lifted up the lowly (*hypsose tapeinous*). (Lk. 1:51–2)

God scatters the proud in their evil imagination, the *dianoia* of their hearts, in order to "lift up (ὑψόω) the lowly, a creative act of the good imagination. Thus, *dianoia* appears to refer most directly to the Hebrew Scripture sense of the *yetsêr* and suggests what the evil and good imagination may mean in the New Testament.

The evil imagination, e.g., is associated with the pride of the powerful (*hypereiphanos*). The good imagination, on the other hand, is associated with "lifting up the lowly." As such, the key verb ὑψόω (*hypsoo*) resembles the elementary act of aesthesis, i.e., the lifting up of a foreground out of a background and giving the foreground value.[62] Such

60. Ibid., s.v. "μετάνοια."
61. Ibid., s.v. "διάνοια."
62. I am referring to that school of Semiotic Aesthetics known as the Prague School of Semiotics whose most prominent figure was Jan Mukarovsky. Mukarovsky saw the essential semiotic element in aesthetics (poetry was his example) as "foregrounding," selecting a piece of the background and making

"lifting ups" are mentioned over and over again in the Scriptures each time giving new sense to what a theological aesthetics might look like. The Septuagint, for example, often uses *hypsoo* to refer to the joyful exaltation of God, an exaltation "which on the presupposition of abasement means glorification."[63] Indeed, Hans Urs von Balthasar identified the "glory of the Lord," *Herrlichkeit*, as the basis for his theological aesthetics. The New Testament use of *hypsoo*, however, in connection with *dianoia*, or the imagination, means not so much "the glory of the Lord" but the "joyful exaltation of the Lord" especially in the context of abasement, in other words, the "lifting up the lowly." The Magnificat of Mary, then suggests a truly biblical aesthetical principle—"lifting up the lowly." A theology of imagination now becomes evident. Its foundation is a semiotic aesthetics whose aesthetic principle—*lifting up the lowly*—founds an anthropology of the imagination.

A Semiotic Aesthetics

The most concrete example of such a semiotic aesthetics at work is the Church's celebration of the Paschal Mystery, the Eucharist. The "lifting up" of the "lowly" wine and bread founds the *real presence* of the crucified Lord of glory. The Eucharist, then, is an act of the good imagination guided by the same imagination that created the world and now acts as the basis for a new creation. As such, it is an imagination guided by the aesthetics of God, the lifting up of the crucified Jesus, risen and lifted up again. To the extent that our human imagination engages the divine imagination, we are lifted up as well, the lowly human creature of dust now exalted to share a banquet with God. This lifting up takes place semiotically, in terms of real signs and symbols. It also takes place aesthetically, a totality of meaning and reference flooding and formed by the senses. What this semiotic aesthetics also reveals that it is both a "making" and a "beholding," a way of life as well as a view of life. The anagogical imagination, then, reveals is that human understanding involves more than an act of "knowing." Human understanding has a redemptive dimension, a dimension of "making." Human life is ultimately anagogical, a lifting of the spirit towards its source. When human understanding fails, the consequences are more than ignorance or un-enlightenment but death and suffering.

---

it prominent through non-discursive means such as rhythms or uniqueness. cf. "The Esthetics of Language" in *The Prague School Reader of Esthetics, Literary Structures, and Style,* selected and translated from the original Czech by Paul L. Garvin (Washington, D.C.: Washington Linguistic Club, 1955).

63. *Theological Dictionary of the New Testament,* s.v. "ὑψόω."

The *Anagogical* Imagination

A theology of imagination, then, ought to recognize that human understanding involves the "heart," which includes not only the moral *leb* of the Old Testament but also the intellectual *nous* of the New Testament. Together, these revealed dimensions of human being articulate a holistic view of human ways of life—affective, volitional, and cognitive—which are at the same time expressions of the human imagination. Such dimensions coalesce in what might be called the *triadic* heart and suggest that the human imagination is more than a psychology but involves the entire human being. The human imagination involves the crafting not simply of a view of life but, more fundamentally, a way of life. As such, what a New World aesthetics proposes is not something like Tracy's *analogical imagination* but the *anagogical imagination*.[64] The *anagogical* imagination is a life of discernment that continually transforms the human creature towards the Glory of the Lord. As such, the *anagogical* imagination calls us to live as communities not of interpretation[65] but as communities of aesthetic discernment.

Conclusions

Those familiar with the work of the famous anthropologist, Clifford Geertz, will interpret the content of this paper as a sort of "thick" description of theological interpretation.[66] This may be the case. As such, many will find the "thickness" of the paper rather uncomfortable. My only defense is that such "thick" descriptions are unavoidable in our day. Theological reflection is called more and more to demonstrate the richness of the tradition rather than take one original insight and expound on it *ad infinitum*, such as in the work of the great German theologians and philosophers. Theology today, I believe, is called to make connections rather than dissect them. It is with that goal in mind that this study was made. It is the richness of the study, I believe, that ought to be its value rather than the unity of its thought (although that too is important). Having given this apology, there are some important points brought out in the study.

First, I believe that the study of spirituality more and more needs the concomitant contribution of the theologian. Christian spirituality

64. See my critique of David Tracy in García-Rivera, "A Matter of Presence."

65. I am thinking here of a contrast with Josiah Royce's notion of Christianity as a community of interpretation as described in his *Problem of Christianity* (Chicago: University of Chicago Press, 1968).

66. Clifford Geertz, *The Interpretation of Cultures: Selected Essays* (New York: Basic Books, 1973)

may be studied in terms of cultural, social, ritual, and linguistic categories but somewhere along the way its basis in the faith must be considered. Hispanic/Latino spirituality presents such a case. Hispanic/Latino spirituality is not some pious adjunct to the Spanish-Speaking tradition of the American (in the continental sense) Catholic Church but a foundational element. Hispanic/Latinos, indeed, all Latin Americans, interpreted, reflected, and made faith *one's own* through their spirituality. Through it they brought insights from indigenous, African, and Roman theology into an authentic inculturation of the faith's tradition. Such spirituality ought not to be studied simply in search of syncretic elements, cultural idiosyncrasies, or even socioeconomic eventualities but, rather, as faith expressions of a deeply felt and profoundly understood Christianity.

Second, the importance of a viable Christian cosmology is underlined in this study. I hope this study makes clear how important a role cosmology plays in so much of theology. As such, the contribution of indigenous America with its concern over cosmic order ought not to be underestimated. Today, as science presents us a universe without intrinsic value, Hispanic/Latino spirituality proclaims with power and vigor that the universe is actually a *cosmos*, a universe, yes, but a universe full of intrinsic value. More important, such indigenous contribution helps reconceive Christian theodicy. We are, in the language of Vatican II, pilgrims, communities of discernment in the midst of a great suffering. Suffering, an ever present reality, is not the foundation of our discernment. Rather, the Glory of the Lord, Beauty itself, charges the world with values as signposts to a vision scarcely imagined. Such vision is ours to have through the anagogical imagination that transforms us as we discern the vision towards which our pilgrimage is pointed. Moreover, such vision is cosmic; not only we but the entire cosmos is transformed through the anagogical imagination. The aesthetic metaphysics of reality itself require it.

Finally, Hispanic/Latino communities are actually communities of discernment. La Virgen de la Caridad del Cobre denotes one such community. Imagine the multitude of other Hispanic/Latino communities that discern in the middle of their pilgrimage, from their seats in a tempest-tossed boat, the "middle" of reality from which they sense a vision of a wonderful world yet to come, a world full of wisdom and beauty, a world, indeed, that is a *cosmos*.

5

The Place of Hispanic Theology in a Theological Curriculum

Systematic and Pastoral Implications

ANA MARÍA PINEDA, R.S.M.

This is an auspicious time for Hispanics in the U.S. Catholic Church. Since the 70s Catholic lay and religious leadership embarked on a journey, a series of "encounters," among them the Encuentro Nacional Hispano de Pastoral of 1972, 1977, and 1985.[1] These Encuentros gave voice to the restlessness, longings, and dreams of U.S. Hispanics as they struggled to articulate the kind of relationship they sought within the U.S. Catholic Church.[2] Among many of the blessings experienced by Hispanics during that period of making history and making memory was the incredible journey of theologizing. The Encuentro processes in themselves were formative experiences that provided Hispanic participants with a context in which to learn theology as a community. In the ensuing decades, the Hispanic presence in the United States has caught the attention of society at many levels.

In the area of theology, this interest has produced diverse consultations (small dialogue conferences) and given impetus to numerous research projects. These projects have challenged the world of theological

1. See United States Catholic Conference, *Hispanic Ministry: Three Major Documents* (Washington, D.C.: United States Catholic Conference Office of Publishing and Promotion Services, 1995). This publication contains three significant documents that were products of the period of active engagement that U.S. Hispanic Catholics embarked upon in the 70s as they articulated their desire to be a valid part of the Church.

2. See United States Catholic Conference, *Proceedings of the II Encuentro Nacional Hispano de Pastoral* (Washington, D.C.: United States Catholic Conference Office of Publishing and Promotion Services, 1978). This particular document gives voice to theological concerns and questions regarding theological preparation for Hispanic leadership for both ordained and non-ordained ministers.

education, for theologians are now called to identify their precise role in preparing ordained and non-ordained religious leadership for ministry in the Hispanic community.[3] The importance of such an endeavor sheds light on vital questions that impact the quality of pastoral and academic undertakings in today's world. In this article I will highlight three significant studies that have provided us with important information about the theological education of U.S. Hispanics and the implications of that education for faculties of schools of Theology, seminaries, and departments of Religious Studies in universities across the country.

DEMOGRAPHICS

The importance of such an endeavor cannot be isolated from the fact that the Hispanic presence in the United States is sizeable. Population figures indicate that in 1990 the Hispanic population was over twenty-two million, twenty-six million in 1995, and projected to reach thirty-one million by the year 2000. The U.S. Bureau of the Census estimates (mid-level estimates) that Hispanics will number forty-five million in 2010, sixty-one million in 2020, and over one hundred million by the year 2040.[4] Political and economic realities in Latin America have contributed to the increase in Hispanic immigration to the United States. The median age of Hispanics is among the youngest and the birth rates of Hispanics the highest in the United States. These factors promote the increase in the U.S. Hispanic population.

3. Examples of consultations and/or research projects that addressed the question of theological education and preparation of Hispanics and non-Hispanics for active engagement with the U.S. Hispanic communities: the 1987 study undertaken by the Fund for Theological Education (FTE), entrusted to Dr. Justo L. González; a forum on Hispanic vocation and formation held in June 1988, sponsored by the U.S. National Conference of Catholic Bishops and directed by Gary Riebe-Estrella, S.V.D.; an eight-year endeavor to study the role of schools of theology in preparing ordained and non-ordained ministers to work in the Hispanic communities, begun in 1989 by Catholic Theological Union in Chicago under the leadership of CTU President Donald Senior, C.P., and directed by Ana Maria Pineda, R.S.M., director of Hispanic ministry.

4. These figures were generously provided by Dr. David Maldonado, Associate Dean for Academic Affairs of Southern Methodist University (SMU) in Dallas, Texas as part of a paper delivered at a consultation on Hispanic American Protestantism at SMU on 18–19 October 1996.

Hispanic Protestant and Hispanic Catholic Dialogue

In addition to the growth and vitality of the U.S. Hispanic population, another factor that has entered into the conversation more forcefully in the last several decades is the growing ties forged among Protestant and Catholic Hispanics.[5] In effect, another kind of "common ground" effort has given clear evidence that while their denominational histories have shaped them in unique ways, nevertheless their cultural values and traditions link them inseparably. For these communities, the issues of theological education for Hispanics is vitally important. Ultimately it poses the question of dignity, regardless of their denominational affiliations.

The FTE Theological Education of Hispanics Report

In 1987 a study to assess the theological education of Hispanics was undertaken with a grant from the J. Howard Pew Charitable Trust by the Fund for Theological Education (FTE). Since its founding in 1954, FTE had a history of supporting the theological education of women and minorities. As the population of Hispanics increased significantly, FTE anticipated the need to be better informed on the state of Hispanic theological education in order to prepare for the new challenges of the future. The study was entrusted to Dr. Justo L. González, a respected professor of Church history and a well-known figure in theological education for Hispanics. While the study specifically focused on the role of FTE in Hispanic theological education, its findings reached beyond FTE.

The report demonstrated several urgent needs in order to augment a pool of qualified Hispanics professors that could contribute to theological enterprise. The underprivileged status of women in the Hispanic theological enterprise required that special attention be given to them. There was the further need to establish a data bank on Hispanics holding a doctoral degree in order to identify qualified candidates for available professional positions. In order to expand the number of theologically qualified Hispanics, it was noted that support should be given to Hispanics who were committed to contributing to the Hispanic communities in the United States. Financial support was recommended for

5. Examples of these have been the growing collaboration in consultations such as that on Hispanic Protestantism held at SMU in 1996. Several advisory/consultative committees have engaged voices of Hispanic Protestants and Catholics, e.g., the Lilly Endowment's consultation on Hispanic concerns held in Indianapolis in 1995 and the Pew Charitable Trust's work on designing a scholarship program for the theological education of Hispanics in 1995.

institutions such as Bible institutes and local Churches that provided Hispanics with ministerial training because the vast majority of Hispanic ministers had not attended accredited theological institutions. During this present interim period, while the numbers of trained Hispanics theologians is small, non-Hispanic faculty needed to be sensitized to be able to respond more appropriately to Hispanic students in their theological institutions.

While the FTE study surveyed existing programs and endeavors aimed at providing theological education for Hispanics, in his report González recognized the need for further studies that would investigate the implications of theological education for Hispanics. The final report was presented not only to FTE but also to theological institutions across the country who would ultimately benefit from its findings. The González report made it clear that the question of theological education for Hispanics was just beginning to be posed and that more extensive consideration would be required in the theological enterprise.[6]

THE ROLE OF SCHOOLS OF THEOLOGY AND HISPANIC MINISTRY

In the 80s the Catholic Theological Union in Chicago (CTU) began to wrestle with the question of the role of schools of Theology and Hispanic Ministry as it took initial steps to broaden its programs. As the enrollment of Hispanic/Latino[7] students began to increase, they asked about the proper role of a graduate school of theology in preparing ordained and non-ordained religious leadership for ministry in the Hispanic community, particularly in an urban, multicultural Hispanic context. The presence of Hispanic/Latino students in the classroom raised fresh and challenging theological questions that required serious consideration and attention.

Beginning in the fall of 1987, an assessment of needs was undertaken by the faculty of the Hispanic Ministry Program. The results of that assessment provided preliminary information to administration, faculty, students, and to the religious superiors of male congregations whose seminarians were enrolled in the institution. It allowed them to understand the important elements in developing a reliable program in

6. Justo L. González, *The Theological Education of Hispanics* (New York: The Fund For Theological Education, Inc., 1988). This study, commissioned by the FTE, was prepared by Dr. González. The findings outlined in this section have been taken from the study.

7. Here Hispanic is used to refer to U.S.-born Hispanics. Latino is used to refer to the increasing number of students born in Latin America who come to the United States for their theological studies.

Hispanic Ministry, one that could prepare ministers for involvement in the diverse U.S. Hispanic communities.[8]

The input indicated that the efforts of such a program had to be totally integrated into the educational structure of CTU. It could not be left on the margins of the theological curriculum or enterprise. At the same time, the faculty was forthright in expressing its need for information and opportunities that would increase their awareness and ongoing understanding of Hispanic reality and culture. The faculty was asking for resources that would support their vocation as theological educators for an ever-broadening constituency, which made it imperative that culture be a theological dialogue partner of theological education. The integration of Hispanic theological concerns and realities would not only influence the faculty of CTU but would also extend itself to Hispanic and non-Hispanic students (ordained and non-ordained) who were being trained to relate to the reality of the universal Church. The inclusion of lay students in this integrated vision of theological formation presented itself as a new challenge that required further exploration. Overall the report urged that such a theological undertaking should be done in collaboration with other educational institutions, establishing contacts with other programs that offered theological training and formation in Hispanic Ministry. Methodologically, the program would draw from regular course work, seminars for faculty, creative liturgies in the Hispanic context, summer sessions, adequate library holdings, and eventually a revision of the curriculum that would place Hispanic Ministry at its heart.[9]

FUNDAMENTAL ISSUES FACING HISPANIC MINISTRY AND THEOLOGY

The assessment of needs provided CTU with valuable insights, information, and challenges. Its implementation would be undertaken in measured steps, assisted in large measure by a generous grant awarded to CTU by the Lilly Endowment in 1989. Under the terms of the grant several projects were included: (1) a major consultation among faculty, key constituents of the school, and Hispanic resource persons nation-

8. While the majority of Hispanics in the United States are of Mexican heritage, it is important to acknowledge the substantial presence of Central and South Americans and Caribbeans.

9. The results of the assessment of needs resulted in a report prepared by Drs. Isidro Lucas and Ana Maria Pineda, R.S.M., which was presented to the administration, faculty, students, and other members of CTU. The written report entitled "An Action Plan for CTU's Hispanic Ministry Program" is on file at CTU, and the summary of those findings in this paper has been selected from that report.

ally; (2) visits to existing Hispanic programs to assess what was being done by other Catholic schools of theology; (3) the sponsoring of a lecture series and study program on the multicultural nature of the U.S. Hispanic community and its religious implications; and (4) the gathering of supporting research data to assist in the consultation and other phases of the planning process.[10]

The national consultation was successful in drawing on the wisdom of the Hispanic community and educational resource persons in order to elicit the central issues facing schools of theology in their attempt to respond to the needs of Hispanic Ministry. Four key areas of concern emerged from the consultation. The first key area of concern centered on the need for faculty development on issues specific to theological education and formation for Hispanic ministry. Specific concerns relating to faculty development were identified: (1) the need for faculty to gain an understanding of Hispanic culture and the attendant problems or barriers posed by racism and sexism; (2) the need to develop an appropriate pedagogy for doing theological formation in a Hispanic context, i.e., one that draws on experience and respects the collaborative values of Hispanic culture; (3) the need to develop models of ministry appropriate for an urban, multicultural Hispanic context. This would require skills and awareness that would encompass such things as: (a) a method that respected "pastoral de conjunto," or collaborative style; (b) understanding of and respect for popular religion; (c) skills in social analysis; (d) the skills and perspectives necessary for community organizing.[11]

The second key area of concern highlighted the educational opportunities needed at several levels for those who would eventually engage in Hispanic Ministry. In concrete terms, the needs of three specific groups were targeted: (1) the need for the theological and pastoral training of pastoral agents beginning ministry for the first time in the Hispanic community, especially those from small ecclesial communities; (2) the need to provide continuing educational opportunities for current pastoral agents; (3) the need to deal creatively with the lack of formal degrees for many of those who have pastoral experience and natural leadership abilities. In order to respond to these needs, the participants in the consultation strongly recommended exploring the possibility of a collaborative effort with other educational institutions and with the local Church. An adequate response to the challenge presented

10. Lilly Endowment Grant No. 890257, awarded to CTU to explore Hispanic Ministry and Roman Catholic Theological Education, 12 June 1989.
11. Final Report for Grant No. 890257, submitted to Lilly Endowment in 1990, on file at CTU, 3–4.

by Hispanic ministry would require the pooling of resources and a commitment to work in a collaborative fashion.[12]

The third key area of concern addressed the establishment of a forum for the development of a U.S. Hispanic theology. It was evident
that in order to gain an awareness, appreciation, and understanding of
the underlying tenets of a contextualized Hispanic theology, it would
be important that Hispanic and non-Hispanic men and women theologians be able to dialogue on the issues. Additionally, encouragement
was needed so that U.S. Hispanic theologians could expand their publications.[13]

The final key area of concern related to the development of continuing education programs in theology for second and third generation Hispanic professionals. Historically, pastoral attention has been
given primarily to immigrant Hispanics. Second and third generation
Hispanics have not been specifically identified by the Catholic Church.
Subsequently, professional Hispanics feel alienated from the Catholic
Church. There is a need to provide faith development for these Hispanics who have perceived the Church to be concentrating its resources on
the recent immigrants.[14]

APPROACHES TO HISPANIC MINISTRY IN SCHOOLS OF THEOLOGY

In the 1989–90 academic year, several U.S. Catholic schools of Theology
were visited by the director of Hispanic ministry at CTU[15] in order to
assess the approaches being used to prepare ministers for Hispanic
ministry. Seven sites were selected on the basis of either the enrollment
of Hispanic students or the presence of an established program in Hispanic Ministry.

The visits provided an excellent opportunity to initiate conversations with faculty and administrators of schools of theology regarding
their individual responses in preparing leadership for Hispanic ministry. With one possible exception, the visits made it evident that, despite
many good faith efforts, the world of Catholic theological education
still has a long way to go to meet the particular challenges of the Hispanic community in the United States. While a number of colleges and
universities have effective programs in Hispanic ministry or Hispanic
studies, traditional Catholic schools of Theology have not yet made ad-

12. Ibid., 4–5.
13. Ibid., 4–5.
14. Ibid., 5.
15. Ana Maria Pineda, R.S.M., was accompanied by a CTU faculty member for several of these visits.

equate provision to meet the massive challenge posed by the pastoral needs of the Hispanic community.[16]

From the interviews of 1990, it emerged that several factors contribute to the problems experienced by most of those responsible for programs in Roman Catholic schools of Theology: First there is an apparent lack of support on the part of the local ordinary. Second, some local ordinaries desire to limit the number of non-seminarian students, consequently limiting the presence of Hispanic laity in schools of theology. Third, the percentage of Hispanic faculty members is small. Consequently, there is a feeling of isolation and lack of support experienced by many Hispanic faculty members. Fourth, there is the need for faculty development to sensitize faculty and teach them the needed skills for doing theology in a cross-cultural context. Fifth, students are geographically isolated from the local Hispanic community, which hinders necessary exchange with the people. Sixth, Hispanic courses are generally limited to electives within the theological curriculum, thereby limiting the impact on the core curriculum. Seventh, there is a lack of flexibility in standard educational prerequisites for enrollment in courses and degree programs of schools of theology, thus limiting participation by Hispanics. Eighth, they lack the resources to identify basic courses that might form the foundation for Hispanic ministry training. Ninth, they employ traditional methods and pedagogy that are not appropriate in training for Hispanic ministry. Tenth, there is often weak institutional commitment on the part of the school as a whole for preparing leadership for Hispanic ministry, leaving the burden to the one Hispanic faculty member. Eleventh, many institutions lack funding for the development of new programs and faculty development. Twelfth, there is a general lack of vision in acknowledging the diversity of the U.S. Catholic Church membership. Finally, in order to offset the excessive reliance on Latin American theology, there is need to foster a U.S. Hispanic theology.[17]

Over the last several years, there have been some advances, particularly on the last issue.[18] This has been particularly promoted by the Academy of Catholic Hispanic Theologians of the United States[19]

16. Final Report for Grant No. 890257, 5–7.

17. Lilly Endowment Grant No. 890257, 8.

18. A dialogue between U.S. Hispanic theologians and Latin American theologians was held in Miami, Florida in October 1995 as part of an Ecumenical Association of Third World Theologians (EATWOT) endeavor. This dialogue clarified the unique nature and contribution of the developing U.S. Hispanic theology, notwithstanding a shared Latin American heritage.

19. For an account of the founding of ACHTUS see Allan Figueroa Deck, ed., *Frontiers of Hispanic Theology in the United States* (Maryknoll, N.Y.: Orbis Books, 1992), xxi–xxiv.

(ACHTUS) at their annual colloquium and by the increased publications of its membership.[20] Nevertheless, many of the challenges that the study revealed continue to challenge theological education today.

THE MULTICULTURAL NATURE OF THE U.S. HISPANIC COMMUNITY

During the Winter 1990 quarter, Catholic Theological Union hosted a lecture series open to the wider theological and Church community, addressing the diverse multicultural reality of the urban Hispanic communities in the United States. The lectures were prepared by expert pastoral and theological resource persons on the national level from different cultural groups within the Hispanic community.[21] Participants in the lecture series expressed appreciation in being exposed to the multicultural and urban reality of U.S. Hispanics. The series benefited both non-Hispanics and Hispanics. Unexpectedly, the participants who most appreciated the exposure to the diversity of Hispanic culture were the Hispanic students themselves, unaware themselves of the range of Hispanic cultures and traditions present in the United States.

In recent years, the multiplicity of Hispanic traditions have been addressed by a small but growing cadre of publications on the diverse nature of Hispanic reality. The Mexican-American experience, however, continues to command primary pastoral and theological attention.

FACULTY RESEARCH SEMINAR ON ISSUES OF METHODOLOGY AND PEDAGOGY IN PREPARING HISPANICS FOR MINISTRY

The success of the 1989–90 grant proposal made it possible for CTU to obtain an award from the Lilly Endowment the following year. The foci

20. Cf. Virgilio Elizondo, *Guadalupe: Mother of the New Creation* (Maryknoll, N.Y.: Orbis Books, 1997); Maria Pilar Aquino, *Our Cry for Life* (Maryknoll, N.Y.: Orbis Books, 1993); Allan Figueroa Deck, *The Second Wave* (Mahwah, N.J.: Paulist Press, 1989); Orlando Espín, *The Faith of the People* (Maryknoll, N.Y.: Orbis Books, 1997); Alejandro García-Rivera, *St. Martin de Porres: The "Little Stories" and the Semiotics of Culture* (Maryknoll, N.Y.: Orbis Books, 1995); Roberto S. Goizueta, *Caminemos Con Jesús: Toward a Hispanic/Latino Theology of Accompaniment* (Maryknoll, N.Y.: Orbis Books, 1995); Ada María Isasi-Díaz, *Mujerista Theology* (Maryknoll, N.Y.: Orbis Books, 1996); Ada María Isasi-Díaz and Fernando F. Segovia, *Hispanic/Latino Theology: Challenge and Promise* (Minneapolis: Augsburg/Fortress Press, 1996); Jeanette Rodriguez, *Our Lady of Guadalupe* (Austin, Texas: The University of Texas Press, 1994).

21. See Ana Maria Pineda and Robert Schreiter, eds., *Dialogue Rejoined: Theology and Ministry in the United States Hispanic Reality* (Collegeville, Minn.: The Liturgical Press, 1995), 9–72. This section provides the published presentations given at this lecture series.

of the grant were several,[22] but for the specific purpose of this presentation it is appropriate to concentrate on the faculty research seminar. The seminar dealt with issues of methodology and pedagogy in preparing Hispanics for ministry and established a sound foundation for later endeavors.

In the 1990–91 academic year, CTU faculty engaged in a yearlong seminar, preparing and presenting papers in consultation with Hispanics in ministry on various areas of theology. They investigated how the Hispanic reality reshapes the articulation of theological formation in preparing ministers for ministry in U.S. Hispanic communities. Using the collaborative model employed in the 1989–90 grant, faculty members who participated in the seminar engaged in a dialogue with theological resource persons of Hispanic background to discover how particular theological and pastoral disciplines could be presented in the context of Hispanic culture.[23] The interaction was intended to heighten the awareness on the part of the CTU faculty of the assumptions and values, both cultural and spiritual, operative in the Hispanic communities. Such an understanding is essential in the development of an appropriate theological education to meet the present challenges and realities.

The faculty seminar proved to be a profoundly transformative experience for the participants. It was evident in the final evaluation that faculty members had grown in their awareness and appreciation of Hispanic culture and values. They found themselves challenged to rethink the approaches used in theological education.[24] Inviting people beyond CTU to participate in the faculty seminar added a Hispanic diversity and quality that otherwise would have been absent. The format of the seminar made it possible for non-Hispanic faculty to interact on equal

22. Theological Education for Hispanic Ministry Grant No. 900691, 19 July 1990–30 June 1992, on file at CTU. The other projects of this grant were: (1) a national symposium on faculty development for those involved in the training of pastoral agents for Hispanic ministry; (2) a collaborative planning process with Chicago-area educational institutions to develop a program for training Hispanic ministers in a multicultural, urban setting; (3) a research project to study the professional experience of Hispanic deacons and their wives.
23. See *Dialogue Rejoined*, 75–177 for the published papers of the seminar.
24. Examples of comments from faculty seminar participants: "My paper allowed me to talk to a lot of people in Hispanic Ministry. From this came a new model for the paper I presented and for [doing] theology." "The fact that we had participants from the Hispanic community has widened our faculty seminar group and allowed us to listen to the *other*." "These seminars have intensified our opening up to local concerns. . . . The powerful exchange we have been engaged in has been not only for the benefit of the faculty but should also reach the students, the Church."

terms with Hispanics. In addition, the dynamics of the seminar established a new way of doing theology—a collaborative or *pastoral de
conjunto*[25] approach. The consciousnesses of the faculty changed as they
read the papers and found themselves looking for answers to new questions. What implications did this seminar present for the theological
disciplines? Did moral and cultural changes vary from one Hispanic
generation to the next? What might the generational bridges be, and
what could be asked about assimilation? Why was a community blessed
with charismatic leadership so under-represented within established
leadership? What were the consequences of the absence of Hispanic
leadership in these structures? How could the learning yielded from a
collaborative process be continued? The success of the seminar was
defined by one faculty member in one word—"dialogue." Listening in
a receptive and critical manner in order to meet the needs of the different groups that constituted "Church" made it possible for a respectful
dialogue to occur where both parties were equal partners in their search
for truth. The overwhelming success of this faculty seminar led to the
creation of other forums for dialogue.[26]

CONSULTATION ON U.S. HISPANIC THEOLOGY

A consultation with a select group of Hispanic theologians and other
theological resource persons[27] was held in 1993 in order to help identify
major issues in developing and articulating a U.S. Hispanic theology, as
well as to assist CTU in ascertaining what role a school of theology,
such as CTU, could play in this process. The purpose of the consultation was to address the following: (1) to make an inventory of previous
efforts in this area; (2) to articulate some of the key issues and factors;
(3) to identify specific research projects that should be undertaken by a
theological community such as CTU in the next decade; and (4) to identify what means and resources would be necessary to carry out such an
agenda.

25. In Spanish, the term *pastoral de conjunto* is understood as the harmoni-
ous coordination of all the elements of pastoral ministry with the actions of
pastoral ministers and structures in view of a common goal: the Kingdom of
God. See Ana Maria Pineda, "Pastoral de Conjunto," *New Theology Review* 3,
no. 4 (1990): 28–34.
26. Grant No. 900691, 1–3. A narrative report on the results of the faculty
research seminar on methodology and pedagogy.
27. Lilly Endowment Grant No. 920317 awarded to CTU at Chicago, July
1992–93, included five specific projects in total. The consultation process with
select Hispanic theologians to help identify major issues in developing and
articulating a U.S. Hispanic theology was one of the five.

This group generated a lengthy list of previous efforts undertaken to develop a distinctly U.S. Hispanic theology. Among those mentioned were the following: (1) the establishment of the Mexican-American Cultural Center in San Antonio, Texas; (2) the creation of the Office of the Hispanic Secretariat in Washington, D.C.; (3) the promotion of the Encuentro Nacional Hispano de Pastoral in 1972, 1977, and 1985 and subsequent documents such as the U.S. National Conference of Catholic Bishops' *Hispanic Pastoral Letter* and *National Hispanic Pastoral Plan*; (4) the establishment of organizations such as HERMANAS and PADRES; (5) the creation of U.S. Hispanic Regional Offices: South East Pastoral Institute (SEPI), North East Pastoral Center, and others; (6) the establishment of lay formation centers such as the former Mundelein Hispanic Institute in Chicago and the Tepeyac Institute in El Paso; (7) the development of newsletters (*HERMANAS, Catechetical Noticias, ACHTUS*), a newspaper (*El Visitante*), media (SEPI), and catechetical material for the formation of lay leaders and youth; (8) the promotion of Hispanic Ministry Programs in seminaries and schools of Theology; (9) the promotion of Hispanic theology by foundations such as the Lilly Endowment and the Pew Charitable Trust to facilitate research projects in this area; (10) the promotion of Hispanic theology by publishers (Orbis, Liturgical Press, Paulist Press, Crossroad, etc.); (11) the funding by foundations of theological resources such as the *U.S. Journal of Hispanic/Latino Theology* (Lilly) and the CUSHWA History of U.S. Hispanic Catholic Project (Lilly); (12) the creation of a Hispanic Publishing House—HARP; (13) the pioneering theological contributions of such Hispanic authors as Virgilio Elizondo and Justo González; 14) the creation of the Instituto de Liturgia Hispana; and (15) the creation of Hispanic theological associations to promote the development and articulation of U.S. Hispanic Theology—La Comunidad and the Academy of Catholic Hispanic Theologians of the United States (ACHTUS).[28]

Several facts surfaced in the process of drawing up an inventory of previous efforts. The task of grappling with what a U.S. Hispanic Theology might look like has been undertaken for approximately twenty-five years on a variety of academic levels. Virgilio Elizondo began the initial effort to articulate a Roman Catholic Hispanic Theology in the United States in 1968. Subsequently, in the 70s, a series of grassroots efforts, for example the promotion of the National Pastoral Hispanic Encounters and the organization of HERMANAS and PADRES, contributed to the articulation of community-based theological values. On a national level, the creation of Hispanic Regional Offices promoted

---

28. Final report on Grant No. 920317, 8–9, on file at CTU.

an articulation of pastoral theology in the leadership formation of His-
panics. The need for theologically sound training of lay leaders in the
Hispanic communities encouraged the birth of centers such as the
Mexican-American Cultural Center in San Antonio and later the
Mundelein Hispanic Institute in Chicago.

In the ensuing years, many diocesan-based centers sprung up
around the country such as the Tepeyac Institute in El Paso, Texas and
the Instituto de Liderazgo in San Jose, California. In the decade of the
80s and the 90s, theological education has been grappling with the establishment of Hispanic ministry programs as part of the general theological enterprise. The production of theological material for pastoral
formation of Hispanics became an insistent need in catechetical training of Hispanics (Grupos Juveniles, Movimiento Familiar Cristiano,
Cursillos, etc.). In the last several years publishers have recognized the
importance of publishing the developing U.S. Hispanic theology. In less
than a decade, two specifically Hispanic theological associations,
ACHTUS and La Comunidad, have begun to articulate the faith experience of the people within their historical, socioeconomic, political, and
cultural contexts. It is evident that the role of certain foundations such
as the Lilly Endowment and the Pew Charitable Trust have been vital
in enabling an ongoing research necessary for the articulation and development of a Hispanic theology.[29]

Hispanic theologians proved to be valuable in surfacing some of
the key issues and factors that need to be taken into account. The plurality of the Hispanic/Latino peoples in the United States presents a
challenge, for the distinct features of each national/generational group
points to the need to develop diverse U.S. Hispanic theologies. Other
issues surfaced that pointed to the necessity of examining the particular contours of the U.S. Hispanic community. Traditionally in Hispanic
cultures, for example, the woman has been the primary transmitter of
the faith, but it is also important to look into what specific contribution
males have made in this area. Another issue was the need to examine
how people pass on cultural/religious values and to examine the impact of that process on acculturation. Art, literature, and music are also
important areas in which one can explore the underlying methods that
need to be employed in the theological enterprise.

The reality of Hispanics is highly contextualized in its social, economic, and political dimensions. The issues that this contextualization
raises are important sources for theology. How does one identify a
method that will assist the theologian in tapping into the theological

29. Ibid., 9–10.

wisdom that resides in diverse Hispanic communities? The emerging new ecumenism among Hispanics also invites a careful study of what particular features are produced by an ecumenical reality that is based in a U.S. setting. Dialogue with other contextual theologies, such as African American, feminist, and other specific cultural groups in the third world also provides a rich source for ongoing investigation into the issues of cultural identity, particularity, and universality. Further issues are raised by the changing character of Church in the United States and the changing paradigms in theological education and in the classical disciplines of theology itself. The implications of these changes for the Hispanic communities in the United States and its experience of faith have yet to be explored.[30]

The consultation identified a number of creative research projects that should be undertaken by theological communities in the next decade. These include: (1) a symposium exploring the pluralistic character of Hispanic communities in the United States; (2) a compilation of Hispanic/Latino proverbs, creation stories, and poetry that express Hispanic experiences of faith; (3) a collection of existing material on popular religiosity; (4) the establishment of an annual cross-disciplinary symposium of scholars to discuss issues relating to methodology and specific application to the Hispanic communities; (5) a series of summer workshops that facilitate dialogue between U.S. Hispanic theologians and Latin American liberation theologians; (6) a series of gatherings promoting dialogue among racial/ethnic U.S. theologies, including Hispanic, African American, Asian American, and Native American; (7) the formulation of an interdenominational study to explore the place and role of Hispanics in various ecclesiastical bodies; (8) the establishment of a center for Hispanic religious arts as a repository for the materials that are part of diverse Hispanic communities.[31]

FACULTY DEVELOPMENT FOR HISPANIC MINISTRY

Consistently expressed by non-Hispanic faculty and administrators (presidents and deans of schools of Theology)[32] was the desire to be more conscious of the values and dynamics of Hispanic culture in order to respond effectively to the needs the Hispanic student body. While

30. Ibid., 10.
31. Ibid., 10–11.
32. This need was identified at a National Symposium on Faculty Development for those involved in Hispanic ministry, which was held at CTU, 14–16 February 1992. Approximately forty-five presidents, deans, faculty representatives, and Hispanic resource persons from fifteen Roman Catholic theology schools and seminaries participated in the consultation and planning.

Hispanic students and faculty often felt that schools of Theology had little awareness of or appreciation for the values of Hispanic cultures, non-Hispanic faculty felt at a loss to meet the challenge adequately and respectfully.

A pilot project designed to educate faculty members of Roman Catholic theological schools for effective ministry with and for Hispanics was held in July 1994 in Chicago at CTU. Ten participants representing eight theological institutions were in attendance.[33] The design of the pilot "faculty development seminar" integrated the basic components needed to assist faculty participants to learn how to become more effective educators of Hispanic theology. The seminar included an "immersion" experience within the Hispanic community in order to impact on the attitudes of faculty and to provide data for reflection. The seminar was interdisciplinary and at the same time provided opportunity for the faculty participants to discuss their own discipline with faculty peers. The seminar intentionally noted the diversity of Hispanic cultures and the implications of regional and urban contexts. Leadership was provided by Hispanic faculty, who were contracted to direct the theological and pedagogical reflections. Lastly, an integral part of the program was an evaluation process directed both to the faculty members' own development and institutional progress toward change.[34]

RESULTS OF THE FACULTY DEVELOPMENT SEMINAR

The seminar was a success. At its end it was clear that the seminar participants had a deeper awareness of and respect for Hispanic cultures and the dynamics of ministry in that context. Their contact with Hispanic faculty and immersion in the community's diverse realities had opened new perspectives in their respective theological disciplines. In other words, from experience they had learned how cross-cultural contexts enriched theology. Working with Hispanic colleagues gave them

33. Lilly Endowment Grant No. 930103, awarded to CTU on 15 March 1993 to support a pilot faculty development program for faculty members of Roman Catholic theology schools who were teaching students for ministry in an Hispanic context. Ten participants were in attendance representing the following eight theological institutions: Sacred Heart School of Theology, Hales Corners, Wis.; Washington Theological Union, Silver Spring, Md.; Wadhams Hall Seminary, Ogdensburg, N.Y.; The Episcopal Theological Seminary of the South-West, Austin, Texas; Jesuit School of Theology, Berkeley, Calif.; Mundelein Seminary, Mundelein, Ill.; St. Meinrad School of Theology, St. Meinrad, Ind.; and Oblate School of Theology, San Antonio, Texas.

34. A description of seminar process is in the final report of grant No. 930103, 2–3.

specific ideas on how they could adjust teaching methods to make a particular course more accessible to Hispanic students. In addition, the participants gained insight into how a core group of aware and sensitive faculty could effect changes in the environment of a specific school of theology to make it more hospitable to persons of other cultures, in this instance, Hispanic students.[35]

Concretely, the participants of the faculty development seminar cited many ways in which the seminar benefitted them in their role as a member of a theological faculty preparing Latino students. For many, the time to focus solely on Hispanic/Latino issues for society, Church, and theology was invaluable. The structure and pacing of the seminar gave them time to converse, plan, and share programs and perspectives with Hispanic and non-Hispanic colleagues. The dynamics of the seminar that promoted quality interaction with colleagues and members of the local Hispanic community gave them concrete experience and knowledge of Hispanic realities. At the same time they confirmed broader perspectives that they had developed from previous experiences, literature, and conversations. Faculty were able to visit libraries and bookstores with good sections on theology and history, including Hispanic-related titles. Hence, seminar participants were able to expand bibliographies, rewrite course syllabi, and obtain resources in Hispanic ministry/theology that they could share with their own theological institutions.[36]

The seminar participants were enriched personally, professionally, and ministerially. The seminar confirmed an earlier assessment that for many Anglo faculty it was not a question of lack of good will but, in some instances, a lack of awareness of the problem and, in others, a sense of inadequacy at how their approach to their discipline or teaching methods could relate to the values of Hispanic cultures.[37] Subsequently, the success of the 1994 faculty development seminar led to the award of a two-year grant for further seminars (1995–96, 1996–97).

PROGRAM OF SCHOLARSHIP DEVELOPMENT FOR HISPANIC STUDENTS

Over the years, the faculty and administration of CTU had taken many steps to find the appropriate ways of preparing ministers to work in Hispanic communities. This had led the institution to a series of consul-

35. Ibid., 3–4.
36. Ibid., 4–5.
37. Ibid., 5.

tations with not only CTU constituency but with presidents, deans, religious superiors, and archdiocesan Hispanic and non-Hispanic leadership. Such consultations provided CTU with insights into fundamental issues facing Hispanic ministry and theology. Subsequently, attention was given to faculty development both internally and beyond the confines of CTU's faculty. With the many efforts already undertaken, it became evident that the environment and programs of the school had changed and had become more responsive to the Hispanic realities and to Hispanic students. The number of Hispanic students at CTU had increased over the years but were primarily provided by the religious communities of men who were corporate members of CTU. If change were to be maintained within a theological institution such as CTU, it was essential that a critical mass of Hispanics be part of the student body. Additionally, there was an urgent need to increase the lay students (men and women) who were actively contributing to the life of the local Hispanic Church but who did not enjoy the same financial support as Hispanic religious at CTU.

The future of Hispanic ministry depended greatly on the development of local religious leaders who would serve the Hispanic communities, and who would receive a theological preparation sensitive to the cultural values of their communities. In order to accomplish this goal, CTU sought financial assistance from the Lilly Endowment to establish a development program that would make it possible to: (1) identify suitable Hispanic candidates who had already demonstrated leadership within their Hispanic community; (2) provide theological education and spiritual formation adapted to the needs of Hispanic students; and (3) work with the local Church to insure their placement following the completion of their academic and pastoral training.

In the 1994–95 academic year, CTU initiated the program of scholarship development for Hispanic students.[38] The Oscar Romero Scholars Program offered Hispanic lay women and men the opportunity to earn a professional graduate degree that prepared them to minister in their communities. It provided grants in aid to qualified Hispanics who wanted to study for ministry in order to serve their communities. In addition to a program of theology courses, the scholarship program included a formation component that made it possible for the Oscar Romero Scholars to participate in activities that enhanced their own spirituality and to integrate spiritual formation, academic understanding, and practical ministerial skills within the context of Hispanic cul-

38. Lilly Endowment Grant No. 940160 awarded to CTU in July 1994, on file at the Catholic Theological Union in Chicago.

tures.[39] In the academic years 1995–97, six Hispanics were admitted into the program. They were reflective of their Hispanic peers, who studied part-time but continued to work, support their families, and maintain their parish involvements. The Oscar Romero Scholars Program held much promise for the preparation of religious leaders to accompany their communities.

CTU's efforts were significant and contributed greatly in its attempt to define the role of a school of Theology in preparing Hispanic and non-Hispanic ministers to serve in U.S. Hispanic communities. It was representative of a growing number of studies that were underway throughout the United States that sought to answer the demands and need for quality theological education for Hispanics. Among these, attention should be given to a significant effort carried out in 1995 under the leadership of Dr. Justo González with the support of the Pew Charitable Trust.

THE PEW CHARITABLE TRUST SURVEY OF HISPANIC THEOLOGICAL EDUCATION

In 1986 the Pew Charitable Trust had awarded a grant to the Fund for Theological Education (FTE), which was carried out by Dr. Justo González. This grant allowed the FTE to establish the FTE Hispanic Scholars Program. In 1992, the Pew Charitable Trust evaluated the FTE Hispanic program and decided to discontinue its support. Dr. Justo González then asked the Pew Charitable Trust to support a study that would develop a comprehensive strategy for funding Hispanic graduate theological education. Dr. Edwin Hernandez, professor of sociology at Andrews University, was asked to create a survey tool that would make it possible to document basic demographic trends and to assess the educational experience and aspirations of Hispanics regarding theological education. An advisory committee was established to shape and direct the study.

By contacting various denominations, schools, and professional associations, they created a list of Hispanic religious leaders who either aspired or had already acquired a degree in theology.[40] They received a

---

39. Description used for the Oscar Romero Scholarship Program brochure of 1995–96.

40. It is important to note that no master mailing list of Hispanics was available for this survey instrument. Consequently, this approach was used in order to create a broad mailing list for the mailing of the surveys.

response from 24 percent of the people contacted providing an adequate and diverse sample.[41]

The survey identified a group of issues facing Hispanics who seek to study for a degree in theology. First, a major obstacle for Hispanic graduate students is the lack of adequate financial support.[42] Lay Catholic students are in particular need of financial aid and assistance in job placement. Second, many students found great difficulty in adapting to the rigors of graduate education and to the overall culture of the school. They expressed a need for more orientation, i.e., *financing, writing and research skills, curriculum choices, qualifying exams, etc.* in order to meet the challenges of theological education. They felt it important to have someone who could help them adjust to the new educational environment. Third, a number of issues concerned the school environment. Students experienced racism and discrimination. There was a lack of Hispanic resources such as library collections, Latino[43] faculty mentors or staff members, curriculum offerings, and community relationships. Students identified the absence of such resources as a major obstacle to their progress. In identifying schools with welcoming environments, students attributed it to the strong leadership on the part of the dean or president of the institution.

Fourth, the presence or absence of *multiple support mechanisms* contributed to the success or failure of graduate students. Students expressed the need for greater support for language exams, dissertations, critical thinking skills, research procedures, and improved writing skills. They found their primary support in families, friends, community ministry, parish, or other religious organizations. Fifth, the feeling of isolation ran deep among those interviewed. It would make a significant difference if communities of learning were created that connected established theologians and practitioners of ministry with fellows. Latina women in particular felt the need for more role models and mentors. Sixth, the mentoring and modeling provided by scholars or ministers

41. 1,923—302 items survey—total number sent 16, 240—total estimated deliverable questionnaires was 7, 919. All the data provided in this section of the presentation has been taken from the final report presented to the Hispanic Theological Initiative (HTI) Advisory Committee. Regrettably, the report was not paginated. This final report is filed at the office of the HTI, 1703 Clifton Road, Suite F–2, Atlanta, GA 30329–4044.

42. As previously cited, all data included in this section are found in the body of the final survey report prepared by Dr. Edwin Hernandez.

43. The report prepared by Dr. Edwin Hernandez favors the use of the term Latino. Consequently, I will be using that term in this section as it pertains to the findings of the national survey and to the subsequent report prepared and presented by Dr. Hernandez.

was identified as an important function in sustaining, guiding, and motivating students to complete their degrees successfully and to aspire to excellence. Hispanic scholars communicate a message to other interested Hispanics that they too can get involved in the field of theology. Some expressed having received effective mentoring from non-Latino professors; nevertheless, a desire remained to see more representation of Latinos on the faculty. Seventh, faculty emphasized the need for opportunities to pursue scholarship after the completion of graduate studies. Nontenured faculty felt torn between different tasks and expectations from the institution and religious community. This suggests that the scholarly activity among many Latinos can be best enhanced in a communal process of support and collegiality as opposed to individuals working by themselves.

Finally, in order to recruit religious leaders and scholars it is important to identify what motivates people to pursue religious vocations and scholarship. Implementing strategies to increase the pool of talented individuals is necessary in order to maintain the viability of religious communities. Bright Latino/a students are pursuing careers in high-paying areas (law, medicine, engineering). Second-career students pursuing theological studies have different needs. Many have received prior training in Bible institutes or diocesan lay training programs. Consequently, greater collaboration between such institutions and ATS-accredited educational centers would be helpful. Many expressed the need to create programs and strategies to increase the pipeline among young people.[44]

From the results of this survey, the Pew Charitable Trust awarded a substantial grant to support a three-year scholarship[45] and formation program for Hispanics in theological education, known as the Hispanic Theological Initiative (HTI). Its goal to was to offer scholarships to promising Latinas and Latinos who could be trained with the best tools available and would give a committed service to each other and to the Church and community.[46] The scholarship program was designed in such a way as to create and nurture a community of scholars. Not only would it increase the availability and quality of Latino candidates for faculty positions but it would also seek to incorporate a strategy for

---

44. From the final report prepared by Dr. Edwin Hernandez.

45. In the absence of the FTE, this grant was to establish another source of educational and financial support for Hispanics interested in theological education.

46. Cf. Program booklet of the Hispanic Theological Initiative, prepared by staff at the HTI, 1703 Clifton Road, Suite F-2, Atlanta, GA 30329-4044 (1997).

community-building designed to mentor, support, and network Latina and Latino scholars.[47]

In itself the building of a community of Latina/o scholars was seen as a critical and decisive component in the approach used by HTI in establishing such a scholarship program. The survey results indicated that the communal element was fundamental in designing an effective scholarship program. A number of approaches were employed. Regional meetings for HTI awardees were organized with the HTI Program Director to monitor progress, concerns, and successes. In these meetings, doctoral students would work closely with an appointed Latino/a senior mentor familiar with their discipline area. In addition, a summer workshop would be held each year for all awardees, mentors, and members of the selection committee. The workshop would provide the awardees with activities to address general and specific needs. Experts in the fields of writing, education, and mentoring would be present as consultants at these workshops to assist with issues that might directly affect the success of the awardees.[48]

In 1997 the first HTI awards were announced. The recipients included eight masters level students, six doctoral students, nine dissertation-year students, and two post-doctoral students. The awardees reflected the diverse Hispanic/Latino U.S. reality. The mix of gender, denominational representation, national heritage, and ordained/non-ordained status spoke in favor of a promising future for U.S. theological scholarship.

CONCLUSION

In the last several decades small but significant steps have been taken toward the assessment and creation of an appropriate theological education for U.S. Hispanics and for the adequate preparation of those wishing to minister to the diverse Hispanic/Latino communities in the United States. If the Church is to be true to its mission, the respectful inclusion of these new voices is not only important but necessary.

47. Ibid.
48. Cf. Brochure of the HTI.

The Latino Body

Church, Family, Ecumenism

6

The Hispanic Challenge to U.S. Catholicism

Colonialism, Migration, and Religious Adaptation

ANA MARÍA DÍAZ-STEVENS

(Materials contained here with a more detailed analysis also appears in Ana María Díaz-Stevens and Anthony M. Stevens-Arroyo, *Recognizing the Latino Resurgence in U.S. Religion: The Emmaus Paradigm*, Boulder, Co.: Westview Press, 1997.)

In Miguel Cervantes's famous book, Sancho Panza asks of Don Quixote: "If the pitcher is struck upon the stone, is it bad for the pitcher or the stone?" Sancho is using a question to tell his master that the stronger reality will always change the weaker, no matter one's intentions. For generations, it was thought that the U.S. Catholic Church was the stone and that immigrant culture was the pitcher. The argument ran that the American way of life, its culture, language, and politics were stronger than any vestige of identity with the "old country." The proverbial clash between the stone and the pitcher, then, can be seen in terms of encounters of cultures and the institutional Church, from the local parish communities up to the bishops of dioceses and national agencies. Here I will offer an outline of historical and sociological understanding of these processes. I will show that there is good news to offer: after years of cultural and military invasion, pious and socio-political occupation and colonization, emigration and dispersal out of our lands, the Hispanics in the United States have reached a point of maturity in our development that empowers us to identify the complex levels in which our presence has challenged, is challenging, and will challenge the institutional Church. The Church is reaching the moment when not only its doctrine but also its culture will be Catholic. Now, in 1997, as we stand on the threshold of a new millennium, it is possible to think that perhaps our

Latino cultures are the *piedra* (stone) and the bureaucratic institutions of the Church are the *cántaro* (pitcher).

I discuss how we have influenced the Church to remake itself on our behalf. Being a sociologist, I am relying on this discipline to inform my perspectives and my interpretation. One of the roles of sociology, as you know, is the gathering of data related to social variables in specific populations. Often this leads to the collection of numbers because numbers are useful for making judgments and developing adequate policies. Basically we need to know our overall numbers proportionate to the total population, as well as distribution patterns (i.e., in regions, in cities). These numbers and other collected data help us to discover all sorts of relevant patterns. In other words, when we find two or more conditions present a significant number of times, we may conclude that these are related. If we take the work of pastoral leaders to be in the realm of making decision or policy to help the Church, this knowledge can help us not only understand each condition better but also anticipate needs and find strategies for practical solutions. How valuable, for example, is the knowledge of growth within specific segments of the population (children, young adults, adults, middle age, elderly) for an informed, adequate planning of urban ministry? Would that information not help us to allocate better time, energy, and resources?

Perhaps I am not saying anything that you do not already know at least in a general way. The gathering of this information is in itself a wonderful thing. But we must go further. We must ask what were the goals and whether they were accomplished. Were these resources, for example, intended to *increase* the number of Catholics? Were they intended to *educate* people in the faith? Were they intended to centralize power for the bishop? Having looked at and analyzed the pertinent historical and sociological facts, we have at the very least a partial picture, somewhat like a silhouette, that affords us a sense of periods or stages in ministry.

In a recent book co-authored with Anthony Stevens-Arroyo, we speak of the Age of Pious Colonialism. In our book, we explain that in the nineteenth century the institutions of the Church subordinated Hispanic expressions of Catholicism as being incompatible with an Americanizing "way of life." We call it "pious" because in the conquered Latino homelands, the people needed the Church in order to exercise their traditional Catholic piety. In the words of Otto Maduro,[1] the Latinos needed the Church in order for their "religious production" to be legitimated

---

1. Otto Maduro, *Religion and Social Conflicts* (Maryknoll, N.Y.: Orbis Books, 1982).

as Catholic by the Church.[2] The bishops and European American priests had the same belief in doctrine and the sacraments that our ancestors had. What was different was the culture and the traditions through which these Catholic beliefs were expressed. The U.S. Catholic leaders did little to encourage the maintenance of our Spanish language or our local traditions. Instead, they often treated the religious expressions proper to our culture as if they were "superstition" or inferior forms of Catholicism. In some cases, our traditions were branded as "paganism" or even as "devil worship." Perhaps the main reason behind these negative policies towards our Hispanic Catholicism was the fear that unless we were "Americanized" our Catholic faith would lead us to resist the invasions, the way that Irish Catholics resisted English Protestants or that Polish Catholics resisted Prussian Lutherans. But whatever the reasons, this policy of subordinating our Catholicism played into the hands of colonialism.

We also call it pious because we recognize that most of the bishops and priests did these things because they really believed it was the correct course of action for the Church. But as a result, when the U.S. bishops imposed a variant form of North American Catholicism over the existent local Catholicism, substituting English for Spanish, they helped the U.S. government assimilate the territory. According to historians such as Rodolfo Acuña[3] and Samuel Silva Gotay,[4] North American Catholicism was meant to Americanize just like other institutions brought by the United States such as civil service, public education, health services, hospitals, and political orginizations. Often the work of the gospel was, unfortunately, subordinated to the goals of assimilation.

The theory of Pious Colonialism helps explain why for so many years, Hispano Catholicism in the United States was one of defensiveness and a collective inferiority complex. For several reasons, one of which was a low percentage of native clergy, Hispano chapels were usually administered by clergy imported from Europe or some priests who had learned Spanish. Hispano aspirants for the seminary or convent were treated in a paternalistic way, and customs of home altars,

2. Anthony M. Stevens-Arroyo, "Latino Catholicism and the Eye of the Beholder: Notes Towards a New Sociological Paradigm," *Latino Studies Journal* 6, no. 2 (1995): 29.

3. Rodolfo Acuña, *Occupied America* (San Francisco: Canfield Press, 1972), 147–9.

4. Samuel Silva Gotay, "The Ideological Dimensions of Popular Religiosity and Cultural Identity in Puerto Rico," in *An Enduring Flame: Studies of Latino Popular Religiosity,* ed. Anthony M. Stevens-Arroyo and Ana María Díaz-Stevens, PARAL Series, vol. 1 (New York: Bildner Center Books, 1994), 133–70.

sung rosaries, and the devotions that gave great meaning to our lives were characterized as "superstitions."

But even within this pious colonialism we discover two distinct forms of governance, and I use a play on words to signify them: *"dicta-dura"* and *"dicta-blanda."* The first one is known for its hard line approach and seeks immediate assimilation with no services or accommodation to Spanish. The second one, a softer approach, is more benevolent and less threatening. It calls for gradual assimilation with some services in order to ease transition to English only and to a European American mindset. It gives the people a measure of autonomy and sometimes a greater measure of independence. An example of autonomy would be the integrated parish in its "basement Church" configuration, while the national parishes would correspond to a more independent situation. With the Hispanic community, it should be noted that the national parishes were the exception, while the "basement Church" approach was the norm, especially in highly urbanized areas.

A second period, roughly from 1967 to 1981, I call "The Period of the Latino Religious Resurgence." Notice, I speak of resurgence because unlike other authors I am very much aware of the fact that (1) Christianity was first brought to the New World from Spain to the Islands of the Caribbean—Puerto Rico being the first apostolic see, dating from 25 December 1513, when the first bishop to the New World, Alonso Manso, arrived at its newly constituted diocese; (2) the Franciscans as well as other religious congregations established themselves in missions in the Southwest approximately a hundred years before the arrival of the Pilgrims at Plymouth Rock; and (3) the movement back and forth between the two continents has kept traditions south of the border very much alive in the north as well. In other words, Hispanic Catholics have always lived in what we today call the United States. Thus, our presence has always been among you as we have struggled to keep our faith and our culture even in the midst of discrimination, neglect, and social invisibility.

The decade of the 1960s and the beginning of the 1970s showed great promise for Hispanics in the Church. It is precisely during the 1960s that this second period of Latino religious resurgence began to unfold, expanding for the next three decades until the early 1980s. The Latino religious resurgence was spurred by other important world events: the Cuban exodus caused by the Cuban Revolution, U.S. intervention in the Dominican Republic, continuing conflict in Central America, the Second Vatican Council (1962–65) with its Catholic Renewal worldwide, the 1964 Immigration Reform Act, the 1965 War on Poverty and Civil Rights Act, the 1967 Bilingual Education Act and the

Farm Workers' strike and boycott, the War in Vietnam, the end of the Luis Muñoz Marín era in Puerto Rico, and the beginning of a strong effort towards politically elected Hispanic representation within the United States. Each one of these movements had its impact upon the resurgence. The War on Poverty, for example, brought to the fore the need for affirmative action via native leaders and specifically Latino community organizations, while the Civil Rights Act, when it lifted the language requirement, made it possible for a greater number of Hispanics who were U.S. citizens to vote in all elections. The Cuban Revolution, U.S. intervention in the Dominican Republic and Central America, and the Immigration Reform Act brought increased numbers of Caribbean and Central American people to U.S. urban regions, at the same time that a dispersal of continental Hispanics was beginning to take place throughout the United States. Furthermore, this new im/migration of *caribeños, centroamericanos,* and *hispanos* brought a number of well-trained professionals, some of whom depended on an increasing number of Spanish-speaking constituents or clientele to maintain their jobs and/or their newly attained political clout.

The Farm Workers' movement and the 1967 grape boycott developed the potential for national solidarity, and it is this idea of national solidarity that is the most important contribution of the Latino religious resurgence. National solidarity means that Hispanics in one place see the connections between their own struggles and those of Hispanics in other regions. In the case of the migrant workers' strike in California, Mexican Americans and Chicanos saw *La Causa* as their own, no matter the state in which they resided. But it should also be said that in far away Puerto Rico, we *boricuas* supported the Chávez strike. Bishop Antulio Parrilla Bonilla, S.J., was in California at the time of the infamous incident at St. Basil's Cathedral where Chicano Catholics were removed from the premises during Christmas Midnight Mass. It was Bishop Parrilla Bonilla who celebrated mass for the Chicanos in a parking lot, just outside of the cathedral.

A second person important in the cause of Puerto Rican solidarity with the Farm Workers' Movement was a Puerto Rican Dominican friar, the late Father William Loperena Soto. He was a member of META (Ministerio para el Trabajador Agrícola) and one of the organizers of ATA (Asociación de Trabajadores Agrícolas), two northeastern-based organizations working on behalf of the pastoral and labor needs of Puerto Rican farm workers. He was a theologian as well as a musicologist who had the distinction of composing *La Misa Jíbara,* the first vernacular mass in the language and music of the people after the Second Vatican Council—a mass that is sung today in Catholic liturgies in Puerto

Rico, the United States, and other Latin American countries. One of Father Loperena's tasks was to make contact and find means of collaboration between the Mexican-American movement (mostly in the Southwest) and the northeastern Puerto Rican organizations. These were two of the many Puerto Ricans in solidarity with the United Farm Workers during the strike and the boycott. Of course, we have to expect that when Puerto Ricans or Cubans or Dominicans, Guatemalans, Educadorians or Colombians need support from Mexican-American Catholics, we will receive it. The message of solidarity as a Hispanic Catholic is: "Amor con amor se paga" (We pay love back with love).

This is not a new message. Even before the Second Vatican Council, pious parish organizations, the Cursillo Movement, the Christian Family Movement, and catechists used the language of the people, autochthonous music, and the liturgy in the Spanish language. It was the decree of the Council that overnight made the Catholic Church in the United States into a bilingual Church. But that decree would not have had its revolutionary impact if our people did not already appreciate the meaning of solidarity and the concept of Hispanic unity.

In the 1970s the Hispanic National Encounters created a social movement within the Catholic Church that ultimately had an impact even within Protestantism. This social movement defined the concrete steps that had to be taken by the institutional Church in order to meet the needs of Latinos. The steps included the consecration of Latino bishops and priests and the naming of Latino pastors. Hispanic pastoral councils and commissions, and a commitment of Church resources to meet Hispanic needs (e.g., meeting places, schools, education of lay leaders, independent or at least autonomous pastoral educational centers in each region/diocese) were also part of this process. Cumulatively, the resurgence produced the goal of a multi-cultural Catholicism in which the role of the European American Catholic Church was to emphasize being "Catholic" over being "American." In other words, this new response brought an end to Pious Colonialism, at least in areas of large Hispanic concentrations.

The third period extends from 1982 to the present. As of this date, we are still in the process of counting the increase and proportionate numbers that the Latino Church generated during the period of the resurgence. When we tally the end results of the efforts of these years, the bottom line is that we have had some very definite improvements. If not, how else could any one say that Pious Colonialism has ended? Unfortunately, however, the change has not been universal. In other words, improvement is not to be found everywhere. Generally, we could say that some degree of improvement can be found in almost all big cities with a significant Hispanic population, but Hispanics in small cities and the suburbs are continuing to experience vestiges of Pious Colonialism.

An added issue, as our numbers increase in definite areas, is the dismantling of our separate organizations in favor of a single agency that will serve the total Church community. When we as Hispanics, or as a sub-Hispanic group, become the numerical majority, how do we use power and resources without falling into the same trap of mistreating the new minorities as we were once mistreated? How do we, for example, propose to train all deacons in a diocese with a majority of Latino candidates, or even a majority of Mexican-American or Puerto Rican candidates?

To say that the Hispanics are a challenge to the Church is an understatement. The distinguished Catholic historian Jay P. Dolan of Notre Dame University has suggested that Hispanics are changing the Catholic Church in the twentieth century as much as did the Irish in the nineteenth century. But while the Irish came at a time when the United States was still expanding, the Hispanics are coming when the only frontiers to conquer are out there in space. The numbers of Hispanics are increasing so rapidly that they can outpace the resources of the total Church. While the Church comes to grips with the special gifts and needs that Hispanics bring, Hispanics have to understand that if present trends continue there will be a time when the number of poor Hispanics in the Church will far outnumber the middle-class European Americans. By reason of percentages alone, we can no longer expect the European American Catholic middle class to bear the burden of financing programs just for us, regardless of our level of poverty and the level of well-being of this middle class. Thus, the challenge is not to the European American Church alone but to *La Iglesia Hispana* as well.

Demographers and other social scientists have made awesome projections for the next five decades. Besides the natural growth of our existing Hispanic population in the United States, there will continue to be an influx of im/migrants from south of the border and the Caribbean islands. This population will continue to be relatively young. As of today the median age of Hispanics is far below that of the European American population. Meanwhile the European American population will continue its trend to reproduce at a lower rate than the Hispanics, and unless a shift of significant proportion occurs, immigration from Europe will not increase this population to compete with Hispanic growth. This will also mean that the European American population will grow older just as the Hispanic population grows younger.

Though it is quite diverse, most studies divide the Latino population into four major ethnicities or nationalities: Mexican, Puerto Rican,
Cuban, and Other. The relative share each of these groups has of the
total Latino population is as follows: Mexican Americans are the largest group (64 percent), followed by Central/South American (13 percent), Puerto Ricans (11 percent), and Cubans (5 percent). A catch-all
category of "Other Latino," including Dominicans and persons who
answered with "Hispanic" as their ethnicity and no specific country,
accounts for the remaining (7 percent). It should be noted, however,
that due to Puerto Rico's colonial status, most statistics of Latino population in the United States (including figures given here) omit the 3.8
million Puerto Ricans who live on the island.

Despite some educational and economic achievements, we must
take into serious consideration the fact that in September of 1996, the
U.S. Census Bureau reported that in 1995 Latinos had dropped below
African Americans in most social indicators of poverty.[5] This is an omi-
nous development because it occurs at a time when Latino immigration
has become a whipping post in U.S. politics with results such as cutting
educational, health, and other benefits and programs to newcomers and
oldtimers as well.

New births and immigration are the two factors responsible for
Latino population growth. Of the two, Latino birth rates (which are
higher than in the general U.S. population) are the principal reason for
yearly increases in the number of Latinos. When Puerto Ricans on the
island are included, nearly 70 percent of Latinos in 1990 were born as
U.S. citizens: thus, the majority of us are not "immigrants."[6] But the
native, or Latino U.S.-born population, while more than twice as large
as the Latin American immigrant or foreign-born population, is not
evenly distributed. Some areas, such as New York City, have higher
concentrations of the foreign-born than native-born. Elsewhere, the conditions may be reversed. Sunseri reports that nearly 95 percent of New
Mexican respondents to his questionnaire came from families established
in New Mexico between 1840 and 1865.[7]

    5. Eleanor Baugher and Leatha Lamison-White, *Poverty in the United States:
1995*, Current Population Reports, series P 60–194 (Washington, D.C.: U.S. Department of Commerce, Bureau of the Census, 1996).
    6. Maria E. Enchautegui, *Policy Implications of Latino Poverty* (Washington,
D.C.: The Urban Institute, 1995), 6; Joan Moore, "The Social Fabric of the Hispanic Community since 1965," in *Hispanic Catholic Culture in the U.S.: Issues
and Concerns*, ed. Jay P. Dolan and Allan Figueroa Deck (Notre Dame: University of Notre Dame Press, 1994), 9; et passim.
    7. Alvin R. Sunseri, *Seeds of Discord: New Mexico in the Aftermath of the
American Conquest, 1846–1861* (Chicago: Nelson Hall, 1979), 44–46.

New births and immigration combined have indeed produced a rapid expansion of Latino presence in the United States.[8] In assessing these numbers, however, one ought to remember that percentage increases are most dramatic when the base numbers are small. When a census track registers only 2,000 individuals, an increase of 2,000 more represents a 100 percent growth rate. But if there are 200,000 individuals, the same increase of 2,000 constitutes only a 1 percent growth rate. Furthermore, in making demographic projections one has to be aware of the fact that high rates of growth are hardly ever sustainable over a long period. Yet, in the Latino case of the past twenty years, the rates have remained remarkably high. Growth in Latino population can be estimated by calculating the difference between projected immigration entries over departures and natural births over deaths. From 1970–1980, there was a 60 percent increase in the number of Latinos in the United States; the decade 1980–1990 saw a 47 percent increase.

The most recent report of the U.S. Bureau of the Census states that by 2010, Latinos will be more numerous in the United States than African Americans. By 2020 there are expected to be 47 million Latinos or nearly 15 percent of the total U.S. population. By 2050, 95 million Latinos will also make us one out of every four persons in the country.[9] Moreover, as the Latino population grows larger, its relatively high birth rates and lower median age indicate that future growth will come mostly from natural demographic increase, not from immigration. In other words, even if tomorrow the borders with Latin American were closed, Latino population growth would still outstrip European American and African American rates of increase, although by not as much. The difference in the percentages under the age of 18 is striking: only 23.3 percent of European Americans (whites) as compared to 35 percent of Latinos. Using 1990 Census data, one can review other significant contrasts between the Latino and non-Latino populations. Latino families are larger; they are younger, have more children, and are growing at a dramatically faster rate (53 percent) than the non-Latino population (7 percent). Among this population, most people have only a high school education. Thus levels of college education are lower (7.5 percent) than the non-Latino rate (19.3 percent).

8. See Moore, "Social Fabric."
9. U.S. Bureau of the Census, *Population Projections of the U.S. by Age, Sex, Race and Hispanic Origin, 1995 to 2050,* Series P 25–1130 (Washington, D.C.: U.S. Department of Commerce, Bureau of the Census, 1996); Katherine Q. Seelye, "The New U.S.: Grayer and More Hispanic," *New York Times,* 27 March 1997. See also Justo González, "The Theological Education of Hispanics" (report to the Fund for Theological Education, New York, 1988).

Poverty is growing rapidly among Latinos. Between 1979 and 1990, poverty within Latino families grew by 6 percentage points, while the African American and European American increase was less than 1 percent each. More recently, between 1993 and 1995 there was a 3.6 percent *increase* in income for African American households and the 5.1 percent *drop* in income for Latinos. In 1996, the Census Bureau reported that 28.5 percent of African American households were poor, a smaller figure than for Latinos, who with 29.2 percent are now the poorer of the two groups. The number of Latino/a families living in poverty grew during the period 1974–1995 by 222.24 percent; for all African Americans the growth rate for families in poverty was 43.81 percent, smaller even than the growth rate (49.02 percent) among all European American families in poverty.

Generally, high rates of poverty are attributable to the increase in female-headed households. While most U.S. families today have more than one wage earner, single parents depend on one salary and/or government assistance to support the family. But it is alarming that even among families with both parents living under the same roof, the poverty growth rate increased 188.85 percent between 1974 and 1995, while that of European American families with two parents increased only by 30.15 percent.[10]

The group of married people worst off in the United States in 1992 were the Mexican Americans, having overtaken the endemic levels of Puerto Rican families. Mexican family poverty has dramatically increased between 1989 and 1992, as has that of "Other Latinos," which includes many recent immigrants from Central America. Cubans in the United States remain the best off of all Latino groups, although they also experienced an increase in poverty from 1980 to 1993, probably because of the Mariel immigration. Despite these high levels of poverty and high levels of unemployment, Latinos have a proportionally lower participation in welfare and food-stamp programs than either European American or African Americans.[11]

Not only do many Latinos fail to collect benefits they could legally have, they also work in worse jobs than any other major group. While in 1979 in the category of "full-time with low annual earnings," Latinos (19.1) and African Americans (17.9) were almost equal, by 1989 Latinos (27.3) were worse off than African Americans (20.7). Even in professional positions, the average income for Latinos is less than for Euro-

10. Strikingly, African American families with both parents present had a drop in total numbers for those in poverty between 1974 and 1995, making for a negative rate of 27.82 percent. Apparently, the civil rights struggles have benefited the African American families.
11. Enchautegui, *Policy Implications*, 13.

pean Americans or African Americans with the same jobs. Whether the Latino or Latina is a manager or engineer, secretary or bus driver, his or her pay is generally less than for people who call themselves "white" or "black."[12] In 1995, while the weekly salary for European Americans working full time stood at $494—more than a hundred dollars more than the weekly salary for African Americans who held full time jobs ($383)—Latinos trailed African Americans in excess of $50 less pay per week. The Latino/a wage-earner receives less pay, has more children to feed, is more likely to expect more children than any other group. Furthermore, he or she is less likely to have a spouse who brings home an additional pay check, though two other members of the household may be employed—even if in a menial job—in order to make ends meet. As Joan Moore has pointed out,[13] poverty in the Latino barrio is long-standing.

Education has been a traditional path out of poverty, and the 1996 Census Bureau report found that the proportion of young Latinos who had completed high school stood at 57 percent, or a bit more than half of all our young people. In contrast, African Americans finishing high school had risen to 87 percent, so that for the first time in the nation's history they have attained relative parity with white youths (91 percent). So while European Americans and African Americans have lowered the percentage of the total population without a high school education, among Latinos today one out of every three persons still lacks a high school diploma (34.7 percent). This is slightly better than 1974 (37.1 percent) but worse than 1984 when the lowest rates were recorded at 34.2 percent.

To put these statistics in perspective, it is important to know what is taking place within specific Hispanic groups. For example, graduation rates rise from the first to the second generation of Mexican Americans but stagnate in the third generation. This trend undermines the argument that Latino poverty can be attributed to the immigrant status and, therefore, will be eliminated as Latinos assimilate in subsequent generations. None of these trends augurs well for the future. While two-thirds of U.S. families in poverty escape that classification within two years,[14] some 80 percent of Latino families stay in poverty over the same period of time. In fact, the group of Latinos who are not immigrants—the Puerto Ricans—are the worst off of all ethnic/racial communities in the United States. If citizenship, political prowess, knowl-

12. Goldberg, "Hispanic Households Struggle as Poorest of the Poor in the U.S.," *New York Times,* 30 January 1997.

13. See Moore, "Social Fabric"; Joan Moore and Raquel Pinderhughes, *In the Barrios: Latinos and the Underclass Debate* (New York: Russell Sage, 1993).

14. Enchautegui, *Policy Implications,* 12.

edge of U.S. law, familiarity with social programs and instruction in the English language were conditions for socio-economic achievement, Puerto Ricans would be the Latin American or Latino group most likely to succeed. Yet, instead of ranking first, Puerto Ricans in the United States rank last—behind even the new immigrants from Latin America. Linda Chavez is a conservative politician who—unlike most of us—wants Americanization and an end to any public programs that preserve or enhance our language and culture.[15] She calls Puerto Ricans an "exception" to the rule that the more Americanized you are, the more likely you are to be acceptable to U.S. society. In my sociological interpretation, I would underscore that Puerto Rico is the place where the colonial contradictions of U.S. rule are most evident. Our country is run from Washington as a colony. Yes, the people of the island elect a representative to sit in Congress, but he cannot vote and cannot even speak—unless he is given permission. We would say that the reason that Puerto Ricans do so poorly in economic terms is because our history has taught us the brutal facts of colonialism and we are the most unlikely to believe that Americanization offers benefits to our culture.[16]

Segregation of Latinos is increasing, not lessening, within U.S. society. A Latino neighborhood, or *barrio*, is defined by the census as a tract with 50 percent or more Latino population. In 1990, 36 percent of all Latinos and 46 percent of all poor Latinos lived in such *barrios*. Moreover, the *barrios* themselves are poor. The census has a precise definition of a poor neighborhood: a poor neighborhood is one where 40 percent or more of the families have incomes below the poverty line. In 1980, 15 percent of all Latino neighborhoods were poor; in 1990, that

15. Linda Chavez, *Out of the Barrio: Towards a New Politics of Hispanic Assimilation* (New York: Basic Books, 1991).
16. In our recent book, *Recognizing the Latino Resurgence,* we question those who blame lack of knowledge of English for Latino poverty. The third-generation Latinos who know English drop out of school more often than the first-generation immigrants from Latin America. Puerto Ricans (who even in their native island study English from the second grade on) are the poorest of Latino groups. Despite such facts, many commentators such as Wayne Cornelius, the director of the Center for U.S.-Mexican Studies at the University of California at San Diego, insist that "limited English proficiency is the single most important obstacle to upward mobility. . . ." See Gary Goldberg, "Hispanic Households." Such a statement may seem true from the narrow perspective of Immigration Studies, in which Dr. Cornelius is a recognized expert, but from a wider, comparative look at Latinos nationwide, the Puerto Rican and Chicano experience indicates that English proficiency is not a cure-all for poverty. There are many other structural factors involved that impact more decisively upon these communities.

percentage had risen to 21 percent.[17] The *barrios* are also increasingly multi-Hispanic, i.e., where Latinos are a majority, but no one national Latino group has more than 50 percent of the population. In 1980, 29 percent of Latino neighborhoods were multi-Hispanic; in 1990, it was 35 percent, more than a third of all Latino *barrios*.

In sum, while demographic projections suggest growing numbers of Latinos in the United States, the indicators of poverty point in the direction of a widening gap between Latinos and the general population. Overall, U.S. median incomes are lower in current dollars today than in 1989 for all groups. The median income of $22,860 for all Latinos is slightly more than that of all African Americans ($22,393), about $10 more per week. But the future prospects for Latinos are worse. Examining the increase in the median family income in the 1990s, we see that the fastest growth was among African Americans, who showed an increase of almost 10 percent in three years, from 1992 until 1995, rising to $22,393 in constant 1995 dollars. While still considerably below the European American median income of $35,766, the African American growth rate of 10 percent was proportionately greater than that of European Americans (2.2 percent). But while the other groups prospered, Latino families lost ground. From 1992 to 1995, the median income for Latinos *dropped* 6.9 percent.[18] In other words, while other groups are moving ahead, either slowly (European Americans) or rapidly (African Americans) during the 1990s, Latinos are going in the opposite direction.

Latinos will replace African Americans as the largest "minority" in the United States by 2010. By 2020, more Latinos will be added each year to the general population than African Americans, Asian Americans, Native American Indians, or all of them combined. The most rapidly growing segment of the European American population are those over the age of 85, and by 2050, there will be nearly 18 million of them. The aging of the European American (not Latino, Asian, Native, or African American) population also points to the year 2034, when more of them will die each year than will be born or enter the United States as immigrants. Not only will the percentage of European Americans in the total U.S. population drop from the 1995 level of 73.1 percent to a bare majority of 52.8 percent, but their total numbers will be less in 2050 than in 2035. When the European American population is further divided by class, religious, and ethnic lines so as to register Catholics, Protestants, Jews, Anglo, Irish, Eastern and Southern Europeans, it will

17. Moore, "Social Fabric."
18. Goldberg, "Hispanic Households."

not be easy to identify who is "majority" and who is "minority" in the United States of the next century.

As far as the Hispanics are concerned, however, their general picture in terms of social, economic, and educational levels is indeed a bleak one. High poverty levels, low educational attainment, high unemployment rates, rapid natural increase, and a continuous movement of immigrants into our communities are elements that contribute to this state of affairs. When all seems to be lost, when there is very little confidence left in the fiscal or government agencies, Latinos—like others before them—have few resources other than their families and faith for support and guidance. Experiencing the poor performance of public schools and its history of low educational achievements for Hispanics, more and more Hispanic families are turning (at very great sacrifice) to Catholic schools for the education of their children. Recent research by Segundo Pantoja, a scholar at the Graduate School of the City University of New York (CUNY), indicates that the need for a good education in the Hispanic community drives even the poorest of Latinos as well as Pentecostals to seek the services of the Catholic schools.

Family values, while under assault by socio-economic factors, are a major factor in Latino identity. Ironically, while the Mexican American family is the poorest in the United States, it is also the ethnic group most likely in the entire nation to preserve the traditional family unit of father, mother, and children living under the same roof. Does the Latino family stick together because of poverty or in spite of it? Would prosperity and upward mobility lead to assimilation and a loss of Latino identity? These are important questions for which as yet there are no simple answers.

Religion is an increasingly important source of hope, especially because so many other reservoirs have gone dry. Religion is a particularly powerful wellspring of Latino identity, cultural cohesiveness and social organization. Latino religion will play a key role in the unfolding of the twenty-first century for both Latinos and for the larger society, in part because religion offers both meaning and moral order to society.[19] Our positive understanding of religion should not be interpreted as a Pollyanna view that all ills can be swept away by a return to the Church. We would not argue that religion can substitute for government programs of assistance to the poor, or for educational reform, or the building of more low-cost housing. We view religion more as a resource for communities and individuals; it can often strengthen and enrich social programs.

19. Robert Wuthnow, *Meaning and Moral Order* (Berkeley and Los Angeles: University of California Press, 1987).

If the Catholic Church does not respond to these challenges, there is a fear that Latinos will leave the Church and become Protestants and Pentecostals. In fact, the media paints a picture in which the Catholic Church has completely failed Hispanics and that within a few years, Pentecostals will replace Catholics as the most numerous Latino group. Statistics on religious membership are somewhat difficult to verify because the census of the United States does not ask any religious identification question. Church estimates about Latino members, however, frequently use census and other statistics for a total number and then apply the percentage of estimated adherents to their denomination in order to approximate the number of believers.[20]

In seeking to improve on these estimates, we looked at the results from the National Survey of Religious Identification (NSRI) of 1991 as found in the prize-winning book, *One Nation Under God*, by Barry A. Kosmin and Seymour P. Lachman.[21] As other recent surveys, the NSRI reported that two out of three Latinos identify themselves as Catholics (65.8 percent) and roughly one out of four as Protestant (24.6 percent, or 25.4 percent including Mormons as Protestants). The findings of Kosmin and Lachman can be compared with a similar identification item in the Latino National Political Survey (LNPS) of 1989–1990.[22] Protestantism is highest among Puerto Ricans and lowest among Mexican Americans—except those in Texas. The sample of the NSRI was large enough to provide numbers for the distribution among Protestants of the different denominations. Baptists are the largest of these denominations (7.4 percent) followed by Christian, i.e., Evangelical Churches (5.2 percent). Other denominations had very few respondents, and many used generic, rather then denominationally specific terms. Moreover, for purposes of accuracy, the NSRI employed weighting in translating the raw numbers to percentages. With all of these limitations, however, the results are illuminating. Overall, this survey found only 2 percent of Latinos identified as Pentecostals. But since the categories supplied in this survey depended on classifications that came from the respondents, it may be asked if the persons who answered that they belonged to the Christian Church, Assembly of God, or Jehovah's Witnesses might be Evangelicals or Pentecostals in other classificatory systems. Likewise,

20. Romea F. Saldigloria, "Religious Problems of the Hispanos in the City of New York," in *Prophets Denied Honor,* ed. Antonio M. Stevens-Arroyo (Maryknoll, N.Y.: Orbis Books, 1980), 166–9.

21. Barry A. Kosmin and Seymour P. Lachman, *One Nation Under God: Religion in Contemporary American Society* (New York: Harmony Books, 1993).

22. See Barry A. Kosmin, *The National Survey of Religious Identification, 1989– 1990* (New York: City University of New York, 1991).

the generic term "Protestant" was used by 2.5 percent of the respondents, with no more specific denominational tag. Without more research, it will be impossible to resolve such ambiguities that arise from most general surveys. But it can be stated rather clearly that, among Latinos, Catholics are two-and-a-half times more numerous than all Protestants and that Latinos identify themselves as "Catholics" twenty times more frequently than as "Pentecostals."[23]

However, we should not be confused by the number game. We have also to understand what the proliferation of Pentecostal Churches in our midst actually means. We may, for example, have ten or twenty new Pentecostal Churches being established within a specific urban sector. As the statistics from Kosmin and Lachman clearly indicate, this does not mean that Pentecostalism has grown ten or twenty times over the one Catholic community in a neighborhood whose building perhaps dates back to the beginning of the century. The Pentecostal Churches may have a membership of twenty, forty, one-hundred and fifty persons, while the only Catholic Church in the neighborhood may have as many as three thousand families. In fact, of all the mainline denominations, the Catholic Church is the only one that has not only maintained its numbers during the past decades but has also registered an increase. Moreover, we should realize that some Protestant denominations have begun to turn more "catholic" when they realize the need of preserving Hispanic culture and identity.

When it comes to developing a pastoral and educational plan for the Hispanic community, various things must be kept in mind. Without adopting a dogmatic position, we think that the changes occurring now in the U.S. economy are more than temporary downturns: they are structural changes.[24] And if the current trends are not reversed, poverty is a

23. With characteristic thoroughness, Kosmin and Lachman also provide a cross-check on their findings by including a comparison with other sources. The Scholastic Aptitude Test (SAT) is one of the few general sources that allow for both ethnic and religious identification. Of course, this is a test only for youth seeking to enter college. It does not represent the older generations, which tend to be more religious than eighteen-year olds. Nor does it account for all Latinos. Therefore, this cannot be said to be a representative sampling. Yet the results from the SAT show a religious affiliation pattern among Mexican, Puerto Rican, and Latino youth that aspire to college that conforms generally to the percentages from the national survey. It is worth noting that among youth identifying themselves as Pentecostal, Puerto Ricans responded nearly three times as often (6 percent) as Mexican Americans (2.1 percent). See Kosmin and Lachman, *One Nation*, 139–40.

24. Martin Carnoy, Hugh Daley, and Raúl Hinojosa Ojeda, *Latinos in a Changing U.S. Economy: Comparative Perspectives on the U.S. Labor Market Since 1939* (New York: Research Foundation of the City University of New York, 1990).

menace that broods over the Latino future. Poverty means low birth weights for Latino infants, lower-quality medical care, hunger, malnutrition, violence in the neighborhoods. These conditions delay a child's physical, cognitive, language and emotional development. How will the Latino family structure negotiate these suffocating conditions?

One of the first things we must understand is that Hispanics are not "new immigrants," though certainly some among us are recent arrivals who have come seeking educational and economic opportunities or the political security so lacking in their own homelands. For some, experiencing themselves or seeing members of their families tortured, exploited, and suffering hunger, the trauma of having to abandon homeland is a constant reminder of how gravely human relationships can deteriorate and how dangerous institutional and political power can become. Others come from families who suffered similar situations during Spanish colonial times and periods of U.S. territorial invasions. Still others have been forced into migration by the U.S. invasion or economic and political intervention in their homelands from the turn of the century on. Here is not the place—though it would be interesting—to examine the role of the Church during these processes and what, if any, pronouncements were made in relationship to these events.

If we are to speak of Hispanics or Latinos and the gifts and challenges they bring to the Church, we must understand the Hispanic im/migrations as well as the Hispanic presence in the United States that preceded these migrations.[25] As I wrote back in the early 70s in an article for the *Chicago Sun-Times*, "Although we are all Hispanics, we are not all alike."[26] We are rich in diversity, a fact that indicates great promise but also tremendous difficulties. I think the next great challenge will not be with the institutional Church: we have fought that war and won most of the battles. The problem is that we have to think of ourselves as members of a growing Hispanic family and learn to work together for the common good. In stressing this national identity as Latinos, I am not denying that first we are *puertorriqueños, cubanos, chilenos, colombianos, dominicanos,* etc. But we must recognize a trend

25. The history of U.S. contact, acquisition, invasion, and domination in the Southwest, the Caribbean, and Central America is being documented from the perspective of the invaded societies. Yet amazingly today, in the Alamo museum, the tour guide may be a Mexican American and may find it difficult to explain why the Tejanos who died defending their soil are categorized and placed with the "foreigners."

26. Ana María Díaz-Ramírez, "Hispanics: All Americans, But Not All Alike," *Together*, magazine supplement of *The Chicago Sun Times*, 7 November 1974, p. 30.

towards a multi-Hispanic reality. This can be seen most easily in Chicago, the Northeastern Tri-State region, California, and Florida. It is in these places where one can say that a truly Hispanic experience is taking place, as Latino peoples descendent from various if not all Spanish-speaking nations come together to negotiate their differences and similarities.

Recently we have emphasized the fact that in the United States, newcomers from the Caribbean and Latin America most often have to identify first with the Hispanic community in order then to negotiate their integration process into the general society. In some cases this integration into the Hispanic community is done through contact with a particular sub-group; such is the case with non-Spanish-speaking Guatemalans within the Mexican American community. In this instance, entrance into U.S. society, mediated by the Mexican American community, requires that the newcomer learn the Spanish language first and then the English language as a means of integration.[27] As this takes place, each Hispanic group is challenged to know itself and respect the other.

While *centroamericanos* and *caribeños* have to understand that Mexican Americans were here first and suffered for their identity and their brand of Catholicism, the Mexican Americans must also accept with respect the fact that other countries have rich and important traditions. After all, 50 years before a shrine was built to Our Lady of Guadalupe in Tepeyac, the first Christian martyr in the New World, Juan Mateo Guatacabanú, spilled his blood for the faith on the neighboring island of Quisqueya, today the Dominican Republic, crying: "Naborí Dios Daká" (I am a warrior-servant of God). If that fact is news to anyone, as a sociologist, I would ask, "Why?" If our theological and historical books treat all Latinos as equally important, then we should know about each other's history and devotions. Nuestra Señora de la Caridad del Cobre and Nuesta Señora de la Altagracia should be as important to us as Latinos as each is to Cubans or Dominicans. I think that in certain areas

27. More recently scholars have been paying attention to this situation. My own writings, those of Anthony M. Stevens-Arroyo, and even more recently a study by Sr. Nancy Wellmeier among Guatemalans in Los Angeles point this out. Guatemalans come to the United States with little or no knowledge of Spanish. In the United States they learn Spanish in order to be integrated into the Latino community first. The integration into the North American community comes second and is mediated by the Latino community. See Nancy Wellmeier, "Marimbas for the Saints: Culture and Religion in a Mayan Refugee Association" (paper presented at the Society for the Scientific Study of Religion Conference, St. Louis, Missouri, 28 October 1995 and at the Association for the Sociology of Religion Conference, New York City, 16 August 1996).

of this common appreciation, we do better than in others. In a hymnal such as *Flor y Canto*, for example, we see a collection of music that reflects a great deal of our diversity.[28] It may be that the Hispanic liturgists are ahead of the Latino theologians.

Indeed, the liturgy has a major role to play in finding this balance between the local traditions close to each nationality and the general respect for the common doctrine that unites us. The fusion and confusion of the world of communications (journalism, novels, television, theater, cinema) continues to have an impact on our identity.[29] Whatever the particular case, these groups are living in close proximity (if not always geographically, nonetheless very real through world of electronics). Thus they are experiencing higher levels of intercultural penetration and accelerated intermarriage trends, which make "Hispanic identity" a more tangible reality. In terms of the Catholic Church, the liturgy among Hispanics has helped develop a new Hispanic consciousness, for it emphasizes our language and that part of our history and culture that is most common to peoples from Aztlán, Central and South America, and the Caribbean.

In a Church such as ours, where the clergy and religious are aging rapidly with little promise of new members taking up the slack, the proper education and use of the laity for the various ministries needed is of the utmost importance. The non-Hispanic Church in the United States perhaps has some lessons to learn from Hispanics, among these the secret of our success in such dire circumstances. The fact that people of Hispanic origin in Latin America, the Caribbean and the United States have lived and survived as Catholics with a limited number of indigenous clergy should be of great comfort to the rest of the Church in the United States, but the Church must not only rely on the good will of these people. What worked in the hinterland of the Caribbean, Central and Latin America may not work today in the urban areas of the United

28. Oregon Catholic Press, *Flor y Canto* (Portland, Ore.: OCP Publications, 1989).

29. For the cinematographer looking to cast the next hero or heroine (or villain, as the case may be), a skin-deep resemblance is more important than a distinct cultural identity. Thus, it becomes possible for Puerto Rican Jennifer López to play the role of the Tejana Selena. On the other hand, while this may seem contradictory to us, for our youth (for whom, I guess, the movie was primarily intended) the image projected by either woman is what makes both of them, separately and combined, role models to be emulated. Perhaps what is important to these youths is not so much that Selena was Tejana, but that she had an *alma latina*. In other words, what animated her was her Latina soul. And that is what inspires Jennifer López's artistic representation of her Latina sister as well.

States. Thus, we must bear the responsibility of an informed and educated laity that can minister to the Church community in the various
and complex needs this community will continually exhibit. In this process of learning and teaching, I believe that special attention must be
paid to the role women have played in the maintenance of our faith.[30]
Consecrated religious women have been present to the people in our
neighborhoods in ways that other institutional religious leaders have
not, and the lay *rezadoras* in our communities have not only survived
but have been further empowered by the migration experience. They
often have greater influence and can claim higher levels of loyalty than
the ordained clergy, basically because the common folk recognize wisdom when they see it and are more willing to trust their own than those
they perceive as outsiders.[31]

Related to the role of consecrated women, I would like to point out
that while the number of North American religious has been steadily
declining, such is not the case in other parts of the world. My fellow
sociologist, Rose Helen Ebaugh, points out in an article in the *Journal for*

---

30. I remember saying once to Fr. Virgilio Elizondo that if I were a theologian instead of a sociologist, I would be writing a theology of *la cocina y el
aposento*, despite the fact that I may run the risk of being burnt at the stake by
some feminist theologians before I had a chance to explain just how revolutionary that theology might be for an understanding of our role as life-giving
and life-changing agents in the Hispanic community. My colleague, Gilbert
Cadena, has written about "Abuelita Theology," and I about the "Matriarchal
Core of Popular Religiosity," and the role of women in what I call
"communitarian spirituality." See Gilbert R. Cadena, "Chicano Clergy and the
Emergence of Liberation Theology," *Hispanic Journal of Behavioral Sciences* 11
(May 1989): 107–21; Gilbert R. Cadena, "Chicanos and the Catholic Church:
Liberation Theology as a Form of Empowerment," (Ph.D. diss., University of
California, Riverside, 1987). See also Ana María Díaz-Stevens, "The Saving
Grace: Matriarchal Core of Latino Catholicism," *Latino Studies Journal* 4 (September 1993): 60–78. There I talk about the role of women in the religion of the
people, especially among Puerto Ricans in the homeland and in the mainland.
I make references to the traditional roles of *curanderas, comadronas, bautizadoras,
rezadoras,* etc. Many times all these roles were held by one person, who also
became the centralizing figure in the local community. I also maintain that
while in migration these roles are not as visible to the receiving society as in
the homeland, they are nevertheless recognizable to those in the local neighborhoods who are in need of them and eager to seek them out. The strength
that people exercising these roles have in the local community often is greater
than that of "official" ministers including priests and consecrated religious
women, especially when they do not share the same ethnic identity as those
they serve.

31. See Ana María Díaz-Stevens, "Latinas and the Church," in *Hispanic
Catholic Culture in the U.S.: Issues and Concerns*, ed. Jay Dolan and Allan Figueroa
Deck (Notre Dame: University of Notre Dame Press, 1994), 249–77.

the Scientific Study of Religion that the places in the world today where religious vocations are increasing are Puerto Rico and the Third World. In fact, in a recent study I found that since the 1930s, there have been nine native religious institutes and congregations for women founded in Puerto Rico, and there is a movement towards autonomy in some of the other religious congregations from the United States and Europe established in Puerto Rico. Does this mean that perhaps someday we will have missionaries from the Caribbean and Latin America ministering to the Catholic Church in the United States?

I think all the Christian Churches, but particularly the Catholic Church in the United States, have to take heed of what Virgilio Elizondo and Roberto Goizueta so forcefully have said (see their presentations in this volume). The suffering and the resurrected Christ must be recognized especially in "the least among you." In the great cities of the United States, as I have statistically demonstrated, "the least," that is, the most needy and poor, are the Hispanics. Elizondo and Goizueta gave in eloquent and poetic language a wonderful theological reflection on what it means for the Church to recognize us as the suffering Jesus and what it means for us to recognize the power of the Christ who constantly reminds us that if he is with us and we with him there is nothing to fear. It has been my task to demonstrate through my own field of statistics and sociological analysis what that face of Jesus looks like in our situation as Hispanics in this country as well as the challenges and opportunities our situation brings to the Church. My words bring the same message. The Church must act now! But by the Church I do not mean only the ordained ministry or the consecrated religious but each one of us as members of the Body of Christ on earth.

Permit me with due respect to go even further. In my opinion, the successes of the Hispano Church in the past have depended less on the priests and even the bishops that have been ordained from within its midst than upon lay participation at the local level. Among Hispanics *pastoral de conjunto* has been a reality for a long, long time. As in Latin America and the Caribbean, the shortage of native clergy has impelled the people at the local level to depend upon their own resources to keep the local Church and its many ministries going. Also as in Latin America, in the United States the *comunidades eclesiales de base* at the local level and pastoral encounters at the local, regional and national levels have been important instruments of the Hispanic's success in planning and organization. These together with local sodalities and movements such as the Cursillo, the Charismatic Movement, and more traditional organizations such as *Damas del Sagrado Corazón, Las Guadalupanas,* the Legion of Mary, and *Las Hijas de María* continue even today to be the backbone of local Church life. The diaconate program, which ordains single and married men to supplement the responsibilities of the priests in the parishes, has also been greatly successful among a people accustomed to accepting grassroots people as religious leaders.

Despite our economic poverty and our difficult situation in this country and elsewhere, the good news is that Latinos in the Catholic Church have given much and are prepared to give even more. When our personal, cultural, and religious resources are tapped, understood correctly, and matched to the needs, ultimately the beneficiary will be not only the Hispanic Catholic community but the entire Church.

Aided by the theological vision of the pastoral and liberation theologians, the U.S. Hispanics have not dichotomized our religious life and our secular and social reality. Less anti-clerical than our counterparts in Latin America, we see no need to consider the responsibilities of the institutional Church apart from the responsibilities of the local congregations. Since in our estimation, despite distinct expressions, the Church is one, there is a mutuality and complementarity in the fulfillment of these obligations. Thus, we speak of the integration of liturgy, catechetics, and social justice (what now is being called holistic ministry), never forgetting the culture and society whence we come and that in which we had to work out our daily lives. The plan of action upon which we reflect has to take into account not only needs that are peculiar to us, but also the needs of others and each group's unique resources.

I have also witnessed a greater desire on the part of Hispanics for the active ministry. Often unable to receive adequate training within the institutional programs of the Catholic Church, many of these people seek education in other Christian seminaries. It may be here that the Catholic Church is having a "brain drain" as these seminary students often choose to "convert" to Churches where their ministry may be recognized officially, often through ordination. I see this trend more often among women than among men, though married men also are among this group.

It is my perception that, recognizing how very difficult it is for Hispanics to shed all the trappings of their Catholic culture, the other Christian Churches will seek to make accommodations in order to tap "this growing market." They will have to construct a new language, new approaches to ministry, even perhaps new liturgical modes to attract and keep their new converts. From the Catholic Church they will copy and adapt programs.

Sociologists are usually expected to make predictions. This is allowed to us because our analysis allows us to say that unless this or that policy is changed, social forces will take us in a certain direction. A sociologist's message today can serve much like the prophets in the Bible who warned the People of God to change their ways. As I see it, the competition from other Christian denominations, plus a downsizing of the clergy, will push the Roman Catholic Church once again towards "innovative" approaches, which will incorporate what in fact the people at the local, grassroots level have found effective for hundreds of years in their land of origin. The role of lay persons, and most especially the role of women—ordained or otherwise—will continue to increase in importance. The end result of all of these activities will be transformative. Based on my knowledge of conflict theory and on my experiences with many years of work at the local as well as at the institutional level, it is my hope and firm belief that competition among the institutions, the shifting of membership, and the challenges presented by personal conversion experiences (from one denomination to another as well as within the same denomination) will serve to invigorate Christianity and religion in contemporary U.S. society.[32]

32. Other studies include Ana María Díaz-Stevens, *Oxcart Catholicism on Fifth Avenue: The Impact of the Puerto Rican Migration Upon the Archdiocese of New York* (Notre Dame: University of Notre Dame, 1993); Ana María Díaz-Stevens, "Latino Popular Religiosity and Communitarian Spirituality" (Occasional Paper presented at the PARAL Symposium, Catholic Theological Union: Chicago, Ill., October 1996); Roberto O. González and Michael La Velle, *The Hispanic Catholic in the U.S.: A Socio-Cultural and Religious Profile* (New York: Northeast Hispanic Pastoral Center, 1985); Anthony M. Stevens-Arroyo, "The Persistence of Religious Cosmovision in an Alien World," in *Enigmatic Powers: Syncretism with African and Indigenous Peoples' Religions Among Latinos*, ed. Anthony M. Stevens-Arroyo and Andrés I. Pérez y Mena, PARAL Series, vol. 3 (New York: Bildner Center Books, 1995), 113–35; Anthony M. Stevens-Arroyo, "Discovering Latino Religion," in *Discovering Latino Religion*, ed. Anthony M. Stevens-Arroyo and Segundo Pantoja, PARAL Series, vol. 4 (New York: Bildner Center Books, 1995), 13–40; Anthony M. Stevens-Arroyo, "Il programma latino: Deamericanizzare e recattolicizzare il cattolicesimo americano," *Religioni e Società: Rivista di scienze sociali della religione* 21 (January–April 1995): 10–29; Anthony M. Stevens-Arroyo, "The Counterhegemonic Role of Barrio Religion" (paper presented at the Annual Meeting of the Latin American Studies Association, Washington, D.C., 29 September 1995); Robert Wuthnow, *The Restructuring of American Religion: Society and Faith Since World War II* (Princeton: Princeton University Press, 1988); Robert Wuthnow, *Producing the Sacred* (Urbana, Ill.: University of Illinois Press, 1994).

7

Latino Leaders for Church and Society

Critical Issues

ALLAN FIGUEROA DECK, S.J.

Little has been written about the emergent role of Latinos in the Churches and society of the United States. Leadership, particularly the leadership *potential* of previously marginal groups like Latinos, Asians, and African Americans, continues to be a matter of great concern among educators, business people, politicians, and social activists alike.[1] These reflections pertain to an experience in leadership education—one of the few of its kind to date—that centers on Latino Catholics. There are four sections to this presentation. The first describes a leadership education initiative undertaken by the National Catholic Council for Hispanic Ministry (NCCHM), a paraChurch federation of Latino Catholic regional and national organizations. The second part contextualizes the initiative within the Latino Catholic presence in the Catholic Church and society. Part three discusses certain critical issues of a cultural and theological nature that impact upon the exercise of leadership among Latinos. The fourth section focuses on implications for the coming third millennium, a time when it is predicted that Latinos will "come into their own" in both the society and Churches of the United States.

THE HISPANIC LEADERSHIP DEVELOPMENT INITIATIVE

In 1993 the National Catholic Council for Hispanic Ministry began to design a Latino leadership education program with a grant from the

---

1. Two articles in Allan Figueroa Deck and Jay P. Dolan, eds., *Hispanic Catholic Culture in the United States* (Notre Dame: University of Notre Dame Press, 1994) are groundbreaking and deserve careful reading: "The Context and Development of Hispanic Ecclesial Leadership" by Marina Herrera and "The Hispanic Community and Church Movements: Schools of Leadership" by Edmundo Rodríguez. See pp. 166 and 206 respectively.

Lilly Endowment, Inc.[2] Over a period of several years almost one million dollars are to be invested in an effort to develop a comprehensive, inclusive program suitable for Latino Church-based leaders. The project began with a series of broad-based consultations in Washington, D.C., Las Cruces, New Mexico, and Los Angeles, California. More than forty Latino/a leaders participated in the consultations that reviewed the status of Latino leadership today. They identified its lights and shadows, positives and negatives. From the beginning NCCHM made an effort to invite Church-based leaders as well as professionals who are not necessarily active in the Church. As a result an interesting, new chemistry came about, one that combines the deep spiritual/religious ethos of Latino cultures with the emergent, modern mindset of new generations of socially and economically mobile Latinos. These consultations set the tone and laid the foundation for the continuing evolution of the program. In addition the project reflects the pan-Latino nature of NCCHM itself; that is, students, trainers, and teachers alike came from virtually all the Latino nationalities—Mexican, Puerto Rican, Cuban, Caribbean, Central and South American. Of equal or perhaps more importance, second and third generation Latinos, for example, Mexican Americans, Chicanos, and Neoricans, participated as instructors and/or trainers and teachers. The rich diversity of the Latino reality in terms of background, language, and social class was taken seriously.

The second phase of the program consisted in the piloting of workshops in areas that had been identified as crucial: skills, a guided practicum, theological foundations, power analysis, cultural factors, and spirituality. The workshops sought to integrate secular insights about leadership, derived mainly from the fields of education and business/management, with the sources for a specifically Christian vision of leadership, namely, with the historical, biblical, and theological underpinnings of ministry and with an apostolic spirituality of the marketplace and public square. Methodologically the curriculum stresses (1) *androgogy*, that is, adult learning approaches, and (2) the *theory-praxis* relationship. Latino Church-based leaders in diocesan and parish ministries, in movements and basic ecclesial communities were invited to participate in a process that builds on their considerable experiences and expertise and addresses their expressed need for further formation in areas they themselves determine, while identifying, sharpening, and fine-tuning the skills already possessed. Participants in the first workshops identified one of their projects already underway or about to begin. This became the basis for the practicum. A total of forty such lead-

2. See National Catholic Council for Hispanic Ministry, *Creating Pathways of Hope* (Los Angeles: NCCHM Publications, 1996).

ers from almost as many organizations participated in the workshops over a two-year period.

The third phase of NCCHM's leadership education program began in the fall of 1996. This phase consists of a second piloting of the entire program over a period of three years. This time the materials for trainers as well as participants will be translated and adapted to English and Spanish-speaking audiences. All the written resources will be made available in the two languages. More importantly, concepts and notions that arise in both leadership education and theology and that are foreign or uncommon in one culture or another will be explored cross-culturally. At the end of this phase, the materials for participants and trainers will be published. This will include a manual, booklets, handouts, audiovisuals, and perhaps a collection of essays on a Catholic/Christian view of U.S. Latino leadership in Church and society. NCCHM hopes to continue to certify those who will deliver this program in pastoral institutes, universities, and dioceses throughout the United States.

Latino Leadership Development in Context

One of the lessons learned during this rich experience of four years is the *bilingual* reality of Latino leadership today in the United States. Initially it was thought that programs would have to be delivered in *either* English or Spanish and perhaps more in Spanish. One group, ostensibly the more recently arrived Latinos, would have to be taught in Spanish and another, the more assimilated Mexican Americans or Chicanos, in English. The experience of actually giving the workshops, however, has so far demonstrated the fact that large numbers of Latinos, indeed the majority, can speak either Spanish or English. Either language can be used in both the conferences and the readings with no need for translation. As one might expect, those who are taking initiative and exercising various forms of leadership in the community are more likely to be well on the way to bilingual proficiency. So far this approach has worked even though occasionally there are Latinos who mistakenly think that proceeding in this bilingual fashion, not doing everything in Spanish and not providing translators, is to favor the "English-only" movement. That, of course, is not at all the intention. Rather, a truly bilingual approach allows youth and the second generation to participate, something that is crucial—even strategic—if the Latino presence is to possess the energy and influence it rightly deserves. English, after all, is the language of second generation Latinos in this country. Indeed, two-thirds of U.S. Latinos are either bilingual or speak only English. One-third speak only Spanish. This is a point that Gregory Rodriguez of the Pacific News Service made in an article in the Los Angles Times on the bilingual and English-speaking Latino markets and mass media.

In working in a bilingual fashion neither NCCHM nor the leadership education program wish to discourage the maintenance and growth of Spanish as an essential resource for Latinos. What is being discovered, however, is the basic role of English as the language of leadership, influence, and therefore of effective ministries, including Hispanic ministry, in the United States. A certain preference for ministry among recently arrived immigrants and the working poor, one totally in Spanish, has unwittingly created an imbalance, one that works against U.S. Latino Catholics in the long run. Thinking strategically, I pointed out many years ago in *The Second Wave*[3] that the *terminus ad quem*, the ultimate target of Hispanic ministry, is the children of the immigrants, the first and second generations, and the youth who are either bilingual or English speakers.[4] These groups are also socially and economically mobile. Neither Church nor Latino leaders have stressed this insight and the result is a decline in Church participation on the part of the youthful generations and, more tragically, of the Latino professional class. These are precisely the groups most likely to assume and exercise effective leadership in this country.

The 1996 elections were a watershed for Latino participation in politics. In reaction to waves of immigrant bashing, particularly in the bellwether state of California, Latinos became U.S. citizens, registered to vote and actually voted in unprecedented numbers. Both major political parties have engaged in soul-searching regarding the effectiveness of their outreach to this dynamic, growing, and youthful force. Latinos are demographically strong in precisely the most politically potent states: California, Texas, New York, Illinois, and Florida. This circumstance highlights the urgency of the question about the nature and quality of the emerging leadership of Latinos in this country.

The role of religion, the Church, and the Catholic cultural ethos of Latinos in the formation of the new Latino social, economic, and political presence is only now coming into focus. Sociologist David Hayes-Bautista has begun to highlight the importance of the Catholic identity of Latinos in his pioneering work.[5] The values that Latinos bring to their decision-making reflect their cultural and religious heritage as well as the powerful influences of U.S. culture and modernity. The Catho-

3. See Allan Figueroa Deck, *The Second Wave: Hispanic Ministry and the Evangelization of Cultures* (Mahwah, N.J.: Paulist Press, 1988), 113.

4. See Gregory Rodriguez, "The Rising Language of Latino Media: English," *Los Angeles Times*, 4 May 1997.

5. David Hayes-Bautista, *The Burden of Support: Young Latinos in an Aging Society* (Stanford: Stanford University Press, 1988).

lic religious and cultural ethos of Latinos provides the framework for the process of accommodation or assimilation they experience today. By no means is the vibrant heritage of the past erased, rather it takes on new life and forms in the more complex cultural matrix of today's United States.

A logical inference to be made in light of this reality is that the formation of new Latino leaders must be rooted in culture and religion, not prescind from these powerful realities. If this is true, it follows then that the Church and the strong religious orientation of Latinos have a critical role to play in the process of leadership development. For at the heart of leadership is the matter of motivation. A persistent view of the transcendent, the religious dimension, is, by all reports, a vital element in the Latino vision of things. That transcendent vision promises to be the source of further empowerment for future generations of Latinos as it was for generations past.

CRITICAL ISSUES IN LEADERSHIP

The dramatic demographic growth of Latino communities in every region of the United States, but especially in the key states of California, Texas, Florida, New York, and Illinois, raises a host of critical questions about the future. One of the more urgent issues arising in this context of rapid change is leadership development. Are new generations of Americans of Latin American origin prepared to assume roles of leadership in society and Church? The absence of Latino leaders is evident in both Church and social structures. Such an absence calls into question the legitimacy and effectiveness of institutions, organizations, and programs purporting to serve the growing Latino communities. Few social and ecclesial challenges, therefore, are as great as this one: to promote the fuller participation of Latinos in Church and society and thus strengthen the Latino communities' sense of responsibility for themselves, their lives, and their institutions.

Where does one begin the effort to discover the path toward an authentic Latino leadership development? Experience shows that traditional American attitudes about leadership and models of leadership development current in the world of education and business are inadequate. They fail to address cross-cultural issues in leadership. They also fail to address adequately the relationship between ecclesial, faith-based understandings of service or ministry to the secular, cultural, and society-based concepts of leadership arising in modern, industrial, and post-industrial contexts of the United States. As a result the values and motivations of Hispanics are not given the attention they need if we are to exercise leadership with conviction and vigor.

A couple of anecdotes may illustrate this thought. Several years ago I was driving across the great Arizona desert. For several hours the strongest signals were coming from the three talk radio shows of Oliver North, Rush Limbaugh, and G. Gordon Liddy. I reached a point of saturation with the mindset of these gentlemen and started to move the dial. A strong signal from a Mexican town along the border was coming in. This was a Mexican talk show and the commentator was saying this: "My thought for today, ladies and gentlemen, is to remind you of the importance and value of humility. We should consider other's views as better than our own; or at least, we should try to find a way to positively interpret what they are saying or hold. . . ." After listening to the three U.S. radio talk shows, what a relief and what a contrast! In very respectful and mellifluous tones, the Mexican commentator was reinforcing a very Mexican value: *humildad,* "humility."

This occurrence made me recall a similar experience just a few months earlier. Several instructors in the Hispanic Leadership Development Initiative met in San Antonio. This was the first time the group had come together and there was plenty of time for introductions. What caught the group's attention was the mildness and modesty of each person in sharing their considerable professional qualifications. It suddenly dawned on us that finding ourselves in a totally Latino environment, we assumed a valued Latino (field dependent) style of interaction, one that places a premium on "knowing one's place" and deferring to others. In our normal work in the Anglo-American context, the approach would be much different. People would naturally be assertive, more direct, and less reserved about letting others really know that one is quite qualified in his or her profession. If one did not know about cross-cultural differences like this, one would never know about the value given to humility by Latinos and how that value may be a source of motivation and meaning to them. More often than not, such "quaint" cultural characteristics are simply dismissed as politically incorrect or remnants of an oppressive, colonial past. But cannot a legitimate question be asked? Is there some value, even wisdom and rightness, about the Latino sense of humility? Must it be brushed aside or can it somehow be tapped for the creation of even more effective leaders? Whom are these Latinos to lead if not other Latinos? Leadership must flow from a sense of proportion, realism, and respect for others. Perhaps a traditional American directness and aggressiveness can be tempered by a Latino sensitivity to others. The emergence of a strong

Latino presence in U.S. society may mean that new nuances and values will be incorporated into the prevailing standards of leadership.

While the literature on multiculturalism grows day by day, the critical issue of cross-cultural or culturally adapted leadership remains unaddressed. For grounding NCCHM's leadership education program it was crucial therefore that an effort be made to clarify the cultural factors that affect the theory and practice of leadership. Similarly, the theological underpinnings of ministry and its relationship to the secular notion of "leadership" remain undeveloped. The work of pioneers like Robert K. Greenleaf and, among Catholics, James D. and Evelyn Eaton Whitehead, Loughlan Sofleld, Dolores Leckey, Philip J. Murnion, William Bausch, and many others, provides an excellent foundation for the practical/pastoral theology of lay leadership in Church and society, but much remains to be done in applying and adapting these insights to the U.S. Latino Catholic experience. For instance, consider the difficulties in the very word "leadership."

The word "leader" or "leadership" is Anglo-Saxon in origin. The concept is expressed in Spanish by the same Anglo-Saxon root: "lide" or "liderazgo." In Anglo-American culture leadership is a very positive thing. Everyone is for it. Curiously enough, outside Anglo-American contexts the reaction to this concept is ambivalent. The U.S. historical experience and the national myth have extolled the importance and value of leadership, initiative, self-responsibility, and related civic virtues. This has much to do with the Protestant sense of personal autonomy and self-responsibility. Following the lead of Max Weber, Latino theologian Roberto S. Goizueta has traced the origins of the North American attitude toward individual accomplishment back to the rise of Protestantism and the Enlightenment experience. Commenting on the result of the individualism fostered by modern European American Protestantism, Goizueta notes the following:

> Individuals come to understand themselves as "separated and isolated" not only vis-à-vis the present with respect to their contemporaries (communities and institutions), but also vis-à-vis the past, with respect to their ancestors (tradition).[6]

In an observation particularly relevant to the issue of the difference between Latino leadership and the prevailing U.S. variety, Goizueta further observes:

6. Roberto S. Goizueta, "U.S. Hispanic Theology and the Challenge of Pluralism," in Allan Figueroa Deck, ed., *Frontiers of Hispanic Theology in the U.S.* (Maryknoll, N.Y.: Orbis Books, 1992), 5.

> The ontological priority of community revealed in U.S. Hispanic praxis suggests . . . that all of us are particular manifestations of an *organic* [emphasis that of current writer] whole before we are individual entities: community—ultimately, the entire human community—is mediated by the particularity of individual identity.[7]

The predicted emergence of Latinos as the largest minority in the United States early in the twenty-first century invites one to focus on the issue of contrasting experiences and bases for the understanding of leadership. Goizueta is pointing to an underlying difference rooted in the very notion of being, in ontology. History provides many sources for grasping the differences in one or another culture's approach to leadership. It is impossible, for example, to understand U.S. history and the extraordinary success enjoyed by the American people in the settlement and development of their nation without adverting to the relatively happy, successful experience of the first Anglo-Americans with their leaders. Few if any other people on earth have a history resembling this one. In contrast, leadership plays a much more limited role in societies where things are preordained, where there are social, political, economic, and cultural patterns deeply and (so it seems) indelibly ingrained.

This contrast was brought home to me many years ago when I served as pastor of an inner-city barrio Church. We were trying to encourage small faith-sharing groups in the homes. To do this it was necessary to train a "leader" for each small community. When few if any "leaders" came forth, I began to wonder what the problem was. I asked people about this. I found that among some Mexican people the prospect of being a leader is not only a threatening, unfamiliar role but also a negative one. They do not value this role and they tend to flee from it. In the family context, of course, it is clear that mother and father, older brothers and sisters, and so forth must be responsible and in that sense assume a clear leadership role. But beyond that inner circle it is unusual for the working poor and the *campesinos* to aspire to anything like "leadership" in society or, for that matter, in Church.

Latino cultures, like most cultures in the developing world, are the product of centuries of stability, of a social equilibrium that does not encourage "moving up and out." Rather, much premium is placed on "keeping one's head down." In the precarious world of the poor, survival is the goal. Leadership is often not an issue.

Political scientist Harry Eckstein has studied efforts made over the past century to promote participation of working-class people in

7. Roberto S. Goizueta, "Rediscovering Praxis," in *We Are a People! Initiatives in Hispanic American Theology*, ed. Roberto S. Goizueta (Minneapolis: Augsburg/Fortress Press, 1992), 77.

sociopolitical action. He studied the efforts of democratic societies such as those of Great Britain and the United States to promote the participation of disenfranchised groups from the lower socioeconomic class in decision-making. He calls this civic inclusion. Part of that process consists precisely in the formation of responsible leaders among groups that have little influence or power in society. He writes:

> There are dramatic discrepancies between what was expected to follow from civic inclusion and what has in fact happened. . . . My proposed explanation of these discrepancies rests on the notion that there exists an authority culture of the lower-classes of society—the beneficiaries of civic inclusion—that has been poorly understood by the higher-class proponents of inclusion. . . . I consider lower-class authority to be a positive and adaptive response to the defining trait of poverty: being compelled to live with and manage high scarcity. The authority-culture of the poor is all the more resistant to change because of this.[8]

Eckstein's point reminds us about the need to factor in both cultural and social class data in the realistic assessment of the Latino experience of leadership.

The Catholic religious heritage of Latinos has also contributed to the people's attitude toward leadership. Much emphasis is given to hierarchy or inherited, natural roles and positions, not to acquired ones. Family structures are clearly hierarchical, but so too are Church structures. By reason of ordination—a sacred conferral of power given to only a few men—leadership is passed on and exercised in the Church. This is not something that one casually or easily attains. For the vast majority of persons, it has been considerably beyond their reach, if not (as in the case of women) totally off limits.

The weight of the hierarchical system may contribute to a strong note of passivity among Latino Catholics in the way they conceive of Church. In the period before the Second Vatican Council's decrees on the proper role of laity in the Church, it was common to hear lay persons refer to their role in the Church in terms of the sacred formula: pray, pay, obey! If this was the case in pre-Vatican II times in the United States, how much more was it so in Latin America! Of course, there have always been outstanding examples of lay leadership in the Church even in pre-Vatican II times. They did not, however, reflect the norm. They were exceptions that proved the rule.

The historical experience of leadership in many cultures outside the Anglo-American one has been negative, abusive. The concept of

8. Harry Eckstein, "Civic Inclusion and Its Discontents," *Daedalus* 113, no. 4 (Fall 1984): 107.

leadership in cross-cultural contexts is therefore often ambivalent. United States Jesuits returning from an international gathering of their confreres in Rome in 1995 mentioned that they were surprised to discover that the typical American emphasis on leadership was a source of some misunderstanding with their brethren from other nations. In their discussion of Jesuit ministries in the fields of education, pastoral care, culture, social justice, science, and mass media, non-U.S. Jesuits resisted referring to these activities as areas of leadership. They preferred to talk of them as ministries. The Christian notion of ministry is not tainted with the weight of abuse that "leadership" has acquired even in modern European countries such as France, Spain, Italy, not to speak of Asian or African nations liberated from colonialism only a few decades ago.

Leadership education cannot therefore presume as much goodwill toward the notion of leadership as one might think. What is needed is a mutual cultural unpacking of the assumptions and historical experiences behind U.S. and Latino notions of leadership. What are the factual, historical underpinnings of the exalted understanding of leadership in the United States? What are their counterparts in the rich and complex Latin American experience? When NCCHM's consultants were asked about the words that come to mind when thinking of leadership within a Latino milieu, they mentioned words such as service, initiative, self-responsibility, and solidarity. But along with them came forth other words: *caudillismo* (tyranny) and *caciquismo* (petty despotism), abusive forms of leadership in authoritarian regimes. Mingled with these negative notions are expressions of machismo, attitudes and expectations regarding male behavior, which often influence the practice of leadership among Latinos/as. These matters are delicate and require considerable reflection and insight if they are to be successfully confronted in ways that avoid the pitfall of stereotyping one culture or another.

Given the complexity of the cultural underpinnings of attitudes toward leadership, it is quite amazing that more has not been written and more initiatives undertaken to develop a specifically Latino understanding of leadership development, one suitable for new generations. In the United States, Latinos seek ways to be Latino but in a manner appropriate to the promise and possibilities of their U.S. citizenship. Crucial to that process of cultural transformation is knowing where one has come from, where one is, and where one chooses to go. A critical, cross-cultural analysis of leadership is the first step in addressing the challenge of leadership formation in a respectful manner. Anything short of that, even with the best of intentions, implies a certain violation of cultural memories, a disregard for experience that borders on cultural imposition or imperialism.

Drawing a conclusion from the seminal thought of Cornell West, it seems to me that a critical cultural awareness works in at least two ways: (1) with respect to the traditional Latino expressions of leadership and (2) with respect to contemporary, Anglo-American models of leadership. The idea here is that there is room for criticism on both sides.[9] Anglo-Americans often suffer what U.S. Latino theologian Justo L. González calls the "myth of innocence": an uncritical, naive understanding of U.S. ways.[10] Leadership as understood and put into practice in the United States today cannot be viewed as unambiguously good. Rather, it is likely to function with prevailing disvalues of the market economy, with individualism, materialism, and a pragmatic rationality that strip people of their moral imagination. Efficiency replaces ethics as human action is viewed primarily in terms of self-interest rather than the common good.

Something similar may be said about leadership in the Church. Attitudes toward Church (ecclesial) leadership must be demythologized by a process of historical, structural, and cultural analyses. Every area of Church teaching and practice has been influenced by the Church's encounter with cultures. For example, Church historians point out that hierarchy was not as emphasized in the first century of Christianity as it came to be in subsequent ones. The Church's adaptation to the Greek and Roman worlds inexorably led to a more rigid definition of roles: bishop, priest, deacon, and eventually the papacy. The more participative, charismatic, and collegial styles of the early domestic (household) Churches gave way to the structured, hierarchical style of the established Church of Constantine.

The point here is not to lament the direction of history, but to illustrate the fact that the actual ways in which leadership is practiced in the Catholic Church have never been static, etched in granite. It has appeared that way to many, but contemporary historical studies make it clear that within a framework of accepted standards established by official Church teaching there always has been and will be, this side of

9. Cornell West insists on the importance of taking a critical stance toward *both* African American and the dominant European American cultures, not just one or the other. He abhors a soft kind of multiculturalism that suggests that a mindless negativity toward hegemonic European American culture or an uncritical affirming of all or any third world culture is all that is needed for a just and humane world. See West's "Beyond Eurocentrism and Multiculturalism," in his *Prophetic Thought in Postmodern Times* (Monroe, Maine: Common Courage Press, 1993), 3–23.

10. Justo L. González, *Mañana: Christian Theology from a Hispanic Perspective* (Nashville: Abingdon Press, 1990), 10.

the parousia, room for development.[11] This idea is important for today's Church-based Latino. For the Latino, the sense of the sacred has often sacralized authority and in so doing so removed it from historical scrutiny, placing it, as it were, "on a pedestal." A contemporary Catholic understanding of leadership or ministry in the Church and the world requires that leadership be revisited not in terms of our long and sometimes unhappy tradition, but in terms of the demands of the Gospel itself. In the Second Vatican Council the Catholic Church began to address its understanding of the role of the laity precisely in terms of the leadership of Jesus Christ whom we are called to emulate (in leadership) and to follow. A critical theological review of leadership in the Church is currently underway. It includes the controversial issue of women's role in leadership. This review must also be brought to the attention of Latinos/as. They need a *theological grounding* for their contemporary understanding of leadership in the Church, one in dialogue with (1) the emerging cross-cultural and historical analyses mentioned above; and with (2) new approaches to the understanding of Jesus Christ himself who is for Christians the leader *par excellence*.[12]

LATINO LEADERSHIP FOR THE COMING MILLENNIUM

Jesuit missiologist Marcello Azevedo reflected on the context of U.S. Latinos in his keynote address at the August 1996 Hispanic Congress Raíces y Alas in Chicago.[13] He makes several points that are relevant to the present and future role of Latinos in the Church and society of the United States. He stresses the need for Latino leaders to reflect inten-

11. An impressive array of theologians have traced the historical development of ministry and office in the Church. There seems to be broad agreement about the development of ministry from the primitive Church to the present. One of the more challenging and insightful of these studies is that of Thomas Franklin O'Meara, *The Theology of Ministry* (Mahwah, N.J.: Paulist Press, 1983), 76–91.

12. Many contemporary christological studies approach the mystery of Jesus Christ in terms of the humanity of Jesus. This "christology from below" stresses the identification of Jesus with human experience and, while acknowledging Jesus' power and divinity, stresses his struggle to incarnate God's love and justice. See, for example, Jon Sobrino, *Christology at the Crossroads: A Latin American Approach* (Maryknoll, N.Y.: Orbis Books, 1978); or J.J. Mueller, *Practical Discipleship: A United States Christology* (Collegeville, Minn.: The Liturgical Press, 1992).

13. Marcello Azevedo, "Hispanic Leaders: Faith and Culture in the New Millennium," in National Catholic Council for Hispanic Ministry, *Creating Pathways of Hope* (Los Angeles: NCCHM Publications, 1996). See also the Fall 1997 issue of *Chicago Studies*, which reproduced Azevedo's talk.

tionally on the issue of inculturation, that is, the question regarding the way in which they will actively participate in the U.S. experience. Leadership requires an *intentional* attitude: U.S. Latinos do not have to merely assimilate, the way traditional Catholic groups have done in the past. Rather, the openness to culture in today's United States and the Church's contemporary emphasis on inculturation combine to provide an opportunity for the nation's twenty-eight million Latinos to exercise a more critical attitude toward their mainstreaming. It is not a question of merely blending in with the existing U.S. culture nor simply "holding out" for the traditional ways of Latin America. Azevedo believes that something new is coming about. He cites the findings of UCLA researcher David Hayes-Bautista. Latinos in California are assimilating to U.S. ways, but they are also holding on to several features of their past: their language (while learning English, of course), their work ethic, their religious interests, and their strong family orientation. There is a notable subgroup of Latinos who consciously opt for bilinguality and biculturality. They focus on *negotiating* their relationship to the dominant cultural patterns of Anglo America.[14]

The present moment offers Latinos the opportunity to assume the role of a "bridge people" with roots in both Latin America and the United States. They are not merely Latin Americans who have been transported to new soil, nor another ethnic group to be Americanized. The multicultural awareness of the waning days of the Second Millennium, globalization, and the human rights movement lay the foundation for Latinos to develop their own way of being American. This new way involves elements of continuity and discontinuity. Azevedo argues that the powerful religious orientation of Latinos must provide a basis for the elaboration of this new way of being "American." He stresses the role of evangelization, that is, the encounter of cultures with the values and message of Jesus Christ. This is the starting-point for an authentic Latino Catholic leadership. It requires knowledge of all the cultures involved, of the Latino cultures as well as of other cultures in the United States, of traditional and modern as well as postmodern cultures, together with a clear sense of other cultures in the complex religious and ecclesial context of the United States. In the first decade of the coming millennium, everything points to the emergence of Hispanics as the majority in the Catholic Church of this country. According to Azevedo,

14. David Hayes-Bautista, Aída Hurtado, R. Burciaga Valdez, and Anthony C.R. Hernández, eds., *Redefining California: Latino Social Engagement in a Multicultural Society* (Los Angeles: UCLA Chicano Studies Research Center, 1992), 79–85.

this will be a presence capable of transforming some postulates and values of North American culture from within.[15]

In addition to the impact of cultural awareness on leadership development, there is also a theological development. In May 1997 the Secretariat for Family, Laity, Women, and Youth of the National Conference of Catholic Bishops (NCCB) sponsored a colloquium titled "Toward a Theology of Ecclesial Lay Ministry." The colloquium arose in the context of the extraordinary explosion in lay ministries in the Catholic Church after the Second Vatican Council. The focus of the colloquium was on describing this vast experience, identifying some of its more salient features, and grounding it in a solid contemporary theological understanding found in biblical studies, Catholic theological scholarship, and the magisterial teaching of the hierarchy.

One of the issues that surfaced at the colloquium particularly relevant to the issue of Latino Church-based leadership is the contemporary Catholic Church's emphasis on evangelization. According to the teaching of Pope John Paul II, a teaching widely accepted and commented upon in the Church throughout the world, the Church is "in its entirety evangelizing."[16] That is, the Church's very identity is found in *mission*. That mission requires ecclesial structures that look outward as well as inward. The mission is fundamental, not optional. It consists in promoting the encounter of the Gospel of Jesus Christ with cultures, all cultures. This means developing structures that enable the faithful to communicate that faith to others. If the Church, then, is to be fundamentally this *evangelizing* force, it must possess the ministerial structure to accomplish the task. There is a clearly perceived crisis, however, in regard to the ability of the Church's current ministerial structures to deliver the required service. The emergence of the laity is driven by the need to multiply services as well as the number of persons authorized in some way to reach out on behalf of the Church. One of the notions, controversial to be sure, that arose within the context of the colloquium was this: the ministerial priesthood can no longer be viewed as adequate to the exigencies of a Church that is truly *evangelizing*. It is not a ques-

15. David T. Abalos has produced an impressive strategic vision of the Latino participation in the transformation of the U.S. culture along the lines of justice and love. He stresses the need for all cultures "to let go": "A multicultural society is one that is ready to discover what it is that we need to nourish and what to let go. Above all, we have to be prepared to critique all cultures in our society because all of them are in bad shape." See his *Strategies of Transformation Toward a Multicultural Society* (Westport, Conn.: Praeger Publishers, 1996), xv.

16. The implications of what Pope John Paul II calls "the new evangelization" are thoroughly developed in Alfred T. Hennelly, ed., *Santo Domingo and Beyond* (Maryknoll, N.Y.: Orbis Books, 1993), 80 ff.

tion of eliminating the ministerial priesthood, but rather of reconfiguring its *modus operandi* in such a way that greater scope is given to all the range of services and outreach required by an evangelizing Church.

The idea that laity substitute for priests who are absent is not theologically grounded. The Second Vatican Council taught that all are called to some form of service in the Church by reason of baptism. Ministry is every form of service that promotes the reign of God and is authorized by the hierarchy. Laity have a considerable role in that call to ministry. The emergence of a new emphasis on the laity's active participation in and responsibility for the Church is crucial for Latino leadership. This does not refer only or even principally to Latino service within the Church itself as clergy or ecclesial lay ministers. Rather, it refers especially to the call of the laity to be leaven in the world, that is, in the transformation of the socioeconomic, political, and cultural orders. The religious impulse in Latino cultures can now be focused not only on service within the Church but, more importantly, on service in the world in accordance with a Gospel vision. This integration of the religious and the secular vocations is fundamental if the tremendous motivation and energy latent in Latino religiosity is to find a constructive expression.

The emergence of a new theology of the laity at this time in the history of the Church in the United States provides a basis for a more effective Latino ecclesial leadership, one that empowers more people to assume responsibility for their Church as well as for their society. The lack of a more integral theology of the Christian vocation and ministry has historically contributed to an unfocused Latino Catholic identity and presence in both Church and society. Laity were expected to remain as spectators more than actors in the story of their Church and society.

Implicit in the articulation of a new theology of ministry is a renewed respect for the giftedness of the Christian faithful and a recognition of the charisms that flow from the Spirit and cannot be generated through merely human means. Latinos will thus be encouraged to serve in accordance with their particular gifts. This does not mean suppressing the hierarchical aspect of the Church, the drive toward order that is a mark of the Catholic tradition, but rather the discovery of new ways for collaboration and subsidiarity in roles and functions. In particular this means finding new ways for women to exercise more forms of leadership in the community and to be *officially recognized* as true leaders and ministers.

CONCLUSION

The experience of designing and executing a leadership development initiative for Church-based Latinos provides a rich source for realistically addressing the critical issues facing Latinos as they assume more prominence in society and the Churches. These reflections are a tentative effort to share some of the concerns raised in the process of carrying out a rather extensive leadership development initiative. This is hardly the final word. These reflections, however, do serve to point out the need for critical reflection on experience that is shared, commented upon, and even debated.

In the course of carrying out this initiative two important areas emerge as in some ways defining and inspiring the vision of leadership implicit in the entire venture; namely, evangelization as the encounter of the Gospel with cultures and ministry as the service of both the ordained and the non-ordained in the promotion of God's reign on earth. The project facing Latinos today and tomorrow revolves around the challenge of developing a contemporary leadership that is at once rooted in the particularity of the Latino cultures and faith traditions and rooted as well in the universality of the Catholic communion. The subjects or protagonists of this renewed leadership for the third millennium are Latinos themselves.

While Latinos are only part of the larger transformation taking place in today's world and Church, their youthfulness, vitality, and demographic growth logically place a great deal of responsibility on their shoulders. Emerging theologies of ministry and ecclesiologies will give even more urgency to the task of leadership development. These new visions of Christian discipleship in the world put a premium on the participation and commitment of all. There are many indications that the Catholic Church is poised to move ahead in its understanding and practice of discipleship in the world. The recent Colloquium on Ecclesial Lay Ministries held at the University of Dayton is an example. The ongoing discussions about the role of women in the Church is another instance of the direction in which the understanding of leadership is going. A new paradigm of lay participation and diversity is emerging within the larger communion that is the Church. It is driven by the reality of a global Church whose mission is to evangelize. That means that the Church cannot be content simply to maintain itself but must expand and reach outward beyond the comfortable bounds of parish, diocese, nation, social class, and race.

In dialogue with all people of good will, Latinos are uniquely positioned to contribute to this development since they are a "bridge people," rooted in several races (native American, African, European), nationalities, cultures, and social class experiences. They are now well on their way to being "American," but "American" on their own unique terms. They will therefore be important interlocutors in a conversation that can only become more urgent and demanding as the new millennium unfolds. The factors that have made the diversity of cultures, classes, and races a central issue of the century coming to an end are not going away. Rather, the coming century will require more creativity than ever in finding ways of *convivencia*, that is, "living together." The orientation of Latino cultures to *convivencia* is perhaps as good a starting-point as any for the serious agenda of leadership, whether ecclesial or secular, in the millennium to come.

8

Ecumenism in the U.S. Hispanic/ Latino Community

Challenge and Promise

JEFFREY GROS, F.S.C.

When I was growing up in Memphis, I thought Hispanic Americans were Presbyterians because that was the faith of our next-door neighbor, Ramón Díaz. As I came into sixth grade geography at Immaculate Conception, I began to find out that Catholic history and demography were quite different from my own experience. I now see that as Christians develop our understandings of our own faith community, the different traditions of our fellow Christians, and the imperative toward Christian unity that is central to our identity in Jesus Christ, we move along quite different paths.

I would like to focus some questions about how best to promote the unity of the Church from the perspective of the U.S. Hispanic Catholic community. My approach will be more programmatic and institutional than either pastoral or abstractly theological. That is the gift I bring to the discussion.[1]

All of us will bring our own gifts to the discussion with the common focus: How do we best serve the pastoral needs in and with the U.S. Hispanic community, and how do we best serve the unity of Christ's Church in the Hispanic context?

My challenging questions are addressed to three specific communities in the Catholic Church: the theologians, the bishops and those who assist them, and the pastoral agents. Of course, our ecumenical partners in the Hispanic community and beyond are important interlocutors, and they should enable us to answer our questions better.

---

1. Dr. Gros's presentation retains the form of an invitation to dialogue. In this written form we have only slightly modified the oral style of presentation to underscore the need for on-going discussion on this issue. *Eds.*

With five million Protestant Hispanics in the United States, we might have a better opportunity for ecumenical interchange than any other Spanish-speaking community in the world. The ecumenical imperative is our common calling. All who live in the real, if imperfect, communion are partners by baptism in this pilgrimage toward unity.

I will organize my remarks around three themes: I will first review the present ecumenical commitments of the Catholic Church and where we are moving at this moment. Second, I will raise the specific issues that seem a priority in the U.S. Hispanic community. Third, I will make a necessary excursus into the question of adapting to pluralism, a topic often spoken of as the "problem of the sects" in the Latin American Catholic literature.

THE ROMAN CATHOLIC ECUMENICAL SITUATION

The Roman Catholic Church has gone through a monumental set of institutional changes in the last thirty years, of which the ecumenical conversion is among the most dramatic. In the last few years, the magisterium itself has focused on these changes in its publication of *Directory for the Application of Principles and Norms on Ecumenism* (1993), John Paul's encyclical *Ut Unum Sint* (1995), and the two Apostolic Letters, *Tertio Millennio Adveniente* (1994) and *Orientale Lumen* (1995). In all of his discussions of the New Evangelization, Pope John Paul continually emphasizes the priority of ecumenism.[2]

These official texts are only the tip of a veritable iceberg of thirty years of ecumenical agreement on key theological, ethical, and pastoral themes that have divided the Churches for fifteen centuries, of participation together in ecumenical councils on local, national, and international levels, and of steady—if uneven—programs of conversion and formation, calling all of our Catholic people into faith in Christ's will for the Church and zeal for promoting the ecumenical priority at the center of Catholic identity.

Both the magisterial leadership and the grass roots developments have been received unevenly across this largest member Church of the ecumenical movement. In some places, the ecumenical vision grows, so that the urgency for deeper sacramental and ecclesial fellowship creates a holy impatience. In other places like Latin America and Eastern Europe, other pastoral priorities or demographic considerations have made the assimilation of this element of renewal slower than, for ex-

2. Cf. John Paul II, "Linking Evangelization and Ecumenism," *Origins* 26, no. 9 (1996): 139–41.

ample, liturgical, biblical, or social renewal. It is becoming increasingly clear to me that the reception of this dimension of Vatican II has its own, unique challenges for inculturation as do liturgy, Bible study, and catechesis.

In the U.S. Hispanic community, the theologians have assumed some important ecumenical leadership, encouraged by the Academy of Catholic Hispanic Theologians of the United States and its *Journal of Hispanic/Latino Theology*. The first Virgilio Elizondo award was presented to the United Methodist theologian and ecumenist, Justo González. The journal's editorial board is fully ecumenical, including Dr. Samuel Solivan of Andover Newton Theological Seminary. The journal provides a source for ecumenical leaders as they ask how best to facilitate and interpret the ecumenical priorities of Hispanic Americans. However, a careful reading of some of the work of the Academy and the *Journal* will also indicate some of the challenges.[3]

The relationships at the grass roots are often with Churches that move beyond the classical horizon of ecumenical theology, for Hispanics show more interest in and affinity for the movemental dimension of Christian life. While the Pentecostal Churches may cause the most problems in the Hispanic community, they are also the most prevalent Christian partner, often sharing culture and class with the newer immigrants. How can the mainstream of the ecumenical movement take account of this fact?

On the other hand, the Hispanic theological community is under-represented in the classical ecumenical literature and in the official dialogues representing the Catholic Church. Much of Latino/Hispanic theology does not take account of the results of thirty years of dialogue. It is difficult to find scholars who are concerned with this dimension of the ecclesiological issue or who are challenged by the questions inherent in the quest for the unity of the Church. Hispanics are represented by two theologians in the formal dialogues of the National Conference of Catholic Bishops (NCCB), and more would follow if scholars writing in the field took an interest. How do we encourage Catholic Latino theologians to take their rightful place in the ecumenical research of the Church?

How does the theological community serve the reception of the results of ecumenical dialogue in the Hispanic community? This is, of course, a question for educators and preachers as well as professional theologians. But the theological community carries a particular charism

3. Orlando O. Espín, "Pentecostalism and Popular Catholicism: The Poor and Traditio," *Journal of Hispanic/Latino Theology* 3, no. 2 (1995): 14–43.

for bringing the vision of unity into the mainstream of Catholic thought in its various cultures and of bringing the aspirations and concerns of particular communities, in this case the U.S. Hispanic communities, into the discussion around the ecumenical table.

As the table widens in the ecumenical experience, the discussion deepens and becomes complex. When talking about Mary, for example, between Catholics and Lutherans (it is still too hot a topic for the Pentecostal dialogue!), the variety and texture of Hispanic devotional life is an important complement to the precision of biblical scholars and the clarity of historians.[4]

The concrete ecumenical situation in regard to episcopal leadership in the United States is quite varied in the Hispanic community, as it is in the full conference of bishops. Just after the Second Vatican Council, the Hispanic bishops were fairly consistent in their support of its ecumenical vision. As we move further away from the experience of the Council, the commitment to its vision varies, but two Hispanic bishops remain strong in their support. Bishop Plácido Rodríguez of Lubbock serves on the Bishops' Committee for Ecumenical and Interreligious Affairs and keeps the range of Hispanic concerns before his fellow bishops with assertiveness and skill. He has also spoken to the concerns of the Hispanic community in ecumenical and Catholic contexts and in several international encounters, including CELAM (the Council of Latin American Episcopal Conferences).[5] Bishop Ricardo Ramírez of Las Cruces, New Mexico has also spoken effectively to the issues.[6] He has proposed a meeting of ecumenical leaders in the U.S. Hispanic community, with the involvement of some of the Latin American community represented by CELAM and CLAI (the Latin American Council of Churches). More will be said about an initial March 1995 meeting generated by Bishop Ramírez's suggestions.

The diocesan ecumenical officer and the ecumenical commission is another dimension of leadership that can bring the Hispanic voice into

4. Jeffrey Gros, "Towards a Hermeneutics of Piety for the Ecumenical Movement," *Ecumenical Trends* 22, no. 1 (1993): 1–12.

5. "El Sacerdote Hispano en el Ecumenismo," an address to the National Association of Hispanic Priests, forthcoming, in English, in *The Priest*. Cf. also National Council of Catholic Bishops, *The Phenomenon of the Sects and the New Religious Movements: A Challenge to the New Evangelization* (Washington, D.C.: United States Catholic Conference Office of Publishing and Promotion Services, 1997).

6. Ricardo Ramírez, "Bringing Ecumenism to Hispanic Christians," *Origins* 22, no. 3 (1992): 40–4; "Together in Pilgrimage Toward the Third Millennium," *Ecumenical Trends* 24 (1995): 81–2, 91–6; "The Crisis in Ecumenism Among Hispanic Catholics," *Origins* 24, no. 40 (1995): 660–6; and "Toward a More Perfect Union: The Challenge of Ecumenism," *Ecumenical Trends* 25 (1996): 155–60.

the ecumenical sphere and the ecumenical discussion closer to Hispanic leadership. Each diocese is directed to have an ecumenical officer and to develop a commission to implement the ecumenical program of the Church.[7] At present, only one diocese has assigned and trained a Hispanic for this role, though in several dioceses Hispanics are quite effectively involved in local and statewide ecumenism. An important challenge before the Church, as an institution, is to engage more Hispanics in diocesan and national ecumenical leadership and provide the necessary training. The ecumenical officers, along with their Hispanic affairs staff counterparts, are initiating a study of ecumenism in the Latino community.

As Roman Catholics only thirty years into this long pilgrimage toward healing the alienation of centuries, we have come a long way. However, this progress entails a tremendous burden to share among our people. For this reason, it is my position that the most challenged group in the Church today, from an ecumenical point of view, are the pastoral agents who have to preach, catechize, and evangelize our people in both the ecumenical vision and the content of thirty years of dialogue.

If we look at the last fifty years, we note three distinct stages in Catholic ecumenism. We have moved, as a Church, from (1) the "getting to know you" stage, to (2) a stage of serious theological engagement, and on to (3) action with Churches to cement the stages toward full communion. Of course various individuals, parishes, and dioceses are at different places in this ecumenical pilgrimage.[8]

The controversies of 431 and 450 with the Assyrian and Oriental Orthodox have been laid to rest, which means that the teaching of early Church history is radically revised. We have recognized theological agreements on eucharist and ministry with the Anglicans, though because of the ordination question we are not yet able to act on them.[9] With the Lutherans we are on the verge of a Joint Declaration on Justification by Faith, the doctrine that is the cornerstone of the Reformation.[10]

7. Pontifical Council for Promoting Christian Unity, *Directory for the Application of the Principles and Norms of Ecumenism* (Boston, Mass., Pauline Books and Media, 1993).

8. John Hotchkin, "The Ecumenical Movement's Third Stage," *Origins* 25, no. 21 (1995): 353–61; Jeffrey Gros, "Reception and Roman Catholicism for the 1990s," *One in Christ* 31, no. 4 (1995): 295–328.

9. Christopher Hill and Edward Yarnold, *Anglicans and Roman Catholics: The Search for Unity* (London: SPCK/CTS, 1994); Rozanne Elder, Ellen Wondra, Jeffrey Gros, eds., *Common Witness to the Gospel: Documents on Anglican-Roman Catholic Relations (1983–1995)* (Washington, D.C.: United States Catholic Conference Office of Publishing and Promotion Services, 1997).

10. H. George Anderson, T. Austin Murphy, and Joseph A. Burgess, eds.,

If these actions by the magisterium are to have any pastoral effect, their translation into preaching and catechetical life are essential.

In addition to the decisions made by the Churches in the third phase of ecumenical development, there is a rich harvest of other dialogues that provides resources for our pastoral contact and also augers well for our pilgrimage toward full communion. Dialogues with Presbyterians and Reformed, Methodists, Disciples of Christ, and Polish National Catholics are all oriented toward full communion.[11] There are other dialogues with the Southern Baptists, Pentecostals and other Evangelicals oriented toward mutual understanding, though not full communion.[12] These dialogues include the results of work with the World Council of Churches, of whose Faith and Order Commission the Catholic Church has been a full member since 1968. They create a major resource for pastoral agents in their task of ecumenical formation.[13]

While most of these important results exist in Spanish, we are in the early stages of providing them in a catechetical form that will serve our pastoral needs.[14] Indeed, a challenge for our catechetical leadership, in all of our communities, including the Hispanic, is to provide educationally competent, user-friendly ecumenical pastoral resources grounded in the dialogues but serving the concrete needs of our people. In the next stage we will be able to move effectively from dialogue to decision only if we incorporate the level of agreement already achieved into our preaching, catechesis, and pastoral life while taking into account the cultural context and pastoral needs of each community.

It is my hope that the Synod for America that took place at the end of 1997 will be a stimulus for deeper collaboration within the hemi-

Justification by Faith (Minneapolis: Augsburg/Fortress Press, 1985).

11. Harding Meyer and Lukas Vischer, eds., *Growth in Agreement: Reports and Agreed Statements of Ecumenical Conversations on a World Level* (Mahwah, N.J.: Paulist Press, 1984); Joseph Burgess and Jeffrey Gros, eds., *Growing Consensus* (Mahwah, N.J.: Paulist Press, 1995); Jeffrey Gros and Joseph Burgess, eds., *Building Unity* (Mahwah, N.J.: Paulist Press, 1989).

12. "'Perspectives on Koinonia,' Final Report of the International Roman Catholic/Pentecostal Dialogue (1985–1989)," *Pneuma* 12, no. 2 (1990): 117–42; Baptist-Roman Catholic International Conversation, "Summons to Witness to Christ in Today's World," 1984–1988, *Information Service*, 1989, 5–14; Jeffrey Gros, "Southern Baptists Affirm the Future of Dialogue With the Roman Catholic Church," *Ecumenical Trends* 24, no. 2 (1995): 4–6; Basil Meeking and John Stott, *Evangelical Roman Catholic Dialogue on Mission* (Grand Rapids, Mich.: Wm. B. Eerdmans Publishing Company, 1986).

13. Michael Kinnamon and Brian E. Cope, eds., *The Ecumenical Movement: An Anthology of Basic Texts and Voices* (Grand Rapids, Mich.: Wm B. Eerdmans Publishing Company, 1997).

14. Adolfo Gonzalez Montes, *Enchiridion Oecumenicum*, vols. 1 and 2 (Salamanca: Universidad Pontificia, 1986, 1993).

sphere on every level, especially social justice and ecumenism.[15] In any case, it should be an opportunity for Catholics in the United States to realize that they are both a minority and latecomers to this hemisphere, and that we have much to learn from the Iberoamerican, Native American, and African American majority.

THE ECUMENICAL CHALLENGE OF THE HISPANIC CATHOLIC COMMUNITY

When we began the renewal of the Council in the 1960s, we were quite naive. We presumed that there would be immediate conversion to this process of reconciliation for which we had been praying for decades and a relatively uniform reception for the new and clear priority of ecumenism in the Roman Catholic Church. We soon learned the dynamics of reception, the politics of ecclesial life, and the complexity of inculturation of the conciliar vision.

When I worked in the South Bronx parish of St. Augustine's in the late 60s, the parish was Hispanic and African American with mostly Irish American staff. We had very good ecumenical collaboration with the Methodist parish, which was Hispanic, and the Episcopal parish, which was Jamaican. When I returned to New York City in the 80s and was placed on the ecumenical commission by Cardinal O'Connor, we tried with no success to get a representative recommended by the Hispanic Affairs office of the Archdiocese to be on the commission. This experience, and many others, have made it clear to me that ecumenism, like liturgy and spirituality, has to be inculturated into each community according to the gifts, needs, politics, and challenges of each. Likewise, like almost any other dimension of Church life, ecumenism is able to be politicized in ways that inhibit renewal and allow subjective and ideological elements to challenge the process of evangelization.

In this section, I would like ask about the ecumenical officer's service to the reconciling mission of the Church in the context of the His-

15. Lineamenta for the Synod of Bishops' General Secretariat for Special Assembly for America, "Encounter with the Living Jesus Christ: The Way to Conversion, Communion and Solidarity in America," *Origins* 26, no. 10 (1996): 146–64; Jeffrey Gros, "An Agenda for Unity of the Church in the Western Hemisphere: Encounter with the Living Christ: The Way to Conversion, Communion and Solidarity in America," *Journal of Hispanic/Latino Theology* 4, no. 2 (1996): 6–33; Jeffrey Gros, "A Synod for America: One More Stage of Reception," *Ecumenical Trends* 25 (1996): 146–54. Special September issues of the Canadian journal *Ecumenism* and the CELAM journal *Medellín* will be devoted to the ecumenical dimension of the Synod, with articles from Latin America, Canada, and the United States.

panic Catholic community. We still lack information about the specific ecumenical programs and successes among the variety of U.S. dioceses and the Hispanic ecumenical priorities of each.

What are the views of the diocesan Hispanic ministry coordinators regarding their ecumenical task? How do they see the ecumenical dimension of that ministry? What are the ecumenical successes in their contexts? What are the challenges they face in promoting this dimension of the Church's mission? From both ecumenists and Hispanic ministers, it would be useful to know what resources can be shared with other dioceses and what national organizations can do to enhance the ecumenical work in the Hispanic community.

Likewise, it would also be useful to know the best strategy for helping those who come from Spain and Latin America to minister within the U.S. Hispanic community. How do we equip them with the ecumenical formation they need to know the U.S. cultural context, the ecumenical program of the U.S. Churches, and the demography and ecumenical partners of the particular context in which they will minister?

Bishop Rodríguez provided some specific challenges to the Hispanic priests regarding the needs for ecumenical formation of themselves, for the pastoral agents with whom they work and for their people. Of course, it is also important to include ecumenical formation in the training of those from the U.S. Church who will serve in various parts of Latin America. Fortunately, the ecumenical office of CELAM, SECUM, has recently done a survey of the episcopal conferences, which elucidates their ecumenical program.[16] Likewise, CELAM offers courses in ecumenism each year and is in the process of rebuilding the ecumenical structures of episcopal conferences across the continent.[17]

Pastoral leadership in ecumenical relationships needs, of course, to be adapted to the context of the diocese, to the particular ecumenical context, and to the varieties of cultures represented in the Hispanic community. The older settled communities that became part of the United States through the treaty of Guadalupe-Hidalgo, the earlier generations of Hispanics, and the newer immigrants all have unique gifts and challenges.

16. Juan Carols Urrea, ed., *Informes Reuniones Regionales* (Santafé de Bogotá: Sección de Ecumenismo y Diálogo Interreligioso, 1996).

17. In 1972 the ecumenical division was downgraded to a section (Sección de Ecumenismo y Diálogo Interreligioso, SECUM) and given the nonecumenical responsibility for "documenting the sects and new religious movements." In the period 1995–1999 an impressive plan has been put into place that will begin to reorganize the ecumenical program in a proactive systematic way. Consejo Episcopal Latinoamericano (CELAM), "Programación Ecuménica de 1995–1999," *Renovación Ecuménica* 27, no. 116 (1995): 6–8.

In the United States, with its five million Protestant Hispanics, interChurch marriages are much more frequent than would have been the experience of recent immigrants. The variety of religious groups active among immigrants, some of whom are less ecumenical or positive about Catholicism than the ecumenical Christian Churches, is often a burden on tightly knit Hispanic family life and confuses the ecumenical agenda.

The centrality and importance of popular religion in the Hispanic community is often quite alien to the culture and priorities of classical ecumenical work, especially with Protestant partners. In the United States we are fortunate that we have some pioneering ecumenical work on Mary, which should become a resource for the Church worldwide.[18]

However, experience and reflection are the ways in which the understanding of popular religion can be enhanced in addition to careful academic work. Ecumenical participation in pilgrimages, for example, enhances understanding and begins to lay the basis for true reconciliation in trust, interest, and sensitivity.

There are many examples I can share, but one summer's period in San José, Costa Rica with the Seminario Bíblico is particularly memorable. Two of us, myself (a Roman Catholic) and a Wesleyan scholar of Pentecostalism, traveled together. I had the opportunity to reflect with him on the variety of Marian pieties: Fatima, Guadalupe, Nuestra Señora de los Angeles, etc. We discussed their devotion, social correlates, and political implications. He shared with me the meaning of the obscure millennial charts, so prevalent among the Protestant dispensationalists of Central America. It has also been gratifying to see the ecumenical volume, *Mary in the New Testament,* showing up in Protestant book stores in Latin America.

There is an ambivalence when we see Catholic practices emerging in Latino Protestant communities, where there are significant numbers of Christians whose culture is Catholic but who came to active faith through Protestant hospitality or preaching. We have to find ways of making painful separations develop, over time, into a ground on which reconciliation can be built.

On the institutional level, Bishop Ramirez has suggested a meeting of ecumenical leaders in the Hispanic community. There has been some

18. Cf. Joseph Burgess, ed., *Christ the One Mediator, Mary and the Saints* (Minneapolis: Augsburg/Fortress Press, 1992); Raymond Brown, et. al., *Mary in the New Testament* (Minneapolis: Augsburg/Fortress Press, 1978); William Rusch, "The Formulation of the Marian Dogmas as an Ecclesiological and Ecumenical Problem," *Dialogue* 25 (1986); George Tavard, *The Thousand Faces of the Virgin Mary* (Collegeville, Minn.: The Liturgical Press, 1996).

reluctance to encourage such an initiative among some Catholic leaders. However, to begin the process there was a meeting of bishops from
the Committees for Ecumenical Relations and for Hispanic Affairs, with
representatives of CELAM invited.[19] The meeting produced modest results, but the process of assessing the ecumenical contribution and needs
in the Hispanic community and creating the first link with CELAM's
ecumenical section, SECUM, was a first for the NCCB.[20]

The commitment and the specific recommendations do set a tone
and provide a basis for further development, should the leadership take
up the task: (1) the specific and diverse Hispanic contexts, the need to
identify the specific character of Hispanic ecumenism, the need to listen to and share the successful ecumenical experiences in the variety of
cultures within the United States and in Latin America; (2) the need to
develop papers to help us understand the various approaches to religious liberty, evangelism/proselytism, the relationship of immigrant
groups and their home cultures, the relationships and roots of
non-Catholic groups to their home denominations and cultures, and
the context of Protestant millennialism and apocalypticism of the year
2000; (3) the possibility of a meeting of U.S. Hispanic Christian leaders,
Catholic and Protestant, on some of the themes mentioned above; and
(4) further meetings of NCCB and CELAM bishops over the ecumenical themes of this consultation and the Synod of America.[21]

Recommendations 2 and 4 have already been taken up, to a limited
degree, in the sharing of information between CELAM and the NCCB;
the ecumenical sections of both are involved in the inter-American bishops meetings. Recommendation 3, the original proposal of Bishop
Ramírez, will require leadership from within the Catholic community,
preferably episcopal leadership, if it is to be successful. Recommendation 1 will require further study, possibly by the Diocesan Ecumenical
Officers, and will require the attention of the seminaries, catechetical

19. NCCB/CELAM, "Fostering Ecumenism in the U.S. Hispanic Community," *Origins* 24, no. 40 (1995): 657–60; "Perspectivas de Ecumenismo en las
Américas hacia el tercer milenio," *Renovación Ecuménica* 28, no. 117 (1996): 9–
10.

20. Since that time, there has been a direct interchange between the Consejo
Episcopal Latinoamericano (CELAM)/Sección de Ecumenismo y Diálogo
Interreligioso (SECUM) and the U.S. National Conference of Catholic Bishops
(NCCB)/Bishops' Committee for Ecumenical and Interreligious Affairs
(BCEIA), with some joint participation in meetings sponsored by the Latin
America Secretariat of the NCCB and staff participation in a SECUM planning
meeting in 1997. This picks up on relationships in place in the 1969–1971 pe-
riod when Bernard Law and Jorge Mejía were on staff.

21. "Ecumenism in the Hispanic Community."

centers, and other institutions responsible for ecumenical formation of those serving the Hispanic community.

Many on the local level will be challenged to find the appropriate ways of adapting the ecumenical agenda to concrete local cultural contests, including local and diocesan ecumenical commissions, ecumenical agencies, state councils of Churches, city ministerial organizations, and various networks in the Hispanic community. They will also need to see to it that concerns of these communities—their successes and challenges—are articulated for the wider Church so that they can provide a basis for ecumenical direction and show national and international leadership how best to be of service to the ecumenical needs of these local situations.

The National Catholic Education Association, for example, has provided some important resources and direction in multicultural education. Similar initiatives in ecumenical formation and in culturally specific ecumenical learning would be welcome pastoral resources. The Liturgical Conference has begun to provide ecumenical bilingual worship resources and to publish articles relevant to Hispanic ecumenical liturgical concerns. As the Protestant Spanish hymnals emerge, it will be fascinating to see how the ecumenical liturgical scholarship and the elements of the various Hispanic cultures not endemic to North Atlantic Protestantism will be integrated.[22]

However, the most significant pastoral impetus will come undoubtedly, at this stage in Hispanic ecumenical development, from those committed and converted Hispanic leaders who equip themselves to provide all of us leadership in knowing how to be attentive to the needs, theological issues, and institutional forms that will best serve the ecumenical dimension of Church ministry for the future.

PLURALISM AND THE NEW EVANGELIZATION

Since 1972 the ecumenical program of CELAM has been diminished.[23] With the emergence of religious pluralism in cultures with a past Catholic

22. Justo González, ed., *¡Alabadle! Hispanic Christian Worship* (Nashville, Abingdon Press, 1996).

23. Cf. Jeffrey Gros, "An Agenda for Unity," 17, Juan Carlos Urrea, "La reflexión episcopal acerca del ecumenismo en América Latina y el Caribe," in the September 1997 issues of *Ecumenism* and *Medellín*, discussed above in note 15. Cf. also Javier Darío Restrepo, *CELAM 40 Años Serviendo e Integrando: Datos Para Una Historia* (Santafé de Bogotá: Consejo Episcopal Latinoamericano, 1995), especially the 1982 exchange of letters between Cardinal Alfonso Lópes Trujillo and World Council General Secretary, Dr. Philip Potter, p. 128.

hegemony, it is necessary to sort out who are the various "others," the minorities with whom one lives, as the Church begins to develop its ecumenical work. Since the Puebla conference (1979) major attention has been given to defend "against the invasion of the sects," or as it might be more easily understood, documenting the emerging plural- ism and developing strategies for a Church in mission.

In Latin America—and therefore in the U.S. Hispanic community as well—it is essential that distinctions be made between the ecumeni- cal Churches, nonecumenical Christian groups, groups of Christian ori- gin like Mormons and Witnesses, and the non-Christian movements of various sorts.[24] Giving priority to these sociological studies is not a task of ecumenism, however necessary they are in outlining Catholic iden- tity in a pluralistic world. It can easily be used as an excuse to avoid the conversion and Catholic priorities entailed in being faithful to Christ's will for the unity of the Church.

The Roman Catholic Church, as the largest Christian Church, espe- cially where it is the majority population, bears a particular responsi- bility for ecumenical leadership. As the largest Church in the United States, Catholic ecumenism is essential if there is to be reconciliation among the Churches. However, in Latin America, there is sometimes a defensiveness about ecumenism for a variety of reasons.[25] Some of this defensiveness has begun to enter into the concerns of U.S. Hispanic leadership because of the activity of some more offensive groups among the new immigrants.

24. CELAM has produced a rich literature to help its episcopal confer- ences understand this new experience of pluralism, and has developed more resources in this field than are yet available on specifically ecumenical themes. Cf. Tony Mifsud, ed., *El Fenómeno de las Sectas in América Latina* (Santafé de Bogotá: Instituto Teológico-Pastoral para América Latina, 1996).
25. Lineamenta no. 42, "In countries where the vast majority of the people have traditionally been Catholic—like Latin American countries—these ecu- menical initiatives are undertaken with caution so as not to endanger the faithful's adherence to the Church's doctrine, their participation in the Church's liturgical and sacramental life, and their practice of traditions and activities which express their faith." Some would question the catholicity of a faith that was not able to promulgate Roman Catholic teaching on the unity of the Church, the call to spiritual conversion and liturgical participation with fellow Chris- tians on the road to unity, or the loyalty and self assurance to maintain a prac- tice through conviction that transcends external cultural supports. Some Latin Americans would see this perspective as patronizing and stereotypical. How- ever, this debate on pluralism is an internal debate among the Latin American episcopal conferences, and does not divide along North-South lines. Cf. Jef- frey Gros, "Culture Wars: The Larger Picture," *New Theological Review* 6, no. 4 (1993): 79–87.

These newly arrived Latino Catholics do not bring with them the experience of pluralism. They also lack the formation to witness to their Catholic heritage in an articulate and assertive fashion within a pluralistic and evangelistic culture.

In the United States we do not use the "sects" language to speak of one another, except in the most common and pejorative way.[26] Even the academic community has moved away from the old Church/sect/denomination typology, in the context of the plurality of religious movements in our culture.[27] The language of the Vatican, "new religious movements," is problematic since some of these groups are almost as old as our nation.

It is our preference to call the other by the language they would prefer to use of themselves, no matter how distasteful their beliefs and practices. We have very different histories, approaches to religious liberty, and experiences of pluralism.[28] It is important for our catechesis to understand the groups that are not ecumenical and are offensive in their practice; yet such understanding does not relate to the ecumenical commitment of the Church in itself.

At a recent meeting of CELAM and NCCB bishops on the theme of "The Sects and New Religious Movements and the Challenge of the New Evangelization," there was considerable debate even about the use of the word "sects." While a vote was not taken, in the final report the word, or any other language designating the "other," was not used because even those bishops who felt the language could be retained did not have sufficient agreement regarding the groups to which it should be applied.

In fact, the pastoral recommendations and proposals for the Synod concerned themselves with Roman Catholic internal biblical, sacramental, and catechetical renewal; positive dialogue with the ecumenical

26. Jean-Pierre Ruiz, "Naming the Other: U.S. Hispanic Catholics, the So-Called 'Sects,' and the 'New Evangelization,'" *Journal of Hispanic/Latino Theology* 4, no. 2 (1996): 34–59. In Latin America, it is increasingly difficult to use "sects" language, since the prefered use in Chile and Brazil, for example, it to talk about "religous pluralism." Cf. National Conference of Catholic Bishops, *The Phenomenon of the Sects*, 10, no. 1.

27. "Vatican Report on Sects, Cults and New Religious Movements," *Origins* 16, no. 1 (1986), 1–10; The Vatican Working Group on New Religious Movements, *Sects and New Religious Movements* (Washington, D.C.: United States Catholic Conference Office of Publishing and Promotion Services, 1995); John A. Saliba, *Understanding New Religious Movements* (Grand Rapids, Mich.: Wm. B. Eerdmans Publishing Company, 1995).

28. Cf. Jeffrey Gros, "*Dignitatis Humanae* and Ecumenism: A Foundation and A Promise," in *Religious Liberty: Paul VI and Dignitatis Humanae*, ed. John T. Ford (Brescia: Pubblicazioni dell'Istituto Paolo VI, 1995), 117–48.

Churches; a renewed Catholic missionary outreach; and the nurturing of a robust, self-confident, and ecumenically informed Catholic spirituality.[29]

Likewise, concerns about proselytism can put some Catholic leaders on the defensive. Like the language of "sects," the definitions are notoriously varied and imprecise.[30] However, even some less than sci-

29. National Conference of Catholic Bishops, *The Phenomenon of the Sects.* One can note that the catechetical directives from CELAM leadership take the same, more positive approach: "Preparar en nuestras sociedades pluriculturales a los catequistas para educar la religiosidad popular, fortalecer la identidad católica, defender al pueblo de Dios contra los ataques sectarios, favorecer la colaboración ecuménica y capacitar para el diálogo interconfessional y con los no creyentes."Consejo Episcopal Latinoamericano, *Hacia Una Catequesis Inculturada* (Santafé de Bogotá: CELAM, 1995), 397.

30. From the Roman Catholic perspective, the understanding of proselytism begins with the question of religious liberty (*Dignitatis Humanae*, Joint Working Group of the World Council of Churches and the Roman Catholic Church, The Challenge of Proselytism and the Calling to Common Witness, 1995, Information Service 91: 1–11, 77–82.). The term is used to describe activities "of Christians to win adherents from other Christian communities. These activities may be more obvious or more subtle. They may be of unworthy motives or by unjust means that violate the conscience of the human person; or even if proceeding with good intentions, their approach ignores the Christian reality of other Churches or their particular approaches to pastoral practice" (§18). It "embraces whatever violates the right of the human person . . . to be free from external coercion in religious matters, or whatever in the proclamation of the Gospel does not conform to the ways God draws free persons to himself in response to his call to serve in spirit and in truth." Proselytism stands in opposition to all ecumenical efforts, and includes such acts as the following: (1) making unjust or uncharitable references to other Churches; (2) making unfavorable comparisons between two Christian communities; (3) using physical or psychological violence to pressure others to one's views; (4) using political, social, and economic power as a means for winning new members; (5) offering education, health care, or material inducements to make converts; (6) exploiting people's needs, weaknesses, or lack of education, especially in situations of distress. Suggested steps forward: (1) encourage prayer for one another among Christians; (2) develop adequate Christian formation, equipping people to share their faith, including ecumenical programs that foster respect and understanding; (3) develop knowledge of and sensitivity to the existing groups in a particular community, especially the distinction between aggressive proselytizing groups and ecumenical partners; (4) avoid prejudicial and inflammatory publications and reporting; (5) learn the history of other groups from their own perspective; (6) work ecumenically to consider how to respond pastorally and firmly to practices of proselytism not in harmony with religious liberty; (7) study ecumenically how service can be transparent to the Gospel and not a means of tension; (8) include in discussions representatives of Christian groups accused of proselytism (§32). Honest Christian hospitality, free sharing of one's convictions and truth claims, and uncoerced calling to

entific studies show that the problems the Church faces are internal and demand Catholic pastoral renewal. They should not stand in the way of ecumenical outreach and ecumenical formation.[31] In the reading of this author, the lessons could be summarized as follows:

(1) We do need to help Catholic people differentiate between the variety of Churches and religious groups with whom they live. *However*, we also want to help enable our people to live in a pluralistic society where the Vatican Council teaching on religious liberty is honored, and our Catholic people are able to sustain their faith and share it evangelistically, like other faithful Christians. We hope our people's Catholic identity and evangelical zeal will be reinforced by pluralism and by ecumenical dialogue. (2) We realize that the experience of pluralism and the open sharing of faith among groups is quite different in cultures other than our own; immigrants often are unprepared for the free interchange of ideas. Our catechetical work must therefore include developing in each individual and family a vision of the Church and its mission. (3) Studies about proselytism have shown that a lack of hospitality, coupled with a certain racism in the Roman Catholic community, results in the loss of new arrivals to the Church. Additionally, Roman Catholic pastoral agents often do not know the Church's distinction between proselytism and appropriate Christian hospitality and evangelism. They need the ecumenical formation to know the work that the Catholic Church has done with other groups on this subject. While some proselytism does occur, its frequency is much less the cause of the loss of Catholics than the kind of Christian hospitality not provided by the Catholic Church but made available by other Christians.

Pastoral effectiveness will entail preparing pastoral agents who can help our people understand and adapt to religious pluralism, move beyond a merely cultural Catholicism without sacrificing any of the gifts of their cultures, and bring a secure and solid witness to the gifts of the Catholic Church to the pluralistic religious culture in which they live.

For those of us who have been used to dealing with Witnesses at the door since the age of ten, who have Mormon and Pentecostal relatives in the family or who have lived most of our lives amid fundamen-

---

active Christian faith nominal Christians is not considered proselytism. "It is not enough to denounce proselytism. We need to continue to prepare ourselves for genuine common Christian witness through common prayer, common retreats, Bible courses, Bible sharing, study and action groups, religious education jointly or in collaboration, joint or coordinated pastoral and missionary activity, a common service in humanitarian matters and theological dialogue" (§35).

31. Eleace King, *Proselytism and Evangelization: An Exploratory Study* (Washington, D.C.: Center for Applied Research in the Apostolate, 1991).

talist majorities, our Catholic identities are quite clear. We are used to expressing the content of our faith to others in civil discourse or even argument. We certainly know the difference between fellow ecumenical Christians and the *sectarian* spirit, even when it shows up among Catholics.

We have experience with some aggressive groups from the evangelical community who have grown to be more collaborative through Catholic collaboration, like Bill Bright's Campus Crusade and Chuck Colson's Prison Fellowship. Some evangelical groups, like World Vision International have even produced a nonproselytizing policy of collaboration with Catholics and Orthodox when they work among them. Of course, for collaboration an ecumenically formed Catholic partner is necessary.

However, part of the cross cultural sensitivity to which we are called in any community, including the Hispanic, is to understand how this pluralistic environment is experienced by fellow Catholics, how we can equip one another for dealing with it, and how we can take a proactive stance in both evangelical and ecumenical outreach. One does not need to affirm or deny the religious value of living in a pluralistic context to know this is the reality of the Catholic future. It is in this context that we form our identity and toward which we direct our ministry.

Ecumenism is central to the New Evangelization as outlined in the thinking of Pope John Paul, and it is an integral part of the reception of Catholic identity as outlined in Vatican II. As the ecumenical priority of the Catholic Church is inculturated in the United States, Hispanic communities will be enriched by learning from one another and the new challenges the Lord will provide us on the pilgrimage toward full unity.

As Pope John Paul reminds us: "The quest for Christian unity is not a matter of choice or expediency, but a duty that springs from the very nature of the Christian community. Concern for restoring unity pertains to the whole Church, faithful and clergy alike. It extends to everyone, according to the ability of each, whether it be exercised in daily Christian living or in theological and historical studies, to believe in Christ means to desire unity; to desire unity means to desire the Church; to desire the Church means to desire the communion of grace that corresponds to the Father's plan from all eternity. Such is the meaning of Christ's prayer: '*Ut unum sint.*'" [32]

---

32. John Paul, *Ut Unum Sint* (Boston, Mass.: Pauline Books and Media, 1995), §9. Consejo Episcopal Latinoamericano, *La Encíclica, Ut Unum Sint: Comentarios* (Santafé de Bogotá: Sección de Ecumenismo y Diálogo Inter-religioso, 1996).

9

Bearing False Witness

JOSÉ ANTONIO RUBIO

There are two Catholic biblical stories that have always appealed to me: one is the story of Susanna, the other is the story of Tobit's wife, Anna. The story of Susanna (Daniel 13), like so many in the Bible, has a disconcertingly modern ring to it. Two lecherous men, both elders of the community and well-respected, falsely accuse Susanna of committing adultery (a capital offense) because she will not give in to their sexual advances. The story of Anna is more domestic—it could happen today in any family—and a bit comical:

> At that time my wife Anna worked for hire at weaving cloth, the kind of work women do. When she sent back the goods to their owners, they would pay her. Late in winter she finished the cloth and sent it back to the owners. They paid her the full salary, and also gave her a young goat for the table. On entering my house, the goat began to bleat. I called to my wife and said: "Where did this goat come from? Perhaps it was stolen! Give it back to its owners; we have no right to eat stolen food! But she said to me, "It was given to me as a bonus over and above my wages." Yet I would not believe her; and told her to give it back to its owners. I became very angry with her over this. So she retorted: "Where are your charitable deeds now? Where are your virtuous acts? See! Your true character is finally showing itself!" Grief-stricken in spirit, I groaned and wept aloud. Then with sobs I began to pray. (Tob. 2:11–3:1 NAB)

I mention these stories because they come from sections of the Bible called *canonical* by the Catholic Church and *apocryphal* by Protestant believers and because they could be parables for the way Catholics and Pentecostals sometimes relate to each other: at times like the elders in the story of Susanna, saying false things about each other; at other times like Tobit, not believing what the other says about herself.

We see this particularly when we look at popular religious literature. Articles in theological journals tend to be respectful and accurate, but few laypeople read them. On the other hand, the books that have a wider readership are the ones that tend to bear false witness, and these

JOSÉ ANTONIO RUBIO

are the works that form attitudes and perceptions among large groups of believers. This paper, then, will discuss popular books that are readily available in religious bookstores and compare them with articles in theological journals. Such a comparison is both fair and necessary because it is popular literature that has the wider readership and the most impact.

PENTECOSTAL MISINFORMATION AND MISCONCEPTIONS

On the Pentecostal side, one book in particular that is fraught with misinformation is Jimmy Swaggart's book, published in 1986, *Catholicism and Christianity*.[1] Jimmy Swaggart is a Pentecostal Televangelist with a large following who wrote his book long after the Catholic-Pentecostal dialogue was well underway. The book is very polemical against the Catholic Church, for its very title implies that Catholicism is not a part of Christianity. I realize that Jimmy Swaggart has been disfellowshipped from the Assemblies of God and as of this writing has not been reinstated. Nevertheless, he is Pentecostal and is highly visible; many people watch his television program and buy his books. Although *Catholicism and Christianity* is written in English, his television show is dubbed into Spanish and broadcast on Spanish-language television in the United States and throughout Latin America. The ideas and opinions that appear in the book are also preached on the television program.

In this book Jimmy Swaggart makes many assertions that are simply not true. He avers, for example, that "The Catholic Church teaches that the layman should not read the Bible. . . ."[2] This is not true. He uses the present tense, but it would not even be true if he had used the past tense. I have often heard that Catholics were not encouraged to read the Bible before the Second Vatican Council, but that statement does not coincide with my own experience. I grew up before the Council, and as long as I can remember we always had a Bible at home and read it. While Jimmy Swaggart's statement does not coincide with my personal experience, I know that he is not the only Pentecostal who believes that Catholics are forbidden to read the Bible. Cecil Robeck, while acknowledging that it is not true, mentions that many Pentecostals nevertheless still believe that "the Roman Catholic Church is not serious about the Bible."[3]

In discussing the Inquisition, Jimmy Swaggart writes, "In totality, it is estimated that the Roman Catholic Church murdered some *twenty*

1. Jimmy Swaggart, *Catholicism and Christianity* (Baton Rouge, La.: Jimmy Swaggart Ministries, 1986).
2. Ibid., 15.
3. Cecil M. Robeck, "Evangelization or Proselytism of Hispanics? A Pentecostal Perspective," *Journal of Hispanic/Latino Theology* 4, no. 4 (1997): 59.

million people during the existence of the Inquisition."[4] There may not even have been twenty million people in those countries of western Europe that had an Inquisition. As an example of how false the statement is, one can mention that in three hundred years of the Inquisition in all of Hispanic America only eighteen Protestants were executed.[5] This is not to defend the Inquisition: it cannot be justified today and one execution is one too many. On the other hand, it is irresponsible to claim twenty million executions; it goes beyond exaggeration. *The New Catholic Encyclopedia*, while not giving numbers when speaking of those given the death penalty by the Inquisition, avers that "this penalty, however, was something exceptional."[6] The *Encyclopedia Judaica*, hardly a pro-Inquisition source, does give some statistics: "It is estimated that in Spain, from the establishment of the Inquisition down to 1808 [when it was abolished], the number of heretics burned in person was 31,912. . . ."[7] This is quite a difference from twenty million. Publishing such an over-exaggerated figure as twenty million is bearing false witness and can only add fuel to the fires of anti-Catholic sentiment.

Another incorrect statement that Jimmy Swaggart makes is that, according to Catholic teaching, "a mortal sin immediately consigns a person to hell, whatever his other spiritual condition. . . ."[8] This statement does not show a correct understanding of the Catholic concept of mortal sin, nor does it take into account the mercy and compassion of God. In this and other statements, he presents a rigid, legalistic Church that is very different from my own experience of Church.

In discussing Catholic devotion to Mary, Jimmy Swaggart writes, "In scores of letters we have received, Catholics maintain that they do not worship Mary. . . . However, . . . the Catholic Church has, in effect, declared her divine and thus renders her worship that should be reserved only for the deity. . . . Yes, Catholics do worship Mary."[9] Here the issue is not only misinformation, but also not believing official Church documents and the testimony of *scores* of Catholics—like Tobit not believing his wife Anna. From my own personal experience, I know that many Pentecostals and other non-Catholic Christians also believe that Catholics do worship Mary. In light of this, simple integrity requires an honest attempt to explain official Catholic doctrine fairly.

4. Swaggart, *Catholicism and Christianity*, 31.

5. Enrique D. Dussel, ed., *Introducción General a la Historia de la Iglesia en América Latina*, Historia General de la Iglesia en América Latina, vol. 1, no.1 (Barcelona: Ediciones Sígueme, 1983), 665.

6. *The New Catholic Encyclopedia*, s.v. "Inquisition."

7. *Encyclopedia Judaica*, s.v. "Inquisition."

8. Swaggart, *Catholicism and Christianity*, 55.

9. Ibid., 107.

Jimmy Swaggart's attitude stands in sharp contrast to that of another Assemblies of God member, the late Jerry Sandidge. His articles, however, have appeared in theological journals and therefore do not have as wide a readership as Swaggart's book. They are not available in Spanish. In an article that appeared in *Pneuma*, the journal of the Society for Pentecostal Studies, Sandidge avers "that Pentecostals have no 'view' or 'theology' of Mary unless it would be in negative terms,"[10] and he admits that Pentecostals are "basically repelled by the whole subject in the first place."[11] Nevertheless, he calls on other Pentecostals to "stretch ourselves and seek to understand more perfectly current Roman Catholic teaching concerning Mary, the Mother of Jesus."[12] He goes on to state:

> For most Pentecostals it is rather easy to object to the Roman Catholic teaching regarding Mary. We have not understood her role in Catholicism. Usually, we object on an emotional level rather than a theological level. But to do this falls short of what is required both by Christian grace and academic respectability.[13]

He adds:

> If there are objections to Catholicism by classical Pentecostals, they should be based upon the latest statements and documents of the Catholic Church and not upon extreme cases, medieval excesses, or even pre-Vatican II practices. It is necessary to read the documents of Vatican II and then to read the books and journal articles by scholars reflecting the spirit and direction of Catholic theology today.[14]

Finally, Jerry Sandidge appeals to Catholics to see Pentecostal concerns, objections and even charges of "idolatry" as stemming "from the Pentecostals' sincere desire to honor Jesus Christ as the only One (besides the other members of the God-head) to Whom worship is due."[15]

CATHOLIC MISINFORMATION AND MISCONCEPTIONS

But, if the shoe fits on one foot, it surely fits on the other. Catholics have been just as guilty in spreading misinformation about Pentecostals. In fact, as Kilian McDonnell writes, "The guilt for bad relations between Catholics and Pentecostals is a two-way street, but it is an unequal street.

10. Jerry L. Sandidge, "A Pentecostal Response to Roman Catholic Teaching on Mary," *Pneuma* 4, no. 2 (1982): 34.
11. Ibid.
12. Ibid., 35.
13. Ibid., 38.
14. Ibid., 41.
15. Ibid., 41.

In this matter Catholics have more to repent of than the Pentecostals. We Catholics need to recognize this, admit our guilt, and take the initiative for reconciliation."[16] Again, it is popular books that are at fault, while less-read articles appearing in theological journals tend to be accurate and fair. In this section, two authors whose works are readily available in Spanish-language Catholic religious bookstores in this country will be contrasted with articles from theological journals.

Juan Díaz Vilar is a Jesuit from Spain who works in New York. He travels widely throughout the country giving conferences and has written many books on a wide variety of topics. His best-known work is probably *Las Sectas: Un desafío a la Pastoral*.[17] (The book is available also in an English language edition.) In it Díaz Vilar describes the beliefs of six *sects*: Seventh Day Adventists, Jehovah's Witnesses, Mormons, Pentecostals, Iglesia de Unificación (Unification Church), and Niños de Dios (Children of God). My first objection to the book is the association of these six groups with each other. I am not sure that Pentecostals want to be associated with the Unification Church or that Jehovah's Witnesses want to be associated with Pentecostals. Placing these groups within the same context is problematic. But, more problematic is the use of the word "sects." In our postmodern culture, the power to name is the power to define. Michel Foucault has spoken of the power to define as the power to locate socially. Thus, the power to name a group as a "Church" or a "sect" matters. In the book of Genesis, Adam names all the animals to show his superiority. If I can then name a group a "sect," by that fact alone I am claiming superiority. I can say that I am only using a scientific, sociologically neutral term after Max Weber or Ernst Troeltsch. But the reality is that to most ears "sect" is not a scientific, neutral term. "Sect" is a derogatory or at least a pejorative term, and to call a group a "sect" gives the group a competitive onus in the free market of religions.

In contrast to Fr. Díaz Vilar, Thomas Rausch, another Jesuit, remarks in the theological journal *One in Christ*:

> Catholics have often been guilty of stereotyping Evangelicals and Pentecostals. Without bothering to distinguish the varieties of Evangelical Christianity, they have tended to dismiss all Evangelicals as fundamentalists. Even the Vatican has failed to distinguish between Evangelical and Pentecostal Churches and groups such as the Mormons and the Jehovah's Witnesses, lumping them all together in its official

16. Kilian McDonnell, "Improbable Conversations: The Classical Pentecostal-Roman Catholic International Dialogue," *One in Christ* 23 (1987): 23.
17. Juan Díaz Vilar, *Las Sectas: Un desafío a la Pastoral*, 3rd rev. ed. (New York: Northeast Hispanic Pastoral Center, 1991).

documents under the term "sects.". . . . In 1993 Cardinal Edward
Cassidy, President of the Pontifical Council for Promoting Christian
Unity, noting that the Catholic Church was in "fruitful dialogue" with
Evangelical and Pentecostal Christians, stated that they should not
be designated as "sects." However, the Cardinal's caution is not al-
ways observed. . . .[18]

Making note to Cardinal Cassidy's statement, Cecil Robeck states
that "it is also important to note that the term "sect" is not a helpful
way of categorizing Hispanic Pentecostals. . . . This fact must be communicated to all levels of the Catholic Church. . . . Continued
name-calling and pigeonholing will only drive a wedge further between
the various parties."[19]

In speaking of Pentecostals, Díaz Vilar also writes about their
"miopía histórica"[20] and "su infantil interpretación de la Biblia."[21] While
one legitimately can question a restorationist view of history that seems
to cancel nineteen hundred years of history and ignore any possibility
of the development of doctrine and what one perceives to be a lack of
scriptural scholarship, it is not necessary to do so by using terms like
"myopic" and "infantile."

Another common objection to Pentecostalism that Díaz Vilar cites
is the issue of social justice. "El *compromiso social* no sólo no lo acentúan,
sino que en general lo ignoran. Generalmente evaden todo lo que sea
compromiso social. . . . Lo malo de esta espiritualidad, entre otras cosas,
es su *falta de compromiso social*."[22]

While it is true that many Pentecostals are not committed to social
justice issues, one could say the same thing about some Catholics. And,
many Pentecostals, particularly Latino Pentecostals, are deeply committed to issues of social justice. Reyes Tijerina who is "a Pentecostal
minister, led the struggle to recover lost land grants in northern New
Mexico;"[23] Eldín Villafañe has been developing a Pentecostal social ethic

18. Thomas P. Rausch, "Catholic-Evangelical Relations: Signs of Progress,"
One in Christ 23, no. 1–2 (1987): 41.
    19. Robeck, "Evangelization or Proselytism," 57.
    20. "myopic view of history," Díaz Vilar, *Las Sectas*, 73.
    21. "their infantile interpretation of the Bible," Ibid., 74.
    22. "They not only do not emphasize a *commitment to social justice*, but in
general they ignore it. They generally avoid anything that might resemble commitment to social justice. . . . What is wrong with this spirituality, among other
things, is its *lack of commitment to social justice*," Ibid., 71, 72.
    23. Edwin E. Sylvest, "Hispanic American Protestantism in the United States,"
in *On the Move: A History of the Hispanic Church in the United States*, ed. Moisés
Sandoval (Maryknoll, N.Y.: Orbis Books, 1990), 127. See also Eldín Villafañe, *The
Liberating Spirit: Toward an Hispanic American Pentcostal Social Ethic* (Grand Rapids,
Mich.: Wm. B. Eerdmans Publishing Company, 1993), 96, 97.

in his book, *The Liberating Spirit: Toward an Hispanic American Pentecostal Social Ethic.*[24]

Several articles that have appeared in theological journals point out that it is unfair to accuse Pentecostals of not being committed to social justice. Kilian McDonnell writes: "though it has been traditional to refer to the lack of social involvement in the evangelical Christians in general and the Pentecostals in particular, Hollenweger shows that the situation is more nuanced than that."[25] In writing about the Brazilian Assembléias de Deus, Walter Hollenweger says that for them, "Political and social engagement goes hand in hand with evangelization."[26] John Burdick mentions that Pentecostals in Brazil are active in neighborhood associations, labor struggles, and even radical party politics.[27] Cecil Robeck mentions, "that there are Pentecostals in Latin America who value major elements of Liberation Theology, who supported the Sandinista government in Nicaragua, who aided the Socialist President Salvador Allende to rise to power in Chile. . . ."[28]

Reporting on the founding of A.M.E.N., a national association of Hispanic Evangelicals that includes Pentecostals, the *Christian Century* wrote:

> An abiding interest in social causes marks a dramatic difference between Hispanic and Anglo evangelicals. Anglos tend to emphasize the personal relationship between each believer and Jesus, and to discount—often as Catholic heresy—any emphasis on good works as a means of salvation. But Hispanics say an approach that de-emphasizes good works neglects the realities of their communities in the U.S. . . . Miranda dismisses the works-and-faith split as an Anglo phenomenon."[29]

Here in the United States Pentecostals often work with the poor in inner cities, or in prison ministry, or with those involved in drugs or alcohol. In San José one Pentecostal Church has a Gang Task Force whose members are on a street corner where gang members often hang out every Friday and Saturday night, Bible in hand, trying to diffuse the

24. Grand Rapids, Mich.: Wm. B. Eerdmans Publishing Company, 1993.

25. Killian McDonnell, "New Dimensions in Research on Pentecostalism," *Worship* 45 (1971): 217.

26. Walter Hollenweger, *The Pentecostals*, trans. R. A. Wilson (London: SCM Press, 1972; reprint, Peabody, Mass.: Hendrickson Publishers, 1988), 80.

27. John Burdick, "Struggling Against the Devil: Pentecostalism and Social Movements in Urban Brazil," in *Rethinking Protestantism in Latin America*, ed. Virginia Garrard-Burnett and David Stoll (Philadelphia: Temple University Press, 1993), 20–44.

28. Cecil M. Robeck, "Southern Religion with a Latin Accent," *Pneuma* 13, no. 2 (1991): 103.

29. "Hispanics Turn Evangelical," *Christian Century* 111, no. 36 (1994): 1183–4.

violence that has so tragically plagued our cities. One could ask, how many Catholic parishes have similar gang task forces?

In concluding the section on Pentecostals, Juan Díaz Vilar asks, "¿Es posible el ecumenismo con los Pentecostales? En general, no, porque donde existe el proselitismo no es posible el diálogo ecuménico."[30] The charge of proselytism is one that has often been leveled at Pentecostals.

"Proselytism," like "sect," is a word that often is used in discussing the activities of Pentecostals. But what exactly does it mean? Like "sect," it did not begin with a negative connotation but was actually a positive word. For example, in the sixth chapter of the Book of Acts, one of the first deacons is Nicolaus "a *proselyte* of Antioch" (Acts 6:5). In the story of the first Pentecost we are told that there were present "Parthians and Medes and Elamites and residents of Mesopotamia, Judea and Cappadocia, Pontus and Asia, Phrygia and Pamphylia, Egypt and the parts of Libya belonging to Cyrene, and visitors from Rome, both Jews and *proselytes*" (Acts 2: 9–10, RSV). Now, however, the word has negative connotations. And often it is hard both to determine its meaning and to distinguish it from evangelization. According to Jean-Pierre Ruiz, a report of the World Council of Churches on Christian witness, proselytism, and religious liberty stated that "objective criteria alone cannot adequately distinguish between the two." Ruiz avers that "the distinction between evangelization and proselytism depends very much on who is doing the distinguishing."[31]

The above mentioned WCC document, "The Challenge of Proselytism and the Calling to Common Witness: A Study Document of the Joint Working Group between the Roman Catholic Church and the World Council of Churches," lists some characteristics of proselytism. They include: making unjust or uncharitable references to other Churches' beliefs and practices and even ridiculing them; comparing two Christian communities by emphasizing the achievements and ideals of one, and the weaknesses and practical problems of the other; employing any kind of physical violence, moral compulsion and psychological pressure . . . ; using political, social, and economic power as a means of winning new members for one's own Church; using explicit or implicit offers of education, health care, or material inducements or using financial resources with the intent of making converts; manipulative at-

---

30. "Is ecumenism possible with Pentecostals? In general, no, because where proselytism exists ecumenical dialogue is not possible." Díaz Vilar, *Las Sectas*, 74.

31. Jean-Pierre Ruiz, "Naming the Other: U.S. Hispanic Catholics, the So-Called 'Sects,' and the 'New Evangelization,'" *Journal of Hispanic/Latino Theology* 4, no. 2 (1996): 44.

titudes and practices that exploit people's needs, weaknesses, or lack of education especially in situations of distress. . . .[32]

Even this list raises some questions. Who is a member of my Church? Who is unChurched? If I was baptized and confirmed as an infant and then had no other religious training at all and grew up in a household that never went to Mass, is it proselytizing if I am approached by a Pentecostal? Cecil Robeck, in an article that appeared in the *Journal of Hispanic/Latino Theology*, feels that Catholics sometimes believe that simply being Latino means that any attempts at ministry to them is proselytism. Referring to the characteristics of proselytism of the WCC report, he writes, "Within the Americas, one or more of these charges is often raised against almost any non-Roman Catholic group who seeks to minister among the Hispanic or Latino communities."[33]

What about televangelism? If I turn on a television program and watch it and then leave the Catholic Church to become a Pentecostal, is that proselytism? What about help that a Church might give in earthquakes, floods, or tornadoes. If I am a victim of some disaster and a non-Catholic Church helps me, and I attend a service out of gratitude and then leave the Catholic Church, would it have been better that I not have received any aid? This reminds me of the story told by Manuel Gaxiola-Gaxiola that "one Archbishop has declared that 'sects are worse than AIDS.'"[34] When is the offer of education, health care, or material aid proselytism, and, more importantly, who makes that decision? Is there legitimate room for persuasion in preaching?

Cecil M. Robeck sees proselytism as occurring when "Christians do not recognize the genuineness or fullness of ecclesial claims made by other communities that call themselves Christian."[35] Is that not what is happening when Catholic doctrine is misrepresented by Pentecostals or when Catholics use terms like "sect" to refer to Pentecostals? Is this not bearing false witness?

Another Catholic priest who has written extensively about Pentecostals is Flaviano Amatulli. Fr. Amatulli, who works in Mexico, was called an authority on "sects" by Allan Deck. Among his many books are *Diálogo con los Protestantes, La Iglesia Católica y el Protestantismo, Las*

---

32. World Council of Churches, "The Challenge of Proselytism and the Calling to Common Witness: A Study Document of the Joint Working Group Between the Roman Catholic Church and the World Council of Churches," *Ecumenical Review* 48, no. 2 (1996): 216.

33. Robeck, "Evangelization or Proselytism," 43.

34. Manuel J. Gaxiola-Gaxiola, "Latin American Pentecostalism: A Mosaic within an Mosaic," *Pneuma* 13, no. 2 (1991): 124.

35. Robeck, "Evangelization or Proselytism," 42.

222   JOSÉ ANTONIO RUBIO

Sectas: Problema y solución.[36] Although his works are printed in Mexico, they are readily available in the United States. Over 100,000 copies of these books have been sold. Like Díaz Vilar he calls Pentecostals "sects" and accuses them of proselytizing.

In Chapter XII of his book, *Diálogo con los Protestantes,* entitled "Principales agrupaciones de Hermanos Separados" (The Main Groupings of the Separated Brethren), he lists alphabetically a number of non-Catholic religious groups. Sandwiched between "Adventistas" and "Anglicanos" are "Aleluyas." He explains, "El pueblo llama 'aleluyas' a los 'pentecostales,' las 'asambleas de Dios,' y las 'Iglesias de Santidad' y a otras agrupaciones protestantes, por repetir continuamente 'aleluya' en sus reuniones."[37] Although that is a popular term that is often applied to Pentecostals, that is not the way to list them in a serious book. It is another example of the "name-calling and pigeonholing " to which Cecil Robeck has referred.

In his book, *La Iglesia Católica y el protestantismo,* Amatulli lists the "Sectas Pentecostales: . . . La Iglesia de Dios (Church of God) . . . El Pilar de Fuego (Pillar of Fire) . . . La Iglesia de Santidad (Holiness Church) . . . La Iglesia del Nazareno (Church of the Nazarene) . . . etc."[38] While the Church of God is a Pentecostal denomination, the Pillar of Fire was founded by Alma White, who divorced her husband because he spoke in tongues! The Holiness Churches are not Pentecostal nor is the Church of the Nazarene. The Church of the Nazarene is a Church of the Wesleyan-Holiness tradition and was originally called *The Pentecostal Church of the Nazarene.* They dropped the term *Pentecostal* in 1919 specifically because it was associated with speaking in tongues, a practice with which they do not agree.[39] In general Amatulli seems to equate Holiness Churches with Pentecostal Churches. Precisely because this is a popular book, one would expect that someone who is an expert should know the difference. Any standard religious reference book or encyclopedia would provide the correct information.

I do not doubt the sincerity of any of these writers, nor do I deny that it is legitimate to explain one's religious beliefs vis-à-vis those of others. However, one needs to make sure that one is correctly interpret-

36. All three were published by Apóstoles de la Palabra in Mexico, D.F.; *Diálogo con los Protestantes* in 1984 and both *La Iglesia Católica y el Protestantismo* and *Las Sectas: Problema y solución* in 1993.

37. "The people call 'Pentecostals,' 'Assemblies of God,' and 'Holiness Churches' and other Protestant groups 'Alleluias' because they continually repeat 'Alleluia' in their services," Amatulli, *Diálogo,* 117.

38. Amatulli, *La Iglesia Católica,* 121.

39. Cecil M. Robeck, "Pentecostals and the Apostolic Faith: Implications for Ecumenism," *One in Christ* 23, no. 1–2 (1987): 126.

ing the beliefs of others. Inaccurate books such as these—on both sides—can only enflame the fires of ill will; they all are examples of bearing false witness.

SOME SUGGESTIONS FOR THE FUTURE

Therefore, what are we to do? First of all, we are to obey the decalogue: "Thou shalt not bear false witness against thy neighbor!" This has to apply not only to individuals, but also to Churches. Kilian McDonnell avers that "Catholics have mistaken notions of what Pentecostals really teach, and vice versa."[40] Not bearing false witness will mean that these mistaken notions will need to be corrected. Cecil Robeck insists that:

> stereotypes of what was, or what might have been, misunderstandings based upon partial truth, and faded memories of old battles from years gone by . . . . The continued propagation of timeworn stereotypes, the anamnesis of ancient divisions, and the failure to investigate fresh evidence, and to allow in others the opportunity for growth and change, perpetuates the bearing of false witness.[41]

Jean-Pierre Ruiz insists that in addition, "For U.S. Hispanic Catholics, that will mean referring to evangelical and Pentecostal Hispanics in the terms according to which they identify themselves rather than with terms that these 'others' resent."[42] This would also mean according to Cecil Robeck, ceasing "name calling, nor making accusations to third parties without first addressing the perceived offender in a direct and loving manner."[43]

Secondly, we need to listen to the ecumenism at the grass roots that is going on between Catholics and Pentecostals. Vinson Synan refers to this when he calls the Pentecostal movement "the most ecumenical force in the world," and qualifies his statement by saying, "I speak here of actual grassroots ecumenical worship and fellowship that has been experienced by literally millions of Christians of practically all denominations."[44] Thomas Rausch insists:

> there can be no real ecumenical progress until Christians in local congregations begin to recognize each other as sharing a common faith and thus as brothers and sisters in the Lord. Thus what is particu-

40. Kilian McDonnell, "The Death of Mythologies: The Classical Pentecostal/Roman Catholic Dialogue," *America* 172, no. 10 (1995): 19.

41. Robeck, "Pentecostals and the Apostolic Faith," 126.

42. Ruiz, 58, 59.

43. Robeck, "Evangelization or Proselytism," 56.

44. Vinson Synan, "Pentecostalism: Varieties and Contributions," *One in Christ* 23, no. 1–2 (1987): 108.

larly significant in relations between Evangelical-Pentecostal Christians and Catholics are the new relationships presently being formed
at the grass roots. In what is a surprising development to many
ecumenists, representatives of these traditions are beginning to recognize the number of concerns they share in common. . . . Even more
significantly, they are beginning to cooperate in ways which only a
few years ago would have seemed impossible.[45]

Ecumenism at the grass roots occurs on the local level when Pentecostal and Catholic clergy meet with each other. Sometimes they appear together to give invocations or benedictions at civic or social affairs. Other times they will both be members of local ministerial alli-
ances or service clubs. At other times they will officiate jointly at a funeral of a member of one Church who has many relatives who belong
to the other. Contacts are made, friendships are formed, and attitudes
are changed. Peter Hocken feels that precisely "the friendships and contacts built up over years have led a growing number of Evangelicals
and Pentecostals to rethink their blanket condemnations of the Roman
Catholic Church."[46]

Equally important are the contacts between lay Catholics and Pentecostals. These occur in various ways. Sometimes a family will be com-
posed of members who are Catholic and members who are Pentecostal.
Many times there are tensions, and sometimes families are so divided
that family members will even refuse to speak with one another. In other
families, however, there is a great deal of mutual charity and respect.
Catholic family members will attend weddings or other functions in a
Pentecostal Church and vice versa and discover that differences exist
alongside similarities. Lay ecumenism also takes place through the charismatic movement in the Catholic Church. Pentecostals may attend a
Catholic charismatic congress. They hear the talks or attend a prayer
service and see Catholics speaking in tongues. They may also attend a
healing service and lay hands on someone who is ill. They may even
attend a Charismatic Mass and be moved to receive communion. This
experience of lay ecumenism among Catholic Charismatics and Pentecostals has often led to a reevaluation of the Pentecostals' attitude toward Catholicism. This is too important an issue to be left to clergy and
other professionals. We need to listen to what the people at the grass
roots are saying to the Churches.

Third, we need to preserve our own identity. There can be no dialogue if we are all the same. I do not want Pentecostals to light candles

45. Rausch, 43.
46. Peter Hocken, "Ecumenical Dialogue: The Importance of Dialogue with
Evangelicals and Pentecostals." *One in Christ* 30, no. 2 (1994): 109.

before a statue of the Virgin Mary. On the other hand, I do not want them to say that I am not a Christian because I do. There are legitimate differences between us and legitimate concerns. Pentecostals can raise legitimate questions about Catholic devotion to Mary and the saints and its biblical basis. I personally think that it was Protestant concerns about devotion to Mary that brought about the attempt to base Marian devotion on the scripture and the liturgy in Pope Paul VI's instruction *Marialis Cultis*.[47] We have heard the objection that there were excesses in the past, and we are trying to clean up our act. But there is room in Christianity for legitimate devotion to Mary. Catholics too can raise legitimate concerns about Pentecostals' sense of history, about restorationism, historical development, and exegesis. We can raise concerns about "the inability to be true to the logic of their fundamentalistic and dogmatic hermeneutics . . . [and] the quite unbiblical erection of two crisis experiences (conversion, baptism in the Holy Spirit), or three crisis experiences (conversion, sanctification, baptism in the Holy Spirit) . . . elevating New Testament patterns into New Testament laws."[48] But while we do this, we need to affirm each other's identity as Christians. We need to raise our concerns with passion but also with charity.

Fourth, Catholic and Pentecostal clergy need to have coffee with each other. My grandmother used to say, "Hablando se entiende la gente." [We understand each other by talking.] We need to *hablar* on an informal basis and get to know each other. Douglas Foster, a pastor of the Churches of Christ told me that I need to "go up to a Pentecostal pastor and unobtrusively say 'would you like to have coffee with me?'" I said, "What if he refuses?" Doug answered, " . . . well, you've got to be persistent."

Fifth, as Latinos we need to be involved. Our voices need to be heard. I attend the meetings of the National Workshop on Christian Unity, The National Association of Diocesan Ecumenical Officers (NADEO), and the Society for Pentecostal Studies, and I see very few other Latinos. It is interesting to note that in the International Catholic-Pentecostal Dialogue, for the first quinquennium there were no women representatives from either partner and only one representative from Latin America for each side, both from Brazil. For the second quinquennium, again there were no women representatives from either partner. This time there were no Latin American Catholic delegates at all. This is surprising given the significant percentage of Pentecostals in Latin America and the tension that exists there between Catholics and Pentecostals. Bishop Robert McAlister from Brazil was the only Pentecostal participant from Latin

47. Paul VI, *Marialis Cultis* (Boston: Pauline Books and Media, 1974).
48. Kilian McDonnell, "New Dimensions," 217.

America in the second quinquennium. The third quinquennium saw one woman Catholic participant, but again there were no Latin American Catholic participants. There were two woman Pentecostal participants and two Latin Americans, one from Mexico and one from Argentina. Ronald Kydd, a Pentecostal participant in the current phase of the dialogue, has also noted the lack of third world delegates: "This is particularly serious given the fact that large parts of the constituencies of both parties are to be found in these racial and geographical categories and that the highest degree of tension between the groups is to be found in the Third World."[49] He goes on to recount that "several years ago when we pushed seriously to locate a dialogue session in Latin America, the plans ultimately had to be dropped. Authorities in the area judged such action to be too disruptive to be advisable. Can it be possible that only Western, university-trained Catholics and Pentecostals can restrain negative feelings toward each other sufficiently to permit serious conversation? This is an issue that begs resolution."[50] Our voices need to be heard in our denominations and in the dialogues at all levels.

Finally, popular religious books found in Church and religious bookstores need to be accurate and need to promote a new spirit of dialogue and acceptance. The influence of the book or pamphlet that the Churchgoer picks up on Sunday in a Church lobby or bookstore cannot be underestimated. These works may have more impact than all the articles that appear in theological journals. The challenge is not to bear false witness but to bear witness to the truth.

In 1955 Robert McAffee Brown wrote an article about the attitudes of Protestants toward Catholics. I quote it by way of conclusion, substituting the word "Pentecostal" wherever he used the word "Protestant":

> The plea for understanding . . . is always important as a safeguard against distortions of the opposing position and the building up of straw men. . . .
> To whatever extent Catholics are permitted, they should seek to understand [Pentecostal] faith in something other than sheerly polemical terms. . . . But two further pleas must be made, beyond that of understanding. These are the pleas for charity and firmness. Let each side espouse both. Various types of [Pentecostal] "anti-Catholicism" have been under discussion, and an attempt has been made to indict a number of them. The shoe must fit on the other foot as well. For there are types of Catholic "anti-[Pentecostal]ism" just as bigoted and unenlightened, and also just as significant in terms of deep commitment to the Church. Perhaps the most important thing, the greatest gift of charity for which we can hope in this situation, is not to cease disagreeing, but to make sure that we disagree about the right things. We can do this only as we are

49. Ronald Kydd, "Reflections on the Roman Catholic/Pentecostal Dialogue," *The Ecumenist* 2 (1995): 50.
50. Ibid.

firm in holding to those things which compromise the essentials of our faith. And we can do this only as charity motivates our discussion and defines the areas of our disagreements. If these ingredients are present, it may be that the Holy Spirit can lead us closer to one another than we have yet come.[51]

As Mel Robeck has stated, "Suspicion abounds. But ultimately, so does grace."[52]

51. Robert McAfee Brown, "Types of Anti-Catholicism," *Commonweal* 63 (1955/1956): 196.
52. Robeck, "Evangelization or Proselytism," 61.

10

Historical Roots of the Contemporary U.S. Latino Presence

A Latino Protestant Evangelical Contribution

DAVID TRAVERZO GALARZA

INTRODUCTION

The purpose of this presentation is to review the historical roots of contemporary U.S. Latino Christian presence through a historical and social analysis of Hispanic reality. While Latino reality is a heterogeneous phenomenon, key social and historical factors provide a common ground to identify such a thing as Latino or Hispanic reality.[1] Regardless of its complex and disparate makeup, we may submit that "the sum of the common experiences and understandings [of U.S. Latino/Hispanics] . . . outweigh[es] the differences or peculiarities."[2]

In the analysis of Hispanic/Latino reality, we may note that the historical backdrop of 500 years of foreign imperial rule, first by Spanish and then by U.S. control, provides a fundamental reference point for our critical reflection. In this nation, one of the overarching factors that binds Latinos together is a history of Spanish-European and then Anglo-American invasion, conquest, colonization, and Christianization.[3]

1. For the purposes of this work, the term Latino or Hispanic will be used interchangeably, notwithstanding the historical, political, or philosophical arguments in favor of or against the use of one term over another. See Suzanne Oboler, *Ethnic Labels, Latino Lives* (Minneapolis: University of Minnesota Press, 1995) for more discussion.

2. Franklyn W. Knight, *The Caribbean: The Genesis of a Fragmented Nationalism* (New York: Oxford University Press, 1990), xi.

3. Justo L. González, *The Development of Christianity in the Latin Caribbean* (Grand Rapids, Mich.: William B. Eerdmans Publishing Company, 1969); Eduardo Galeano, *Open Veins of Latin America: Five Centuries of the Pillage of a*

Another major emphasis in this critical reflection is to examine the contemporary plight of U.S. Hispanics in light of current predicaments of overt social, political, educational, and economic disparity. A history of disfranchisement and disempowerment is therefore identified.

We will also refer to some of the more recent manifestations of contemporary U.S. Latino Christian presence, especially in their Protestant and more ecumenically-oriented expressions. We might note here that the past Latino colonial history of foreign domination and internal capitulation is currently under reconstruction as innovative efforts attempt to reinterpret and remake such an infamous history.

This presentation will be organized in three parts. First, we will offer a historical framework to examine Latino Christianity within the parameters of both Roman Catholic and Protestant expressions of faith. A few key historical events and illustrations will be identified. Second, we will review the available demographic data to help situate present U.S. Latino reality within a U.S. social context. Significant demographic features such as population trends, employment and income indices, formal educational statistics, and related census data will be highlighted. Third, we will identify what the future has in store by viewing some of the more innovative directions U.S. Latino Christianity is taking today, especially among Latino Protestant communities.

Consequently, the historical roots of contemporary U.S. Latino Christianity may be examined within such a framework of historical, demographic, and institutional developments. We submit that the roots of contemporary U.S. Hispanic presence require the review of past, present, and future directions in order that a more complete scenario of Latino reality and Christian faith may be considered toward the twenty-first century and beyond.

U.S. LATINO CHRISTIANITY: HISTORICAL PERIODS

There are two major historical periods under which to understand U.S. Latino reality and Christianity. They represent the Spanish colonial era and the U.S. neocolonial phase.[4] At the very root of Latino presence in

---

Continent (New York: Monthly Review Press, 1973); Charles Gibson, *The Spanish Tradition in America* (Columbia, S.C.: University of South Carolina Press, 1968).

4. Edwin Sylvest, Jr., "The Protestant Presence (1845 to the Present)," in *Fronteras: A History of the Latin American Church in the U.S.A. since 1513*, ed. Moises Sandoval (San Antonio: Mexican American Cultural Center, 1983), 277–338; Edwin Sylvest, Jr., "Hispanic American Protestantism in the United States," in *On the Move: A History of the Hispanic Church in the United States*, ed. Moises Sandoval (Maryknoll, N.Y.: Orbis Books, 1990), 115–30.

the United States is the actual birth and emergence of the Latino people. Virgilio Elizondo refers to this presence as the painful yet beautiful birth of a new, unique people—a *mestizo* people.[5] Consequently, Elizondo refers to U.S. Latino Christianity as a new "Mestizo Christianity" and the emergence of the radical newness of *Mestizo*-Christians.[6] A deep and rich Hispanic legacy in the United States and the Americas stems from a long and painful birthing process.[7]

Under the Spanish colonial era, the roots of U.S. Latino Christianity were characteristically Roman Catholic. There is also a medieval context that reflected the political and religious objectives of the Spanish expansionist empire. Under the Patronato Real, the Spanish crown was given virtual authority over the religious and political affairs of the Americas.[8] In this era, religion and power were at the heart of the conquest, colonization, and Christianization project of the Americas.[9]

Within this process of Christianization and conquest, the Church was an instrument of societal control. In the name of God and the Spanish crown, the native inhabitants, their lands, culture, and wealth were raped and plundered. The justification for conquest was declared through the Requerimiento—an announcement of Spain's mission and the de facto subjugation of the natives as her subjects.[10] The institutionalization of slavery was justified and practiced through the Encomienda system; aborigines were uprooted forcibly from their villages and placed "in trust" to the Spanish patron (the *encomendero*). The result of the aforementioned two acts led to the fundamental disruption and virtual decimation of aborigine life, culture, and religion by the mid-sixteenth century.[11]

    5. Virgilio Elizondo, *Christianity and Culture: An Introduction to Pastoral Theology and Ministry for the Bicultural Community* (Huntington, Ind.: Our Sunday Visitor, 1975), 123; Virgilio Elizondo, *Mestizaje: The Dialectic of Cultural Birth and the Gospel* (San Antonio, Texas: Mexican American Cultural Center, 1988); Virgilio Elizondo, *Galilean Journey: The Mexican-American Promise* (Maryknoll, N.Y.: Orbis Books, 1983).
    6. Justo L. González, *Mañana: Christian Theology from a Hispanic Perspective* (Nashville: Abingdon Press, 1990), 14; Elizondo, *Mestizaje*.
    7. Elizondo, *Christianity and Culture*; Elizondo, *Mestizaje*; González, *Mañana*; Allen Figueroa Deck, *The Second Wave: Hispanic Ministry and the Evangelization of Cultures* (Mahwah, N.J.: Paulist Press, 1989).
    8. González, *Mañana*, 56; Gibson, *Spanish Tradition*, 35–9.
    9. González, *Mañana*, 56.
    10. Justo L. González, "The Christ of Colonialism," *Church and Society* 82, no. 3 (1992): 22.
    11. Gibson, *Spanish Tradition*; Adolfo Colombres, *A Los 500 Años del Choque de Dos Mundos* (Buenos Aires: Ediciones del Sol, 1989); J. H. Parry, *The Spanish Seaborne Empire* (Berkeley and Los Angeles: University of California Press, 1966); Blanca G. Silvestrini and Maria Dolores Luque de Sánchez, *Historia de Puerto Rico* (San Juan, Puerto Rico: Ediciones Cultural Panamericana, 1992). Silvestrini

Religion therefore played an imperial role in the Spanish project of conquest and colonization. Christianization went hand in hand not only with military conquest but with Spanish European cultural domination. As González submits, Christianization and the Hispanization of the American native inhabitants were one and the same. Cultural imperialism and evangelization were identical.[12]

Three hundred years later, a second conquest, colonization, and Christianization project was institutionalized in the Americas. The U.S. expansionist era swept over the southeastern and southwestern territories that included Florida, Louisiana, Texas, and Mexico.[13] After the U.S. war with Mexico (1846, 1847), we may summarize that "as part of the 1848 Treaty of Guadalupe Hidalgo, Mexico was forced to yield almost half of its land: all of the territory north of the Rio Grande was then transferred to the United States. Mexico lost what is now California, Arizona, New Mexico, and the territory from which the states of Colorado, Kansas, Nevada, Oklahoma, Utah, and Wyoming were formed."[14]

The U.S. nineteenth-century period of expansion and control is also the same era that led to the "Spanish-American War" (1898). The islands of Puerto Rico, Guam, the Philippines, and Hawaii were invaded and conquered. Cuba was "liberated" and kept under U.S. vigilance (the Platt Amendment). In specific reference to Mexican Americans and Puerto Ricans, Elizondo notes: "we can say that in the last five hundred years these peoples have been twice conquered, twice colonized, and twice oppressed—first by Spain in the sixteenth century, and then by the United States, beginning in the nineteenth century."[15] The nineteenth

---

and Luque de Sánchez make mention of a "triple" conquest that included a military, an economic, and an ideological dimension. See especially chapter three.

12. González, *The Development*, 18. In Guillermo Bonfil Batalla's essay "El Problema de la cultural nacional," the author states: "La ideología que pretendía justificar la colonización como una cruzada de redención revelaba precisamente la convicción de que el único camino hacia la salvación era el trazado por la civilización occidental." See Colombres, *500 Años*, 76–7.

13. Joan Moore and Harry Pachon, *Hispanics in the United States* (Englewood Cliffs, N.J.: Prentice-Hall, 1985); Robert T. Handy, *A Christian America: Protestant Hopes and Historical Realities* (New York: Oxford University Press, 1984), 162–96.

14. Edna Acosta-Belen and Barbara Sjostrom, eds., *The Hispanic Experience in the United States: Contemporary Issues and Perspectives* (New York: Praeger, 1988), 89–90.

15. Virgilio Elizondo, "Toward an American-Hispanic Theology of Liberation in the U.S.A.," in *Irruption of the Third World: Challenge to Theology*, ed. Virginia Fabella and Sergio Torres (Maryknoll, N.Y.: Orbis Books, 1983), 50.

century therefore laid the foundations for contemporary conquest and colonization.

In contrast to the predominantly Roman Catholic, medieval, and authoritarian character of the Spanish colonial era, the U.S. imperial epoch may be characterized as Protestant, modern, and somewhat egalitarian.[16] U.S. expansionism, however, was intertwined with the doctrine and practice of Manifest Destiny that engulfed the religious, political, and cultural ethos of the time. Robert T. Handy has referred to this project as the U.S. Christian conquest of the world via the creation of "a Christian America."[17]

At the heart of this hegemonic program was the role of U.S. Protestant Christianity. From the U.S. colonial Puritan ideal of the Christian commonwealth to the nineteenth-century emergence of the Second Great Awakening, the notion of U.S. domination operating under divine providence served to fuel the justification for U.S. expansionism.[18]

One of the least noted features of U.S. Latino Christianity during this second major period is the impact of U.S. Protestantism on U.S. Latino life and religion.[19] Less acknowledged are the emergence and role of the U.S. Latino Protestant Church.[20] An important variable that helps explain part of this neglect is that the emergence of U.S. Latino Protestantism is a fairly recent phenomenon. It is only 130 years young in contrast to more than 330 years of Spanish colonial history. The key point of reference for U.S. Latino Protestantism's birth is the nineteenth-century conquest and colonization of half of Mexico by the United States.[21]

An in-depth review of this rich history is not allowed here, yet one of the more recent works that attempts to survey a history of U.S. Latino Protestantism is a collection of essays edited by Dr. Justo L. González.[22] The specific focus, however, is upon U.S. Hispanic United Methodism.

As González examines this history, a key underlying feature in the review of U.S. Hispanic Methodism is the element that binds together

16. Michael Dodson and Nuzzi O' Shaughnessy, *Nicaragua's Other Revolution: Religious Faith and Political Struggle* (Raleigh, N.C.: North Carolina Press, 1990), 33–101.

17. Handy, *Christian America*.

18. Sylvest, "Protestant Presence," 279–87.

19. Sylvest, "Protestant Presence," 279.

20. Silvest, "Hispanic Protestantism," 115, 116.

21. Sylvest, "Protestant Presence"; Silvest, "Hispanic Protestantism"; Justo L. González, ed., *Each in Our Own Tongue: A History of Hispanic United Methodism* (Nashville: Abingdon Press, 1991); Moore and Pachon, *Hispanics in the United States*, 115.

22. González, *Each in Our Own Tongue*.

any study of U.S. Latino Protestantism—U.S. nineteenth-century conquest and domination. While this review is limited to the Southwest region, the following may apply to U.S. Latino Protestantism as a whole.

> The encounter between United States and Mexican peoples was within the dynamic of the conqueror and the conquered. It is only by taking into account this context of conflict, war, and eventual domination that one can attempt an adequate interpretation of the present reality of the Church in the Southwest, including The United Methodist Church.[23]

Protestantism therefore had an impact upon U.S. Latino reality (especially the Southwest and West) through U.S. territorial expansion due to the U.S. war with Mexico. Shortly afterwards, Puerto Rico experienced the same fate with the "Spanish American War" of 1898.[24] The island of Puerto Rico, which had received an Autonomous Charter from Spain in 1897, was invaded, conquered, colonized, and Christianized by a new rising Empire. Puerto Rico came under U.S. military control in 1898 and remains a U.S. territory today. U.S. Protestantism thus extended its influence with a conquering modality by "rechristianizing" the native people of the land.[25] Christianity and conquest had surfaced again.

Edwin Sylvest suggests an interrelationship between U.S. Protestant Christianity, Manifest Destiny, and U.S. territorial expansionism. Sylvest underscores that territorial expansionism and the notion of divine providence were intrinsically related.[26] The conquest and colonization of U.S. Latinos within the Methodist tradition, for example, was thus a religious task with a national agenda. Expansionism, conquest, and conversion to Protestantism were part of a U.S. national program in a manner akin to the Spanish conquest, colonization, and Christianization process. To "evangelize" was tantamount to the extension of U.S. religious, economic, political, and ideological control.

The roots of U.S. Latino Protestantism are therefore linked to Anglo-American religious and political domination over U.S. Latino reality. Nevertheless, Sylvest suggests that even *if* Manifest Destiny may not have necessarily *motivated* U.S. expansionism, it served to *justify* it.[27] Hence:

23. González, *Each in Our Own Tongue*, 39, 40.

24. Moore and Pachon, *Hispanics in the United States*.

25. Moore and Pachon, *Hispanics in the United States*; Clarence Senior, *Strangers—Then Neighbors: From Pilgrims to Puerto Ricans* (New York: Freedom Books, 1961); Adalberto Lopez, ed., *The Puerto Ricans: Their History, Culture, and Society* (Rochester, Vt.: Schenkman Books, 1980).

26. Silvest, "Protestant Presence."

27. Silvest, "Protestant Presence," 281–3.

Nothing less than the conversion of the world was the mission of the North American Protestant Empire. That process entailed simultaneously expansion to fill and to evangelize the geographical space of the continent and the support of an extensive foreign missionary enterprise.[28]

The relationship between Protestant evangelization and conquest is what the late Dr. Orlando E. Costas identified as the alliance between the foreign missionary movement and a liberal ideology of domination. Costas argued that world mission via the Protestant faith has played a domesticating versus a liberating role.[29] As the Spanish Empire (with a Roman Catholic foundation) institutionalized a dynamic relationship between religion and the subjugation of native life, the U.S. Empire (with a Protestant base) actualized the same. To civilize was to Christianize and conquer in the name of God and country. Costas thus observed that "this system has succeeded not only in subjugating Christian mission, but also has turned it into a tool of domestication, thereby stripping it of its liberating content."[30]

U.S. LATINO REALITY

DEMOGRAPHIC FEATURES

There are four basic demographic features that stand out when we examine U.S. Latino reality today. These include population size and growth rate, a concentrated regional distribution, high urbanization, and real diversity.

Quite striking is the fact that the U.S. Latino population represents the fastest-growing single ethnic group in the nation. It is estimated that there are over 22 million Hispanics in the United States. This represents about 8.8 percent of the total U.S. population.[31] Since 1960 there has been a steady increase that has about tripled in the last forty years.[32] The decade of the 70s, for instance showed a 61 percent growth. From 1980–90 there was reported a 53 percent increase.[33]

28. Silvest, "Protestant Presence," 282.

29. Orlando E. Costas, *Christ Outside the Gate: Mission Beyond Christendom* (Maryknoll, N.Y.: Orbis Books, 1984), 66, 67.

30. Costas, *Christ Outside the Gate*, 58.

31. Jesús Garcia, "The Hispanic Population in the United States: March 1992," in *Current Population Reports, Population Characteristics* P20–465 (Washington, D.C.: U.S. Department of Commerce, Bureau of the Census, 1992), 2.

32. Acosta-Belen and Sjostrom, *Hispanic Experience*, 10.

33. Teresa Puente, "Latino Population Grows 53%, to 22.4 Million: 1980–90," *Hispanic Link*, 18 March 1991, 2.

Frank Bean and Marta Tienda indicate that in the 70s the Latino growth rate was seven times greater than the 9 percent non-Hispanic growth for the nation.[34] The actual number in the 90s is most likely much greater.[35]

In fact, if we take into consideration this growth pattern and census undercount problems,[36] we may actually have closer to 40 million Hispanics in the United States today. Joan Moore and Harry Pachon have suggested that the 1983 count may be 20 million instead of the 14.6 million figure.[37] If this is the case, the 61 percent growth rate for the decade of the 70s is more than doubled.

Second, U.S. Latinos represent a concentrated regional distribution of its population. Approximately 90 percent of U.S. Hispanics reside in nine states.[38] The majority (55 percent) live in just two states (California and Texas) and close to two-thirds live in the three states of California, Texas, and New York. The largest numbers reside in California where the Hispanic population has risen 70 percent from 1980–1990.[39] In California and Texas, the Latino population represents about 25 percent of the total population, while in New York, Colorado and Florida the figure is about 12 percent. The percentage of growth in states such as New Jersey, Georgia, Maryland, and Nevada ranges from 50 and 77 percent to 93 and 130 percent change.[40]

Third, U.S. Latinos are characteristically an urban population.[41] Eighty-seven percent of U.S. Hispanics live in metropolitan areas while only 75 percent of the general population is urban.[42] There is a heavy concentration in central cities but not as great as the African-American population.[43] The U.S. Hispanic population represents about a 60 percent central city concentration as opposed to 70 percent for African-Americans and 35 percent for non-Hispanics.[44]

34. Frank D. Bean and Marta Tienda, *The Hispanic Population of the United States* (New York: Russell Sage Foundation, 1987), 58.

35. Pastora San Juan Cafferty and William C. McCready, eds., *Hispanics in the United States* (New Brunswick, N.J.: Transaction Books, 1985), 9–19; Moore and Pachon, *Hispanics in the United States*, 52–3.

36. Cafferty and McCready, *Hispanics in the United States*, 9–19.

37. Moore and Pachon, *Hispanics in the United States*, 52–3.

38. Puente, "Latin Population Grows," 2.

39. Puente, "Latin Population Grows," 2.

40. Puente, "Latin Population Grows," 2.

41. Frank L. Schick and Renee Schick, eds., *Statistical Handbook on U.S. Hispanics* (Phoenix, Ariz.: Oryx Press, 1991), 2.

42. Geraldo Marin and Barbara VanOss Marin, *Research with Hispanic Populations* (Newbury Park, Calif.: Sage Publications, 1991), 5.

43. Belen and Tienda, *The Hispanic Population*, 147; Schick and Schick, *Statistical Handbook*, 10.

44. U.S. Bureau of the Census, 1988.

Fourth, the U.S. Latino population is a diverse community. There are dynamic and real differences among the various Latino groups in the country.[45] Regionally, the West and the Southwest area represents a predominately Mexican-American constituency.[46] Even here there is some diversity between the older Mexican-American migrant groups, newer Mexican immigrations, and the rise of Chicano nationalism. The Northeastern region is mostly Puerto Rican (61 percent live in New York and New Jersey), with a dispersal away from New York City and toward the South and the Midwest areas.[47] Florida (Southeast) contains the vast majority of Cubans in the United States, mainly residing in the Miami area.[48]

According to the March 1992 Census figures, the compositional make up among the diverse Latino groups in the United States is as follows: Mexican-American—63.6 percent, Puerto Rican American—10.6 percent, Cuban-American—4.7 percent, Central and South American—14.0 percent, Other Hispanic—7.1 percent.[49]

While the larger society identifies the U.S. Latino population as a distinct community, great diversity exists within the particular Latino groupings.[50] There is a rich plurality of histories, along with the diverse societal conditions of each respective group.[51] The Puerto Rican and Cuban American experiences, for example, display grave differences in their respective circumstances for emigrations to the United States. The imposition of U.S. citizenship on Puerto Ricans in 1917 and post-World War II economic transformations on the island and in the U.S. metropolis stands in contrast to the Cuban revolution of 1959 that impacted Cuban immigration to the United States in the 60s. A socialist revolutionary government directly affected this immigration.

Puerto Ricans, however, migrated in large waves already as U.S. citizens in the mid-1940s and 50s due to the faltering of the island's economy.[52] Cubans immigrated as exiles after the revolutionary changes of the 60s in Cuban society. There are also basic distinctions regarding

45. Moore and Pachon, *Hispanics in the United States*, 38–49.

46. Cafferty and McCready, *Hispanics in the United States*, 20.

47. Belen and Tienda, *The Hispanic Population*, 139; Marin and VanOss Marin, *Research with Hispanic Populations*; Cafferty and McCready, *Hispanics in the United States*, 20.

48. Belen and Tienda, *The Hispanic Population*; Marin and VanOss Marin, *Research with Hispanic Populations*, 5.

49. U.S. Bureau of the Census, 1992, 2.

50. González, *Each in Our Own Tongue*, 29.

51. Moore and Pachon, *Hispanics in the United States*; Acosta-Belen and Sjostrom, *Hispanic Experience*; Belen and Tienda, *The Hispanic Population*.

52. David Traverzo, "Towards a Theology of Mission in the U.S. Puerto Rican Migrant Community: From Captivity to Liberation," *Apuntes* 3 (1989): 54.

socioeconomic characteristics of each respective population.[53] The Cuban profile was essentially white, well-to-do, and politically anti-Castro. The Puerto Ricans were basically poor, racially very mixed, and pro-democratic.[54]

At the same time, the U.S. Census reports and other studies have observed some marked social characteristics and socioeconomic conditions that place the U.S. Latino community in stark contrast to the White non-Hispanic society. As we examine below, the U.S. Latino community appears as an unequal partner in the realms of income, employment status, and formal education.

CHARACTERISTICS AND CONDITIONS

One of the most outstanding characteristics of the U.S. Latino population is age. The Hispanic population is younger than the total population. Thirty percent of Latinos were under 15 years of age in contrast to 20 percent for non-Hispanic Whites. Five percent of U.S. Latinos were 65 years old in comparison to 14 percent of non-Hispanic Whites.[55] About 11 percent of Hispanics were 5 years or younger in comparison to 8 percent for the total population.[56] In summary, the median age of Hispanics was 26.3 years as opposed to 35.2 for non-Hispanic Whites.[57]

At the same time, some variation exists within the U.S. Latino population. Mexican-Americans show a low 24.4 years, while Puerto Rican, Central and South Americans, and Other Hispanics have median ages of 26.9, 28.4, and 32.4 respectively. The Cuban-American population is highest with a median figure of 40.4.[58]

In terms of income and earnings, the median income of Hispanic households was about 70 percent of non-Hispanic households.[59] In 1991, the median income of Hispanic families was $23,889 in comparison to $39,240 for non-Hispanic White families.[60] The unequal distribution of income is further noted by the fact that about 19 percent of Hispanic families had incomes less than $10,000 a year as opposed to 6 percent for non-Hispanic White families. In addition, non-Hispanic White fami-

53. Acosta-Belen and Sjostrom, *Hispanic Experience,* 121.
54. Moore and Pachon, *Hispanics in the United States,* 34, 36.
55. Garcia, "The Hispanic Population in the United States," 2.
56. Marin and VanOss Marin, *Research with Hispanic Populations,* 6.
57. Marin and VanOss Marin, *Research with Hispanic Populations,* 6.
58. Marin and VanOss Marin, *Research with Hispanic Populations,* 6.
59. U.S. Bureau of the Census, 1992, 9.
60. U.S. Bureau of the Census, 1992, 9.

lies with $50,000 incomes were twice as many as Hispanic families (36 versus 16 percent).[61]

Total earnings for Hispanic men and women (15 years and over) were also lower than for non-Hispanic men and women. Median earnings for Hispanic men were $14,405, or 60 percent of non-Hispanic White men ($24,302). Median earnings for Hispanic women ($10,397) were 78 percent of non-Hispanic White women ($13,397).

The poverty of earnings is evident, with 75 percent of Hispanic males earning less than $25,000 a year. This was in contrast to 51 percent for non-Hispanic White males.[62] Even further, Hispanic males with earnings of $50,000 or more represented 4 percent of the population versus 15 percent for non-Hispanic White males. Hispanic females (48 percent) had earnings of less than $10,000 in comparison to non-Hispanic White women (39 percent).[63] Thirteen percent of Hispanic women had earnings of $25,000 in comparison to 23 percent of non-Hispanic White women.

Unemployment for both Hispanic males and females is also higher than for non-Hispanic Whites. The figures were 12.2 percent for Hispanic males and 9.8 percent for Hispanic females, versus 7.5 and 5.4 percent for non-Hispanic White males and females.[64]

In formal education, Hispanics lag behind the non-Hispanic population in the United States. Sixty percent of Hispanic young adults (25–34) completed four years of high school or more. The non-Hispanic population was 89 percent. Only 11 percent of Hispanic young adults completed four years or more of college—this compared with 26 percent for non-Hispanics. The college figure does not take into consideration the extremely high rate of Hispanics who begin but do not finish.[65] Among Latino groups, the percentage who have completed a doctoral degree (Ph.D., Ed.D.), for example, amounts to 0.1 percent for Mexican-Americans and Puerto Ricans, 0.7 percent for Cuban-Americans, in comparison to 0.9 percent for White non-Hispanics.[66]

INNOVATIONS AND NEW DIRECTIONS: LIBERATING SIGNS

In spite of a history that includes colonial subjugation, social disfranchisement, and ecclesial collusion, U.S. Latino Christianity has played

61. Garcia, "The Hispanic Population in the United States," 9.
62. Garcia, "The Hispanic Population in the United States," 6.
63. U.S. Bureau of the Census, 1992, 6.
64. Garcia, "The Hispanic Population in the United States," 6.
65. Garcia, "The Hispanic Population in the United States," 3.
66. U.S. Bureau of the Census, 1992, 3.

a somewhat liberating role among both Roman Catholic and Protestant expressions.[67] Especially in the last three decades or so, many hopeful signs have emerged. In Roman Catholic circles, we have witnessed the training and appointment of native priests and bishops. There has also been the mobilization of Latino controlled conferences, programs, and organizations.[68]

In the Protestant arena, the old Anglo-American paternalistic control of Latino ministries and organizations has been shifting. For example, U.S. Latino Protestants have presently established a theological seminary that offers accredited graduate level courses with a Latino-oriented curriculum that is controlled and staffed by Latinos. Although the Hispanic Summer Program (Dr. Justo L. González is its founding director) that began in 1989 does not offer an accredited degree program, the seeds are sown for an eventual U.S. Latino Protestant Theological Seminary. An ecumenical thrust permeates this Hispanic program with strong indigenous Pentecostal, mainline denominational, and Roman Catholic participation.

In 1989, another historic event occurred in the field of academia. At the annual meeting of the American Academy of Religion (AAR) and the Society of Biblical Literature (SBL) in Anaheim, California, La Comunidad of Hispanic American Scholars of Theology and Religion was formed. Under the direction of Rev. Dr. Benjamin Alicea, this scholarly society proposed to "promote and stimulate scholarship for and by Hispanic scholars in the United States, Canada, and Puerto Rico in the broad fields of theology and religion." Although predominantly Protestant with Pentecostal support, the ecumenical orientation was foundational and continues today.

In the summer of 1991, the First Encuentro of Hispanic Education for Ministry founded the Association for Hispanic Theological Education (AETH). The purpose would be to "promote and enhance theological education for Hispanic Americans in Bible institutes, Bible colleges, seminaries, and other programs in the United States, Canada,

67. Moore and Pachon, *Hispanics in the United States*, 114–7; González, *Each in Our Own Tongue*, 58–64; Sylvest, "Protestant Presence," 329–34; Silvest, "Hispanic Protestantism"; 127; Acosta-Belen and Sjostrom, *Hispanic Experience*, 126–8; Raymond Rivera, "The Political and Social Ramifications of Indigenous Pentecostalism," in *Prophets Denied Honor: An Anthology on the Hispanic Church of the United States*, ed. Antonio Stevens-Arroyo (Maryknoll, N.Y.: Orbis Books, 1980).

68. Virgilio Elizondo, Frank Ponce, Patrick Flores, and Robert Sanchez, *Los Católicos Hispanos en los Estados Unidos* (New York: Centro Católico de Pastoral para Hispanos del Nordeste, 1980); Silvest, "Protestant Presence"; Silvest, "Hispanic Protestantism"; Deck, *Second Wave*.

and Puerto Rico." The composition of this association is mixed with Latino Pentecostals and mainline Protestants. This event served as a springboard for the birth of the Commission for the Study of the History of Latino Protestantism. The Latino Church History Academy was subsequently organized in August, 1992. The orientation here was essentially mainline Protestant with some Latino Pentecostals involved.

In the fall of 1991 formal efforts toward the articulation of a Hispanic theology crystallized with a national event sponsored in New York City. "Faith Doing Justice" was an ecumenical endeavor to "raise pastoral concerns and issues that need to be addressed by Hispanic Theology and to identify distinct Hispanic theological understandings." The event was sponsored by Auburn Seminary in partnership with the Fund for Theological Education, La Comunidad of Hispanic American Scholars of Theology and Religion, the Academy of Catholic Hispanic Theologians of the United States (ACHTUS), and the Hispanic Caucus of Union Theological Seminary.

On 1 July 1993, Rev. Dr. Raymond Rivera founded the Latino Pastoral Action Center (LPAC), a division of the New York City Mission Society.[69] LPAC's vision is "to empower the Latino Church to develop holistic ministries in New York City Latino communities." This agenda includes the development of "a network of comprehensive services" and the development of "an independent cadre of indigenous leaders who are selected and legitimized by and accountable to their communities." The Bible Institute School of Ministry Consortium has emerged from LPAC. A key purpose of the Consortium is to sponsor the first Latino designed and controlled Church college-level program in New York City, one that is fully accredited by a Board of Regents. This has been a predominately indigenous Pentecostal effort.

In August 1993 in Chicago, the Christian Community Development Association (CCDA) and the Hispanic Association for Bilingual/Bicultural Ministries (HABBM) sponsored a national summit entitled "Empowering the Latino Church to Transform Our Barrio." This was an attempt to bring together a group of Latino pastors and specialists who engage in community-based and community-oriented ministries. Drs. John Perkins, Manny Ortiz, and Raymond Rivera were keynote speakers. Revs. Luis Madrigal and Noel Castellanos organized this national event. The emphasis was upon the development of "holistic ministries" from a Protestant vantage point.

In 1994, the Alianza de Ministerios Evangelicos Nacionales (A.M.E.N.) was founded in Long Beach, California by a national repre-

69. Emilio Bermiss is the Society's first Latino executive director in its 181-year history.

sentation of Latino Protestant laity and clergy. The fundamental intent
of this para-church association was to provide a public voice and forum
for Hispanic evangelical Christians in the nation. The idea for such a
body emerged out of a 1992 meeting in Philadelphia at the offices of the
Pew Charitable Trusts, Inc. With a cross-section of young and visionary
Latino Protestant leaders, cutting and controversial issues ranging from
the colonial status of Puerto Rico to holistic ministry among the poor
emerged to shape the original agenda and character of this organization. A more moderate and conservative agenda has recently emerged
with some relationships to the right-wing oriented Promise Keepers'
movement.

CONCLUSION

After 500 years of struggle, U.S. Latino Christianity is developing a sense
that new paradigms are required for a new day. The legacy of conquest
blessed by Christianization is today questioned and confronted with
alternative visions of reality. In the forms of Roman Catholicism, mainline Protestantism, evangelicalism, and indigenous Pentecostalism, U.S.
Latino Christianity is deeply diverse yet greatly united in some concrete projects that foster a spirit of cooperation, common ground, and
authentic community. With the above small yet significant illustrations,
the last ten years have propelled such historical projects from coast to
coast toward a new tomorrow—*mañana*. In his book entitled *Mañana:
Christian Theology from a Hispanic Perspective,* Justo L. González refers to
this as a new reformation or a new ecumenism:

> This new ecumenism has a practical and political side. The civil rights
> movement has its counterparts in the Hispanic community, and in
> those counterparts Catholics and Protestants have been drawn to-
> gether. This is true of those involved in the unionization of farm la-
> borers in California, in community organization in the barrios of San
> Antonio and Los Angeles, in the struggle for independence in Puerto
> Rico, and in the search for more political participation in New York
> and Chicago. In these struggles, Protestant and Catholic Hispanics
> march arm in arm and are thus learning to undo many of the preju-
> dices that have divided them. It is true that many Hispanics, both
> Protestant and Catholic, do not participate in these struggles, but for
> those who do, out of the struggle itself a new ecumenism has been
> born.[70]

As we move toward the twenty-first century, we may suspect that
as the U.S. Latino population continues to grow in vast numbers,
strength, and vision, the role of U.S. Latino Christianity will also in-

70. González, *Mañana*, 74.

crease. Both Latino Roman Catholic and Protestant networks, along with more grassroots Pentecostal groups, show that U.S. Latino Christianity will serve as a vital element in the present and future development of a national U.S. Latino agenda. As identified above, such networks and ecumenical efforts are already underway with extraordinary dynamism, auspicious creativity, and new, promising leadership.

In conclusion, whether it is the Roman Catholic, Protestant evangelical, or indigenous Pentecostal expression of Latino Christianity, the past history, the present predicament, and the future innovations all point toward a unique and transforming contribution to the world.[71] Rev. Dr. Jesse Miranda, the first national President of A.M.E.N., summarizes the hope of U.S. Latino Christianity for both Church and society:

> At a time when many view the sun setting on Church and society, ethnic minorities offer freshness and untapped resources. Hispanics bring many gifts to enhance both nation and Church. To a nation with a low birthrate and an aging population, Hispanics bring the vitality of youth. To churches struggling for survival, ethnic ministry brings hope. . . . The hope of Hispanics lies in the repentance of the Church and the correction of past failures. The Church can ally itself with the growth mentality of the nation, as it has done before. Or it can seek to develop a Christian worldview based on the biblical principles of compassion, justice, and righteousness. The Church can follow the nation's

71. Other works on the topic include Archdiocese of Newark, Office of Research and Planning, *Presencia Nueva: Knowledge for Service and Hope—A Study of Hispanics in the Archdiocese of Newark* (Newark, N.J.: Archdiocese of Newark, 1988); Ruth Doyle and Olga Scarpetta, eds., *Hispanics in New York: Religious, Cultural and Social Experiences*, 2 vols. (New York: Archdiocese of New York, 1982, 1989); Justo L. González, *Una Historia Ilustrada del Cristianismo: La Era de Los Conquistadores*, vol. 7 (San José, Costa Rica: Editorial Caribe, 1980); Robert González, and Michael La Velle, *The Hispanic Catholics in the United States: A Socio-Cultural and Religious Profile* (New York: The Northeast Catholic Pastoral Center for Hispanics, 1985); Hispanic Policy Development Project, *The Hispanic Almanac* (Washington, D.C.: Hispanic Policy Development Project, 1990); New Digest, "Hispanics in the Assemblies of God Out Pace General U.S. Spanish Population in Rapid Growth," *Pentecostal Evangel* 19 (1987): 14–5; Tzvetan Todorov, *The Conquest of America* (New York: Harper & Row, 1984); David Traverzo, "Towards a *Relectura* of the History of the Church from a Latino Perspective: Reform, Rediscovery, or Revolution?" *Journal of Hispanic/Latino Theology* 4 (1996): 49–65; David Traverzo, "The Puerto Rican/Latino Protestant Urban Church: Agent of Liberation or Oppression?" *Critica* 11–12 (1995): 2, 8–9; David Traverzo, "A Paradigm for Contemporary Latino Thought and Praxis: Orlando E. Costas' Latino Radical Evangelical Approach," *Latino Studies Journal* 5 (1994): 108–31; U.S. Department of Commerce, Census Bureau, *Condition of Hispanics in America Today* (Washington, D.C.: U.S. Government Printing Office, 1983); Eldin Villafañe, *The Liberating Spirit: Toward an Hispanic American Pentecostal Social Ethic* (New York: University Press of America, 1992).

pattern of cultural self-preservation. Or it can work to dissolve race prejudice and to reconcile social antagonism. The Church may offer the world a privatized, personal, and "spiritual" brand of Christianity. Or it can provide leadership toward a more just and humane society exemplifying the kingdom of God.[72]

72. Jesse Miranda, "Realizing the Dream," *Christianity Today* 33 (1989): 40.

11

Cuando Lleguemos a Casa

The Journey to be Church

VICENTE OSVALDO LÓPEZ, O. CARM.

I hope that some *cuentos de familia*, stories from my Mom and Dad, can illustrate a couple of key questions that I believe are directly related to ministerial preparation. On one occasion while I was teaching a class in the summer pastoral program at the Mexican American Cultural Center (MACC), my parents came to visit me in San Antonio. After they sat in on my class, they joined me at a reception where Gustavo Gutiérrez was surrounded by a large group of students and by representatives of the media. When my Dad asked about all of the commotion, I told him that Gustavo was a world-famous theologian. Dad thought that was nice, but he wanted to know what a theologian was. I told him that a theologian was a man who talked and wrote about God. My Dad proceeded to tell me that he had a question for the theologian. I hesitated and wondered what kind of question my father would consider worthy of a theologian. So I asked him to run it by me.

My Dad told me that he had often wondered why God did not favor *nosotros, los nacidos acá en este país*: why was the favor of God denied to those of us who were Mexicans born in the United States? His question was different than what I expected, but I figured it would be a good discussion. So I led my Dad over to where Gustavo was standing. Before we got there, we ran into Juan Alfaro. I introduced them. My Dad thought a biblical theologian must know about these things as well, and they began to talk. My Dad told Juan that it was obvious to everyone that the United States was the richest, most powerful country in the world. He suggested that surely God had favored our country. Then he said that at one time Spain had been the empire that ruled the world and that even today half the world speaks Spanish. So God must also have favored Spain. He went on to talk about Israel and all of its struggles

244

to become a modern nation and how God has also favored the Jewish people. He even insisted that Mexico had found great favor with God because the Virgen de Guadalupe had appeared there and had made her home there. Now he got to the point and asked Juan: "Why does God not favor those of us north of the border?" Father Juan took great care to explain all about the history of salvation and finally recommended that God's time is not our time. My father pointed to his watch and said: "But Father, this is the only time I have. When will God's favor come to us?"

My mother's favorite saying is "¡Hay está Dios!" (sic, "There's God!"). She is a devout, prayerful, and perseveringly faith-filled woman. She prays novenas to the Niño Jesús de Praga, to San Antonio. She adorns her *altarcito* (home altar) to the Blessed Virgin—the Immaculate Conception—with flowers and candles. As children we knelt at the feet of the Virgen to pray the rosary together. In any family crisis Mom would remind us: "¡Hay está Dios!" Her words still reverberate in my ears to this day. When our family is together and we are reminiscing, someone will always mimic her with great joy; "¡Hay está Dios!" My Dad always responds: "I know, *hay está Dios*, but who is going to pay the bills?" "Dios sabe lo que hace" (God knows what He is doing) found new meaning during the terminal illness of my youngest brother, Victor. My mother expanded on the theme: "God's ways are not our ways," and "No hay mal que por bien no venga" (There is no evil that does not come for some good). After my brother died of AIDS in October of 1994, my mother said she had asked God for three things: (1) that Victor would not die alone, (2) that he would not suffer too much, and (3) that he would die at peace with God. When her prayer was answered she said: "Estoy conforme a la voluntad de Dios" (This accords with God's will).

These stories occasion questions that set the general background for my presentation. *Nos inquietan*, they unsettle us because we Church professionals do not deal well with questions of grace and favor. It is always so difficult for us to understand how it is that God is manifest among us. But, if we are to prepare ministers to *acompañar* (join with) the people of faith where do we need to begin? I have been around a few years in this field called Hispanic Ministry in the United States. Father George O'Keefe, O. Carm., my associate at Mt. Carmel Parish in Joliet, used to say: "El diablo no es diablo por ser diablo sino por ser viejo" (What's evil about the devil is that he never goes away).

Yes, I tried them all! Movimiento Familiar Cristiano, Cursillos de Cristiandad, Industrial Areas Foundation (IAF), community organizing, even *cibernética* by Waldemar di Gregori, and that was just from 1971–1975. I was an activist priest who was initiated with Priests Asso-

ciated for Religious, Educational, and Social Rights (PADRES), arrested
with the United Farm Workers, and inspired by MACC. I went to the I
Encuentro, met Mother Teresa of Calcutta at the Philadelphia Eucharistic Congress in 1976, and participated in the II Encuentro. I was looking
for an instrument or a program; anything that would train, mobilize,
instruct and inform the various communities placed under my pastoral
care. Later on, RENEW, the Rito de Iniciación Cristiana de Adultos (the
Rite of Christian Initiation of Adults), Encuentro Conyugal (Marriage
Encounter), the Charismatic Movement, and most recently the
Neo-Catechumenado (the Neo-Catechumenate) have caught my attention. In many conferences and workshops, I encouraged the formation
and the work of *comunidades eclesiales de base* (ecclesial base communities). I spent what often seemed like all of my life organizing Evangelization Missions, working with the Conference of Religious in Hispanic
Ministry (CORHIM), coordinating the efforts of the regional pastoral
centers, and planning with the national network of the Secretariat for
Hispanic Affairs. *Me entregé por completo* (I gave myself competely).

I gave all that I had because I considered them the "signs of the
times." I believed that these were the means that the Spirit was using to
build up the Church, to gather the people, and to train us to be better
ministers. As I look back, I now realize that I was too concerned with
"how to," with a pragmatic, action-oriented approach. In other words,
I could not see the forest for the trees. I don't think I understood fully
the complexity, the arduousness of the commitment implied in the preparation for ministry.

Most of my experience has been outside of the formal academic
institutions sponsored by the Church in the United States. Certainly,
there were forays into seminaries, universities, priest's convocations,
and national gatherings of professional ministers. But even in the context of our highly specialized areas of concentration, I have always felt
that in these contexts many of the issues *del pueblo* (of the people) were
sort of a bothersome novelty, a distraction from the main course of business. Even in a highly rewarding presentation at the National Catholic
Education Association gathering in Dayton, Ohio in 1989, I felt like we
were entertaining folklore rather than committing ourselves to the life
of *el pueblo*.

We are seldom recognized as a part of the mainstream commitment
of the Church. We have so often been unsettling voices clamoring for
inclusion. Our equal share in the educational and ministerial resources
of the Church has yet to become a reality.

I can still remember the scandal when my Uncle Ralph's comments
made the front page of the Arizona newspapers. Either in 1954 or 1955,

he addressed the annual conference of Baptist Ministers and criticized the Catholic Church for not educating Mexican Catholics. As a student in a catholic elementary school, soon to graduate into a Catholic high school, I was offended by his critical statements that had become so public. My uncle Ralph Estrada was president of La Alianza Hispano-Americana, a fraternal benefit society that had "sucursales" (branches) all over the Southwest. He told me that even if it hurt, I should never be afraid to speak the truth. The sign above the front gate to the headquarters of La Alianza in downtown Tucson read: "Ésta es su casa" (This is your home).

Ever since those days I have been worried about the Church's commitment to the education of the Latino Catholics in the United States. Unfortunately, I have never found a serious, generous, or creative response to our needs in the formal, more academic institutions under Church auspices. I certainly have found a creative response in the more popular, informal, ad hoc programs that I mentioned previously. I have often felt struck by the question: How do we mobilize, instruct, train the Latino faithful to know and live our faith? We have never been able to redirect the ongoing priorities of our existing institutions in order to adapt them for the ministerial formation of the *pueblo en marcha* (people on the way).

At long last it has become more clear to me that ministerial formation can no longer be a "how to" question. Formation is a process that must lead us to ask about the motivation and foundation of our action. We need to ask, "What are we doing and why? Where are we going with all of this? What are we preparing ministers to do? Who are we calling ministers to be? Where does all of this formation lead us? What is the role of ministry in the Church of our time?" The National Pastoral Plan calls us "to live and to promote . . . by means of a *pastoral de conjunto*, a model of Church that is: communitarian, evangelizing, and missionary, incarnate in the reality of the Hispanic people and open to the diversity of cultures, a promoter and example of justice . . . that develops leadership through integral education, . . . that is leaven for the kingdom of God in society."[1]

It was an incredible process that more than ten years ago forged and winnowed that statement into being. Maybe the stylized language does not motivate us today. Perhaps, if I put it into my own words, *crear un lugar donde nos podemos conocer, crear confianza, y convivir. Donde podemos compartir los unos con los otros un compromiso mayor con Dios, con*

1. The National Conference of Catholic Bishops of the United States, *National Pastoral Plan for Hispanic Ministry* (Washington, D.C.: United States Catholic Conference Office of Publishing and Promotion Services, 1987), §17.

su Iglesia, y con nuestros hermanos y hermanas.[2] Where all of us can recognize the promise: "Ésta es su casa."

I am absolutely convinced that God's fidelity to the "pueblo de Dios en marcha" has allowed the Spirit of Jesus to call us to communion and to community. Even in the face of the culture of death, in our extreme individualism, in the violence, the greed, the self-absorption of our age, we have been gathered together in the name of the Lord Jesus. We are once again challenged to commit ourselves, our resources, the Church, and the resources of the Church for the development of those who are most in need.

I have often reflected on the life of my aunt Maggie who was the Church organist in Sonora, Arizona for twenty-five years. She played at all of the Sunday Masses, at first communions, funerals, marriages, and all the special events. The faith of that small mining town came alive with music on Christmas, Easter, during the *Mes de Mayo* (month of May) and so many other times. She practiced faithfully with her "muchachas" (girls) and they sang like songbirds in this Mexican community in the hills of southern Arizona.

Father Angel Esteve, O.C.D. was the pastor of Sonora, and he used to stop by Aunt Maggie's store. The sweet smoke of his cigar would fill the air as they planned parish activities. They always found ways to welcome the visiting priests and sisters who would come for summer catechism. Together the hospitality of the parish was a gift to all. I am told that as a babe, I was carried in my mother's arms to the *coro* (choir) for Mass. I can still remember the evenings where the priests and sisters would gather around the piano in my aunt's living room to sing and to dance. As my grandmother watched and my *tías* and *primos* (aunts and cousins) and I joined in the celebration, I understood that this was Church, that I was "en mi casa."

Aunt Maggie was always very generous. Strikes were a common occurrence in the copper mines during those years. She would often extend credit (*fiaba a la gente*—she trusted people), so that school clothes, shoes, women's dresses, and work pants for men were available when they were needed. It is not enough for us to "do" Church. We get so caught up in our need to "hacer" (do things). Ministerial preparation is a process of becoming, we are called to "ser iglesia" (be Church). I am not convinced that the vision of Church that we articulated in the National Pastoral Plan is so different from the challenge faced by the early

2. [We need] to create an environment in which we get to know one another, foster confidence, and live fraternally. Here we will be able to share with one another a deeper commitment to God, God's Church, and our own brothers and sisters.

Christian communities, which we read about in the Acts of the Apostles
(Acts 2:42–47 and 4:32–35).

We do live in the tension between two models of Church. The authoritarian and hierarchical remains of a clerical culture are stretched
and challenged by the communal, shared, and consensual struggle of
the *pueblo en marcha*. We do find a value in order, efficiency, and productivity. At the same time we live in a more dynamic, loosely knit gathering of multiple forces attempting to serve basic community needs.

These two models pull constantly at one another. Pastoral agents
and our formation programs are often caught trying to serve two masters at once. I call it the "encrucijada" (crossing). It is a painful and
often exasperating existence trying to bridge two perspectives and two
seemingly contradictory means to the realization of the kingdom. Even
though the tension and the conflict seem like a distraction and can be
terrifying, I sense that they are necessary. Somehow conversion is the
bridge from the Church of the monument to the Church of the living. Is
it not the cross that leads us through purification and death to the promise of new life? However reluctant the journey, it is a process of down-
ward mobility.

In 1971 as we initiated the work of PADRES, I believed that our
problems would be solved once we had bishops and Hispanic priests. I
had the same feeling in 1977 with the priorities of the II Encuentro:
political responsibility and integral education, etc. It seemed so clear
that the small-group process and the work of base communities would
lead us into a new way of being Church.

By 1988, Cardinal Bernadin told the conference of Bishops that the
National Pastoral Plan was the "blueprint for action not only for Hispanic Catholics but for the Church of our country." This was "el grito
de la voz profética" (the cry of the prophetic voice). We have struggled
to create models for education and formation, for reflection and community. We must reclaim our *mística familiar* (family-based spiritual theology), a spirituality that is historical, ecclesial, biblical, and catholic. It
is a *mística* of many nations, languages, and ways of being. We are con-
voked to be one people in the Spirit of Jesus who makes his *morada entre
nosotros* (dwelling among us).

When I embarked on this journey in Hispanic ministry in 1971, I
believed that our numbers would prove to be convincing and that our
needs would be compelling. Later I thought that if all pastoral agents
would learn Spanish, we could make it work. If only the priests, sisters,
and seminarians would learn Spanish, then we could communicate with
one another. My work at MACC and in the Encuentro Process gave me

the assurance that culturally sensitive ministers would serve our community best.

I have now come to believe that the fundamental question is one of
vision and spirit. What is the model of Church for which we will declare ourselves? It is from the perspective of this vision that we must
develop our processes of formation.

12

Hispanic Family Life Ministry

GELASIA MÁRQUEZ MARINAS

At their 1990 meeting, the National Conference of Catholic Bishops unanimously adopted a resolution reaffirming "The Plan of Pastoral Action for Family Ministry." One of the goals of the approved plan is: "to raise the awareness of the Church to the sacramental nature and mission of Christian marriage as well as to the realities now facing families."[1] Similarly, one of the elements that the *National Pastoral Plan for Hispanic Ministry* includes for pastoral planning is the analysis of the reality wherein the Church must carry out its mission.[2]

In what follows I will describe some of the empirical elements in the day-to-day reality of immigrant Hispanic families undergoing cultural transition in the United States. An analysis of this transition will increase the knowledge needed for the pastoral care of Hispanic families and the ministerial preparation of Hispanic family-life ministers.

Hispanics and Caribbeans come from more than twenty-six nations. There are significant differences among these nationalities. The language, economic resources, and educational systems vary dramatically from country to country. Also individual countries are often very ethnically diverse. The historical experiences of these immigrants are very different from other U.S. citizens and European immigrants; therefore, the manner in which they identify themselves ethnically often cannot be assimilated to the usual paradigms.

Most Hispanic families embrace two different cultural environments simultaneously. Moreover, approximately one-half of married Hispanics were married before emigrating. These people have unique developmental issues. They may be at different stages of maturity depend-

1. The National Conference of Catholic Bishops, *Family Ministry: A Pastoral Plan and a Reaffirmation* (Washington, D.C.: United States Catholic Conference Office of Publishing and Promotion Services, 1991).
2. The National Conference of Catholic Bishops, *National Pastoral Plan for Hispanic Ministry* (Washington, D.C.: United States Catholic Conference Office of Publishing and Promotion Services, 1987).

ing upon how they define themselves as persons. They may be still forming their own identity while responding to the demands of a new culture. In addition, the development of their family may have been stopped
or interrupted to deal with specific, urgent issues such as procuring
housing and work or learning a language.

THEORETICAL FRAMEWORK FOR DESIGNING PROGRAMS FOR THE PASTORAL CARE OF HISPANICS

In spite of the extensive literature on intercultural adjustment and psychosocial development, we still lack a theoretical and conceptual framework for working with newcomers and immigrant families. During my
years of study, research, and practice working with immigrant Hispanic
families, I have developed the following scheme. It is intended as a
frame of reference for the design and development of programs for the
pastoral care of these families. Basically, I see the process of transition as
involving three separate but interrelated components.

   1. The "culture" of the family. An understanding of the functioning
of any family requires not only knowledge about the family's internal
structure and processes but also attention to the larger social environment. The neighborhood, peer group, Church, school, and workplace,
as well as the larger political, governmental, and economic situation
touch family members directly. For this reason, we need to give attention to the "culture" of this family and how that cultural environment
shapes the family structure and its external activities and projections.

   Every family belongs to a defined cultural community, for every
family identifies itself with a common group, whether this be in terms
of race, religion, nationality, or some mixture of these categories. This
community serves as a social and psychological referent and, through
historical circumstances, creates a sense of being a people.[3] The relationship between the family and its cultural community involves mutuality and reciprocity, social articulation and recognition. It creates a
sense of belonging and historical continuity for the family and for its
members.

   Every family is involved in a continuous interchange with its economic and sociocultural environment in the accomplishment of its daily
tasks.[4] Because culture is a set of values by which a people judge, accept, and live what is considered important within the community, the

3. M. Gordon, *Assimilation in American Life: The Role of Race, Religion, National Origins* (New York: Oxford University Press, 1964).
4. U. Bronfenbrenner, "Ecology of the Family as Context for Human Development," *Developmental Psychology* 22 (1986): 723–42.

cultural values and ethnicity of the family mediate its interactions with the external world. These in turn strongly affect family mechanisms for coping with and adapting to the ethnocultural environment.[5]

Consequently, through the process of socialization parents instill in their children culturally specific ways or preferred modes of perceiving and relating to others and of understanding the verbal and nonverbal symbols essential for communicating, remembering, and thinking, as well as for problem-solving and for the use of meaning and logic. Similarly, this inculturative or socializing process shapes the children's self-concept and self-esteem while they "absorb" the culture of their parents and "locate" themselves within their first society, their home, and its sociocultural expectations.

2. Adaptation to the new culture. Immigrant family members have been conformed, shaped, and socialized by their culture of origin, which had provided the context and the original content of their personality development. Consequently, migration ruptures the continuity of experience present in the immigrants' previous sociocultural context. To migrate is therefore to be born again, not only because of the social nature of human personality and its inextricable relationship to the cultural environment in which a person gains his/her identity, but because the person has to restructure his/her cognitive and affective abilities—introducing new meanings, gestures, and words to function effectively and developing the coping mechanisms required for life in the new place. In addition, the immigrant Hispanic family must undergo change collectively—as a small society—so that it can (1) continue to be the matrix of its members' psychological development; (2) accommodate itself to the new society and its culture; and (3) insure some continuity with its own culture. This process of learning a new set of coping mechanisms must be done over time in such way that family continuity is maintained while making restructuring possible.

3. The need for continuity in a changing family. The process of transition or progressive change from one culture to another is possible only through continual interaction with the new culture. Various stages are required before the immigrant feels a sense of belonging to the new environment. Additionally, during the transition from one culture to the other, the immigrant couple must repeatedly adapt to the demands of the new culture. Their personal identity must be continually reformed, not only for their personal adjustment, but also so that their children might achieve a sense of dignity, worthiness, and acceptance. When this transition is slow, regardless of the cause, the behavior of the immi-

5. M.K. Ho, *Family Therapy and Ethnic Minorities* (Newbury Park, Calif.: Sage Publications, 1987).

grant family—still out of step with the new culture—may appear aberrant to members of the new society.

In sum, the members of immigrant Hispanic families are immersed in a threefold process: (1) each family member's own personality and psychosocial developmental process as child, adolescent, or adult; (2) each family member's process of adaptation and adjustment to the new sociocultural environment through the adaptation to the new culture; (3) societal changes in family structure for the continuing fulfillment of the family's own functions to insure some continuity with the culture of origin and family traditions. To be sure, family-based customs and traditions may generate rigid psychosocial endowments that render the individual unprepared for the ravages of migration and further adaptation to host cultures. Such processes generate defensive postures to ward off societal norms, encourage the use of defenses that split off affect from content, and may even result in antisocial behaviors.

SOME POSSIBLE RESPONSES

The possible responses to immigrant families in cultural transition may vary. They range from a combination of information, education, opportunities for emotional ventilation and support, and contact with other families who have similar difficulties in making professionals available during times of crisis. Obviously, all these methods of intervention need to be addressed in the migrant's native language and culture. Moreover, since the family is the person's most important, reliable, and external resource for psychosocial development as well as the key social group that intervenes between the macro-system and the family member, the family has to be the matrix of the process of healing after migration.[6] As De Voss[7] argues, the adaptation of a minority group in a larger society may depend more on the internal stability of the family roles and the community cohesiveness in that particular group than on factors in the external environment.

What would be the overall goal of Hispanic family ministry? Based on the previous statements, one must first assist Hispanic families in their struggle to be contributing members of the U.S. Church and society, as well as encourage Hispanic families in their efforts to maintain their Christian and cultural sense of self, meaning, and worth while they cope with a new and radically different environment. Two pos-

6. S. Minuchin, *Families and Family Therapy* (Cambridge, Mass.: Harvard University Press, 1974).

7. G.A. De Voss, *Response to Change: Society, Culture and Personality* (Berkeley and Los Angeles: University of California Press, 1976).

sible objectives for fulfilling this goal are: (1) to help families and their members in the development of a new sense of self by allowing them the possibility of reconciling a variety of internal issues in a coherent and acceptable identity; and (2) to support immigrant families in the processes of changing their internal organization and structure by allowing them to explore alternative ways of relating as family.

The psychological, social, and spiritual healing after migration usually consists in the use and/or creation of intermediary structures that mediate between the individual and the new culture. None of this can take place in a vacuum. One favorable setting for intercultural adjustment is the parish where bilingual, bicultural liturgies, programs, and activities bring together members of different ethnic groups who share the same Catholic identity. "It was the (parish) community who gave the immigrants of the last century the strength and stability to move steadily into the mainstream . . . [I]n a strange world it was the basis of their identity, their social satisfaction, their security, their strength."[8] One integrates, however, from a position of strength, not from a position of weakness. Therefore, some circumstances must be carefully planned. For example, contact between the members of the various ethnic groups must be fostered in a manner that establishes respect and equal regard. One example would be presentations at a bilingual parish that are delivered in both languages.

CONCRETE INTERVENTIONS

Education is an important step in regaining the sense of belonging. In any social group, the individuals have built up habits, attitudes, values, and norms that fit together in an articulated system (culture) and permit a complete adjustment in the social and geographical context where those elements develop. However, they become disorganized in any other social situation. Culture, including its subjective aspects, can be systematically taught and learned in an educative environment where the confusing ambiguity of its members is probed rather than avoided and where immigrant Hispanics not only maintain their sense of self-meaning and worth, but also learn to cope step by step with the challenges of the new and different environment. The provision of factual information helps the different generations to gain an understanding of what is "expected" within each other's world.

Moreover, counseling should be provided to enable the family to cope constructively with stress from the different social, political, eco-

8. J. Fitzpatrick, "The Hispanic Poor in a Middle Class Church," *America* (11–13 July 1988).

nomic, and cultural environment and to counteract their pervasive influence. This form of intervention must be directed toward strengthening family structure, enhancing flexibility and improving role functioning, reinforcing the ability of friends, community and the larger social system to offer effective and appropriate support, and promoting a clearer bicultural identity by helping family members to define values and beliefs that also will enable them "to increase their tolerance for difference."

This therapeutic intervention must be concrete, directive, immediate, problem-focused, and action-oriented. It must serve as catalyst for change, help families tolerate anxiety, acknowledge the inadequacy of established patterns, mobilize resources, explore alternatives, and create new behavior patterns.[9]

Both the educational and therapeutic interventions presuppose the assessment of the relevant migration and acculturation stresses and of the presence of typical transitional problems and conflicts. Given the diversity of geographical origins, languages and dialects, socioeconomic status, educational backgrounds, and immigration status, it is important to assess: (1) migration patterns (migration occurs for diverse reasons and the adjustment of the family depends on the extent to which its original expectations compare with its reality); (2) country of origin along with its political, economic, and educational situation; (3) age and developmental stage of family members at the time of migration in order to understand what experiences are stored in which language; (4) socioeconomic status and educational background of family members prior to migration; (5) current availability of support systems (friends, Church, ethnic community, members of the extended family); (6) degree of harmony between both cultures (the relative stress of migration is in part determined both by the country and culture of origin, and by the country and culture of adoption).

SUMMARY

The U.S. Bishops' *Pastoral Letter on Hispanic Ministry*[10] encourages and urges all U.S. Catholics "to explore creative possibilities for responding

9. See Gelasia Márquez Marinas, "Helping Hands: A Counseling Program for Hispanic Families in Cultural Transition" (presentation given in April 1993 at the 25th Annual Conference of National Association of School Psychologists in Washington, D.C.).

10. The National Conference of Catholic Bishops, *Hispanic Ministry* (Washington, D.C.: United States Catholic Conference Office of Publishing and Promotion Services, 1983).

innovatively, flexibly, and immediately to the Hispanic Presence." Recent Church documents, especially the Apostolic Exhortation *Familiaris Consortio* emphasize that "family ministers ought to apply themselves to understanding the situations within which marriage and family are living today, in order to fulfill their task of serving."[11]

In working with this conceptual framework as frame of reference for developing the pastoral care and the ministry-formation of those who are going to work with Hispanic families, we hope that we might affirm, support, and welcome Hispanic families to the Church and to the U.S. society.

---

11. John Paul II, *Familiaris Consortio: Apostolic Exhortation on the Family* (Washington, D.C.: United States Catholic Conference Office of Publishing and Promotion Services, 1981), §4.

The Extended Body

Faith Generates a Culture

13

The Sacramented Sun

Solar Eucharistic Worship in Colonial Latin America

JAIME LARA

Anthropologists and liturgical historians have long disagreed over the evangelization of the Americas: whether the dominant dynamic was one of syncretic confusion between pre-Columbian and Christian beliefs and practices, or whether there was a conscious, selective, and deliberate inculturation on the part of the missionaries.[1] I would like to tackle the question head on by focusing on one particular visual image: the sun. In this study I will first suggest that the dominant religious belief of Mesoamerican and Andean natives was related to the sun and solar worship.[2] Second, I will suggest that the mendicants deliberately attempted to rehabilitate solar imagery for evangelizing purposes—relating it to the Christian God, to Christ, and to Christ's Eucharistic presence. In this they had ample European precedents. Lastly, I will suggest that this inculturation of the sun had its manifestation in popular piety and in the liturgical arts.

Solar cults had their origin in the Near East, in Egyptian and Babylonian mythology.[3] The Hebrew Bible is replete with references to

1. The methods of evangelization are discussed in Robert Ricard, *The Spiritual Conquest of Mexico: An Essay on the Apostolate and the Evangelizing Methods of the Mendicant Orders in New Spain 1523–1572* (Berkeley and Los Angeles: University of California Press, 1966); A. Ybot Leon, *La Iglesia y los eclesiasticos españoles en la empresa de Indias*, 2 vols. (Barcelona: Salvat, 1954); Pedro Borges, *Métodos misionales en la cristianización de América* (Madrid: Consejo Superior de Investigaciones Cientificas, 1960); and Jacob Baumgarten, *Mission und Liturgie in Mexiko*, 2 vols. (Schöneck/Breckenried: Neue Zeitschrift für Missions-Wissenschaft, 1972).

2. Armand Labbé, *Religion, Art and Iconography: Man and Cosmos in Prehispanic Mesoamerica* (Santa Ana, Calif: Bower Museum, 1982); Manuel Ballesteros Gaibrios, *Cultura y religión de la América prehispánica* (Madrid: Biblioteca de Autores Cristianos, 1985), 179–204, 227–54.

3. *The Sun: Symbol of Power and Life*, compiled by Madanjeet Singh (New

sun worship, usually in a negative context by condemning it in the Jews' neighbors.⁴ But the recent discovery and analysis of the Dead Sea Scrolls, particular that one known as the Temple Scroll, have suggested to some scholars that at one time the Hebrews may have incorporated sun worship as part of a cult to YHWH. The Temple Scroll speaks of a gilded staircase leading to the roof of the Holy of Holies where the high priest was to perform certain rituals at dawn, which may have been related to a later-suppressed worship of certain angelic beings as intermediaries of YHWH. Certain passages in the Torah, in the Mishna commentary, and in the Essenes' scroll, *The War of the Sons of Light*, suggest this. The subject has been hotly debated and is far from resolved.⁵ Be that as it may, Jewish ritual art confirms the use of the Greco-Roman god Helios as a symbolic representation of the Divine. The floor mosaics of several Late Antique synagogues display a zodiac with Helios in the center panel parading through the heavens in his quadriga of four horses.⁶ Recently this author was privileged to witness the discovery of another Helios floor mosaic in Galilee; it has just been published (fig. 1).⁷

The Psalms confirm solar imagery for God. For example, Psalm 57 states: "Rise up above the heavens, O God, let your glory shine its light on earth!" Psalm 19 agrees: "In the heavens God has placed a tent for the sun; it comes forth like a bridegroom coming from his tent, rejoices like a champion to run its course. At the end of the sky is the rising of the sun; to the furthest end of the sky is its course. There is nothing concealed from its burning heat." Psalm 72 includes the prayer, "May His Name be blessed forever and endure like the sun." Habakkuk 3 proclaims: "Covered are the heavens with his glory... His splendor

York: Harry Abrams, 1993).

4. See, for example, Ezekiel 8:14–18.

5. H.V. Parunak, "Was Solomon's Temple Aligned to the Sun?" *Palestine Explorer's Quarterly* 110 (1978): 29; Morton Smith, "The Case of the Gilded Staircase: Did the Dead Sea Scroll Sect Worship the Sun?" *Biblical Archeology Review* (September/October 1984): 50–5; Jacob Milgrom, "Challenge to Sun-Worship Interpretation of the Temple Scroll's Gilded Staircase," *Biblical Archeology Review* (January/February 1985): 70–3; Glen Taylor, *Yahweh and the Sun: Biblical and Archeological Evidence for Sun Worship in Ancient Israel* (Sheffield: JSOT Press, 1993).

6. Erwin R. Goodenough, *Jewish Symbols in the Greco-Roman Period*, 12 vols. (New York: Pantheon, 1965), 12:45, 65–67, 153–5, 185–8 and passim. Christ is represented as the Sun in the center of a zodiac ceiling in the Chapel of the Rosary of the Dominican Church, Santo Domingo, Dominican Republic. See Santiago Sebastián López, *El Barroco Iberoamericano: Mensaje iconográfico* (Madrid: Encuentro Ediciones, 1990), 15 f.

7. Ze'ev Weiss and Ehud Netzer, *Promise and Redemption: A Synagogue Mosaic from Sepphoris* (Jerusalem: The Israel Museum, 1996).

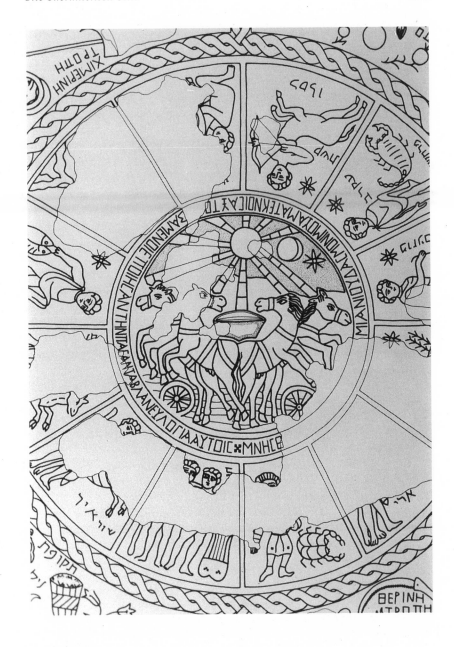

Fig. 1. Detail of the synagogue floor mosaic of Sepphoris with Helios, fifth
century C.E. drawing, The Israel Museum.

spreads like the light; rays shine forth from beside him where his power is concealed."

The prophet Malachi (3:20) also spoke in solar terms, which Christians would later make use of in the liturgy of Advent: "The day that is coming is going to burn up the evildoers, says YHWH Sabaoth, but for you who fear my name, the Sun of Righteousness will shine out with healing in his wings." Thus images of divine judgment could be associated with the sun and with winged beings, that is, images with feathers. Sol Justiciae and Sol Salutis became titles that could be used for God or his Messiah. In Jewish and Christian thought, the sun was a personal, living being; one of the angelic powers whose worship St. Paul railed against in his Letter to the Colossians (Col. 2:18).[8]

Christians perhaps had more reason to use solar imagery for Christ. Jesus, after all, had called himself the Light of the World. Just prior to his birth, Zechariah prayed for salvation in solar terms, that ". . .the dawn from on high shall break upon us to shine [like sunshine] on those who dwell in darkness. . ." (Luke 1:78–9). The Book of Revelation indicates that Jesus' angelic appearance to John the Seer had "a face like the sun shining with all its force" (1:16). The same book describes the Heavenly Jerusalem in a new light: ". . .the city did not need the sun or the moon for light, since it was lit by the radiant glory of God and the Lamb was its light."

Liturgical scholars believe that the dating of Christ's birth on 25 December was a deliberate attempt to replace the pagan feast of the Invincible Sun with the true Sun of Justice, as John Chrysostom so often states in his homilies.[9] Christian liturgical time has been structured since the earliest days around the year, the month, and the day. The daily "turning points," so to speak, occur at sunrise and sunset with the recitation of Morning Prayer and Evening Prayer. An examination of the development of the Daily Office shows that the rising sun has been continuously seen as a "sacrament" of the rising of Christ, the sun of righteousness; while the setting sun is the "sacrament" of Christ the light that the darkness of death can never quench.[10] Ὁ Φῶς Ἱλαρόν (Oh Gladsome Light) is just one of a multitude of ancient sunrise-sunset hymns from the Divine Office.

8. Philippe Seringe, *Les symboles dans l'art, dans les religions et dans la vie de tous les jours* (Paris: Helios, 1988), 289–95.

9. Franz Joseph Dölger, *Sol Salutis: Gebet und Gesang im christlichen Altertum, mit besonderer Rucksicht auf die Ostung in Gebet und Liturgie* (Munich: Aschendorff, 1925); Edward Lipinski, "Le culte du soleil," *Orientalia Louvaniensa Periodica* 22 (1991).

10. Paul Bradshaw, "Christian Worship as an Architecture of Time" (conference paper delivered at Yale University, Institute of Sacred Music, Fall 1997).

From about the time of Constantine's reputed experience of the sign of the cross in the sky comes a mosaic in a tomb under St. Peter's basilica. Discovered in the 1940s, the spectacular find displays Christ riding through the heavens in a quadriga as the deathless Helios (fig. 2).[11] A similar image, a bust of Christ as Helios, was created in mosaic on the triumphal arch of St. Paul's-outside-the-Walls in the fifth century, under the patronage of the great liturgical poet, Leo the Great.[12] An examination of early Christian liturgical manuscripts would demonstrate the same quadriga and sun-rising imagery, as seen, for example, in the Ascension scene of the Rabbula Gospels of the sixth century. In the thirteenth century St. Paul's added another solar-Christ symbol to its mosaic repertoire. The Byzantines had had an image of the Hetimasioi, the "empty throne" on which the eschatological cross reigns in heaven until it will return as the "Sign of the Son of Man," according to Matthew 24.[13] When the image was adopted at St. Paul's in Rome, a bust of Christ as well as the instruments of the passion were added, and the name was changed. It was called the *solisternium*, the "throne of the sun," thus giving solar connotations to the return of the cross at the Parousia for the Final Judgment.[14] It is no coincidence that such images were reused in sixteenth century Mexico, as I hope to show. By that time Sol had long been a common image on outdoor stone crosses (fig. 3) and on Romanesque facades, especially in Spain on the pilgrimage route to Compostela.[15]

In the thirteenth century, Francis of Assisi took the celestial light as his kin in the "Canticle of Brother Sun." In the fifteenth century another Franciscan, Fray Bernardine of Sienna had reworked the solar imagery for the novel devotion and worship of the Holy Name of Jesus. He created an apocalyptic symbol: a solar shield of gold rays against a sky-blue background to surround the quasi-magical Name (fig. 4).[16] Popular pi-

11. John Moffit, "Helios, Christ, and Christmas," *Arte Cristiana* 78 (1990): 437–41.

12. Jerzi Miziolek, "When Our Sun is Risen: Observations on Eschatological Visions in the Art of the First Millennium," *Arte Cristiana* 82:245–60; 83:3–22.

13. Charles Picard, "Le trône vide d'Alexandre et le culte de trône vide," *Cahiers archeologique* 54.

14. Luciano Bartoli, *La chiave: Per la comprensione del simbolismo e dei segni nel sacro* (Trieste: Lint, 1982), 265.

15. Manuel Guerra, *Simbología Románica: El cristianismo y otras religiones en el arte románico* (Madrid: Fundación Universitária Española, 1978), 171–99. For crosses with solar symbols, see *The Ruthwell Cross*, ed. Brendan Cassidy (Princeton: Princeton University Press, 1992), 108 and plate 20.

16. E. Gurney Salter, *Franciscan Legends in Italian Art: Pictures in Italian Churches and Galleries* (London: Dent, 1905), 183–7. Etienne Delaruelle,

Fig. 2. Mosaic of Christ-Helios, early fourth century. Grotto of St. Peter's
Basilica, Rome.

Fig. 3. The Ruthwell Cross, Durham England, north side, eighth century.
Durham University.

Fig. 4. Shield of the Holy Name of Jesus, detail of a seventeenth century
colonial painting.

ety used these Name-shields in superstitious rites and as apotropaic
devices or talismans to ward-off evil.[17] Ignatius of Loyola would later
incorporate it into the emblem of the Jesuits.

On the eve of the discovery of the Americas, Sir Thomas More wrote
his *Utopia* in which he describes and praises the inhabitants of the mythical island republic as sun worshippers. Although erroneous, the religious instinct of the Utopians is laudatory because they have chosen
the material object that is closest to the true God. More appears to have
been influenced by the Christian Kabbalists of the Florentine Academy,
especially Pico della Mirandola. In More's praise of sun worship as a
preliminary step toward faith, he was echoing the words of the early
Christian philosopher, Dionysius the Areopagite, in the fourth book of

"L'Antichrist chez S. Vincent Ferrier: S. Bernardin de Sienne et autour de Jeanne
d'Arc," in *La piété populaire au Moyen Age* (Torino: Bottega d'Erasmo, 1975),
329–54.

    17. John Lenhart, "The Devotion to the Holy Name of Jesus and Supersti-
tion," *Franciscan Studies* 29 (1948): 79–81.

the *Divine Names*, where he wrote that, apart from humans and angels, no creature shows forth the attributes and excellencies of God as clearly as does the sun.[18] In the Americas of the eighteenth century, Tomaso Campanella would repeat this utopian theme in his political work *La Città del Sole*, the City of the Sun.[19]

MEXICO

When the mendicant missionaries encountered the Aztecs of central Mexico in 1519, they were repulsed as well as fascinated by their practices, which centered on the bloody cult of the sun. Aztec cosmology and eschatology spoke of five suns or time cycles that corresponded to several creations and destructions of the world. At the time of the conquest, the Aztecs were living in the time of the fifth and last sun, called *ollin* or "movement." They were awaiting an apocalyptic end, which just happened to coincide with the arrival of the Spanish. The Aztecs feared that the sun would be smothered in its nightly disappearance below the horizon unless its was fed the blood of human sacrifices.[20] The *cultus satanicus*, as the Christians called it, consisted of preparing willing or unwilling victims and adorning them with crowns of flowers or feather-down. They were laid down and stretched X-wise, like Saint Andrew's cross, on a mirrored altar made of black volcanic glass, which is known as obsidian. The chest cavity was opened with an obsidian knife, and the live heart was extracted and offered to the sun (fig. 5). The solar god, Tecatlipoca, had as his attribute a black obsidian mirror.[21] The friars could not help but see a satanic parody of the Catholic sacrifice of the Mass in the crowning and outstretching of a man whose

18. John B. Gleason, "Sun-Worship in More's Utopia," in *Le soleil à la Renaissance: Sciences et mythes* (Brussels: Presses Universitaires de Bruxelles, 1965), 433–46.

19. Luigi Firpo, "La cité idéale de Campanella et le culte du soleil," in *Le Soleil à la Renaissance: Sciences et Mythes* (Brussels: Université Libre, 1965), 325–40; Mario Góngora, "El Nuevo Mundo en el pensamiento de Tomás Campanella," *Anuario de Estudios Americanos* 31 (1970): 385 ff. Cf. Dionysius the Areopagite, *De Divinis Nominibus*, IV.4 in *Corpus Dionysiacum I: Pseudo-Dionysius Areopagita De Divinis Nominibus*, ed. Beate Regina Suchla (Berlin: Walter de Gruyter, 1990), 147.

20. Inga Clendinnen, *Aztecs: An Interpretation* (Cambridge: Cambridge University Press, 1991), 236–63; Mercedes de la Garza, "Análisis comparativo de la *Historia de los Mexicanos por sus pinturas* y la *Leyenda de los soles*," *Estudios de Cultura Náhuat* 16 (1983): 123–34.

21. Maria Teresa Jarquín Ortega, *El culto y las representaciones solares en el arte y la arquitectura del México antiguo* (Mexico: El Colegio Mexiquense, 1996), passim.

Fig. 5. Aztec human sacrifice, sixteenth century manuscript. Codex Vaticanus
Latinus, 3738, Pl. 74.

blood was similarly redemptive, for it too kept the sun and the world going. A eucharistic element was even detected because, after the killing of the victim, his body became an anthropophagic communion meal.[22]

The mendicants deliberately attempted to replace this pagan sacrifice with that of Calvary and its unbloody sacramental repetition, as the chronicles so often state. In this task they had papal approval and encouragement, for in the year 1558 Paul IV issued a bull for all the Indies, in which he stated:

> The days which the Indians, according to their ancient rites, dedicated to the sun and to their idols should be replaced with feasts in honor of the true sun, Jesus Christ, and his most holy Mother and the saints whose feasts days the Church celebrates.[23]

It is thus no wonder that solar symbolism was incorporated into images of the cross.[24] Mexican *atrio* crosses of the sixteenth-century display the eschatological emblems of the instruments of the passion and the sun, moon, and stars on shaft and cross beam. The bust of Christ on Veronica's veil may be displayed at the intersection. More spectacularly, an obsidian mirror could replace the Holy Face of Christ (fig. 6).[25] Aztec and Maya religious iconography had, for centuries, featured cross-like cosmic trees with mirror glyphs attached to them.[26] Such mirrors on crosses could not but be read by the indigenous populations as solar symbols whose vital liquid was, in the Christian dispensation, the blood of the voluntary victim of Golgotha. Such notions of sacrifice, blood, and sun were strengthened by mounting the crosses on stepped

22. David Carrasco, "Cosmic Jaws: We Eat the Gods and the Gods Eat Us," *Journal of the American Academy of Religion* 63 (1995): 429–63. For the positive and negative reinterpretations of these "eucharistic" rituals, see Mónica Patricia Martini, *El indio y los sacramentos en Hispanoamérica colonial* (Buenos Aires: Consejo Nacional de Investigaciones Científicas y Técnicas, 1993), 188–93.

23. As quoted in Gabriel Guarda, "La liturgia: Una de las claves del barroco americano," in *El Barroco en Hispanoamérica: Manifestaciones y Significación* (Santiago de Chile: Universidad Católica de Chile, 1981).

24. For the following discussion on crosses, see my "El Espejo en la Cruz: una reflección medieval sobre las cruces atriales mexicanas," *Anales del Instituto de Investigaciones Estéticas* 68 (1996): 5–40.

25. Santiago Sebastián López, et al., *Iconografía del arte del siglo XVI en México* (Zacatecas: Universidad Autónoma de Zacatecas, 1995), 39–56.

26. Linda Schele and Mary Ellen Miller, *The Blood of Kings: Dynasty and Ritual in Maya Art* (New York: Braziller, 1986), 176–7. Mirrors had magical properties in the religion of the Incas as well; see Erland Nordensklöld, "Miroirs convexes et concaves en Amérique," *Journal de la Société des Americanistes* 18 (1926): 103–10.

Fig. 6. Atrium cross with obsidian disc, Tajimaroa, Michoacan. Instituto de
Investigaciones Estéticas, UNAM.

bases with corner spikes affecting the appearance of the horns of the altar of holocausts in the atrium of the Jerusalem temple—thus making a connection to Old Testament sacrifices of the paschal lamb. The imagery went even further at Cuernavaca where the cross is imbedded in a *cuauhxicalli*, a pre-conquest stone box for catching freshly sacrificed human hearts (fig. 7).[27] I have recently discovered that well into the seventeenth century the Nahautl word used by Christian indians for the base of the atrium cross was *momuxlti*—the same word previously used for the mirrored pagan altars of sacrifice.[28] Thus it is my contention that in Mexico a unique conflation of solar imagery and Christ's Eucharistic sacrifice on the cross was accomplished.[29]

Such a theory seems to be confirmed by anthropologists who study the present-day indigenous descendants of the Maya. The Zinacantecans and Chamulas of the state of Chiapas, for example, speak of Jesus as "our Father the Sun." This solar-Christ delimits the spatial boundaries of their universe and also maintains the critical temporal cycles that regulate their agricultural activity and ritual life.[30] The *campesinos* of Ichcatepec, Xalapa also identify Christ with the sun using the name *Totiotzi* for both, a word that means both sunlight and goodness. The Ichcatepecans observe a daily cult wherein the eldest member of the household offers incense and Christian prayers three times a day. The rite takes place facing the rising sun at the door of the house, which is incensed during the recitation of the Our Father. Similar communal rites take place during Holy Week in what has been called the "Passion and Death of Christ the Sun."[31]

27. Elizabeth Wilder Weismann, *Mexico in Sculpture 1521–1821* (Cambridge, Mass.: Harvard University Press, 1950), 20 f.

28. Günter Zimmermann, *Die Relationen Chimalpahins zur Geschichte Méxicos*, 2 vols (Hamburg: Cram, de Gruyter & Co., 1963), 2: 124 f.

29. For possible European precedents for such iconography, see Carla Ferguson O'Meara, "In the Hearth of the Virginal Womb: The Iconography of the Holocaust in Late Medieval Art," *Art Bulletin* 63, no. 1 (1981): 7–88.

30. Gary H. Gossen, "Temporal and Spacial Equivalents in Chamula Ritual Symbolism," in *Reader in Comparative Religion*, 4th ed., ed. William A. Lessa and Evon Z. Vogt (New York: Harper and Row, 1979), 135–49; Eva Hunt, *The Transformation of the Hummingbird: Cultural Roots of a Zinacantecan Mythical Poem* (Ithaca, N.Y.: Cornell University Press, 1977), 137–51: Manuel Marzal, *El Sincretismo Iberoamericano*, second ed. (Lima: Pontificia Universidad Católica del Perú, 1988), 39–74; Manuel Marazal, et al., *The Indian Face of God in Latin America* (Maryknoll, N.Y.: Orbis Books, 1996).

31. Luis Reyes García, *Pasión y Muerte del Cristo Sol*, Cuadernos de la Facultad de Filosofía y Letras 9 (Xalapa: Universidad Veracruzana, 1960), passim.

Fig. 7. *Cuauhxicalli* box reused for the base of an atrium cross, Cuernavaca,
Morelos. Weismann, *Mexico in Sculpture.*

THE ANDES

In moving on now to the Andean region, we see that a similar dynamic
related to Inca cosmology has occurred wherein the sun is called *Inti* or
Viracocha, creator. The Inca lords considered themselves to be sons of
the sun and wore solar symbols on their vesture (fig. 8). Human sacrifice was also a part of Andean solar cults.[32]

In their desire to rehabilitate *Sol* for evangelization purposes, some
of the mendicant chroniclers and their Inca converts to Christianity went

32. Sabine MacCormack, *Religion in the Andes: Vision and Imagination in
Early Colonial Peru* (Princeton: Princeton University Press, 1991), 139–81.

Fig. 8. Detail of a Peruvian Corpus Christi painting, artist unknown,
seventeenth century. Museo de Arte Religioso, Cuzco.

to great extremes to explain that solar worship was a pre-evangelical disposition given by Divine Providence, a sort of preparation for the full Gospel of Christ, the *Sol Justiciae*. For instance, Bartholomé de las Casas, the great defender of the Indians thought that the Andean peoples had a general concept of God that was so close to the truth that "one need only to help them substitute the Creator, the Sun of Justice, for the material sun. To the Creator they will then offer, with less labor than is required for sacrifices of flour and feathers, the sacrifice that the true God asks for, which is their souls."[33]

In Incan cosmology the earth's navel or world center was the imperial city of Cuzco and its temple of the Sun, Coricancha, today the Church of the Dominicans.[34] The Christianized Inca, Garcilaso de la Vega, could still remember its original arrangement, or so he thought. The sacred center of Coricancha was the Hall of the Sun. Nearby, arranged around a cloister, were five other halls dedicated to the Moon and ancillary planets. The temple had a staff of priests and consecrated virgins not unlike a Christian monastery. In the Hall of the Sun was housed the golden image of the deity, which Garcilaso took to be a gold disk in the form of a round solar face surrounded by rays and flames of fire. Mummies of deceased Inca rulers were displayed on either side of the Sun's image. The last Inca mummy faced the sun in an act of adoration, much like our Perpetual Adoration of the Blessed Sacrament.[35] Garcilaso's memory may not have been all that accurate, and it may have been colored, as I believe, by Catholic Eucharistic devotion. When the Dominicans converted the temple into their Church, they used the opening in the rear wall as a Eucharistic balcony (fig. 9). From this outdoor balcony exposition of the Sacrament in its *custodia* or liturgical monstrance took place on a regular basis, therefore replacing the gilded cult image of the sun, which had been destroyed, with the new cult object, the consecrated host in its gold or silver *ostensorium*.

Confirmation of this practice is seen in several other Andean Churches of the seventeenth and eighteenth centuries that have "Eucharistic balconies" that open eastward onto a "Garden of the Sacrament" (fig.10). One archeologist has even discovered traces of reflective glass in several of these balcony chapels, suggesting that they may have been lined with mirrors.[36] Since exposition of the Sacrament usu-

33. Marazal, *El sincretismo*, 21–38.
34. Robert Lehmann-Nitsche, *Arqueología peruana: Coricancha, el templo del sol en el Cuzco y las imagenes de su altar mayor* (Buenos Aires: Coni, 1928); Raymundo Béjar Navarro, *El Templo del Sol o Qorikancha* (Cuzco: Yañez, 1990).
35. Sabine MacCormack, 212–25.
36. Jorge Bernales Ballesteros, "Capillas abiertas en el Perú," *Arte y*

Fig. 9. Cuzco, Dominican Church, formerly the Temple of Coricancha.

Fig. 10. "Eucharistic balcony," Church of Zurite, Cuzco, Peru, sixteenth or early seventeenth century.

ally occurred in colonial times immediately after Morning Mass, it is
tempting to imagine the new sun, Christ the Eucharistic host, in the
gilded *custodia* surrounded by mirrored walls, and illuminated by the
rays of the rising sun coming from the east. Such a daring inculturation
appears to have been favorably looked upon at least until the end of the
eighteenth century.[37] The missionaries may also have had luck on their
side. The papal bull that we quoted above[38] encouraged the evangelizers to replace the feast days of the sun with Christian feasts. By a happy
set of circumstances, the Inca solar harvest feast, the Inti Rami, was
celebrated at the winter equinox. In the Southern Hemisphere, this occurs in late May or early June, thus coinciding with the greatest feast of
the late Middle Ages, the feast of Corpus Christi.[39] Once again a Eucharistic connection could be made at such a harvest event, and the sacred
host in its *custodia* could act as the centerpiece of the spectacular processions, which have been recorded in colonial paintings (fig. 11).[40]

Latin American colonial religious art is filled with solar imagery. Since
the images were by and large created by artists under the supervision of
Church officials, no one questioned their orthodoxy. Another matter entirely is how they were received and understood by the indigenous popu-
lace. One finds in the research of Teresa Gisbert de Mesa the following
examples: (1) in a solar window in the Church of Andahuailillas, Peru (fig.
12), the dove of the Holy Spirit in an Annunciation scene has been replaced
by solar window because of the prohibition on representing animals in
ecclesiastical art, for fear of zoolatry—obviously there was no fear of using
the sun for the third person of the Trinity;[41] (2) in a painting of the Blessed
Trinity (fig. 13), God the Father uses the same sun symbol on his vesture
as the Inca lords in Figure 8;[42] (3) a mural on the interior wall of the

Arqueologia 2, no. 4 (1975); Jose de Mesa y Teresa Gisbert, *Arquitectura Andina*
(La Paz: Colección Arzans y Vela, 1985), 145–62; Ramón Gutiérrez, et al.,
Arquitectura del altiplano peruano (Cuzco: Libros de Hispanoamérica, 1987), 75;
Ramón Gutiérrez, *El Valle del Colca* (Buenos Aires: Libros de Hispanoamérica,
1986), 83.
37. For official ecclesiastical solar imagery in Mexico, see Louis M. Burkhart,
"The Solar Christ in Nahuatl Doctrinal Texts of Early Colonial Mexico,"
Ethnohistory 35, no. 3 (1988): 234–56.
38. See note 23 above.
39. MacCormick, 139–81.
40. Santiago Sebastián López, *El Barroco Iberoamericano*, 83–108.
41. Teresa Gisbert, *Iconografía y mitos indígenas en el arte* (La Paz: Linea
Editorial, 1994), 29–35. Notice the Hebrew and Latin names for God that surround the window.
42. Ibid., 88–90.

Fig. 11. Detail, "Exaltation of the Eucharist," Leonardo de Flores, seventeenth century. Church of Achocalla, Bolivia.

Fig. 12. "The Annunciation," mural painting by Luis de Riaño, c. 1626. Church of Andahualillas, Peru.

Fig. 13. "The Trinity," artist unknown. Museo Histórico, Cuzco.

Church of Colquepata, Peru depicts a human figure who makes an act of adoration to the sun setting behind a hill (fig. 14).[43]

Much like the Chamulas and Icatapecans of Mexico, present-day Andean peoples conflate Jesus Christ with the sun. Unofficial Christian confraternities of Sun-Christ exist today in the Charcas province of Bolivia. The local population consider themselves to be "soldiers of the sun," and they annually celebrate a Mass of the Sun at Corpus Christi in which the solar body of Christ is ingested as a eucharistic seed that merges with the fecundating energy arising from Mother Earth.[44]

But this preoccupation with the sun was not limited to Amerindian natives with syncretic tendencies. It was also encouraged by the missionaries in their art, their music, and their theatrical performances. One of the first, if not *the* first New World play took place in Mexico in 1526 and was entitled "The Conversion and Baptism of the Last Four Kings of Tlaxcala."[45] The playwright, a mendicant friar who knew well the Apocryphal Gospels, recounts the extra-biblical story of the fall of Lucifer (the angel of light) and his cohorts while detailing the historical event of the first Mexican conversions. The kings of Tlaxcala dialogue among themselves saying:

> Was this Christ I saw, brighter than sun light, who spoke of a Holy Cross and won my heart? Although my idol be angry and should kill me, I shall take the new faith preached by these children of the Sun.

And later they pray:

> Lord, in whom I believe without having seen, why has Your love made me wish to adore you? Let the children of the Sun come and bring with them your Holy Sacrament in which I believe in spite of our idols.

The play ends with angels appearing, intoning a Eucharistic hymn: ". . . If you ask for bread in God's name, God's own substance shall be given you as bread."

The solar theme is taken up in Baroque poetry by one of the most outstanding spiritual writers of the seventeenth century, Sor Juana Inés

43. Ibid., 29–35.

44. Tristan Platt, "The Andean Soldiers of Christ: Confraternity Organization, the Mass of the Sun and Regenerative Warfare in Rural Potosí, 18th–20th Centuries," *Journal de la Société des Américanistes* 63 (1987): 139–89; N. Ross, "Los ritos fúnebres y las fiestas sagradas de la costa del norte del Perú en la integración de los pueblos, con enfoque especial en los ceremoniales de la Semana Santa y del Santísimo Sacramento de Catacos, Piura," in *Rituales y Fiestas de las Américas* (Bogotá: 45th Congreso de Americanístas, 1988).

45. Carlos Casteneda, *The First American Play* (Austin: University of St. Edward, 1936).

46. Sor Juana Inés de la Cruz, *Obras Completas* (Mexico: Editorial Porrúa,

Fig. 14. Wall mural, Church of Colquepata, Peru. Teresa Gisbert.

Fig. 15. Tabernacle door, Colombian, sixteenth century. Seminario Mayor de Bogotá.

de la Cruz, in her poem entitled *En el Sol de la Custodia*. Here is a partial translation:

> In the sun of the monstrance / God placed his throne / and as a gallant Groom / came forth from his bridal chamber. / Whenever a new temple is dedicated / he goes to the new Church as to his Bride, opening wide his arms of love. / Whenever might be the day on which the Bride-Church comes to her happy union / Christ celebrates again his wedding feast in the bridal chamber of the sun.[46]

From a slightly earlier date comes a polyphonic Eucharistic motet written in Puebla, Mexico, *En aquel pan. . . miré mi Sol.*

> In that bread which hides Him / I saw my hidden Sun / and although my senses sought / only my faith could discover him / . . . Seeing him clearly does not take place in the heights / where one may ascend / but rather within the dark cloud / which embraces the brightest sun.[47]

We have already referred to the visual arts as a means of inculturating the sun in a Eucharistic context. Three exceptional examples come from Colombia, one toward the end of the sixteenth-century, the other two toward the end of the seventeenth. The first is the door of a Eucharistic tabernacle, which is now in the collection of the Seminario Mayor de Bogotá. Once again the ancient image of the youthful god Helios greets the Christian worshipper (fig. 15). He fulfills the prophecy of Malachi in that he is the Sol Justiciae, the sun with spiritual healing in his plumed wings.[48] While this image may have meant one thing to the classically trained theologian and cleric, one can only wonder what it might have meant to the Chibcas and Muiscas whose cult images had been small gold figurines adorned with colorful plumes.

The second is from the colonial city of Tunja. The Convent of Santa Clara originally was outside the city limits, and its chapel acted as an evangelization center for the local Indians. On the ceiling directly over the high altar is one of the most delightful wooden sculptures in all Colonial art (fig. 16).[49]

1992), 312.

47. *Música del Período Colonial en América Hispanica* (Bogotá: Fundación de Música, 1995), musical recording. The composer of "En aquel Pan que le encumbre mi fe" is Juan de Padilla, 1605–1673.

48. Martin Doria, *La pintura del siglo XVI en Sudamérica* (Buenos Aires: Instituto de Arte Americano e Investigaciones Estéticas, 1952), fig. 69.

49. Little has been written on this sculpture. See *Tesoros de Tunja* (Bogotá: El Sello Editorial, 1989), 94–9.

50. Museo Colonial de Cali, Arzobispado de Cali, Colombia.

Fig. 16. Ceiling detail over high altar. Convent of Santa Clara la Real, Tunja, Colombia.

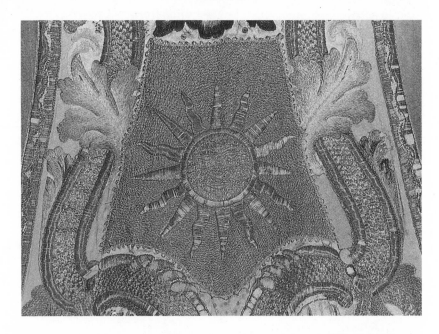

Fig. 17. Chasuble with solar ornament. Museo Colonial, Cali, Colombia.

The third Colombian example is Eucharistic vestments, whereon the sun is prominently seen on the bourse used to cover the chalice, and as a mirror on the chest of the celebrant's chasuble (fig. 17).[50]

This leads us to consider our last set of images: the Eucharistic monstrance. My research leads me in the direction of saying that the monstrance, in its well-known form as a sunburst with rays emanating from the white host, is a New World, not a European invention. No such monstrance is known in Europe before the second quarter of the seventeenth century. Europeans either used the Gothic ostensorium, which was tower shaped, imitating a Gothic Church, or the Renaissance monstrance form of a circular ring.[51] The later example may appear at first sight to be solar, but in actuality is an inverted crown, sometimes with gothic filigree. The first such ring monstrance is thought to have been that depicted in Raphael's painting *The Dispute over the Sacrament* in the Stanza della Segnatura of the Vatican palace, dating from 1509.[52] About the same time intellectual members of the papal court were intrigued by hermeticism and were writing a Christian interpretation of the Jewish Kabbala, which we mentioned above in reference to Sir Thomas More's *Utopia*.[53] In rereading Neoplatonic thought, they were moving in the direction of a heliocentrism, which they interpreted also as a Christocentrism.[54]

Nevertheless, it appears that solar iconographic associations to the Eucharistic host first took place in the New World, where from an early date Christ's Eucharist presence is called the Sol Sacramentado, the

51. Josef Braun, *Die christliche Altargerät in seinem Sein und in seiner Entwicklung* (Munich, 1931); Josef Braun, *Die Reliquiare des christlichen Kultus und ihre Entwicklung* (Fribourg, 1940); Franz X. Noppenberger, "Die eucharistiche Monstranz des Barockzeitalters" (Ph.D. diss., Ludwig Maximilians Universität, Munich, 1958), esp. 18–25; Michel Andreu, "Aux Origines du Culte du Saint-Sacrement: Reliquaries et Monstrances Eucharistiques," *Melanges Paul Peeters*, Analecta Bollandiana 68 (Brussels: Societé des Bollandists, 1950), 397–418; Manuel Tres, *Las Custodias Españolas* (Barcelona: Editiorial Litúrgica Española, 1952), 72 ff; Charles Oman, *The Golden Age of Hispanic Silver 1400–1665* (London: Victoria and Albert Museum, 1968), xxviii–xxix; Maria Jesús Sanz Serrano, *La orfebreria sevillana del barroco* (Seville, 1976), 1:154–7.

52. Noppenberger, "Die eucharistiche Monstranz," 18.

53. For Spain, see Catherine Swietlicki, *Spanish Christian Cabala: The Works of Luis de León, Santa Teresa de Jesús, and San Juan de la Cruz* (Columbia, Mo.: University of Missouri Press, 1986).

54. Heinrich Pfeiffer, *Zur Ikonographie von Raffaels Disputa: Egidio da Viterbo und die christlich-platonishe Konzeption der Stanza della Segnature* (Rome: Università Gregoriana Editrice, 1975), esp. 222 ff.

55. Constantine Bayle, *El culto del Santísimo en Indias* (Madrid: Consejo

Sacramented Sun, or the Divino Sol, the Divine Sun.[55] As I stated above, European examples of the sunburst monstrance are late, and some of the earliest European examples were actually crafted in the New World and thence imported to the Old.[56]

In the Americas of the Baroque period, spectacular Eucharist show-cases were created by native gold and silversmiths (fig. 18). A seven-teenth-century bicephalous eagle-monstrance from Popayán, Colombia is unique (fig. 19). The double-headed eagle was a symbol of the Spanish Hapsburg monarchs who considered themselves "defenders of the Eucharist." But there was also a legend among the Incas around the Popayán region about a bicephalous eagle who was the only bird than could soar as high as the sun and not be burned—a sort of Andean phoenix bird myth. The double-headed eagle appears frequently on altars as well. Once again we have the question of Spanish Catholic iconography and a possibly different reception by an indigenous audience.

Alas, the problems associated with a confusion surrounding the sun may have caused a late negative reaction to such attempts at incultura-tion. Several of the Andean Eucharistic balconies discussed earlier were bricked-up around the end of the eighteenth century in what appears as a deliberate attempt to suppress the liturgical outdoor exposition. From the year 1795 come the *Constitutions of the Diocese of Guamanga, Peru*. The second section deals with abuses around the Blessed Sacrament:

> We all know that the Indians in their pagan unbelief adored the sun, taking it to be the true God, to whom they made temples and offered sacrifice. It is our obligation to erase all memory which they still make of this superstitious and unlawful cult. Therefore, we order that every silver veil of the tabernacle, known today as "the Sun," which is used to cover the Blessed Sacrament, be removed and destroyed, because many people weak in faith, when they see this sun in such a sacred place, believe that the sun has something of divinity. We have even seen some people make an act of adoration when this solar image is placed there. In an obstinate way, they eagerly give more attention to a piece of silver or "sun" than to the tabernacle itself. Experience has demonstrated this to be true because we have found idols and other pieces of idolatry in the same altars and tabernacles.[57]

Superior de Investigaciones Científicas, 1951), passim; Ramón Gutiérrez, *Arquitectura del altiplano*, 75; Ramón Gutiérrez, *Arquitectura virreynal en Cuzco y su región* (Cuzco: Libros de Hispanoamérica, 1987), 212.

56. Marta Fajardo de Rueda, *Oribes y Plateros en la Nueva Granada* (Bogota: Banco de la República, 1990), Exposition catalogue, Museo de Arte Religioso, May–July 1990.

57. See "Adiciones ineditas a 'La Imprenta en Lima,'" *Fenix* 8 (1952): 451–3.

58. See Luis Balquiedra, "The Liturgical Principles Used by the Mission-

Fig. 18. Eucharistic monstrance, seventeenth century. Catedral de Bogotá,
Colombia.

Fig. 19. Bicephalous eagle monstrance, eighteenth century. Museo de Arte
Religioso, Popayán, Colombia.

CONCLUSION

In summation, I would like to suggest that, as regards the inculturation of the Christian faith and liturgy in the Americas, the mendicants were operating out of two general principles: dynamic equivalence and ritual substitution.[58]

1. Dynamic equivalence. The mendicants purposely selected pre-Columbian rites and religious objects that were not objectively tied to idolatry and that could be invested with a Christian interpretation without too much catechesis. Thus feathers, mirrors, jewelry, dances, musical instruments, poetic expressions, sacred geography, and even tortillas were reworked to accommodate them to the new religion.

2. Ritual substitution. While extirpating idolatry and destroying the temples with the *cultus sangrientis* (their "bloody liturgies"), the missionaries simultaneously erected Churches on top of the very same holy sites. They sought to fill the ritual vacuum with the sensorial and kinesthetic splendor of the late medieval liturgy that they had brought with them. This was nowhere more evident than in the use of the visual arts, and in the constant processions, musical spectacles and liturgical theatrics they created for the neophytes.[59] By ritual substitution and symbolic equivalency, they changed the root metaphor of a civilization from sacrificial human blood and ritual cannibalism that kept the sun spinning in its orbit to that of the Sun of Justice whose blood was willingly poured out on the cross and whose body could be ingested sacramentally. By changing the root metaphor, it appears to this author, they christianized a continent. The notions of New World sunlight, Christ, his cross, and the resplendence of divine δόξα (glory) were intertwined and thereby made into unique contributions to Christian theology and literature (fig. 20).

What relevance this historical presentation may have for Hispanics in the Church of the twentieth-century United States, I leave up to reader. If nothing else, it shows at least the sophistication of the evangelizers of the New World and their desire to accommodate the faith and its liturgy to the novel situation. In spite of all the injustices that were done during the Conquest and even in the name of Christ, the Sacramented

---

aries and the Missionary Background of the Christianization of the Philippines," *Philippiniana Sacra* 30, no. 88 (1995): 5–79.

59. See Jaime Lara, "Urbs Beata Hierusalem Americana: Stational Liturgy and Eschatological Architecture in Sixteenth-Century Mexico" (Ph.D. diss., GTU/University of California, Berkeley, 1995) and more recently, Jaime Lara, "Precious Green Jade Water: A Sixteenth-Century Adult Catechumenate in the New World," *Worship* 71 (1997): 415–28.

Fig. 20. Frontispiece. Francisco de Ossuna, *Norte de los estados . . . en las provincias de las Indias,* 1550.

Sun does evidence a certain respect for the cultures and religious instincts of the native populations.[60] In this the evangelizers anticipated by five centuries the *Constitution on the Sacred Liturgy* of the Second Vatican Council, which in paragraph 37 gives the principal of inculturation:

> The Church respects and fosters the genius and talents of the various races and peoples. The Church considers with sympathy and, if possible, preserves intact the elements in these peoples' way of life that are not indissolubly bound up with superstition and error. Sometimes in fact the Church admits such elements into the liturgy itself, provided they are in keeping with the true and authentic spirit. . . .[61]

I suggest that we see the Sacramented Sun—solar Eucharistic worship—in this light. It is part of the unique heritage of the Hispanic presence in these United States.

60. *Inculturación del Indio,* Serie Cátedra V Centenario, ed. Luciano Pereña, et al. (Salamanca: Universidad Pontificia de Salamanca, 1988), 80, ". . .nos lleva a probar que en la primera evangelización no hubo una total aculturación o transculturación—como generalmente se sostiene—sino una genuina inculturación; en otras palabras, que los primeros misioneros, después de haber llevado a cabo una *kenosis* y movidos por el *agapé,* no vinieron a destruir valores sino a construir con ellos el templo espiritual de la Iglesia y cultura cristiana. . . ."

61. *Sancrosanctum Concilium,* n. 37, in *Documents on the Liturgy 1963–1979: Conciliar, Papal, and Curial Texts* (DOL), comp. the International Commission on English in the Liturgy (Collegeville, Minn.: The Liturgical Press, 1982), 1.37.

14

Catholic Social Doctrine and Mexican American Political Thought

MARIO T. GARCÍA

I

As the Latino population in the United States continues to grow and to diversify, more scholarly attention is being paid to it. In the last two or three decades, we have witnessed a veritable boom in research in this area along with academic and research centers focused on the Latino experience either as a whole or in its various parts. Yet despite this increase in the knowledge base, scholars have had unfortunately little interest in the religious dimension of the Latino experience. In Chicano Studies, for example, there is almost no teaching curriculum in religion and only now the beginnings of substantive research in this area. The reason for this gap has to do with the more secularized orientation of the Chicano Movement during the late 1960s and early 1970s that gave rise to Chicano Studies. The Movement—with the exception of the farmworkers struggle—did not privilege religious themes and increasingly saw the Catholic Church as just another institution of domination. While this critical view of the Church was to some degree justified, it nevertheless led to the downplaying of the role of religion in Chicano life and in the early development of Chicano Studies.

The marginalization of religion during the period of the intense and militant Chicano Movement—the most dramatic and widespread explosion of social protest by Mexican Americans in this century—has had unfortunate consequences. While attempting to understand the history and experiences of Mexican people in the United States, Chicano Studies has omitted one of the critical foundations of that experience: religion and spiritual life. No society or culture, and certainly not the Chicano/Latino experience, can truly be appreciated without understanding the great influence that religion—both formal and popular

292

manifestations—plays in these cultures. This has nothing to do with the scholar's own religious beliefs, but everything to do with a recognition that religion is a central cultural variable.

One area where I believe that we need to integrate the theme of religion in Chicano/Latino Studies is in the changing political identity of Chicanos as well as of other Latino groups. Political identity has been one of my central research concerns as I have employed a generational approach in my historical studies concerning the changing character of the Mexican communities in the United States.[1] It seems to me that political and ethnic identity and consciousness in the Mexican American context has been directly and indirectly influenced by religious beliefs. This has not been the only influence as Mexican Americans and other Latinos have experienced their own particular process of acculturation or transculturation within the United States. Certainly secular American political and cultural influences—themselves not fully devoid of religious influences—have had a profound impact on the "Americanization" of Latinos. Political and ethnic consciousness is a complicated process and one which is constantly being reinvented between and even within political generations. I would like to suggest that religion plays an important role in this reinvention.

To illustrate this, I want to examine the religious influences manifested in Mexican American political thought in one key period in Chicano history. This is what I and others have referred to as the period of the Mexican American Generation.[2] This was that generation of Mexican Americans, many but not all of immigrant parents, who came of political age prior to or during the Great Depression and World War II and who struggled with dual and even multiple identities: Mexican and American and everything in between. This struggle with ethnic and political identity was made even more difficult due to the subaltern position of most Mexicans in the United States, especially in the Southwest: pools of cheap labor reinforced by severe forms of racial discrimination and segregation. One result of this generation's struggle with identity and social status was the emergence of new ethnic leadership through organizations such as the League of United Latin American Citizens (LULAC), the Mexican American Movement, the Spanish-Speaking Congress, the Unity Leagues, the American G.I. Fo-

1. See Mario T. Garcia, *Desert Immigrants: The Mexicans of El Paso, 1880–1920* (New Haven, Conn.: Yale University Press, 1981); *Mexican Americans: Leadership, Ideology, and Identity, 1930–1960* (New Haven, Conn.: Yale University Press, 1989); *Memories of Chicano History: The Life and Narrative of Bert Corona* (Berkeley and Los Angeles: University of California Press, 1994).

2. See Garcia, *Mexican Americans*.

rum, the Community Service Organization, the Asociación Nacional México-Americana, as well as through representation in key CIO unions in the Southwest. This leadership in turn started the first significant civil rights struggles by Mexican Americans in this century, predating the later Chicano Movement.

In these civil and human rights efforts from the 1930s through the 1950s—the key period of the Mexican American Generation—it appears that some areas of Mexican American political thought were influenced by Catholic social doctrine. While much work needs to be done to explore this relationship in all of its dimensions, I want to at least suggest this influence by examining two key political figures whose views helped to shape Mexican American political thought for this period through their roles, not as professional politicians or professional intellectuals, but as community leaders and community intellectuals. These two are Alonso Perales of San Antonio and Cleofas Calleros of El Paso.

II

In case studies of the Mexican American Generation, Alonso Perales and Cleofas Calleros represent two particular strands of Mexican ethnic and political evolution. Perales symbolizes that smaller body of Mexican Americans whose origins within the United States has nothing to do with mass immigration from Mexico. Rather, Perales descended from those Mexican Americans in locations such as south Texas, northern New Mexico, southern Arizona, and parts of California whose roots go back to the early Spanish colonizing efforts in the northern frontier of New Spain and the subsequent Spanish/Mexican settlements in this borderland. These Mexican Americans saw themselves as natives to the Southwest and the Anglos as the strangers and intruders.

Yet despite their native roots, these Mexican Americans constituted what I call the "conquered generation" in Chicano history. Their central political experience involved the U.S. conquest of what became the Southwest and their subsequent dispossession and disempowerment in the new American social order.

Perales's family came out of this colonized experience. Perales was born in Alice, Texas in 1898. His experience paralleled that of a small but still influential group of more middle-class Mexican Americans who, despite the new Anglo ruling economic order, were able to retain some political and economic status in still predominantly Mexican south Texas as merchants, politicians, teachers, and a few attorneys. Indeed, Perales was even more fortunate in that he was able to attend college in Washington, D.C. He served in World War I and on his return to Texas became a lawyer. He also became one of the leading Mexican American community leaders in San Antonio and south Texas. He was one of the founders of LULAC in 1929. This became the predominant civil rights group for Mexican Americans in Texas. He likewise served as a diplomat, being asked by both Republican and Democratic administrations to participate in diplomatic missions to Latin America. Perales's views on Mexican American issues were promoted by his numerous essays beginning in the 1930s published in the leading Spanish-language newspaper of Texas, *La Prensa* of San Antonio. These essays included a weekly column, which ran from the late 1940s to the late 1950s.[3]

Cleofas Calleros, on the other hand, represented another strand among Mexicans in the United States. This was the large-scale immigrant population flowing out of Mexico by the turn of the century and increasing during the period of the Mexican Revolution of 1910. Calleros's immigrant parents belonged to what I further call the "immigrant generation" in Chicano history. While there have obviously been subsequent immigrant generations of Mexicans, the initial mass one between 1900 and 1930 stands as the only one that with a few exceptions came to dominate the Mexican-based experience on this side of the border. In no other period in Chicano history have immigrants played such a dominant role than in the early part of the twentieth century. They, for the most part, overwhelmed the previous Mexican American population of the nineteenth century. Communities such as San Antonio and Los Angeles were transformed into immigrant communities.

Calleros was born in a small town in Chihuahua in 1896, two years earlier than Perales. He came to El Paso in 1902 with his parents. There along the border, Calleros grew up and became Mexican American. In Calleros's case, unlike Perales, his early socialization is clearly of Catholic origins. He attended Sacred Heart Catholic elementary school in south El Paso, the major immigrant *barrio*. However, unlike Perales, Calleros's education was limited to the eight grades available at Sacred Heart. Nevertheless, Calleros became a self-taught community intellectual as a local historian of the early Spanish/Mexican experience in the El Paso area and, like Perales, as a regular newspaper columnist, although in an English-language paper, the *El Paso Times*. Like Perales, Calleros also served in World War I and returned to his home town to became a major community leader especially through his many years as the representative of the Bureau of Immigration of the National Catholic Welfare Conference.[4]

3. See basic facts on Perales's life in Alonso Perales, *En Defensa de Mi Raza* (San Antonio: Artes Gráficos, 1937).

4. See clippings in the Cleofas Calleros Collection, Southwest Collection,

III

Although Perales and Calleros were undoubtedly influenced in their political thinking by the liberal social thought that came to be concretized in the New Deal, they also appear to have been influenced to one extent or another by Catholic social doctrine. This influence was centered on key papal encyclicals such as Pope Leo XIII's classic *Rerum Novarum* (1891) and Pope Pius XI's *Quadragesimo Anno* (1931) issued on the 40th anniversary of *Rerum Novarum*. Both of these encyclicals proposed views of humanity and society that Perales and Calleros in their own writings, columns, and reports reflected. The key influences, especially of *Rerum Novarum*, involved the proclamation that all people are equal in the eyes of God and, despite social and class difference in a new industrial order, that all men must be treated with dignity and justice. In the case of working-class people—the majority of Mexicans in the United States—this meant, as Pope Leo XIII stressed, that workers, besides being treated humanly by their employers, were entitled to a just wage for their labor. "Among the most important duties of employers," Leo XIII wrote, "the principal one is to give every worker what is justly due him. . . . To defraud anyone of the wage due him is a great crime that calls down avenging wrath from Heaven."[5]

In addition to *Rerum Novarum*'s insistence on justice for working people, the other significant part of the encyclical that resonated in the works of both Perales and Calleros is its stress on the priority of the collective good over individual attainment. *Rerum Novarum* is hardly a socialist text and indeed both *Rerum Novarum* and *Quadragesimo Anno* were written to combat socialism and communism. However, to do so both Leo XIII and Pius XI understood that the excesses of what they called "liberalism" or capitalism had to be curtailed. This meant that while both pontiffs accepted the acquisition of private property as a natural right, they also recognized that such a right carried obligations. Both employers and workers had to always keep in mind the social good of the community in the face of the jungle of uncontrolled individualism. "But if the question be asked," inquired Leo XIII, "How ought man use his posessions? the Church replies without hesitation: "As to this point, man ought not regard external goods as his own, but as common so that, in fact, a person should readily share them when he sees others in need.'"[6]

El Paso Public Library.

5. Leo XIII, *Rerum Novarum* (Boston: Pauline Book and Media, 1942), 19.
6. Ibid., 21–2.

Perales and Calleros were both staunch Catholic laymen. Historian and fellow Catholic Carlos Castañeda referred to Perales as possessing "una visión de profeta" (a vision of a prophet).[7] Calleros was often called the "apostle of the border."[8] Calleros, as noted earlier, had attended a Catholic elementary school. Both were also close to Catholic religious leaders such as Archbishop Robert E. Lucey of San Antonio, who in his own teachings, writings, and ministry, especially to his large Mexican constituency, expressed and practiced Catholic social doctrine emanating from both *Rerum Novarum* and *Quadragesimo Anno.*

In Perales's case, the direct influence of the encyclicals is less evident. However, his identification with Catholic social doctrine indirectly appears in some of his writings and statements. Perales consistently stressed the inalienable rights of Mexicans in the United States, whether native-born or of immigrant background. Clearly, these were views influenced by Jeffersonian principles, but given Perales's own strong Catholic attachments and relationships, this stress on natural rights and human dignity also drew consciously and unconsciously from Catholic social teachings.[9] Moreover, Perales was not shy about making it clear that there was no inconsistency between holding strong religious views and being American. In one of his columns in *La Prensa* he agreed, for example, with John Valls, the district attorney of Laredo, Texas, who noted that "the community that recognizes God and the dictates of one's conscience and the rights of man, possesses the spirit of true Americanism." Perales further agreed with Valls that the real patriots were those who held the constitution of the United States in one hand and the Bible in the other.[10]

Perales never directly referred to the encyclicals in his writings; the closest he came to doing this was by liberally quoting in one of his columns a speech made by Father John J. Burke, the Executive Secretary of the Bishops' Committee for the Spanish-Speaking of the Southwest, to the 1947 convention of the National Catholic Women's Conference in El Paso, which Perales attended. In this speech, Father Burke echoed a theme that Perales had been articulating for many years: the dignity of every human being as a creation and mirror of God who hence deserve to be treated as such. One could not be Christian and Catholic and practice discrimination toward fellow humans. "One can understand a pa-

7. See quote in Perales, *En Defensa,* iv.
8. Kenneth Duane Yielding, "The Apostle of the Border: Cleofas Calleros," seminar paper, Department of History, Texas Western College, May 1960, Southwest Collection, El Paso Public Library.
9. Perales, *En Defensa,* ii.
10. Ibid., 29–30.

gan and an atheist behaving like this and even treating a person like an animal," Father Burke stated and Perales agreed, "but it is difficult to understand a Catholic who recognizes his neighbor as a brother in Christ and treating that person as anything but as a child of God."[11]

In his writings where he specifically addressed the issue of religion, Perales not only encouraged Mexican Americans to practice their religion especially as Catholics, but he applied the theme of Catholic social doctrine with respect to perfecting the human condition here on earth and not just waiting for salvation and justice in Heaven. This theme, of course, would later on be elaborated even more by liberation theology. Perales in a 1945 column noted that while in the end one's destiny was controlled by God, still one had an obligation as a Christian to struggle in this life to achieve one's God-given rights, including social justice.[12] He reiterated this two years later when he wrote: "We have to understand how to help ourselves. That is, with the help of God, our progress depends in large part on ourselves."[13]

In Calleros's case, the influence of Catholic social doctrine on his political views are much more direct. This was the result of his own involvement not only with Church lay organizations such as the Knights of Columbus, the Catholic Welfare Association of El Paso, and the Diocesan Council of Catholic Men, but more significantly with his long-term association, beginning in 1926, with the National Catholic Welfare Conference (NCWC) as head of its Immigration Bureau in El Paso. The NCWC, which was organized in the United States in 1919, was a direct outgrowth of Catholic social doctrine beginning with *Rerum Novarum*. Its specific mandate when approved by Pope Benedict XV was for the purpose of "unifying, coordinating, and organizing the Catholic people of the United States in works of education, social welfare, immigration aid, and other activities."[14] Part of the charge of the NCWC especially through its Department of Social Action was "to promote the social teaching of the Church and to integrate, under the guidance of the Bishop, the application of this teaching to the complex social problems of the country."[15] The Department of Social Action focused on what it called the "industrial question" by "making known, exploring, and trying to show the application to America of Leo XIII's great Encyclical *The Condition of Labor* (*Rerum Novarum*); of the incomparable Encyclical of Pius XI, *Reconstructing the Social Order* (*Quadragesimo Anno*)."[16]

11. As quoted in *La Prensa*, 26 October 1947, 3.
12. *La Prensa*, 18 November 1945, 6.
13. *La Prensa*, 28 December 1947, 3.
14. See document "National Catholic Welfare Conference," 31, Calleros Collection, Southwest Collection, El Paso Public Library.
15. Ibid., 26.
16. Ibid., 27.

As a result of Calleros's work with local relief and recovery programs during the depths of the Great Depression in El Paso, he requested copies of *Rerum Novarum* from the Director of the Bureau of Immigration of the NCWC in Washington, D.C. He received copies not only of *Rerum* but of *Quadragesimo Anno*.[17]

As a way of more specifically applying Catholic social doctrine to Mexicans in the United States, in 1943 the NCWC, with the support of Archbishop Lucey of San Antonio, sponsored a Conference on Spanish-Speaking People of the Southwest in San Antonio, which Calleros was invited to attend. It is not known whether Perales, who was friends with Calleros, also attended. Coming in the wake of the Zoot-Suit Riots in Los Angeles a month earlier when armed forces personnel indiscriminately attacked Mexican Americans in the streets of Los Angeles, the conference aimed at coming up with strategies to deal with issues of poverty and discrimination facing Mexicans, both native-born and immigrants, in the Southwest. In his opening address, Archbishop Lucey made it very clear that the conference and the work of its delegates was inspired by Catholic social thought as applied to the Mexican American condition. "If I were asked to mention one outstanding problem that weighs most heavily upon our Mexican people I would say that it is the burden of undeserved poverty." Lucey added in words that Calleros undoubtedly agreed with:

> These people are our people. They are the most numerous body of Catholics in the whole Southwest. They are God's children created to His image and likeness. All of us, English and Spanish-speaking Catholics, have been blessed with the same heritage of Christian faith. We receive with them the same sacraments, at the baptismal font, at the altar, in the tribunal of repentance and the last anointing on our bed of death. With them we believe, we pray, we are governed. With them we strive for salvation in a blessed immortality.[18]

Whether apparent as in the case of Calleros or more indirect as in the case of Perales, Catholic social doctrine appears to have been part of the "intellectual baggage" that both leaders brought to their views on Mexican American issues.

17. See Calleros to Bruce Mohler, El Paso, 28 July 1933; and Mohler to Calleros, Washington, D.C., 2 August 1933, Cleofas Calleros Collection, ACC 933, Box 31, Folder 3, Special Collections, University of Texas at El Paso (UTEP).

18. See typescript copy of Archbishop Lucey's address to the Conference on Spanish-Speaking People of the Southwest, San Antonio, 20 July 1943 as well as additional correspondence on the conference in Calleros Collection, Southwest Collection, El Paso Public Library.

IV

In their capacities as community leaders, both Perales and Calleros spoke
out on a range of issues that paralleled the Church's social doctrines.
First and foremost was concern over the treatment of labor in the case
of Mexican workers in the United States, both native-born and immigrants. Catholic social thought beginning with *Rerum Novarum*, of course,
stressed the need for employers to treat workers humanly, including
the distribution of just wages. Both Perales and Calleros echoed this
theme with respect to Mexican workers. They agreed that Mexican workers did not receive a just wage. At a two-day regional meeting of the
Catholic Conference on Industrial Problems in Los Angeles in 1930,
Calleros in his address to the group observed that the Mexican as a
laborer was considered by employers as an asset, but that the full importance of his work was not appreciated and hence not paid a fair
return.[19] Perales in quoting Father Burke's talk in 1947 seconded this
critique. "One of the sins that cries out for God's vengeance," Father
Burke exclaimed, "is the denial to the worker of a just wage and our
pontiffs have stressed that a just wage is one that makes it possible for a
man to live in reasonable comfort and frugality with his family."[20]

A just wage made it feasible for workers, including Mexicans, to
achieve a higher standard of living. But this unfortunately was not the
case with Mexican workers. In 1931 Calleros noted that he was in the
process of doing a survey in El Paso to determine how many contrac-
tors paid their workers, predominantly Mexicans, less than $2 a day—
less than what Calleros regarded as a living wage.[21] "There is no doubt
but that the Mexican is exploited; he is never paid a living wage,"
Calleros told a Texas Conference of Social Welfare in Waco, Texas in
1938. "As a matter of fact industry generally considers him so many
pounds of flesh performing any given task for the least possible wages."[22]
Perales believed that employers should raise salaries for their Mexican
workers out of both humanistic as well as economic motives: "In order
for the Mexican to educate himself and his children and to live in good
and sanitary housing it is absolutely indispensable that he receive for
his labor a wage that will permit him to live a normal human life. I
firmly believe that if employers who hire Mexican workers would raise

19. See clipping, *Los Angeles Times,* 31 March 1930, Calleros Scrapbook,
Southwest Collection, El Paso Public Library.
20. As quoted in *La Prensa,* 16 November 1947, 3.
21. See clipping, *El Paso Times,* 9 June 1931, Calleros Scrapbook.
22. See Calleros, "Social and Welfare Problems with Mexicans in Texas,"
typescript, Calleros Collection, Acc 933, Box 31, Fld. 3 in Special Collection,
UTEP.

their wages that they would be performing not only a humanistic act but that it would benefit the whole community economically."[23] In again quoting from Father Burke, Perales agreed with Burke's encouragement to Catholic women who employed Mexican domestics to raise the wages of their employees. "Pay them an adequate wage," Father Burke exhorted, "even if your neighbor doesn't." He also encouraged the Anglo women to organize campaigns in favor of better wages for young Mexican females who worked in five and dime stores, in department stores, and in factories. "Nobody knows how many young single women have been forced into dishonorable work," Father Burke concluded, "due to being unable to gain a living wage."[24]

Both Perales and Calleros acknowledged that the false stereotyping of Mexican workers as lazy and unproductive too often was manipulated by employers to justify paying them low wages. "Of course," Calleros noted in 1938,

> we always hear the cry that he (the Mexican) is paid low wages, because he is naturally lazy. We find lazy workmen amongst all racial groups but we seem to capitalize in the poor Mexican's patience, brand him as lazy and offer him low wages, which by necessity, he has to accept. Hundreds of personal interviews with employers and foremen invariably bear out the fact that a Mexican workman is highly competent when shown a given task and is properly instructed in the proper performance and in the way it must be completed. Those who are lazy, or become lazy on their jobs, are forced to become so by the 'lazy-low' wages paid.[25]

Perales further observed that one of the false arguments used by employers of Mexican women in stores and factories as well as of domestics was that these women by nature had low standards of living and consequently it would do no good to raise their wages because they would squander it away.[26] Calleros's and Perales's critique of such stereotyping to justify low wages was endorsed by Archbishop Lucey who, in his address to the Conference on Spanish-Speaking People, observed:

> One of the myths seriously entertained by some English-speaking Americans is that Mexican workers are lazy, slow and improvident. He would indeed be an optimist who would declare that no Mexican workers deserve that description. But the same is true of all nationals—a few are improvident but the vast majority are normal, hard working people. . . . And right here a thought occurs to me which I believe has validity. How hard would an Irishman work if you paid

23. Perales, *En Defensa,* 67.
24. As quoted in Perales's column, *La Prensa,* 16 November 1947, 3.
25. See Calleros, "Social and Welfare Problems."
26. *La Prensa,* 2 November 1947, 3.

him twenty cents an hour? How much exuberance, vitality and enthusiasm could any people show who had been underpaid, undernourished and badly housed for half a century?[27]

Such unjust and nonliving wages came to be called "Mexican
wages." Calleros and Perales noted that these were the lowest wages
paid to any workers in the Southwest. Perales observed that when a
Mexican received employment he was forced to accept less pay than an
Anglo or non-Mexican of equal experience or lack of experience.[28]
Calleros remarked in 1930 about the "Mexican wage": "The employer
believes that because of the mere fact he is a Mexican he is supposed to
receive a smaller wage and is expected to live on less."[29]

Besides bringing attention to the injustice involved in the "Mexican
wages," Perales and Calleros also supported public policy to eliminate
such an injustice. Perales, for example, in a 1937 column encouraged
other Mexican Americans to support New Deal legislation such as the
Black-Connery Wage and Hour Bill before the Congress that would
mandate a minimum wage, maximum hours of work, and prohibit in-
terstate transportation of goods produced by child labor. All three aspects of this bill, Perales stressed, would improve the Mexican workers'
position in the United States. "We Mexican Americans," he wrote, "who
truly wish our people to progress should immediately support this legislation. We should realize that as long as our people are paid less than
a living wage that would allow them to live as human beings, we cannot progress."[30] At the 1930 Los Angeles Catholic Conference on Industrial Problems, Calleros undoubtedly supported the proposal by Father
Thomas J. O'Dwyer, Director of the Catholic Welfare Bureau of Los Angeles, who in his address to the conference noted that low-wages were
the single cause of poverty and called for legislation to correct this problem. "It is our duty," he said, "to sponsor and support in every way
possible legislation that will procure for the workman his fundamental
right to a living wage, adequate protection against industrial hazards
and an income that will provide properly for old age."[31]

Regrettably, several years later in 1962, Calleros observed that the
practice of paying "Mexican wages" to Mexican workers still was occurring in the Southwest with the consequences of continued underdevelopment for the Mexican. In reacting to an article that blamed Mexicans for their lack of progress, Calleros angrily responded: "The real

27. As quoted in clipping, 20 July 1943, Calleros Collection, Southwest
Collection, El Paso Public Library.
28. *La Prensa,* 3 December 1939, 3, 6.
29. See clipping, *The Denver Post,* 30 September 1930, Calleros Scrapbook.
30. *La Prensa,* 1 August 1937, second section, p. 7.
31. See clipping *Los Angeles Times,* 30 April 1930, Calleros Scrapbook.

reason that they live in deplorable conditions is due to the fact that the majority are not paid a living wage, and that is our fault. How can we expect them to live with all the thrills and frills of our 'standard of living' if we do not pay them a living wage?"[32]

Mexican wages and the lack of a living wage in turn was symptomatic of the fact that Mexican workers were also relegated to what were literally called "Mexican jobs." These were the lowest and most menial unskilled jobs in the Southwest. "Mexican jobs" were justified, as with "Mexican wages," by the stereotype that Mexicans were incapable of more skilled labor and that, like blacks, they were more physically suited than Anglos to perform menial labor. Both Perales and Calleros consistently called attention to job discrimination in the case of Mexicans and encouraged the upgrading of job opportunities for Mexicans. Mexicans were not only initially hired in these "Mexican jobs," but even after acquiring work experience and even some education, they in most cases were still denied job mobility. "There is no such thing as promotion," Calleros noted of Mexican workers. "It is for that reason that he cannot adjust his ways because he is not given the means to adjust his life to the 'American way of life.'"[33] Calleros further observed in 1930 that in a recent survey that he had made in El Paso, he had discovered that Mexicans who had acquired some education were still denied better jobs. Moreover, in a visit to Kansas City, he observed that some Mexican female high school graduates were discriminated in job opportunities and were forced to take unskilled jobs in factory work. Such discrimination discouraged many Mexicans from acquiring more education either for themselves or for their children.[34] In a speech before a convention of teachers of adult night schools, Perales noted that such night schools needed to train Mexicans for better skilled jobs and that this training had to be linked with equal employment opportunities. "I am one who believes," Perales told his audience, "that my community is deserving of the opportunity to learn the same knowledge and skills and to acquire the same jobs and professions as are available to those of Anglo background."[35]

In addition to supporting livable wages and better jobs for Mexicans, neither Calleros nor Perales appear to have made any distinction between Mexican Americans and Mexican nationals in the United States. Both believed that neither group should be discriminated against in

32. See Calleros to Mohler, El Paso, 29 August 1962, Calleros Collection, Southwest Collection, El Paso Public Library.

33. Calleros, "Social and Welfare Problems."

34. See clipping, *Southern Messenger,* 16 October 1930, Calleros Scrapbook.

35. *La Prensa,* 29 December 1940, 2.

employment, education, and in public facilities. Both groups, in keeping with Catholic social doctrine, were deserving of social justice and of dignity as working people. Calleros, in particular, due to his position as head of the Bureau of Immigration of the NCWC, paid attention to the rights of immigrants.

This attention was especially critical during the early years of the Great Depression when efforts were made in the Southwest and elsewhere to scapegoat Mexican immigrant workers as one of the causes for the Depression by the false charge that they were taking jobs away from "real" Americans. This resulted in large-scale deportations and repatriation drives that forced close to half a million Mexicans out of the country, many of them illegally since this included the U.S.-born children of immigrants. From his position in El Paso, Calleros witnessed this tragic story of the "repatriados" or repatriates. "Words fail to describe the condition of some of these unfortunates reaching the border," Calleros stated in 1932. "They are penniless, hungry, with troubled minds as to their future, as to what to expect in Mexico, and with a feeling that they are being forced out of the United States through racial and other contributing causes."[36]

As head of the Immigration Bureau of the NCWC, Calleros was responsible for most of the U.S.-Mexico border region. His main task with respect to the "repatriados" was to insure that they were adequately provided for while they waited to return to Mexico, since relief agencies including federal ones often refused to help them.[37]

Moreover, Calleros worked to prevent those who were U.S. citizens or who were legal residents from being illegally returned to Mexico. The issue of nationality was not one that U.S. immigration officials concerned themselves with in the process of deporting or repatriating Mexicans. If you were of Mexican descent, it was assumed that you were a noncitizen and possibly an illegal alien. Race and cultural background seemed to be the criteria for determining one's nationality. In a later 1972 interview with historian Oscar Martínez, Calleros still expressed outrage at this lack of discrimination on the part of officials. In "a Depression when it comes in any country," Calleros told Martínez,

> the ones who suffer are supposed to be aliens. And very few Americans know the difference between being a citizen and being a Mexican national. They look at them and say, "Oh, you are a Mexican." The average American does not believe in the constitutional rights for others. As a matter of fact, he doesn't even know what the Consti-

36. See untitled clipping, 18 January 1932, Calleros Scrapbook.
37. See Calleros, "New Mexican Immigrants Into the United States," typescript, undated, Calleros Archives, vol. 16, Carbon Copy Letters, 1958–1960, Southwest Collection, El Paso Public Library.

tution says. So the thing was nationally—from El Paso to Vermont and from the Carolinas to California—to get rid of the Mexicans, just like that. And within six months over 400,000 individuals of different ages had been sent to Mexico.[38]

In a 1934 report, Calleros observed that of the Mexican "repatriados" he had dealt with, more than 80 per cent were U.S. citizens. For those, especially children and teenagers, who had grown up on this side of the border, a new life in Mexico proved to be traumatic. Hence, many families or individuals returned to the border crossing areas such as El Paso where Calleros attempted to secure their entrance back into the United States on the basis that they were American citizens.[39]

Calleros was particularly concerned about families being separated. In some cases one of the parents who could not prove legal residence in the United States was deported or "convinced" to repatriate back to Mexico leaving the rest of their family including small children on the north side of the border. Calleros worked to prevent such family separation or to reunite those families by documenting the legal residence of the deported or repatriated parent.[40]

In his work with the "repatriados" and with Mexican immigrants over the years, Calleros reinforced the Catholic Church's efforts to include immigrants within the fold of Catholic social doctrine. While much of the Church's work in the United States concerned European immigrants, Calleros expanded these services and protection to the U.S.-Mexico border. Calleros's work was recognized as early as 1929 when Father John J. Burke, the General Secretary of the NCWC, said of Calleros: "If we could have a few men with the experience and ability and Catholic spirit of Mr. Calleros, going through the country, both speaking to the Mexicans directly and interesting Catholic native Americans in the importance and pressing nature of this problem."[41]

V

Calleros's and Perales's reaction to the so-called "Mexican problem" included one of the important additions that both men made directly

38. Interview with Calleros by Oscar Martínez, 14 September 1972, Institute of Oral History, UTEP, Transcript No. 157.

39. For excerpts from Calleros's 1934 report see Mohler to Alice W. O'Connor, Washington, D.C., 11 August 1936, Calleros Collection, ACC 933, Box 2, Folder 2, Special Collection, UTEP.

40. See, for example, Calleros to Mohler, El Paso, 12 October 1933, Calleros Collection., ACC 933, Box 31, Folder 3, Special Collection, UTEP.

41. Rev. John J. Burke to Frank Gross, Washington, D.C., 21 September 1929, Calleros Collection, ACC 933, Box 3, Folder 2, Special Collection, UTEP.

and indirectly to Catholic social thought. That is, while encyclicals such as *Rerum Novarum* and *Quadragesimo Anno* addressed very well the issues of class conflict with respect to industrial workers in Europe, they did not deal with the additional social injustice of race prejudice. This omission was particularly noticeable in the United States where race conflict was as significant as class conflict. Aware of the importance of race in American culture, both Perales and Calleros focused not just on the class injustices suffered by Mexicans in the Southwest, but the racial ones as well.

Perales, for example, stressed the basic and fundamental equality of all people irrespective of race. Human beings, despite ethnic differences, were all equal beings. And no group was inferior or superior to another. This, argued Perales, certainly applied to Mexican-Anglo relations. "The Mexican people," he wrote, "do not pertain to a fundamentally inferior race. The history of our people proves this." Indeed, he stated: "Mexicans are descendants of two great peoples: the indigenous and the Spanish."[42] Perales noted that being proud of his Mexican background and of his American citizenship only convinced him further of the equality of all peoples.[43]

The problem in race relations in the United States and specifically in the Southwest, Perales contented, had nothing to do with race per se, but with attitudes. Anglos believed themselves to be superior to Mexicans even though this was not true. Perales appeared to be arguing that the notion of race represents not a scientific construction, but a social and a political one in order for one group to acquire power and privileges over another. If attitudes created a race problem, then for Perales the solution was to transform these attitudes rather than the system that hosted them. In this view, Perales was consistent with Catholic social thought, which in the case of class conflict did not see capitalism as at fault, but rather the excesses of capitalism. While Perales certainly understood the economic consequences of the race problem in the Southwest, he seems to have attached greater weight to race issues as first and foremost an ideological conflict. Throughout most of his writings, Perales emphasized that race relations would not improve in Texas, for example, until a solid body of Anglos came to the conclusion or were brought to the conclusion that Mexicans were equal human beings and deserving of mutual respect. Furthermore, he believed that what was also needed was for Anglos to provide Mexicans with the equal opportunities to prove themselves as equal and as capable as any other group.[44]

42. Perales, *En Defensa,* 10.
43. Ibid., 82, 85.
44. Ibid., 3, 11, 23, 51, 69, 100.

If Mexicans were equal to others based on natural human rights, they were also equal, Perales argued, on the basis of law and of their contributions to American society. Perales reminded Anglos that under the Constitution of the United States, Mexicans, whether citizens or immigrants, were equal in the eyes of the law.[45] Moreover, during World War II, Perales did not hesitate to point out the loyalty of Mexican Americans to the United States. They were putting their lives on the line for their country and because of this were deserving of being treated as equally as any other American ethnic group. About half a million Mexican Americans were fighting the "good war" and Perales believed that they were entitled to come back to a Texas where they would have equal rights and equal opportunities with other Texans. "Our hope," he wrote in 1944, "is that when our brothers return from the warfront that they will find if not a more truly democratic Texas at least a political climate much healthier than when they left to go to war." Perales added that the following slogan needed to apply:

> Equal in the trenches, but also equal in the factories, in the stores, in the schools, in the Churches, in the restaurants, in the barbershops, in the theaters, and everywhere else.[46]

The most onerous manifestation of racial injustice for Perales and Calleros, as well as for the rest of the Mexican American Generation, consisted of educational discrimination including school segregation for most Mexican American children. Since the turn of the century when mass immigration from Mexico commenced, the practice of the public schools in the Southwest was to establish segregated and inferior schools in the *barrios* and in the countryside for Mexicans. These were the so-called "Mexican schools" that despite their designation revealed little if any sensitivity to the cultural backgrounds of the students. Instead, they provided limited educational opportunities stressing vocational education. As segregated schools, they were inherently unequal.

Both Perales and Calleros understood this and spoke out against such segregation and inferior education. Perales observed that education in the United States was not a privilege, but a right that was being deprived Mexican American children. This deprivation was particularly troublesome to Perales because he further understood that education was the key avenue for Mexican American mobility. It would not only open the doors for better jobs and livable wages—what the encyclicals called for—but would also assist in the social and political inte-

45. Ibid., 27.
46. *La Prensa*, 4 June 1944, 1–2; 22 April 1945, 6.

gration of Mexican Americans. "Education is the most important factor," Perales stressed in 1928, "since human progress depends on it."[47]

Perales also made it clear that the only explanation for the exclusion of Mexican Americans from equal education with Anglo children
was racism. He rejected the often-repeated response by school administrators and school boards throughout the Southwest that the "Mexican schools" existed only to deal with special pedagogical issues appli-
cable to Mexican American students such as language difference. Perales
conceded that perhaps some initial special instruction had to be provided for those Mexican American children who entered school speaking only Spanish, but that such separation should be limited to the first
few years. "With reference to the segregation of our children in Texas
schools," Perales wrote, "that segregation which exists beyond the third
grade is purely racial. . . . and it is illegal and we also know that school
officials always come up with an excuse to skirt the spirit if not the
letter of the law."[48] Indignant about such practices in Texas, Perales in
1932 went so far as to declare to the annual LULAC convention that if
ever the U.S. Supreme Court would approve the segregation of Mexican American children in the public schools that he would give up his
U.S. citizenship in protest.[49]

Calleros further pointed out that the denial of equal educational
opportunities and facilities to Mexican Americans represented part of
the denial of social justice to Mexicans in the United States. Calleros in
particular attacked the practice of the public schools utilizing questionable and biased intelligence tests as applied to Mexican American children in order to justify continued segregation and inferior education.
He especially reacted to a 1940 report on such tests in El Paso by a Dr. I.
M. Epstein who concluded that an even lower educational standard
than the one already being applied in the south side "Mexican schools"
needed to be implemented in keeping with what Epstein concluded
was the lower mental capacities of most of the Mexican American children. According to Epstein, the Mexican American students tested significantly lower than Anglo students in the north side schools with the
results suggesting that most of the Mexican American children were
mentally retarded, feebleminded, or slow learners.[50]

Calleros, in a letter to the *El Paso Times* that minced few words,
attacked the Epstein report and its conclusions as racist. "The report is

47. *La Opinión*, 25 August 1928, 3.
48. Perales, *En Defensa*, 14.
49. See clipping in *La Prensa*.
50. See clipping, untitled, no date, Calleros Scrapbook, vol. II, Southwest
Collection, El Paso Public Library.

unfair and highly colored with racial prejudice," Calleros asserted. "It brands the south side school children as dumbbells and of low mentality." Calleros instead pointed out what he believed to be the real factors behind the educational underdevelopment of the Mexican American children. This included a disproportionate number of halftime classes, overcrowded classrooms, and inferior school buildings. "To these may be added the following facts which also contribute," Calleros noted:

1. The segregation of children by racial classification.
2. The flagrant racial prejudice of some school officials and teachers.
3. The constant evidence of some officials and teachers in having the so-called "Mexican" child feel that he is inferior to his so-called "white" companion although both are, believe [it] or not, of the white race.[51]

If Epstein's report concluded that the educational practices as applied to the south side schools was a failure, Calleros observed, then that failure had nothing to do with the children and everything to do with the school system itself. Moreover, this failed system was in the hands of Anglo administrators who could impose reforms, but that such changes would not come about as long "as the system persists in some of their racist tactics and in giving the south side schools the 'leavings or discards.'" Calleros concluded that the problem lay with a fundamental contradiction in the public schools:

The fact is that too much good American citizenship is preached and very little practiced. So-called 'Mexican' children are constantly reminded that they are expected to be good citizens and the same reminders turn right around and deny them the same privileges accorded other human beings.[52]

If educational discrimination represented an affront to the dignity of Mexican Americans, so too was discrimination in public facilities. Both Perales and Calleros protested such discrimination and called for particular measures, including legislation, to eliminate it. According to Perales, such discrimination was widespread throughout Texas. In 1942 he supported efforts by both the U.S. and Mexican governments to investigate discrimination against Mexican contract workers in Texas—the *braceros*—but at the same time pointed out that such discrimination, especially in public facilities, had a very long and ugly history. Perales noted that he personally possessed data on at least 150 cities and towns in Texas where at a minimum ten commercial establishments refused

51. See clipping, *El Paso Times,* 10 May 1940, Calleros Scrapbook, vol. II, Southwest Collection, El Paso Public Library.
52. Ibid.

services to Mexicans, both citizens and immigrants.[53] In one particular case, Perales in 1937 protested to the mayor of San Angelo about the segregation of Mexicans along with blacks in the balcony of the municipal auditorium. "I write to energetically protest against the insult to the dignity of Mexicans," Perales wrote, "and to solicit your assistance so that this humiliation not be repeated."[54] Perales further noted that such discrimination also pertained to restaurants, barbershops, and many other establishments.[55]

Calleros, for his part, later recalled how wide and distasteful this discrimination was: "There were towns in Texas where Mexicans were actually forced to walk on the street, denying them the privilege of using the sidewalk; services were refused in most restaurants and movie houses."[56]

Perales in particular advocated legislation to outlaw such affronts toward Mexicans. In 1941 he wrote to Undersecretary of State Sumner Wells informing him of an incident in New Braunfels, Texas where a group of Venezuelan air force pilots who were in training in San Antonio were told to vacate certain tables in a public park because those were reserved for whites, while some other tables were for Latin Americans. Besides such an incident harming inter-American relations advocated by Franklin Roosevelt's Good Neighbor Policy, Perales inquired of Wells if the President could ask Congress to pass a law prohibiting such discrimination. He reminded Wells of the large numbers of Mexican Americans serving in World War II. He further informed the secretary of another incident in Lockhart, Texas where a group of Mexicans were ordered to leave a public Fourth of July dance, being told that this was a celebration only for Americans and for whites.[57]

During the war, Perales supported making the Fair Employment Practice Commission into a permanent arm of the federal government and of expanding its work to include investigating incidents of discrimination in public facilities. He also attempted, unsuccessfully, to get the Texas state government to pass antidiscrimination laws concerning public facilities.[58]

53. *La Prensa*, 21 December 1942, 3.
54. Perales, *En Defensa*, 73.
55. *La Prensa*, 4 June 1944, 1–2.
56. Calleros, "LULAC and Its Origin," typescript, Calleros Archives, vol. 16, Carbon Copy Letters, 1958–1960, Southwest Collection, El Paso Public Library.
57. *La Prensa*, 12 October 1941.
58. *La Prensa*, 18 March 1945, 2; 27 February 1944, 3, 6.

VI

On these issues, as well as in their efforts to acquire adequate and equal public resources for Mexican residents in Texas communities, Perales and Calleros embodied a consciousness and a commitment to achieving social justice and the common good for Mexicans in the United States. These themes of social justice and the common good with respect to labor, wages, education, and the dignity of Mexicans as human beings complemented and resonated directly and indirectly with Catholic social doctrines. What this suggests is that Mexican American political thought during the period of the Mexican American Generation, as exemplified in the writings and praxis of both Perales and Calleros, possessed a religious and a specific Catholic dimension that needs to be acknowledged and examined even more closely in other writers and activists of this formative period in Chicano history.

15

Community and the Sacred in Chicano Theater

Marcos Martínez

The role of the Catholic Church in the colonization of the New World placed an indelible stamp upon the various societies that have emerged since the initial encounter between Spain and the Americas. The theater, once a proselytizing and colonizing tool, remains an effective means for communicating the immediacy and relevance of the sacraments and the social and political needs of parishioners. Any discussion about the sacred in Chicano Theater must consider the presence of Christian faith and the indigenous belief systems it attempted to supplant or destroy. This paper provides an opportunity for clergy and professionals involved in lay activities within the Catholic Church to reflect upon and address issues and themes present in Chicano Theater. Additionally, I consider how the consistent presence of sacred forms in our community (Easter Passion Plays and *Pastorelas*), and the continual presence of a relationship to God as a dramatic theme coincide with issues of social justice in Chicano Theater. These elements are part of an existing informal framework that includes theater artists, the Church, and the Chicano community that may have unexplored potential for collaboration and community development.

Overview of the Presence of the Sacred in Chicano Theater

I use the word "sacred" to mean "venerable, worthy of respect, set apart for worship."[1] The word "community" includes both the geographical location of the *barrio* and the psychic domain of Latino and non-Latino Catholics responsive to Chicano/Latino issues and art. "Chicano" refers specifically to the Mexican American experience; "Latino" encom-

---

1. *American Heritage Dictionary*, 3rd ed., s.v. "sacred."

passes a broader range of communities that share some of the same
linguistic, social, political, and cultural concerns.

The use of sacred elements in the formation of *mestizo* culture in the
southwest United States cannot be discounted when examining the history of Chicano Theater. In his study of New Mexico history Ramón
Gutiérrez offers insights on the Church's reliance on the use of drama
to proselytize Native Americans and transform their cultures:

> The reorganization of Puebloan temporal rhythms was also under-
> taken by establishing a rival ritual calendar that was incarnational
> and Christocentric—focused on Christ's birth and death rather than
> on cosmological events. For this the friars depended primarily on the
> *autos sacramentales,* didactic religious plays based on New and Old
> Testament narratives, popular Christian traditions, and episodes from
> the history of Mexico and New Mexico's conquest. Historians and
> literary critics for some time have regarded these plays as quaint folk-
> loric curiosities, ignoring their powerful political content and the val-
> ues their rhetorical gestures were intended to communicate. The text
> of every *auto* had a subtext concealed in the costumes, generational
> casting, and dramatic actions. Every text had its context. Drama was
> not pure entertainment but a moving, pedagogical instrument. The
> explicit purpose of the *auto* was to inculcate the Indians with a highly
> ideological view of the conquest, simultaneously forging in their
> minds a historical consciousness of their own vanquishment and sub-
> ordination as the Spaniards wanted it remembered.[2]

Native ceremonies banned at the behest of Church officials were
replaced with dramatizations of scriptures, the mounting of traditional
Passion Plays to commemorate Holy Week, and Shepherd's Plays during the Christmas season. These plays continue to be performed up to
the present, marking the best of the Church's theatrical tradition in the
Southwest. Without proceeding into anthropological discussions about
the development of Hispanic communities in the American Southwest,
it is clear that existing traditions of theatrical representation remain, if
not close to, at least considerate of the Church. This may have been
especially true in earlier periods when priests were often among the
few literate members in a community. It became less the case with the
development of mercantilism and the introduction of public schooling.

Nicolás Kanellos's exhaustive study of Hispanic Theater in the
United States explores the presence of sacred elements and Church relationships among professional theater companies. In San Antonio at
the turn of the century, the Compañia Dramática Solsona performed *El*

2. Ramón A. Gutiérrez, *When Jesus Came, the Corn Mothers Went Away: Marriage, Sexuality, and Power in New Mexico, 1500–1846* (Stanford: Stanford University Press, 1991), 83.

ángel conciliador as reported in *La Fe Católica*, 7 May 1898.[3] Later, in 1930
The Asociación de Señoritas Esclavas de la Virgen performed the secu-
lar one-act comedy, *Levantar muertos* by Eusebio Blasco and Ramos
Carrión, and the "juguete cómico," *Los apuros de un fotógrafo* at the
Nuestra Señora de Dolores church hall.[4] According to Kanellos, the use
of venues also provides a glimpse into the relationship between the
Church and the promotions. In San Antonio

> church and community auditoriums were somewhat better equipped
> for professional productions. The first and most important of these
> was the San Fernando Cathedral auditorium. Used since the turn of
> the century for professional, amateur, and charity performances, the
> San Fernando had built a long and intimate relationship with the
> Mexican community. In fact, San Fernando Cathedral developed out
> of one of San Antonio's original missions and probably had an un-
> broken history of religious theatre, *pastorelas,* and pageants. In 1929,
> a lay organization associated with the cathedral emerged as favoring
> theatrical arts: Hijas de María (Daughters of the Virgin Mary). This
> lay society began sponsoring plays by San Antonio's professional
> actors to raise funds for the church. For the most part, most of the
> performances sponsored were of secular drama, except during feast
> days, Easter week, and special occasions.[5]

In addition to the obvious preoccupations of consistently producing community and professional theater companies is the underlying
sense of sacrifice that accompanies theater work. One may argue that
the vocation of theater activist bears some similarities to that of a priest.
Both are involved with the hearts and minds of people, and both use
public and private time to bring meaning into the life of a community.
There is a reciprocal quality to these vocations. In the theater, the medi-
ums of acting and production are often inseparable from the message,
while in the Church the message, or text, is the medium of communication.

In some theater groups the notion of what Peter Brook refers to as a
holy theater is the central core of the work, and sacred elements are
consciously used and explored to convey meaning. "The act of performance is an act of sacrifice, of sacrificing what most men prefer to hide—
this sacrifice is his gift to the spectator. Here there is a relation between
actor and audience similar to the one between priest and worshipper. . . .
This theater is holy because its purpose is holy; it has a clearly defined

3. Nicolás Kanellos, *A History of Hispanic Theatre in the United States: Origins to 1940* (Austin: University of Texas Press, 1990), 72.
4. Ibid., 86.
5. Ibid., 87.

place in the community, and it responds to a need the churches can no longer fill."[6]

THE SACRED IN CONTEMPORARY CHICANO THEATER

In dealing with the presence of the sacred in Chicano Theater, I want to focus some attention on the effect the Church had not only on the theater but on the society it helped to mold. Since 1965 and depending upon the place, depictions of the Church as a retrograde influence existed simultaneously with its role as a supporter of the theater. Colonization and the Church's historical association with wealth and the state have provided fodder for anticolonial and anticlerical arguments about the Church's legitimacy as a voice for the community. Yet, generally throughout the Church's history in the Southwest, it has been a consistent source of support for theatrical activity and the community's voice.

In a discussion about the spiritual foundations of Chicano Theater, Dr. Jorge Huerta maintains that "today's *teatros* are following a missionary tradition, but with a totally different purpose."[7] In the following discussion I will examine how elements within this theater movement that emerged in part from a colonial proselytizing tradition are both similar to and different from its colonizing precursor.

The presence of the sacred has by no means been diminished despite the fact that Chicano Theater in its politics has often cast the Church as antagonist. While Christian faith may be the obvious focus for sacred concerns, recognition of indigenous spirituality and deities has also figured prominently in Chicano Theater and the Chicano Movement, both forces for social justice and anticolonial issues. How social justice is perceived to be a sacred concern has to do with the spiritual aspect of the dignity of the human condition. The ever present image of La Virgen de Guadalupe on the banners of the United Farm Workers during marches, gatherings, and rallies attests to the place of faith in struggle. The Virgen's sacred image is invoked to protect the community. Indeed, the story of the discovery of the Virgen by Juan Diego is itself a wedding of the European and indigenous sacred. According to the legend, La Virgen appeared to Juan Diego near the shrine to Tonantzin at Tepeyac. *El indio* Juan Diego was not credible until he brought European roses as proof of his faith and contact with La Virgen. This is as much a story about the affirmation of indigenous faith as about discovering La Virgen.

6. Peter Brook, *The Empty Space* (New York: Avon Books, 1968), 54.
7. Jorge A. Huerta, *Chicano Theater: Themes and Forms* (Tempe, Ariz.: Bilingual Press, 1982), 187.

Spiritual concerns figure prominently in the work of Luis Valdez, in which the ethic of Chicano ideology asserts that the sacred is the indigenous sacred. From actor training to the work on stage, Valdez demonstrates a constant preoccupation with the sacred. This recognition of the specifically indigenous sacred can also be seen as part of the unbroken spirit of resistance towards European hegemony. In *La gran carpa de los rasquachis*, "Quetzalcóatl, who was the Redeemer figure for all of Mesoamerica, becomes Valdez's symbol of hope for the people of Aztlán. It was this indigenous deity who taught the Toltecs fine arts, science, and the agricultural craft that would make them the leading nation of America long before Cortés or Moctezuma."[8]

In addition to the use of indigenous deities in his theater, Valdez employs the Maya phrase "In lak'ech" which in Spanish is "tú eres mi otro yo" (you are my other self). This concept also forms the basis for the "Veinte Pasos," an actor training technique Valdez developed and used with his company. Yolanda Broyles-Gonzales, in her book *El Teatro Campesino: Theater in the Chicano Movement*, attempts to describe and articulate the significance of this technique and offers many examples of indigenous spiritualism within this training model. Often, as with most attempts at describing theater training, her description suffers from the inability of words to capture the vibrant physical life and energy of theatrical work that happened in the past. Yet, she succeeds in providing clear and forceful examples of sacred concerns inspired from outside of Christian and European belief systems.[9] *La Virgen del Tepeyac*, *La carpa cantinflesca*, *Bernabé*, and *El fin del mundo* are some of the plays in which elements of the indigenous sacred can be found in the work of Luis Valdez.

Seasonal *pastorelas* and several other plays also deal directly with sacred or holy concerns. *El Jardín* by Carlos Morton is an adaptation of the Adam and Eve story vis-à-vis the Chicano experience. Luis Santeiro's *Our Lady of the Tortilla* revives the phenomenon of sacred sightings in unexpected places. *Petra's Pecado* by Rupert Reyes is a riotous bilingual comedy that combines a mistaken sin with the confessional and Petra's own guilt. Rudolfo Anaya's *The Farolitos of Christmas* has a promise to the *Santo Niño* as the driving centerpiece that motivates the principal characters. In Anaya's *¡Ay, Compadre!*, prayers to the *Santo Niño* and visits to the *Santuario de Chimayo* fail to rekindle a couple's sex life. In my and Cheyney Ryan's *Holy Dirt*, El Pachuco, from Luis Valdez's *Zoot Suit*, becomes my guardian angel (as in *It's A Wonderful Life*). El Pachuco

8. Huerta, 201–2.
9. Yolanda Broyles-Gonzales, *El Teatro Campesino: Theater in the Chicano Movement* (Austin: University of Texas Press, 1994), 80.

in turn meets my character on the way to the *Santuario de Chimayo*. What all of these works share with the Church's colonial tradition of proselytizing is the propagation of an alternative worldview, except in this case the motive is building audiences for Chicano Theater. We find that today's *teatros* are indeed following a missionary tradition, but the "different purpose" mentioned by Dr. Huerta is anticolonial in spirit, for the purpose is rather that of asserting and redefining the Chicano experience.

The presence of God is often implied when discussing spiritual realms of life, especially with regard to that which is sacred. When God is absent as an interlocutor in man's spiritual dialogue, is the human spirit still capable of being an object of sacred concern? I would hope so. With the human condition as the primary object of investigation in the theater, Chicano Theater has repeatedly focused on the search for justice and equity in the conditions and quality of life. Because it is tied to the dignity of the human spirit, the search for social justice has been regarded by Chicano Theater as a sacred concern. Degrading living conditions have been the subject of many plays that served as a catalyst for action. The *Actos* by Luis Valdez, often used as a primer for Chicano Theater artists, clearly demonstrates this use of subject matter in *Las Dos Caras del Patroncito, Los Vendidos, No Saco Nada de la Escuela*, and *Huelgistas*.[10] In some areas, perceptions of passiveness in the face of oppressive living conditions resulted in a disaffection from the Church.

Depictions of the Church as a retrograde influence are better understood when considering the Church's historical association with colonization, wealth, and the state. These associations frame the anticolonial and anticlerical suspicions within Chicano Theater about the Church's legitimacy as a voice for the community. This is clearly depicted by Dr. Huerta in his discussion of how El Teatro de la Esperanza went about gathering material for their play *Guadalupe*, a docu-drama about the suppression of political activity and union organizing by Chicanos in the town of Guadalupe in Central California. The *teatro* created this piece from newspaper articles, a report published by the U.S. Commission on Civil Rights, and many personal interviews with townspeople. "When the troupe visited the local parish, the Spanish priest noted their presence and, almost as if to taunt them (for he knew why the group was in Guadalupe—everybody did), piously admonished his congregation, "¡Ustedes que siguen a César Chávez, íran directamente al infierno!" Naturally, the group was thus moved to in-

10. Luis Valdez y El Teatro Campesino, *Actos* (San Juan Bautista: Menyah Productions, 1979).

clude a scene showing the collusion between this representative of the Church and the few families who controlled the wealth in *Guadalupe*.[11]

While these kinds of depictions were present for a time, currently they tend to be more the exception than the rule. From the discussion so far one might surmise that all Chicano Theater troupes had similar paths of development and were antagonistic to the Church. Without sacrificing a concern for social justice, La Compañia de Teatro de Alburquerque is a clear departure from that taken by many *teatro* troupes during the 1970s. It illustrates a constructive alliance with the Church that had a significant and lasting impact on the cultural landscape of New Mexico.

LA COMPAÑIA DE TEATRO DE ALBURQUERQUE

La Compañia de Teatro de Alburquerque was founded in the late 1970s by a group of community actors led by José Rodriguez, an actor trained at the Royal Academy of Dramatic Art (RADA). Rodriguez later went on to become a priest. Struck by the number of cultural similarities to his native Puerto Rico, José decided to stay in New Mexico after visiting while on a theater tour. He had been an actor with New York's Repertorio Español.

La Compañia started with a clear agenda of speaking to a community, which, at the time, had limited access to theater and the voice, reflection, and validation a theater should afford its community. There were a few other *teatros* in New Mexico modeled along the same lines as other Chicano *teatros*. They were primarily social activists who did issue-based *actos* and occasionally performed. But from the beginning Rodriguez strived to instill professional standards into La Compañia with the goal of one day becoming a professional troupe. He began consciously to develop a company that would, for some time, be one of the best theaters in New Mexico. What was remarkable about this undertaking is that in the space of about six years, La Compañia went from being rumored locally as a "language experiment" to one of the most respected companies in New Mexico. This was due in part to several members (nine) from his company successively going on to train at some of the best theater training institutions in England and the United States: RADA, London Academy of Music and Dramatic Art, The Juilliard School, Yale University, and the University of California San Diego. This was a significant accomplishment since the University of New Mexico's

11. Jorge A. Huerta, *Necessary Theater: Six Plays About the Chicano Experience* (Houston: Arte Publico Press, 1989), 211.

Theater Program had only one or two Chicanos in their program and had never sent anyone to either RADA or Juilliard, let alone Chicanos.

Initially, Rodriguez focused on Spanish classical theater and Christmas pageants. Later the repertoire would include Latin American plays, original works by New Mexican authors, and American plays. Throughout his tenure as artistic director the work was always informed by Christian ethics. This included gathering people into a circle during rehearsal to define goals and to offer a small prayer. This gathering would serve to bring people together and define the group's purpose within the community. Some professionals who were attracted to our productions and wanted to come to work with us abhorred this practice and left immediately. Another aspect of this ethic was the notion of sacrifice for the greater good during the long hours of rehearsal. This sacrifice not only dealt with the immediate work of mounting a play, but also with the longer range goal of training individuals in a company.

Of utmost importance was the selection of the plays to be performed. Not only were plays selected to develop the company, but they were also considered for the meaning they could bring to the community within a context that elevated the human spirit. Rodriguez's concept of community was palpable and began with the members of his company. The selection of plays was geared specifically towards the progressive development of non-actors into actors who would then become a voice of the community. He engaged in a very humanistic type of community development.

Social justice was another key factor in the selection of material and was a constant point of contention with forces of both the left and the right. La Compañia constantly balanced the pressures of strident and vocal audience members who attempted to assert their views into the season. In retrospect they may have been reacting to the lack of cultural discourse, a void in the Chicano community that went unfilled for years.

During a time when performing in Chicano communities implied having a message or being overtly political, Rodriguez managed to address several constituencies with each production and remain true to his belief in the sacred ability of theater to transform a community. The politics of Jose Rodriguez in La Compañia de Teatro de Alburquerque were to develop a theater that at once entertained and provided a voice for a community that had no established theatrical organ. He valued and developed members of a disenfranchised community by recognizing a deep need for cultural reflection. And he respected and restored a cultural legacy centered around speaking Spanish and asserting Latino cultural values.

New Mexican society is inclined toward colonial romanticism, which is most clearly expressed in fiesta and holiday pageantry. Rodriguez recognized this tendency. An example of how he managed to address normally disparate groups, while addressing social inequity, was his staging of Lope de Vega's *Fuenteovejuna*. The setting was changed from fifteenth-century Spain to territorial Texas during the American occupation in which the villain (*El Comendador*) is a corrupt American. This adaptation addressed the left's desire to portray a quest for social justice within a Spanish-speaking American context. In addition to mounting a Spanish classic in Spanish, this piece played to other constituencies in a large and diverse Spanish-speaking community: the conservatives who wanted to maintain the facade of New Mexico's relationship to Spain and the middle class who wanted to fulfill a desire to see Latino classical theater. A central concern in staging the play had to do with drawing metaphorical parallels to New Mexican society and history. New Mexico's inherited colonial legacies, Spanish and American, requires any theater of consciousness to address issues of social justice and the consequent social order. Given Rodriguez's strong Christian beliefs, issues of social justice were not only inseparable from sacred concerns but were central to his Roman Catholicism.

In addition to addressing social justice and critiquing the social order, Rodriguez engaged in a subversion of the dominant cultural paradigm by training actors in the vicinity of a university often perceived among Chicanos as an Anglo fiefdom. Not only was he successful in training and sending actors beyond the limits and influence of the university, he also had addressed and surpassed a need in the Chicano community largely ignored by Anglo cultural institutions, especially the university. Rodriguez's grooming of local Chicano actors made apparent the de facto exclusion of Chicanos and created an alternative to often mediocre and/or irrelevant theatrical offerings.

La Compañia explored various genres, aside from classical Spanish theater, while pursuing an alternative path to that taken by other Chicano *teatros*. Yet, social justice remained an object of sacred concern, one which threaded La Compañia into the matrix of the Chicano *teatro* movement occurring throughout the United States. This became especially evident in La Compañia's development and production of *La Pasión de Jesus Chavez: A Modern Commentary on the Gospels*. The impetus for presenting *La Pasión de Jesus Chavez* came in part from the need to address social issues within a non-confrontational format. The play was about three undocumented Mexicans who escape a political struggle in their town of Madera and are targeted for death only to end up in an American jail with the possibility of being sent back to Mexico. The three are followers of Jesus Chavez, a Christ figure who opposes a corrupt, class-based status quo. The play combined the Passion of Christ with contemporary social issues including class, exile, sanctuary, prison corruption, and disinformation. The play had many flaws, but its effect on the audience was penetrating and heartfelt.

The story is narrated from within a jail. The significance of this setting could be seen on the back of a convict at the New Mexico State Penitentiary. The inmate had tattooed the image of the play's poster on his own body. In and of itself this would mean little, if the penitentiary had not experienced the most bloody prison riot in U.S. history. Thirty-one inmates were left dead. The riot occurred about a week or two before the play opened. The relationship of the poster image to the inmate's tattooed back was never made quite clear, but the riot, the play, and its subject matter were side by side in the public eye for several months. After the play toured northern New Mexico in 1980, the Catholic Church agreed to sponsor a statewide tour of the play later that year. This piece, perhaps more than any other I know in Chicano Theater, made apparent the relationship between the sacred and social justice. With the exception of *La Víctima* by El Teatro de la Esperanza, the play's effect was unsurpassed. Over the years, La Compañia has presented other plays that feature a strong relationship between the community and sacred concerns. This continues up to the present with the recent Church sponsorship of *La Posada Mágica* by Octavio Solis.

Why should La Compañia's example of the sacred in theater be of note? Despite the relative obscurity of the company, it offers a model for constructive engagement between two important institutions that seek to provide meaning to their communities in a time of limited and dwindling resources. It is clear that despite all the talk of the theater dying out because of technology and film, there remains a basic human need to find meaning in life through other people (actors) as a group (audience). It is the social basis of this dilemma that can serve as a point of mutual benefit between Chicano Theater and the Church. La Compañia's example suggests how Church values can help Chicano Theater to develop community voices through theater.

INITIATIVES

The major current of contemporary Chicano/Latino Theater in the United States arose out of a movement for social justice relying on the agency of socio-political consciousness for propulsion. The winds of change did not ease the hunger instilled by scores of amateur groups. However, until recently, institutional support necessary to train profes-

Poster advertising *La Pasión de Jesus Chavez*

sionals for this market has been slow at best. The present situation presents a rush to fill the dearth of plays, playwrights, trained actors, and directors able to address a demand made evident by plays and movies such as *La Familia, Zoot Suit,* and *Like Water for Chocolate.* The need to interpret characters and create plays for the Chicano/Latino community accounts for the necessity among theaters to create new community partnerships and continue to develop those already in place.

Both the Church and Chicano Theater might begin actively to view the nurturing of talent and artistic voices in a community as direct community development. What this might mean will depend upon each set of players. Particular initiatives that come to mind include hosting workshops and offering the use of space to support theatrical activity such as rehearsal and performance.

During my tenure as artistic director of La Compañia, I would bring certain plays to church halls, and they would always draw substantial audiences. Most often they were attended by people who never went to the theater, and so we were afforded an opportunity to increase our audiences. In addition, priests would usually allow leafleting after each mass. This would enable us to direct patrons to other showings. However, the issue was always one of appropriateness of subject matter, which aroused the spectre of censorship.

Another possibility is to sponsor playwriting contests with commissions that leave artists enough room to be able to create without the fear of censorship. There are many gray areas that belong more to developing relationships and negotiation than prescribed actions. A specific endeavor could be the cosponsorship of a playwriting contest about the family. A suggestion for a thematic guideline might include "a family struggling with a particular issue or emotional problem." I am not suggesting that this will create great artists but what the Church can hope for is to aid or guide artistic endeavors that elevate and privilege the human being and spirit. The immediate objective need not necessarily be art. It need only create and engender dialogue about the way we live.

Additionally, opportunities are created to address a need for the cultural reflection in the Chicano/Latino community mentioned earlier. The dearth of plays that speak directly to the Chicano/Latino community influenced my own career path as a theater artist. My own efforts at playwriting have responded to the need to develop works that voice concerns, aspirations, and stories in the Chicano community that are to date rarely present in the broader American Theater.

These initiatives can be part of a mosaic of change from some of the stories that inflict on some and perpetuate upon others a continual state of anomie and nihilism. Communication across culture, discrimination, the sanctity of human life, and issues concerned with the development of a diverse society must be treated with love as a key factor. And I can think of only one institution that dedicates itself completely to the tasks of sacred love.

16

Spain in Latino Religiosity

WILLIAM A. CHRISTIAN JR.

In my reading of prior published colloquia and conferences, I note a model repeatedly used to explain the Spanish component of U.S. Latino religiosity: (a) the religiosity brought from Spain was pre-Tridentine; (b) the religion brought from Spain was essentially that brought before the mid-sixteenth century (implicit in a); (c) it was more that of lower-class laypersons than of clergy; (d) it was combined or synthesized with elements of indigenous and/or African religion; (e) the religiosity of most Latino people is "popular religiosity" (with the implication that the religion of other people and other Latino people is not, or may not be, "popular"). I suggest that each point in this schema be examined critically.

Spain has maintained a presence, and particularly a clerical presence, in Latin America and the United States up to the present. Spain has been sending priests and male and female religious to Latin America in considerable numbers since the sixteenth century. Bishops were often Spanish until the early nineteenth century at least. According to Rutilio del Riego, one-third of the 1,415 Hispanic priests in the United States around 1980 were from Spain.[1] And Spanish laypersons in commerce have been a constant presence in many parts of Latin America, also up to the present. Is there a good reason to suppose that Spanish influence ended with Cortés and the first Franciscans? Cursillos de Cristiandad, spread to the United States by Spanish laypersons in the 1950s, was surely just one of a series of movements and devotions that came to the New World in waves from Spain. There would have been others from Rome and from France. Spain in turn has been influenced, through returning migrants, by Mexican devotions and devotional tone. "Indianos" brought back to the North of Spain devotion to the Mexican

1. Isidro Lucas, *The Browning of America: The Hispanic Revolution in the American Church* (Chicago: Fides/Claretian, 1981).

Guadalupe.[2] And Spanish clergy have brought liberation theology back (and forth) from Latin America to seminaries and parishes in their homeland. An example of a largely "post-Tridentine" devotion is the special attention to the passion through confraternities, and the emphasis on the crucified Christ, which many studies emphasize as a distinctive feature of Latino religiosity. In Spain these confraternities developed throughout the sixteenth century, and in the seventeenth and 18th centuries dramatic images of the crucified Christ became enshrined in parish Churches, generalizing votive devotion previously directed to a few special images like the Christs of Burgos and Orense, and the Christ of San Agustín in Sevilla. Indeed a concentration of devotion on Mary, Christ as Child, and Christ Crucified to the gradual exclusion of local and localized saints is thought to be one long-term *effect* of the Council of Trent.[3] But in practice how this happened was by the substitution of devotion to local or specialized saints with devotion to localized, specific images of Mary or Christ as general helpers.[4]

Hence, in my opinion, the Council of Trent did not seriously affect the local nature of Spanish or Mediterranean devotion, but rather, if anything, reinforced it. The aspects usually selected as "pre-Trent" in Latino religiosity are also "post-Trent" and would have been brought to the New World not just in the first wave of conquest and Christianization, but over the following centuries as well. In Spain the main elements of this religiosity were shared by clergy, both secular and religious, and laypersons alike: devotion expressed through images, a landscape regarded as strewn with sacred places, elaborate attention to death and dying,[5] an expressive connection to sacred figures, strong brotherhoods, a theatrical, affective depiction and reenactment of the passion and the nativity. Not until the neo-Jansenism of the late

2. Carmen González Echegaray, *La Patrona de México en las montañas de Santander* (México, D.F.: Jus., 1973).

3. William A. Christian, Jr., *Local Religion in Sixteenth-Century Spain* (Princeton, N.J.: Princeton University Press, 1981), 178–80; Marie-Hélène Froeschlé-Chopard, *La Religion populaire en Provence orientale au xvii* siècle (Paris: Beauchesne, 1980); Marie-Hélène Froeschlé-Chopard, "Les Saints du dedans et dehors en Provence orientale," in *Luoghi sacri e spazi della santità*, ed. Sofia Boesch Gajano and Lucetta Scaraffia (Torino: Rosenberg and Sellier, 1990), 609–29. For Trent see also Sara Nalle, *God in La Mancha: Religious Reform and the People of Cuenca, 1500–1650* (Baltimore: Johns Hopkins University Press, 1992); Henry Kamen, *The Phoenix and the Flame: Catalonia and the Counter-Reformation* (New Haven, Conn.: Yale University Press, 1993).

4. Christian, *Local Religion*, 181–208.

5. Nalle, *God in La Mancha*; Carlos M. Eire, *From Madrid to Purgatory: The Art and Craft of Dying in Sixteenth-Century Spain* (Cambridge: Cambridge University Press, 1995).

eighteenth century would a substantial portion of the Spanish clergy seriously question these elements.

Some scholars use the pre- and post-Trent distinction to explain some of the differences in the religiosity of Spanish-speaking immigrants from Central and South America to North America from that of other North American Catholics. I wonder if some of these differences are not better explained by differing kinds of European Catholicism, a northern variety heavily marked by mobilization against and competition with Protestantism, and a southern variety, that of Italy, Spain, and Portugal, for which Protestantism was never a serious alternative. (The more doctrinal, austere northern European Catholicism was just as appropriate in the United States, where the society was even more plural and the faith equally endangered.) The comparative study of European Catholicisms is in its infancy, but what work there is shows striking differences from country to country in the landscape features that are the sites for shrines and the divine figures to whom shrines are dedicated.[6] The country most distinctive in this regard is Ireland. The Irish influence on the tone and the agenda of U.S. Catholicism has been tremendous, and one working hypothesis for differences between "Latino" and "Anglo" Catholicism might, instead of pre-Trent and post-Trent, be the difference between northern vs. southern Europe, or, more precisely, Ireland vs. Spain.

It is assumed that Spanish Catholicism combined with native American and/or African elements to create the various kinds of Catholicism practiced by Spanish-speakers in the United States. Syncretization or synthesization is evident in many Catholic communities in Latin America, but just how, aside from possibly a greater belief in spirits, Mexican-American Catholicism has been influenced by pre-Christian beliefs is not clear. The spirit beliefs evidenced in the questionnaire responses to study of Mexican-American Catholics in Orange County, California,[7] are not dissimilar to those to be found in parts of rural Spain.[8] The appeal of Kardecian spiritism to Puerto Ricans may be explained in part by Taíno or African spirit beliefs,[9] but spiritism was equally attrac-

6. Mary Lee Nolan and Sydney Nolan, *Christian Pilgrimage in Modern Western Europe* (Chapel Hill, N.C.: University of North Carolina Press, 1989).

7. Jeffrey S. Thies, *Mexican Catholicism in Southern California: The Importance of Popular Religiosity and Sacramental Practice in Faith Experience* (New York: Peter Lang, 1993).

8. María Cátedra, *This World, Other Worlds: Sickness, Suicide, Death, and the Afterlife among the Vaqueiros de Alzada of Spain* (Chicago: University of Chicago Press, 1992).

9. Dominga Zapata, "The Puerto Rican Experience in the United States: A Pastoral Perspective," in *Dialogue Rejoined: Theology and Ministry in the United States Hispanic Reality*, ed. Ana Maria Pineda and Robert Schreiter (Collegeville,

tive to Spaniards and Portuguese, long alert to the presence of the dead, before it was repressed by their respective national Catholic regimes. There are substantial, perhaps inevitable, areas of overlap between agrarian religious culture in Spain, Africa, and pre-Columbian America, and as Spain's rural rituals become better known, scholars are finding them in, for instance, remote Andean ceremonies long thought to be quintessentially native American.[10] Careful ethnographic studies of the different kinds of Latino religious communities are sorely needed (those of other kinds of American Catholics, which would be useful for comparison, are also scarce).

Too often Spain is referred to as one religious culture, whereas Spain's regions have stark differences in the relation of clergy to laity, in the popularity of religious brotherhoods, in the centrality of Holy Week, in the popularity of nativity plays or creches, in the holy figures chosen as patrons, and the quality of the devotion accorded these figures. A serious examination of the sources of Latino religiosity will want to consider the particular varieties of Spanish religious experience.

I also question the generally-accepted notion of "popular" religiosity. Is there another kind? Is Latino religiosity any more "popular" than Catholicism as practiced elsewhere? Surely the distinction is between religious norms and religious practice.[11] While canon law is universal, Catholicism as practiced is widely varied. As in Islam and other major religions, Catholicism forms a kind of mosaic around the world. Catholicism in the United States is a mosaic microcosm of the world mosaic.[12] One way to look at "popular" Catholicism as a social construct is to see it as something the speaker considers distinct from her or his own variety, which he or she arbitrarily considers normative. Accepting Latino Catholicism as "popular" thus implicitly, and unjustifiably, validates some other variety of practice.

There are other Spanish elements of Latino Catholicism. I list some possible ones:

Minn.: The Liturgical Press, 1995), 43–60. Cf. Anthony M. Stevens-Arroyo, *Cave of the Jagua: The Mythological World of the Taínos* (Alburquerque: University of New Mexico Press, 1988).

10. Thomas Abercrombie, "Rural Indians In and Out of the Urban Bolivian Public Sphere: Carnival and the Carnivalesque in Colonial and National Consciousness" (paper presented at the Agrarian Studies Colloquium, Yale University, 28 March 1997).

11. Jean-Claude Schmitt, "'Religion populaire' et culture folklorique," *Annales E.S.C.* 31 (1976): 941–53.

12. Dolores Liptak, *Immigrants and Their Church* (New York: Macmillan, 1989).

Collective, corporate responsibility before God and the saints. In Spain collective, town-wide contractual vows with divine protectors were made by municipal councils or village assemblies into the nineteenth century. Every family who lived in the town was bound by such vows in perpetuity, unless the vows were dispensed by ecclesiastical authority. Such collective responsibility was concomitant with the communal aspect of Spanish polities—the existence of communal meadows, backlands, grain deposits—and the shared consequences of epidemic disease and drought. This collective relation to the divine meshed with pre-Columbian religious organization in the new world,[13] and the closed corporate aspect of rural communities in contemporary Latin America has long been recognized. One might look for the extent to which corporate religiosity subsists in historic Latino communities in the United States, what if any of it survives immigration, and whether, as with the Farm Workers, it still has power when called on. I wonder whether there is still a notion that grace can have a social component—that it can apply to groups, not just individuals.

Personal patronage. Persons too have divine friends and protectors, special patrons they can call on for help. Such patronage, like its human parallel, may be stronger in Mediterranean Europe than in northern Europe, and in Latino Catholicism than in some of the other varieties.

Women as family religious experts. Several essays point to the existence of *rezadoras*, informal prayer experts and healers, as characteristic of Latino religiosity. These religious virtuosi are also characteristic of contemporary Spain. And in most parts of Spain, as in Italy, women are the family representatives on religious matters, both to the Church and to the divine. There are indications that such was the case in the sixteenth century as well—for instance, the overwhelmingly feminine ownership of private religious artwork.[14]

Specific devotions and fiestas. Most major Hispanic American shrines have at least a genealogical connection with Spanish or European originals, like Our Lady of Guadalupe, La Caridad, and La Regla. The repertoire of Saints is essentially that of Spain. I already referred to the often unsuspected Spanish origin of many fiesta rituals, costumes, and dances.

Kinds of epiphanies. Many of the numerous alleged apparitions, images that seem to weep or manifest emotions, or faces that appear on walls, in windows, or even on *burritos* have a cultural lineage that can be traced back to specific templates in specific zones in Spain. That this

13. James Lockhart, *The Nahuas After the Conquest: A Social and Cultural History of the Indians of Central Mexico* (Stanford: Stanford University Press, 1992).
14. Nalle, *God in La Mancha.*

process is ongoing is demonstrated by alleged miracles and visions of the Cristo de Limpias, which spread to the New World by way of Cuba, Mexico, and Peru from their point of origin in the Spanish province of Santander (now Cantabria) starting in 1919.[15]

An underlying question is which elements can "travel" (like wine) away from a matrix of a sacred landscape, an ancestral community, and a dominant religion and survive in a plural society in which Latino-American Catholics are not only part of a Catholic minority, but

15. William A. Christian, Jr., *Moving Crucifixes in Modern Spain* (Princeton, N.J.: Princeton University Press, 1992), 89, 175, 180.

16. Further works on the subject include William A. Christian, Jr., *Apparitions in Medieval and Renaissance Spain* (Princeton, N.J.: Princeton University Press, 1981); Jay P. Dolan and Gilberto M. Hinojosa, eds., *Mexican-Americans and the Catholic Church, 1900–1965* (Notre Dame: University of Notre Dame Press, 1994); Jaime R. Vidal, "Towards an Understanding of Synthesis in Iberian and Hispanic American Popular Religiosity," in *An Enduring Flame: Studies of Latino Popular Religiosity*, PARAL Series, vol. 1, ed. Anthony M. Stevens-Arroyo and Ana María Díaz-Stevens (New York: Bildner Center Books, 1994), 69–95.

Contributors

Peter Casarella

Associate Professor of Systematic Theology at The Catholic University of America where he helped design the concentration in Hispanic Ministry for the Master of Divinity degree. Edited, with George Schner, S.J., *Christian Spirituality and the Culture of Modernity: Essays in Conversation with Louis Dupré* (William B. Eerdmans Publishing Company, 1998). Instructor in the Instituto de Formación Pastoral, Apostolado Hispano, Diocese of Arlington.

William A. Christian, Jr.

An independent scholar who lives in Las Palmas de Gran Canaria, Spain and recipient of numerous awards, including fellowships from the Guggenheim and John D. and Catherine T. MacArthur Foundations. Author of many books and articles on the religious history of Spain, e.g., *Visionaries: The Spanish Republic and the Reign of Christ* (University of California Press, 1996), *Moving Crucifixes in Modern Spain* (Princeton University Press, 1992), and *Local Religion in Sixteenth Century Spain* (Princeton University Press, 1981).

Allan Figueroa Deck, S.J.

Adjunct Professor of Hispanic and Theological Studies at Loyola Marymount University in Los Angeles and Director of the Loyola Institute for Spirituality. Cofounder and first president of the Academy of Catholic Hispanic Theologians of the United States (ACHTUS) and founder and first president of the National Catholic Council for Hispanic Ministry (NCCHM). Edited, with Yolanda Tarango and Timothy M. Matovina, *Perspectivas: Hispanic Ministry* (Sheed and Ward, 1995). His *Second Wave: Hispanic Ministry and the Evangelization of Cultures* (Paulist Press, 1989) has become a standard text in seminaries, universities, and pastoral institutes throughout the United States.

Ana María Díaz-Stevens

Associate Professor of Church and Society at Union Theological Seminary in New York. Author of numerous publications, including the award-winning *Oxcart Catholicism on Fifth Avenue: The Impact of the Puerto Rican Migration upon the Archdiocese of New York* (University of Notre Dame Press, 1993) and, with Anthony Stevens-Arroyo, *Recognizing the Latino Resurgence: The Emmaus Paradigm* (Westview Press, 1997). Cofounder of the Program for Analysis of Religion Among Latinos (PARAL) and of the Puerto Rican Studies Association.

Virgilio P. Elizondo

Founder and first president of the Mexican American Cultural Center as well as the founder and first director of the Incarnate Word Pastoral Institute, both in San Antonio, Texas. Recipient of numerous awards and honorary doctorates, including the Laetare (Notre Dame) and Quasten (The Catholic University of America) medals. Presbyter of the Archdiocese of San Antonio where he has served as Rector of the San Fernando Cathedral and in various other pastoral, educational, and administrative roles. Published numerous books and articles related to Hispanic theology and culture, including *Galilean Journey: The Mexican-American Promise* (Orbis Books, 1983), and, most recently, *Mestizo Worship: A Pastoral Approach to Liturgical Ministry* (The Liturgical Press, 1998) with Timothy Matovina.

Mario García

Professor of History and Chicano Studies at the University of California at Santa Barbara. Recipient of numerous fellowships, including Guggenheim, Ford Postdoctoral, and Woodrow Wilson Center. Wrote *Memories of Chicano History: The Life and Narrative of Bert Corona* (University of California Press, 1994) and *Desert Immigrants: The Mexicans of El Paso 1880–1920* (Yale University Press, 1981).

Alejandro García-Rivera

Assistant Professor of Systematic Theology at the Jesuit School of Theology in Berkeley, California. Vice-president of ACHTUS, winner of two Catholic Press Association awards, and associate editor of the *Journal of Hispanic/Latino Theology*. Published *St. Martin de Porres: The "Little Stories" and the Semiotics of Culture* (Orbis Books, 1995). His forthcoming work on theological aesthetics will be entitled *The Community of the Beautiful: A Theological Aesthetics* (The Liturgical Press).

Raúl Gómez, S.D.S.

Associate Professor of Pastoral Studies and Director of the Hispanic Studies Program, Sacred Heart School of Theology, Hales Corners, Wis. Past president of the Instituto de Liturgia Hispana. Edited, with Heliodoro Lucatero and Sylvia Sánchez, *Gift and Promise: Customs and Traditions in Hispanic Rites of Marriage/Don y promesa: Costumbres y tradiciones en los ritos matrimoniales hispanos* (Instituto de Liturgia Hispana/OCP Publications, 1997), along with articles on Hispanic and Mozarabic liturgy. Former advisor to the Bishops' Committee on the Liturgy and member of its Subcommitee on Hispanic Liturgy.

Roberto Goizueta

Associate Professor of Theology at Loyola University of Chicago. Former president of ACHTUS and former associate editor of *The Journal of Hispanic/Latino Theology*. Wrote *Caminemos con Jesús: Toward a Hispanic/Latino Theology of Accompaniment* (Orbis Books, 1995) and edited *We Are A People! Initiatives in Hispanic American Theology* (Augsburg/Fortress Press, 1992).

Jeffrey Gros, F.S.C.

Associate Director of the Secretariat for Ecumenical and Interreligious Affairs of the U.S. Catholic Conference and Director of the Commission on Faith and Order of the National Council of the Churches in the U.S.A. Edited, with William G. Rusch, *Deepening Communion: International Ecumenical Documents with Roman Catholic Participation* (Paulist Press, 1998) and, with Joseph A. Burgess, *Building Unity* (Paulist Press, 1989). Also authored *An Introduction to Ecumenism* (Paulist Press, 1998).

Jaime Lara

Professor at Yale Divinity School. Has also held appointments at California State University at Los Angeles, the Universidad Nacional de Colombia, St. Patrick's Seminary, and the Jesuit School of Theology at Berkeley. Former vice-president of the Instituto de Liturgia Hispana and past member of Bishops' Committee on the Liturgy. Author of numerous essays on *religiosidad popular*, liturgy and architecture, the liturgical roots of Hispanic folk religion, and the medieval sources of Latin American colonial religion.

Vicente López, O. Carm.

Pastor at St. Jane Frances de Chantel Parish in North Hollywood, Calif. Served as Vicar for Hispanics in the diocese of Tucson and Associate Director of the Secretariat for Hispanic Affairs at the National Conference of Catholic Bishops. From 1989–1994 directed the Carmelite Provincial Commission for Hispanic Ministry, in which he opened a mission in Torreón, Coahuila, México and a seminary for Latino students in Houston, Texas.

Gelasia Márquez Marinas

Bilingual School Psychologist. Author of Helping Hands, a counseling program for Hispanic families in transition. Has implemented policies for initiating Hispanic Family Life programs at national, regional, and diocesan levels and lectured throughout the United States on the implications of Hispanic culture for the mental health provision, the role of schools in supporting multicultural families, and the contribution of the Hispanic family to the U.S. Catholic Church. Received two journalism awards from The Catholic Press Association.

Marcos Martínez

Assistant Professor at California State University San Marcos as well as director, playwright, and actor. Founding member and former Artistic Director of La Compañia de Teatro de Alburquerque. Has given workshops on Chicano theater and/or the Suzuki Method of Actor Training at the Smithsonian Institution, The Catholic University of America, the National Theater of Ghana, and the Universidad Autónoma de México.

Ana María Pineda, R.S.M.

Teaches in the Department of Religious Studies at Santa Clara University. Former Director of Hispanic Ministry, Catholic Theological Union, Chicago, Ill. Edited, with Robert Schreiter, *Dialogue Rejoined: Theology and Ministry in the United States Hispanic Reality* (The Liturgical Press, 1995). Wrote numerous articles on culture as a locus for theology, *pastoral de conjunto*, Hispanic pluralism, and the Hispanic oral tradition. Past secretary to ACHTUS and member of Ecumenical Association of Third World Theologians (EATWOT).

José Antonio Rubio

Presbyter of the Diocese of San José, Calif. Director of the diocesan Office of Ecumenical and Interreligious Affairs. Catholic delegate to the Faith and Order Commission of the National Council of Churches. Participant in Catholic-Pentecostal dialogues on the local and national level. Past member of the Bishops' Subcommittee on Hispanic Liturgy.

Jean-Pierre Ruiz

Assistant Professor and Chair of Theology and Religious Studies at St. John's University, Jamaica, New York. Former president of ACHTUS and since 1996 editor-in-chief of the *Journal of Hispanic/Latino Theology*. Author of *Ezekiel in the Apocalypse* (Peter Lang, 1989) and numerous articles on biblical hermeneutics in the third world context, the apocalypse of John, liturgy and the apocalypse, and the relations of U.S. Hispanic Catholics to the so-called "sects." His forthcoming commentary on Ezekiel will be published by The Liturgical Press.

Juan Sosa

Executive Director of the Office of the Ministry of Worship and Spiritual Life of the Archdiocese of Miami. Former advisor to the Bishops' Committee on the Liturgy and a member of its Subcommittee on Hispanic Liturgy. Founding member and former president of the Instituto de Liturgia Hispana. Has published numerous articles on popular piety in Spanish and English as well as liturgical music in Spanish.

David Traverzo Galarza

Assistant Professor in the Department of Black and Hispanic Studies at Baruch College of the City University of New York. Has written on Latino religion, ethics, and politics with a concentration on Puerto Rican history, the U.S. Puerto Rican migration, and social ethics from an evangelical Latino perspective.